Nigeria's Digital Diaspora

Rochester Studies in African History and the Diaspora

Toyin Falola, Series Editor
The Jacob and Frances Sanger Mossiker Chair in the Humanities
and University Distinguished Teaching Professor
University of Texas at Austin

Recent Titles

Mediators, Contract Men, and Colonial Capital: Mechanized Gold Mining in the Gold Coast Colony, 1879–1909
Cassandra Mark-Thiesen

Muslim Fula Business Elites and Politics in Sierra Leone
Alusine Jalloh

Race, Decolonization, and Global Citizenship in South Africa
Chielozona Eze

Plantation Slavery in the Sokoto Caliphate: A Historical and Comparative Study
Mohammed Bashir Salau

African Migration Narratives: Politics, Race, and Space
Edited by Cajetan Iheka and Jack Taylor

Ethics and Society in Nigeria: Identity, History, Political Theory
Nimi Wariboko

African Islands: Leading Edges of Empire and Globalization
Edited by Toyin Falola, R. Joseph Parrott, and Danielle Porter-Sanchez

Catholicism and the Making of Politics in Central Mozambique, 1940–1986
Eric Morier-Genoud

Liberated Africans and the Abolition of the Slave Trade, 1807–1896
Edited by Richard Anderson and Henry B. Lovejoy

The Other Abyssinians: The Northern Oromo and the Creation of Modern Ethiopia, 1855–1913
Brian J. Yates

A complete list of titles in the Rochester Studies in African History and the Diaspora series may be found on our website, www.urpress.com.

Nigeria's Digital Diaspora

Citizen Media, Democracy, and Participation

Farooq A. Kperogi

University of Rochester Press

First published 2020

University of Rochester Press
668 Mt. Hope Avenue, Rochester, NY 14620, USA
www.urpress.com
and Boydell & Brewer Limited
PO Box 9, Woodbridge, Suffolk IP12 3DF, UK
www.boydellandbrewer.com

ISBN-13: 978-1-58046-982-1
ISSN: 1092-5228

Library of Congress Cataloging-in-Publication Data

Names: Kperogi, Farooq A., 1973– author.
Title: Nigeria's digital diaspora : citizen media, democracy, and participation / Farooq A. Kperogi.
Description: Rochester : University of Rochester Press, 2020. | Series: Rochester studies in African history and the diaspora, 10925228 ; 87 | Includes bibliographical references and index.
Identifiers: LCCN 2019032330 | ISBN 9781580469821 (hardcover) | ISBN 9781787446540 (pdf)
Subjects: LCSH: Online journalism—Nigeria—History—21st century. | Citizen journalism—Nigeria—History—21st century. | Minorities and journalism—United States. | African diaspora.
Classification: LCC PN5499.N5 K64 2020 | DDC 070.4—dc23
LC record available at https://lccn.loc.gov/2019032330

This publication is printed on acid-free paper.

MIX
Paper from responsible sources
FSC® C013056

Printed and bound in Great Britain by TJ International Ltd, Padstow, Cornwall

To my father, Adamu Kperogi, who passed away on December 31, 2016, for molding me to become who I am today

Contents

Acknowledgments

The foundation for this book was laid at Georgia State University. I owe enormous debts to Michael Lane Bruner, who is now chair of the Department of Communication Studies at the University of Nevada, Las Vegas, for helping me to crystalize my germinal thoughts on liberatory politics and diasporic media formations in digital platforms, and to Ted Friedman for inciting my curiosity about citizen journalism. Leonard Ray Teel, now emeritus professor, whose journalism text I studied as an undergraduate at Bayero University in Kano, Nigeria, gave me access to his rich personal library in international journalism.

This book, above all, emerged from my deep, longstanding experiential immersion in the deliberative politics and practices of the Nigerian digital diaspora in the United States. Many diasporic Nigerians in the United States contributed immensely in shaping my perspectives and deepening my appreciation of the many and varied phenomena described in this book. I want to especially acknowledge Moses Ochonu of Vanderbilt University, whose abiding friendship and enduring scholarly engagements with me, dating back to our undergraduate days in Nigeria, have been central to my growth in academe. This book bears the imprints of our periodic, extended conversations about Nigeria and its expanding, increasingly consequential digital diaspora. Philip Adekunle, founder of the Nigerian Village Square, has been a treasured digital friend who supported this book from its inchoate state in ways he is not even aware of. He has played critical roles in inaugurating and deepening platforms for discursive democracy in the Nigerian diaspora and at home, and has influenced the evolution of Nigerian citizen journalism and online activism. I also want to recognize Sonala Olumhense, the storied, highly esteemed syndicated newspaper columnist whose uncompromisingly searing critiques of the dysfunctions of the Nigerian state from his New York location have inspired hundreds of thousands of Nigerians at home and abroad. His unwavering passion for upholding probity and influencing the politics and policies of the homeland from his exilic location has been a source of inspiration to me—and to many more people than he can ever know.

In the course of writing this book, I profited from the insights of many home-based Nigerian journalists. Ibraheem Musa, former editor of *Weekend Blueprint*, shared insightful thoughts with me about the changes that digital-native citizen and professional media outlets have brought to the ecology of news in Nigeria. Lasisi Olagunju, editor of the *Saturday Tribune*; Nuruddeen M. Abdallah, the *Daily Trust*'s investigations editor; Martins Oloja, former editor of the *Guardian* and current executive head of its editorial board; Ajibola Amzat, former features editor of the *Guardian* and current editor of the International Center for Investigative Reporting (ICIR); Musikilu Mojeed, editor-in-chief of *Premium Times*; and Joel Nwokeoma, editorial page editor of the *Punch*, all generously invested time and energy to share with me their perspectives on the contours, ethical quandaries, and challenges of the evolving, perpetually kaleidoscopic journalistic landscape in Nigeria in the face of the emergence and evolution of diasporic and homeland online journalism.

I would also like to thank Abdulbasit Kassim, doctoral candidate at Rice University and valued mentee of mine, whose persistent but gentle nudges pushed me to complete this book. Each time he called me, he never failed to ask about the progress I made in writing the manuscript of this book. His unceasing inquiries about my progress became one of the biggest prods for the completion of this book.

My good friend John Brown and his kind wife, Delilah Brown, have become an indissoluble extension of my family and a great source of emotional security for me. I am grateful to them for the remarkable generosity they have continually shown me and my family over the years. Jim Schiffman, Nneka Logan, Abdullahi Bego, Bamidele Ademola-Olateju and her husband, Ademola Olateju, are also treasured friends whose unfailing loyalty and kindness mean a lot to me.

My father, Adamu Kperogi, who died on December 31, 2016, at the age of ninety-two—and to whom I dedicate this book—was my principal source of inspiration while he lived. He wasn't just my father; he was also my teacher, my mentor, my emotional and moral fortress, my greatest cheerleader, and my all-time hero. I would never be who I am today, much less write this book, were it not for the efforts he invested in bringing me up to be curious, questioning, and critical, and to cherish knowledge for its own sake. Six qualities defined my father: trust, truth, faithfulness, kindness, hard work, and a profound aversion to superstition, ignorance, and deceit. He made manifest some of these qualities in the names he chose for his first three children. His first son, my older brother, is (Al-)Amin, which is Arabic for "the trustworthy." My name, Farooq, is Arabic for "one who distinguishes truth from falsehood"; and my younger brother is named Abdulmumin, which means "servant of the faithful." He told me the choice of our names was deliberate. From our impressionable years, he let us know the meanings of our names and the importance he attached to those meanings. Through his constant reminders of the moral burden of my name in my formative years, he caused me to internalize the imperative of speaking the truth, including to power, even at the expense of my personal safety and comfort. My mother, Hauwa, also shares the credit for bringing me up. I thank her immensely for her unquestioning love and for the unfailing emotional nourishment she provides me in both good and bad times.

I also want to express my gratitude to the production and editorial staff at the University of Rochester Press for their helpfulness, patience, and cooperation from the proposal to the production stages of this book. In particular, Sonia Kane, Jacqueline Heinzelmann, and Rio Hartwell have been nothing short of remarkable. Toyin Falola, the series editor whom I like to call the undisputed patriarch of African academics in North America, deserves commendation for his mentorship and for his enduring inspiration in multiple ways. I would also like to thank two anonymous reviewers whose critical comments and suggestions for improvement have made this book a lot better than it would have been. Publication of this book was made possible, in part, by a grant from the Publication Subvention Fund of the Office of the Dean of the College of Humanities and Social Sciences at Kennesaw State University. I would like to thank Dean Shawn Long and Senior Associate Dean Thierry Leger for making this possible. I am also grateful to Barbara Gainey, director of Kennesaw State University's School of Communication and Media, for her moral support and for providing funds to purchase indexing software for this book.

Finally, were it not for the support and understanding of my wife, Maureen, and our children, Sinani, Maryam, Adam, and Ramat, this book would never have been completed. Words alone aren't sufficient to do justice to the depth of gratitude I owe them for their understanding when I stayed away from home for prolonged hours to complete this book. Sinani, in addition, graciously designed the cover image of this book. Maureen's loving encouragement, moral and intellectual support, and consistent thoughtfulness were particularly crucial to the completion of this book. I can't say enough how much of a priceless gift she has been to my life. Her parents, Edwin Erinne and Cecelia Crump Erinne, have accepted me as their son and continue to provide immeasurable moral support for my aspirations.

Maureen's siblings—Erica, Cedric, Jennifer, Jacqueline, and Olivia—are the most supportive in-laws anyone could ever wish to have. Their unconditional love and support for my family and me have been crucial to my success these past few years in more ways than I can persuade them to believe.

Farooq A. Kperogi, Kennesaw, Georgia
November 2019

Introduction

The terms *Cyberia* and *Nigeria's digital diaspora* are used interchangeably in this book to denote the dispersed collective of Nigerians on the Internet. "Cyberia" is used as a lexical and semantic double entendre. It simultaneously encapsulates the original meaning that Arturo Escobar assigned to it when he coined it in 1994[1] and its sense as a portmanteau word that blends "cyber" and "Nigeria."[2] Escobar deployed this term to capture the epistemic and discursive location of the emergent, postcorporeal cyberculture of the 1990s and to "describe, in part, how various groups appropriate or reject new technologies based on cultural, political and economic factors."[3] But this term also signifies the notional and substantive convergence of cyberculture and Nigeria. "Cyberia" is conceptualized here as the space on the Internet where Nigerians congregate for public-sphere deliberations, for quotidian dialogic encounters, and for increasingly multiple forms of engagements both with themselves and with the state.

To be sure, "Cyberia" itself traces its lexical descent from the term *cyberspace*. It is the consensus of Internet scholars[4] that the first use of "cyberspace" is attested in the first volume of William Gibson's prescient 1985 trilogy and citation classic *Neuromancer*. In this fictional projection of the world, the concept of cyberspace is ideated by the following oft-cited passage: "Cyberspace. A consensual hallucination experienced daily by billions of legitimate operators, in every nation, by children being taught mathematical concepts. . . . A graphical representation of data abstracted from the banks of every computer in the human system. Unthinkable complexity. Lines of light ranged in the non-space of the mind, clusters and constellations of data. Like city lights, receding . . ."[5]

Michael Benedikt derived inspirational strength from this Gibsonian schema of "consensual hallucination" to conceive of cyberspace as a "new universe, a parallel universe created and sustained by the world's computers and communication lines."[6] Kevin Hughes, for his part, defines cyberspace as "an interconnected, computer-mediated environment in which all prior media are represented."[7] Cyberspace has also been defined as a bioelectronic ecosystem that subsists anywhere there are phones, coaxial cables, fiber optic lines, or electromagnetic waves.[8] However, over the course of time, there has been a dramatic semantic extension of the notion of cyberspace beyond its hitherto essentially technical purview. The contemporary conception of cyberspace that enjoys scholarly currency across various disciplines in the humanities and the social sciences encapsulates all the psychosocial and sociopolitical variables that online interaction has spawned, and grapples with the reality that technologies are relentlessly permeating the entire fabric of modern societies at all levels and with respect to all subsystems.[9]

From a sociotechnical point of view, cyberspace can be thought of as the replication, in online platforms, of a whole range of normative offline sociocultural interactions.[10] Manuel Castells made the persuasive argument that the popular conception of cyberspace as "virtual reality" misses the point about the sociotechnical interactional environment that its existence necessarily breeds.[11] He suggested that in light of the "real-world" approximations that cyberspace creates, it should be theorized as "real virtuality." The cartography of cyberspace can therefore be said to be hallmarked by both the nonvirtual spatialities of the "real word" and the organizational singularities of the virtual world. Other scholars of the Internet, in celebrating the unexampled capacity of cyberspace to be an interface between "real" and "virtual" realities, pronounced cyberspace as the veritable harbinger of the "death of distance" and the disappearance of spatial orderings, such that all points are equally accessible from any position.[12] Paul Adams points out that discourses of cyberspace and online activity are often characterized by references to space and place. He said the now familiar references to "portals," "sites" complete with "back doors," and "chat rooms," "lobbies," "classrooms," and "cafés" all linked together via "superhighways," with "mail" moving communications from one location to another suggest that cyberspace possesses a recognizable geography more or less contiguous with the conventional spatial organization of the physical world to which we are habituated.[13] However, it has been suggested that such ways of talking are little more than convenient metaphors that help us conceptualize an environment that, in reality, is inherently discontinuous with the nonvirtual world of physical objects, locations, and coordinates.[14]

Timothy Luke's conception of cyberspace sums it all up and provides a departure for articulating cyber Nigeria, which exists in both Nigeria and its digital diasporas:

> Cyperspace, then, is essentially a metaterritorial domain—everywhere, nowhere, here, there, anywhere, somewhere else—and its political possibilities, especially for the rising blocs of digerati who ceaselessly tout its benefits, are metanational in quality and quantity because of digitalization. The virtual institutions of e-commerce, e-structures, and e-government all require new "e-haviors" in cyberspace, and those platforms for shared interactivity promise to constitute something like "e-publics." The metanation of cyberspace is a contradictory cluster of contrary oppositions inside of each nation, but also outside of it; for each nation, but also not only for it; by each nation, but also not of it. As a "meta" factor, computer networks share actions and structures in common with territorial nationstates, but the telematic metanation is already always more: a deterritorialized domain of domains whose virtual/fractal/digital/viral institutions coexist behind, beyond or beside the nation-state system.[15]

Consequently, the newfangled reality that cyberspace has begotten is not only reproducing—in newer, bolder forms—the time-honored thrills and problems of human interaction but is also facilitating wholly hitherto unthought-of modes of social actions that dissolve the spatial and temporal boundaries that had traditionally governed human relational engagements. The breadth of relational processes embracing cyber interactions has also actuated new ways of thinking about the effects of virtual technologies on discursive democracy, online journalism, citizen media, virtual diasporas, and civic engagement.

When Escobar theorized Cyberia in the 1990s, Nigeria, like most African countries, was stuck in the world's digital fringes, or what Manuel Castells called the "black hole of informational capitalism."[16] At the time, no scholar "envisioned the popularity of blogging or its impact on journalism and the mass media,"[17] even in resource-rich countries, much less on the digital margins of the world. However, with more than 100 million active Internet users as of April 2019, representing more than 27 percent of Africa's 4.3 billion Internet population,[18] the foundations for the convergence of Nigeria's media-savvy diaspora in the West and the homeland digital public sphere isn't hard to conceive. This convergence has spawned a frenetic virtual public sphere and the evolvement of an engaged diasporic citizen-media formation. In this book, I analyze the emergence, growth, development, reach, and influence of unexampled diasporic, citizen-led online spaces for politically and symbolically consequential online journalism about the homeland.

A New Cyberian Media Landscape

A momentous informational revolution has been sweeping across Nigeria's media landscape since 2005. The dominance of the traditional media in the country is being challenged, and occasionally supplanted, by an emergent, as yet amorphous but nonetheless consequential, diasporic online citizen-journalism formation, reversing time-honored notions of the contours of informational flows between diasporas and homelands and the role of ordinary individuals in the transmission of information across geographic and temporal boundaries. Ordinary Nigerians who are now permanently located in the United States by virtue of voluntary geographic displacement have taken advantage of the enhanced discursive opportunity structures that the Internet enables to set up citizen media sites that not only serve as valuable vaults of information for many everyday Nigerians and traditional journalists back home but that also expose corruption in government and ethical infractions in homeland media practice. The purveyors of these inchoate but nonetheless politically potent diasporic online media have neither robust institutional support for their operations nor are they affiliated with the state.[19]

It was Hamid Mowlana who first perceptively isolated three historically foremost vectors of cross-border informational flows. He identified them as national governments, transnational corporations, and individuals.[20] However, as Karim H. Karim has aptly noted, the preponderance of international communication and globalization scholarship over the years has tended to be disproportionately concerned with the first two at the expense or even the exclusion of the third.[21] In fact, individuals who operate outside the institutional structures of governments and corporations have played significant roles in transborder data flows. This fact is becoming even more salient with the extraordinary expansion and reach of the Internet, which is enabling the emergence of a vast multitude of what the Latin American scholar Michel S. Laguerre has called "virtual diasporic public spheres,"[22] or what Jennifer Brinkerhoff has called "digital diasporas."[23]

Although the term *diaspora* is historically deployed to refer to communities of Jews who were dispersed to far-flung lands from their homeland in Israel thousands of years ago, it has now been semantically extended to denote communities of deterritorialized ethnoscapes from the global South.[24] According to Gabriel Sheffer, "Modern diasporas are ethnic minority groups of migrant origins residing and acting in host countries but maintaining strong sentimental and material links with their countries of origin—their homelands."[25] The increasing ease of international transportation, economic pressures, and educational tourism, and the widening transnational tentacles of multinational corporations that seek talent from diverse corners of the world have all conduced to the elective migration of people from the "rest" to the "West" and the evolution of diasporic communities.

The progressively diminishing importance of the nation-state in the age of globalization, which Arjun Appadurai controversially characterized as the imminence of the "end of the era of the nation-state," is also bringing into bold relief the importance of nonstate and noncorporate actors in the new information age.[26] As Appadurai observes, in place of nation-states, "transnations" of diasporic communities play increasingly defining roles in shaping the structure and substance of the processes of globalization. He argues that as electronic media "increasingly link producers and audiences across national boundaries, and as these audiences themselves start new conversations between those who move and those who stay, we find a growing number of diasporic public spheres."[27]

More recently, Nancy Fraser has extended this notion of the emersion of ever more politically and socially consequential but spatially dispersed nonstate actors in the contemporary, globalized epoch to account for the growth of public spheres that are transnational in form and essence. Specifically, she uses the term "transnational public sphere" to denote the profusion of nontraditional communicative arenas for the articulation and mobilization of political will formations that "overflow the bounds of nations and states."[28] These transnational diasporic public spheres, as Janet Conway and Jakeet Singh have noted, may be "comprehensive publics, counter-publics, weak publics or strong publics."[29] Such conceptions extend Appadurai's notion of diasporic public spheres in one important respect: they free it from a narrow preoccupation with the dynamics of the flows of migratory elites from the periphery to the core of the global power structure and link it instead with the politics and discourses of transnational political will formation and mobilization by nonstate actors.

What is missing, however, even in Fraser's more sophisticated analysis of transnational diasporic public spheres—and in the analysis of most scholars who study transnational diasporic public spheres—is a recognition of the progressively central roles that the online media, especially the citizen online media, of diasporic public spheres now play in the articulation and mobilization of political will formation across the bounds of nations and states.[30] Even scholars who have studied the role of the Internet in the enablement of transnational public spheres have generally failed to focus attention on the role of the web-based citizen media of diasporic public spheres.[31]

In a related but slightly different context, Ulf Hannerz problematizes this deficiency as a manifestation of the inadequacy of disciplinary conversation between migration and media studies—even though, as he points out, migration and mediatization "are continuously intertwined."[32] I would say, however, that what the lack in transnational public sphere scholarship evinces is the inadequacy of disciplinary dialogue between the still embryonic but nonetheless vibrant field of transnational online journalism research and the more theoretically grounded area of public sphere theory. This book fills that void by studying how the citizen online media of a peripheral but transnational virtual diasporic public sphere have functioned as veritable sites for transformative transborder informational and political intercourse between a deterritorialized ethnoscape and the media and state institutions of its homeland.

Over the past decade, the Nigerian diasporic public sphere has transcended media and migration scholars' notions of the concerns and preoccupations of deterritorialized ethnoscapes.[33] During this period, we have seen the robust growth and flowering of web-only, citizen-generated, and sometimes alternative, diasporic Nigerian online news outlets that have risen above the traditional thematic preoccupations of diasporic media. Such U.S.-based, Nigerian-owned online news outlets as SaharaReporters.com, PointBlankNews, ElenduReports.com, TimesofNigeria.com, Huhuonline.com, NigeriaVillageSquare.com, and others have become rich sources of information for local Nigerian newspapers and for Nigerians in the homeland. They—particularly Sahara Reporters and, before it, NigeriaVillageSquare.com and Elendu Reports—have also called attention to acts of corruption in Nigeria and challenged abuse of power in ways the local media are not equipped to do. Through archival, documentary, and observational evidence, this book focuses on select diasporic online media—which straddle the traditions of citizen and alternative journalism—and evaluates their impact on politics, policies, and journalistic practices in Nigeria.

Although it is customary for some scholars to conflate citizen media and alternative media, I distinguish them in this book and apply this distinction to my objects of inquiry.[34] In the new media literature, as we will see in more detail in chapter 1, citizen journalism is conceptualized as online "news content produced by ordinary citizens with no formal journalism training."[35] It needs to be noted, though, that this definition does not preclude people with formal journalism training who partake in nonprofessionalized, user-generated news-gathering and dissemination practices. Alternative journalism, on the other hand, is not merely nonprofessionalized and noninstitutionalized journalism produced by ordinary citizens; it is also purposively counterhegemonic and "closely wedded to notions of social responsibility, replacing an ideology of 'objectivity' with overt advocacy and oppositional practices."[36] Although citizen journalism (at least as the term is widely understood in new media scholarship) is enabled solely by the emergence of the Internet, alternative journalism antedates the Internet by several years. And whereas all online alternative media, to the extent that they are products of journalism by ordinary citizens outside institutional and professional structures, are citizen media, not all citizen media are alternative media. To be alternative media, citizen media have to be expressly oppositional and actuated by a progressive, emancipatory political agenda.[37] Since all the online media analyzed in this book are run by ordinary diasporic Nigerian citizens who are not affiliated with any professional news organization, they qualify as citizen media. But not all of them are alternative media because they are not all explicitly political and counterhegemonic in their reportorial temperaments, as chapters 4, 5, and 6 show.

As subsequent sections of this book reveal, however, these categories are not neat, unchanging, or invariably mutually exclusive. News sites that began as alternative media can transmute to being ordinary citizen media, and profit-driven citizen media can occasionally exhibit the characteristics of alternative media. What is not in doubt, though, is that the Nigerian diasporic online news media, whether they are merely citizen or alternative media, have dramatically altered the journalistic landscape in Nigeria and have caused major shifts in homeland state policies in novel, unique ways.

Why Studying Diasporic Online Media Is Important

The primary reason this study is necessary is that the emergence of Nigeria-focused diasporic online citizen media has not only broadened the breadth and diversity of informational resources for Nigerians both at home and in the diaspora but has also inaugurated a sometimes noticeably hostile and at other times ambivalent relationship between traditional, mainstream media practitioners in Nigeria and the plethora of exilic online citizen journalists who increasingly seem to be building their legitimacy on the strength of their capacity to undermine the credibility of traditional journalists in the homeland. Diaspora citizen journalists also have easy access to news sources and privileged news-gathering practices that have sometimes put traditional Nigerian journalists to shame. Similarly, the citizen online media of the

Nigerian diasporic public sphere have lately been at the vanguard of instigating politically consequential discourses that have had and continue to have far-reaching implications for politics and governance in the homeland. An indication of the ever-increasing importance of the sometimes adversarial online citizen journalism of the Nigerian diasporic public sphere is the growing tense relationship between critical online citizen journalists in the diaspora and the Nigerian government, a relationship that sometimes has led to the arrests of a number of high-profile diasporic online journalists who had cause to travel to the homeland for routine business.[38]

No scholarly work has systematically captured the burgeoning phenomenon of diasporic citizen online media, which is simultaneously changing and challenging the practice of corporate, institutional journalism and dramatically influencing the state policies of a distant homeland, or other dimensions of the emerging hallmarks of the transnational citizen online journalism of the Nigerian diaspora in the West. If Nancy Fraser is correct that a transnational public sphere is defined by its capacity "to be a vehicle for mobilizing public opinion as a political force [and by its capacity to] empower the citizenry vis-à-vis private powers and permit it to exercise influence over the state," then the noncorporate, nonprofessional online citizen and alternative media of geographically displaced but politically and socially consequential Nigerian exiles in the West undoubtedly qualify as a veritable transnational diasporic public sphere and are therefore worthy of careful scholarly study.[39] These newfangled Nigerian diasporic media might very well be the prototype of an evolving, Internet-enabled, translocal, and mutual informational and cultural exchange between the educated, deterritorialized ethnoscapes of peripheral nations, whose exile in the West endows them with symbolic and cultural capital, and the private institutions and governments of their homelands.

It was Debra Spitulnik who first called attention to how what she calls "small media" in Africa—by which she means alternative, citizen discursive spaces that ordinary individuals and small groups can be in command of, such as the Internet, audiocassettes, and so on—can function as "vital and pervasive undercurrents and reservoirs of political commentary, and potential mobilization."[40] Courtesy of the dizzying ease of cross-border data flow, made even easier by the phenomenal expansion of hitherto restricted Internet and mobile-phone technology on the African continent only a few years after her essay appeared, what Spitulnik identified as a probability is materializing in ways that likely exceed her prognostications.[41]

In the conventional scholarship on sovereignty, state-civil society relations, and diaspora studies, it is customary to emphasize domination and one-dimensionality in cultural flows.[42] However, this book argues that the participation of members of the Nigerian digital diaspora in the politics and discourses of their homeland illustrates that citizens, especially in the age of the Internet, are not merely powerless subjects and receivers of informational flows from the institutions of the state and from corporate mass media. Through the instrumentality of online citizen media, even from their exilic locations in the West, they can be active consumers and producers of informational resources and even purveyors of political power in ways that amply exemplify translocal reciprocality.

This book will be the first to systematically chronicle and explore the rising power, through the instrumentality of online citizen media, of the digital public sphere of a previously politically disempowered diaspora in the West. Traditionally, because of what Brinkerhoff called their "hybrid identities," diasporans had always been comparatively politically inconsequential in the politics of their homelands.[43] In particular, their media-use patterns had consisted in (and in most other contexts still consist in) the consumption of news from the homeland rather than participation in the generation and reporting of news from, about, and for the homeland. Historically, where vibrant diasporic media existed, their creators and consumers did little more than deploy them mostly to negotiate their identities as voluntary and involuntary exiles, promote solidarity, and nurture collective national memories that were often sanctified by nostalgia and the desire to suture the ruptures that so readily emerge in a state of uprootedness that is concomitant with geographic displacement to new sociocultural habitats—what Arif Dirlik has called the "mournful discourses of marginalized diasporics."[44] The media were never used as instruments to change homeland state policies, or as reservoirs of information for citizens back "home," or as tools for political mobilization.

The online citizen media of the Nigerian diasporic public sphere have transcended these time-honored structural trademarks of diaspora media in ways that seem to have no parallel so far. This book, therefore, makes important contributions to the existing literature on critical diaspora discourse. It illustrates, through the diasporic alternative and citizen journalism of the Nigerian digital public sphere, that in the process of deterritorialization, societies of departure and arrival are inextricably interlinked in the delineation of human motions, a delineation characterized not "by linear and unidirectional motions . . . but by 'circulations' of peoples and commodities that are in the process of creating new spaces."[45]

This book also captures, on a transnational scale, the nascent ambivalent relationship between citizen journalism and institutional journalistic practices. The extant literature concerning the consequences of the proliferation of citizen media on traditional journalistic practices is almost exclusively preoccupied with the experiences of the more advanced parts of the world; it does not capture the singularities of peripheral, transitional nations such as Nigeria, where the Internet is only just becoming demotic, where the tension between traditional and online journalism is assuming unpredictably unique forms every moment, and where alternative and/or citizen online journalism imposes on itself the simultaneous task of fighting corrupt governments and equally corrupt, co-opted, traditional mainstream media in the homeland.[46] By tracing the evolution of the citizen journalism of the Nigerian digital diaspora; exploring its variegated manifestations and forms; capturing the relational and professional tensions between online citizen journalists in the diaspora and traditional journalists in the homeland; and showing how all this has altered journalistic practice and statecraft in Nigeria, this book contributes to scholarship not only on the tension between online and traditional journalism but also on the reconfigurations of the loci of political and symbolic power that are taking place in the age of globalization and the Internet. It therefore joins and advances disciplinary conversations in media and migration studies, globalization, online journalism, deliberative democracy, and public sphere theory.

It also contributes to the body of work on the notion of resistance in critical media theory and cultural studies. For instance, it explores such questions as: How much resistance (a subject with which cultural studies have been preoccupied) can web-based alternative media that are compelled to survive by attracting advertisements put up to the system they purport to fight? In their bid to reverse the disabling cynicism of much of the Frankfurt School, cultural studies scholars have been obsessed with investigating instances of resistance to the power structure by citizens at the lower end of the social scale. As Thomas Frank has satirically noted, in echoes of Meaghan Morris' apt observation of the tendency of cultural studies scholars to read rebellion in every banal form of pop culture consumption, "Their books teem with stories of aesthetic hierarchies rudely overturned; with subversive shoppers dauntlessly using up the mall's air conditioning; with heroic fans building their workers' paradise right there in the Star Trek corpus; with rebellious readers of women's fashion magazines symbolically smashing the state."[47] He was ridiculing such cultural studies scholars as John Fiske and Henry Jenkins, who aver that the capacity for "oppositional" readings of media texts is evidence of "resistance" to cultural hegemony.[48] However, as Douglas Kellner has argued, such "oppositional" readings occur at no cost to the reader and certainly without any consequence to the capitalist hegemony they are supposed to be "resisting." It is merely a weak struggle for "meaning" and "pleasure."[49] So where might resistance lie in the emerging forms of web-based alternative citizen media, or what Chris Atton has called "radical online journalism"?[50]

Similarly, this book elaborates on traditional notions of media imperialism and advances the conversation about media flows in international communication scholarship. The concept of media imperialism has dominated scholarship in international communication for decades. The argument of scholars who first propounded the theory of media imperialism is that the flow of cultural goods across the world is disproportionately skewed in favor of countries in the West, which are at the core of the world system, and to the disadvantage of countries in the third world, which are at the periphery of the world system. The early proponents of this theory, interestingly, are American scholars whose geographic and cultural realities put them at the core of the world system.[51] Writing in the 1970s, Herbert Schiller pointed out that, for instance, 65 percent of the world's news and cultural products originated in the United States, a reality that relegated the rest of the world to being consumers of American media and cultural products.[52] Wilbur Schramm also pointed out that the uneven distribution of mass media in the world has meant that the realities of the peoples of the third world are either ignored or distorted by the dominant Western media.[53]

Over the last few decades, however, fresh theoretical insights into the nature of global flows have challenged the accuracy of the media imperialism paradigm. One such insight is the theory of contraflows, which shifts scholarly attention to instances of the subversion of the dominant conception of global flows. Arjun Appadurai, for instance, calls attention to the fact that globalization has not necessarily translated into the homogenization of the world or, for that matter, the westernization of non-Western societies. What has happened, he says, is that in cultural and informational flows, the global often fuses with the local to produce the "glocal."[54] As Daya Thussu points out, "The global (which in essence means Western or more accurately American) offering interacts with the national and the local in ways that produce often hybridized, 'glocal' media products, hallmark of a postmodern cultural sensitivity."[55] This reconsideration of the nature of global flows has given rise to the concept of contraflows.

In his essay "Mapping Global Media Flow and Contra-Flow," Thussu develops a typology that divides the main media flows in the world into three categories: global, transnational, and geocultural. He draws a distinction between what he calls the "dominant flows," which spring forth from the global North, and the "subaltern flows," which he defines as "contra-flows originating from the erstwhile peripheries of global media industries."[56] This is similar to Straubhaar's asymmetrical interdependence thesis within the context of a developing bifurcation in global cultural interchange between the "global popular" in movie production and "glocalization" in television production.[57]

The notion of contraflows has become popular and can even be said to have achieved a position of dominance in international communication scholarship. As a result, the perception of a unidirectional flow of informational and cultural goods from the Western "core" to the third world "periphery" has been contested by many scholars who insist that global flows are inherently multidirectional.[58] Such scholars theorize globalization as a force that animates—or at least has the potential to animate—ethnic, cultural, religious, and linguistic resistance to the homogenizing and imperialistic tendencies of the Western media and the neoliberal gospel of their owners. Annabelle Sreberny-Mohammadi, for example, points out that popular notions of Western cultural and media imperialism blur the intricate and mutually reinforcing nature of interaction over centuries between diverse and progressively more hybridized cultures.[59]

Similarly, Anthony Giddens points to the phenomenon of inverse colonization instantiated by the proliferation of alternative loci of cultural influence in the periphery and, in fact, the increasing exportation of this influence to the core, such as the export of Brazilian television programs to Portugal, its ex-colonial overlord, and the hispanicization of southern California.[60] More generally, it is argued, global media enterprises have been forced to adapt to local cultures and to link up with local partners in order to sustain their expansion. The identity of diasporic communities, it is argued, can now be nourished not only through treasured postcards and the evanescent recollections of grandparents but also through daily media feeds that sustain endangered ethnic minority identities.[61]

The emergence, popularity, and ubiquity of the Internet have further complicated this process. Although the wealthiest nations of the world still have an edge in access to the Internet, its nature has helped to complicate informational flows dramatically. Information from peripheral countries is reaching core countries at a higher volume—and at a faster rate—than was ever thought possible. This has enabled coalition building between people who are vastly physically separated. This book takes off from these interventions about the perpetually kaleidoscopic nature of informational and cultural flows in the age of globalization, but departs from them and advances their application to the changing face and phase of global news flow in ways that account for what I call Western diaspora media cultural capital. Although the media flow that I grapple with in this book is still geographically from the West, it is initiated by people who have been territorially displaced from the periphery to the core by the forces of globalization and who have not only internalized a Western journalistic ethos but also have tremendous access to information that is not available to their counterparts in the homeland.

I argue that territorial displacement in the emerging global age does not simply alienate; it also invests people with the social and cultural capital to exert influence in the domestic public sphere from which they are uprooted in ways that complicate and dramatize the antinomies between diasporic public spheres and the national politics of nation-states. Location in the West, particularly in the United States, confers on diasporic Nigerians the sort of cultural and symbolic capital that enables them to be strategically inserted in the politics and informational flows of their homeland. This reality has profound implications for the ways we theorize globalization, media flows, and media imperialism.

Structure and Outline of the Book

It is obvious from the foregoing that citizen journalism on the Internet constitutes the fulcrum around which this changing phase of transnational news flows revolves, which is what this book is concerned with. In order to empirically map and situate the evolution, significance, and impact of Nigerian diasporic online citizen journalism, I analyze:

- how the online citizen and alternative media of the Nigerian diaspora have influenced traditional journalistic practices in Nigeria
- how and why the online citizen and alternative media of the Nigerian diaspora caused the Nigerian government to change state policies
- how and why online citizen news media emerge in the Nigerian digital diaspora with their current characteristics
- specific ways in which the online media of the Nigerian digital diaspora disrupted traditional notions of news flows between the media of the homeland and the people in the diaspora

- which dominant influences—such as advertising, political affiliations, emancipatory politics, and so on—actuate the citizen journalism of the Nigerian diaspora
- how they instigated the flowering of a robust online-only domestic media formation
- how the journalistic practices of the Nigerian diaspora might complicate notions of citizen and alternative journalism

This book is divided into eight chapters. This introduction is a broad overview of the subject matter of the book, the disciplinary conversations it joins and extends, the significance of its thematic preoccupation, and the research questions that undergird it.

Chapter 1 reviews and coalesces the extant literature on diaspora media, citizen online journalism, alternative media, public-sphere theory, and various conceptions of informational flows. It lays out the conceptual outlines of the book, identifies the gaps in the existing literature, points out the contributions this book makes to the disciplinary conversation, and highlights the broad theoretical framework that informs this book.

Chapter 2 traces the historical trajectory of resistant and emancipatory journalism in Nigeria and finds linkages between this tradition and this book's object of inquiry. It particularly focuses on a phenomenon that has been called "guerrilla journalism" in Nigeria, which flourished in the 1990s in the face of a particularly brutal military dictatorship that reigned between 1993 and 1998. With the restoration of democratic rule in 1999, the insurgent journalism of the guerrilla media era in Nigeria all but fizzled out, and the erstwhile radical, uncompromising, and adversarial media were co-opted and compromised. This chapter locates the emergence of diasporic citizen online media within the context of this extinct media tradition, especially because some of the diasporic media initially had working agreements with the remnants of the guerrilla media in Nigeria to share and cross-promote stories.

Chapter 3 historicizes the Nigerian diaspora in the United States and chronicles its record of early adoption of technology and deliberative democracy. It locates the emergence of Nigeria's vibrant diasporic citizen media formation to the history and character of the Nigerian diaspora in the United States and joins the debate on Habermasian conception of the public sphere. Chapter 4 is one of the compositional phases and evidentiary bases of the book. It traces the history of online journalism in Nigeria and locates its evolution in Nigeria in the context of broader discussions about global online journalism. It then provides detailed histories of specific, high-profile, and influential diasporic citizen media sites, pointing out their most important stories, reportorial temperaments, limitations, and differential motivations.

Chapter 5 examines specific case studies that instantiate the transformational interventions of diasporic citizen media in homeland politics and policies, including being the diasporic watchdogs of the homeland watchdogs. The cases are organized and thematized to illuminate those in which online citizen media stories have led to homeland governmental policy changes and those in which the diasporic online media exposed high-level corruption in the local news media. This selection conforms to the outlines of critical, extreme, and paradigmatic case studies. The implications of these cases are explored and related to the broader theoretical and empirical concerns of the book. Chapter 6 discusses the reactions of the Nigerian government to the piercing, unaccustomed, and disruptive scrutiny of governance by the new, geographically distant diasporic media outfits. Chapter 7 explores networked social media journalism, an emerging phase of journalism in which traditional Nigerian news organizations lag behind some of their diasporic and digital-native homeland counterparts. It also discusses the plethora of online-only Nigerian-based newspapers that have emerged in the last couple of years and shows how these media derived inspirational strength from the success of the Nigerian diasporic citizen media formation.

The last chapter highlights the implications of the findings of this book and draws conclusions based on these findings. The findings, where applicable, are compared with existing theoretical formulations to discover patterns, themes, key issues, nuanced divergences, and new insights. Since this book is ultimately about the nature and consequences of emergent forms of informational flows between the diasporas and homelands of peripheral, transitional nation-states in the age of globalization and the Internet, in this chapter I draw connections between existing theories of media flows, transnational public spheres, resistance, and the findings of the research. I also show the limitations of the study and recommend areas for future research.

Chapter One

Citizen and Alternative Journalism: Mapping the Conceptual Contours

Citizen journalism and alternative journalism are core constructs in this book and have been used to characterize emergent models of decentered, non-oligopolistic journalisms. An awareness of the differences between them is central to the preoccupations of this book. In this chapter, I define alternative and citizen models of journalism, map their conceptual contours, and point out their intersections in the age of the Internet. In reviewing the corpus of research that has been done in conceptualizing citizen and alternative journalism, I reveal the gaps in the extant literature. How might we conceive alternative journalism? How is it different from and similar to citizen journalism? And how are these categories useful for this book?

Although it is customary for some scholars to conflate citizen media and alternative media, I argue in this book that they are different.[1] In the new media literature, citizen journalism is traditionally conceptualized as online "news content produced by ordinary citizens with no formal journalism training."[2] It needs to be noted, however, that citizen journalism does not necessarily preclude people with formal journalism training so long as they partake in nonprofessionalized, user-generated news-gathering and dissemination practices. Alternative journalism, on the other hand, is not merely nonprofessionalized and noninstitutionalized journalism produced by ordinary citizens; it is also purposively counterhegemonic and "closely wedded to notions of social responsibility, replacing an ideology of 'objectivity' with overt advocacy and oppositional practices."[3]

Whereas citizen journalism (at least the way this term is widely understood and applied in new media scholarship) is enabled largely by the emergence of the Internet, alternative journalism not only preceded the Internet but is as old as journalism itself. And although all online alternative media—to the extent that they are products of journalism by ordinary citizens outside institutional and professional structures, are citizen media—not all citizen media are alternative media. To be alternative, media citizen media have to be expressly oppositional and actuated by a progressive, emancipatory political agenda.[4] However, these categories are not neat, unchanging, or invariably mutually exclusive. For one thing, as will be demonstrated throughout this book, notions of what constitutes progressive, emancipatory political agendas vary widely from country to country. For instance, a comparative study of the editorial dispositions of British and Nigerians newspapers shows that "what is 'conservative' in Britain is 'liberal' in Nigeria," which underlines "the fragility and instability of facile ideological labels."[5] Similarly, news sites that began as alternative media can transmute into quotidian citizen media, and profit-driven citizen media can occasionally exhibit the characteristics of alternative media.

In what follows, I review the trajectory of the scholarship on alternative and citizen journalism and explore the intersection between alternative journalism and citizen journalism in the age of the Internet. This helps in contextualizing and foregrounding the book's core thematic and theoretical concerns.

Conceptions of Alternative Journalism

Sahara Reporters, one of the exilic citizen media sites analyzed in this book, is characterized here as having practiced "alternative journalism" before its decline between 2018 and 2019. But what is alternative journalism? What are its definitional outlines and limitations? Can notions of alternative journalism be mediated and inflected by geographic, sociohistorical, and political specificities? In other words, is there a conception of alternative journalism that is equally valid and applicable in both first- and third-world contexts and in both democratic and emerging democratic contexts? Would a media formation that qualifies as "alternative" in the United States be validly so in Nigeria and vice versa?

Although the emergence of alternative journalism is almost coterminous with the birth of mainline journalistic practice, comparatively little scholarly attention has been devoted to its growth, form, content, impact, and future.[6] The last twenty years, however, have witnessed a vigorous profusion of scholarly interest in alternative journalism.[7] This is certainly partly a consequence of both the popularity and ubiquity of the Internet and the expansion of the discursive space that it enables, evidenced in the blossoming of several web-based citizen and alternative media. But although many critical media scholars have robustly and carefully captured the emergence, constraints, motives, practices, prospects, singularities, and dominant thematic preoccupations of alternative media, there is no universally agreed upon conception of what alternative journalism is.[8]

As Chris Atton has noted,[9] until relatively recently, the only definitive scholarly study of alternative journalism was John Downing's influential 1984 book on the subject.[10] For Downing, the distinctiveness of alternative journalism lies in its self-conscious subversion of the elaborate hierarchies typical of professional news organizations and in its explicitly nonconformist and counterhegemonic political agenda. The kind of media formation this engenders is often well suited to the progressive, anticapitalist agenda of social movements, which are usually marginalized in the mainstream media. Downing draws clear contrasts between alternative media and the mainstream media. He maintains that the operations of the mainstream media are animated by profit motive; are organized according to predetermined, exclusive professional and routinized standards; and are hallmarked by entrenched hierarchies. In other words, as Atton observes, Downing's conception of alternative media privileges "media that are written and run by non-professionals, by groups that are primarily activists for progressive social change."[11]

As more critical media scholars became interested in the systematic study of alternative media, however, conceptions of what constitutes alternative journalism have become much more complicated than Downing's simplistic, if historically contingent, binaries. Since the publication of Downing's book, at least ten other notable scholarly works—among them another one by Downing in which he revises his earlier approach, have been published, all of which have sought to more carefully capture the complexity of alternative journalism.[12] Similarly, at least six journal issues have devoted exclusive attention to the subject of alternative journalism.[13]

As Patricia Gibbs and James Hamilton have pointed out, part of the difficulty of providing an all-encompassing definition of alternative journalism is that the term is often merely a convenient label that encapsulates—or seeks to encapsulate—a variety of nonhegemonic media practices that are vastly diverse in aims, goals, and specificities, and that replace or supplant "more specific designations such as the 'labor press,' 'feminist press,' or 'underground media.'"[14] Vincent Campbell agrees. He says terms such as "alternative press" tend to be used as "broad-brush collective terms for a disparate body of practices," although common themes can often be isolated from these practices.[15] Scholars who want to remain faithful to the differential motivations that actuate the practices of alternative media formations often distinguish between "oppositional" alternative media and "advocacy" alternative media to take account of the dominant concerns that inform several different alternative media practices.[16] Although advocacy alternative media often function as the mouthpieces of organized social movements, oppositional alternative media usually are not wedded to any definite political cause or social movement. They are often just purposive vaults of nonhegemonic news.

However, even though the term *alternative media* would appear to dissolve the exceptionalities that characterize a wide variety of counterhegemonic, insurgent media practices, Gibbs and Hamilton insist "it is extremely useful to see them together because such a move emphasizes their collective resistance to increasingly monolithic commercialized media systems and products."[17] In fact, in his later work on alternative media, John Downing agrees that in spite of what might seem like the vastly divergent goals of various categories of alternative media, they are actually united by the dual functions they all perform: as "counter-information institutions" and as "agents of developmental power."[18] It is because of this dual function that some scholars have broadly characterized this genre of journalism as "insurgent journalism"[19] or "counter-hegemonic journalism."[20] In other words, alternative journalism's meaning can be realized only in opposition to the established, mainstream media.

Such a discursive delineation provides the conceptual justification for the customary practice in media studies to conceive of "alternative" media in binary opposition to the "mainstream" media, with "'mainstream' seen as maximizing audiences by appealing to safe, conventional formulas and 'alternative' foregoing the comfortable, depoliticizing formulas to advocate programs of social change."[21] It is in the same vein that Tanni Haas conceives of alternative media as "media devoted to providing representations of issues and events which oppose those offered in the mainstream media and to advocating social and political reform."[22]

This means, in essence, that alternative media define themselves—or are defined—only in contradistinction to the mainstream media. Where the mainstream media are impersonal and professionally managed, alternative media are "self-managed."[23] Where the mainstream media are formally structured, alternative media are "non-hierarchical."[24] Where the practices of the mainstream media are motivated by profit, those of the alternative media are motivated by "collectivist-democratic" ideals.[25] By being radically different from mainstream media in structure and content, alternative media seek to comfort a broad range of subaltern populations that are either pushed to the margins of the mainstream media or that are completely excluded from them.[26]

Most important, according to scholars of alternative media, where the mainstream media impose on themselves the responsibility of creating and nurturing an informed citizenry, alternative media practitioners have as their goal the desire to inspire a mobilized citizenry.[27] As Kenya Tomaselli and Eric Louw put it, alternative media practitioners perceive their role more as "facilitators of social communication" than as "sources of information."[28] This explains why scholars of alternative media variously characterize the unequivocally political content of alternative journalism as "mobilizing information,"[29] "information for action,"[30] "action on action,"[31] or simply "useful information."[32]

Other scholars locate the difference between alternative media and mainstream media in terms of their differential conventions of news sourcing. Whereas the routinized professional practices of the mainstream media often predispose them to take recourse to "the systematic accessing of powerful, resource-rich institutions and their definition of events—and to the marginalization of resource-poor social groups and interests,"[33] alternative media actively seek a "different cast of accessed 'officials' and other voices."[34] They adopt what has been dubbed "native reporting," which Atton defines as an alternative news-gathering practice "where social actors, instead of being subjects of the news, become their own correspondents, reporting on their own experiences, struggles and ideas."[35] This nonconformist alternative media reportorial practice finds its most sophisticated expression in what Nick Couldry calls "active witnessing,"[36] which John D. Peters describes elsewhere as a situation in which "one is a privileged possessor and producer of knowledge in an extraordinary, often forensic, setting in which speech and truth are policed in multiple ways."[37]

In other words, for the mainstream media, the primary definers of news are people who occupy the upper end of the social scale, people whose possession of what Pierre Bourdieu called "doxa" (that is, the cultural and discursive unconscious that predisposes us to accord authority to some people and deny it to others), people who get access to the news media as a matter of convention.[38] For the alternative media, the voices of the voiceless tend to take precedence. They give expression to the thoughts, actions, anxieties, and perspectives of people whose lack of social, cultural, and symbolic capital consigns them to the discursive fringes. Predictably, this makes most "professional" news hardly more than the concerns, interpretations, and cultural biases of the privileged few in society. The concerns of the lower rungs of the social order are highlighted only under special circumstances. As Robert McChesney observes, "Professional journalism tends to demand 'news hooks'—some sort of news event—to justify publication. This means that long-term public issues, like racism or suburban sprawl, tend to fall by the wayside, and there is little emphasis on providing the historical and ideological context necessary to bring public issues to life to readers."[39] An additional consequence of this demotion of the concerns of subalterns to the margins and the elevation of the concerns of the upper classes to the forefront is that the society is often burdened with a media formation in which "consumerism, the market, class inequality, and individualism tend to be taken as natural and often benevolent, whereas political activity, civic values, and anti-market activities tend to be marginalized or denounced."[40] It is this media practice that liberatory alternative media seek to reverse and, in its place, inaugurate a media system "where working people, sexual minorities, trade unions, protest groups—people of low status in terms of their relationship to elite groups of owners, managers and senior professionals—could make their own news, whether by appearing in it as significant actors or by creating news relevant to their situation."[41] This is possible because as Tony Harcup reminds us, many people involved with alternative journalism "see their journalism as 'political activity' . . , a perspective that appears to be far from the norm among journalists in the wider industry."[42] However, the Nigerian experience of alternative citizen journalism, with which this book is primarily concerned, is in some ways markedly different from most of the dimensions of "native reporting" that scholars of alternative journalism have identified. Most of the Nigerian alternative online news sites use conventional news sources for their stories. Although they speak with sources that would not have any voices—or that would at best have only marginal voices—in the mainstream Nigerian media, they mostly tap the discontent and internal wrangling of the Nigerian power elite to get exclusive stories that would never make it to the mainstream media.

This is especially possible because Nigerian alternative online news practitioners are geographically displaced from the homeland. This gives their sources assurances of confidentiality. Exclusive pictures of a president's son bathing in a pile of cash and brandishing brand-new guns; video clips of a governor in the strictly Muslim, Sharia-implementing state of Borno dancing with a female musician and splashing loads of cash on her (dancing and music are prohibited in Sharia states); PDF files of court documents showing that important Nigerian government officials were convicted of crimes in foreign lands (which should disqualify them from holding public office); or pictures of the choice property of corrupt Nigerian elites in Nigerian cities and in Western capitals do not fall under the purview of "native reporting," but they are radically alternative nonetheless, and have so shaken the roots of the Nigerian presidency that the late president of Nigeria, Umaru Yar'Adua, was compelled in 2008 to force every person working in his office to swear an oath of secrecy. Nigeria's oldest surviving weekly newsmagazine, *Newswatch*, remarked, "This is the first of such oath-taking at the seat of power" in Nigeria.[43] The only feature that this mode of news gathering shares with native reporting is its unabashed repudiation of the requirements of balance and objectivity, what Sunday Dare, a practitioner of guerrilla journalism (a precursor to Nigerian alternative online journalism that is discussed in more detail in chapter 3) calls "an editorial philosophy of partisan objectivity on the side of the truth."[44] Alternative news practitioners consider notions of "objectivity"—central to the ethos of professional journalistic practices as embedded in a system of domination—as a rhetorical smokescreen to perpetuate the marginality of subaltern populations and naturalize the symbolic and cultural dominance of the privileged classes. Therefore, in alternative media reportorial practices, traditionally marginal groups are purposively privileged. Their voices are no longer incidental noises in the narrative structure of media reports.

Another popular way to conceive of alternative media, especially among Marxist and neo-Marxist media theorists, is to understand them in terms of their location "outside of the forces of market economics and the state."[45] Independence from the constraints of the market and the pressures of the state, Atton contends, imbues alternative media with the capacity to confront "radical questions of citizenship in the public sphere" in ways the mainstream media cannot.[46] Like other scholars of alternative media, he argues that it is this distinctive structural feature that makes alternative media such irresistible magnets for new social movements. It has been observed, for example, that alternative media emerge and flourish "during periods of heightened social tension."[47] In Nigeria, the social tension that justified the emergence of online alternative media in the diaspora is the deepening of corruption and elite irresponsibility in the wake of the restoration of civilian rule, as subsequent chapters of this book illustrate. This is precisely why there has historically been a strong nexus between alternative media and social movements, although in the Nigerian case an organized social movement has not accompanied the emergence of alternative media platforms.

A number of empirical studies also have demonstrated that only alternative-media formations frame social protests sympathetically and cast activists in a positive light.[48] One study found that activists in social movements consume more news from alternative media than do nonactivists. Yet another study showed that although activists extensively get their news from alternative media, they do not ignore the mainstream media.[49] The implication of all this is that because of their constant exposure to alternative viewpoints through alternative media, activists are likely to develop what Stuart Hall called "resistant readings" to the hegemonic codes inscribed in the messages of the mainstream media.[50] That is why Atton has argued that a key feature of alternative media, especially online alternative media, is their "egalitarian mode of address, where intellectuals share media platforms with activists and where it is hoped that elitism is eroded. Here we find the new media used both by grassroots activists and by dissenting academics and other intellectuals participating in a counter public sphere."[51]

This is, however, an inadequate definition of radical online journalism. By limiting it to the exchange of platforms between intellectuals and activists, these definitional constructs have rendered it a victim of the elitism it hopes to escape. This limitation is clearly a consequence of the tendency among alternative-media scholars to associate radical online news practices only with established social movements and to conflate alternative media with social-movement media. As pointed out earlier, although these two kinds of media share many similarities, they are different in significant respects. Whereas social-movement media are distinguished by their association with organized social movements, not all alternative media are embedded in organized social action. Sahara Reporters, for instance, is not the organ of an organized Nigerian social movement; it is an independent media platform anchored around the activist bona fides of its founder, Omoyele Sowore. When we learn to conceive of online media activism outside the limited confines of organized social movements, and to recognize that it can incorporate several varieties of small-group and individual dissent, we will do more justice to notions of radical online journalism.

That is why Roger Silverstone's instructive point that "alternative media have created new spaces for alternative voices that provide the focus both for *specific community interests* as well as for *the contrary and the subversive*" [emphasis mine] is more fitting to this book than all other conceptions of alternative media.[52] Three elements can be isolated from Silverstone's conception of alternative media. First, alternative media are often targeted at specific communities. This is a crucial distinction from the oligopolistic model of mass communication that, for the most part, targets a mass, dispersed, heterogeneous, and anonymous audience. Second, alternative media are ideologically invested in espousing points of view that are contrary to the traditions and conventions of the established order. Third, in order to counter the power structure, alternative media deploy subversive tactics and strategies. These range from self-conscious repudiation of the institutional and organizational structures of the mainstream media to rejection of traditional methods of news sourcing. Silverstone adds that whenever alternative media formations decide to adopt the practices of the mainstream mass media, they often do so with the explicit aim to "pursue a critical or alternative media agenda, from the margins, as it were, or from the underbelly of social life."[53] This dovetails with the character and operations of a few of the Nigerian online news outlets that are examined in this book, particularly in their earliest manifestations. They did not employ the techniques of native reporting but rather adopted, adapted, and subverted mainstream media news-gathering techniques.[54]

From these varying conceptions of alternative media, Atton concludes that the most rewarding way to understand alternative media is to recognize their location outside time-honored, routinized professional news practices:

> Alternative media may be understood as a radical challenge to the professionalized and institutionalized practices of the mainstream media. Alternative media privilege a journalism that is closely wedded to notions of social responsibility, replacing an ideology of "objectivity" with overt advocacy and oppositional practices. Its practices emphasize first-person, eyewitness accounts by participants; a reworking of the populist approaches to tabloid newspapers to recover a "radical popular" style of reporting; and collective and anti-hierarchical forms of organization which eschew demarcation and specialization—and which importantly suggest an inclusive, radical form of civic journalism.[55]

Alternative journalism is radical, he adds, when it is "opposed to hierarchical, elite-centered notions of journalism as a business."[56] This is, of course, problematic because many radical online news outlets are run as businesses of some sort, allowing advertisements to be placed on their websites from which they make money. Similarly, not all alternative journalism is explicitly antibusiness.

A few Nigerian alternative diasporic online media outlets illustrate this. Since even alternative media platforms must first survive before they can be effective, and financial solvency is the lifeline of all media, alternative journalism can simultaneously embrace business and be oppositional. The sort of business they embrace, not business in and of itself, is the key here.

Problematizing the Binary Opposition of Alternative and Mainstream Media

It is obvious from the foregoing that the germinal conceptions of alternative journalism, which are still influential today, locate it in binary opposition to what have been understood as the mainstream media. Perhaps this is not altogether surprising. After all, the very notion of "alternativeness" presupposes not just an opposition to something but, in fact, mutual exclusivity with that thing. Alternativeness connotes not just unconventional choices but also contradictory possibilities.

Lately, however, a few scholars of alternative media have begun to question the ontological utility of this dualist conception of alternative media. In his later works, John Downing concedes that the dualism of his earlier typology imposed definitional and discursive burdens on the notion of alternative journalism.[57] He has identified two fundamental flaws with his earlier approach. He terms the first flaw "anti-binarism."[58] By "anti-binarism," he means his rejection of the then dominant Western and Soviet media models and his insistence that both models were ideologically complicit with maintaining and naturalizing exploitative relations of production. Because he thought both media systems were monolithic and unrepresentative, he argued that neither of them offered any hope. He labels the second flaw "binarism," by which he means the rigid distinction he imposed between alternative journalism and traditional, professional journalism. He points out, however, that the "binarism" was justified by the need to "hammer home merits of alternative ways of communicating politically, however picayune they might appear in the first instance."[59] Downing has acknowledged that these flaws prevented him from appreciating the subtleties and continuums that exist between alternative media and mainstream media, and he ended up with an account that "seriously simplified both."[60]

Many other scholars are recognizing the futility of an "either/or" approach to understanding alternative media. Atton, for instance, following Downing's self-criticism, has argued that it is more useful to talk of the "hybridity" of reportorial practices within the "contemporary media landscape," and has pointed to the "complex, hybrid nature of alternative media in relation to [their] mainstream counterparts."[61] Harcup has also called attention to what he terms the "crossover grouping," that is, current mainstream media practitioners who were previously alternative journalists and vice versa.[62] It is also significant that alternative media are not necessarily invariably progressive and liberatory. André Haller, Kristoffer Holt, and Renaud de La Brosse remind us that the popularity and centrality of such fringe, right-wing, conspiracy US news sites as Breitbart News Network, The Alex Jones Show and Infowars challenge us to expand the epistemological boundaries of the traditional conceptions of alternative media. They point out that to the extent that they "publish alternative reports and interpretations of current events as a direct response to the perception that the perspective they promote (political, ideological, moral, cultural, religious) is being treated unfairly in the mainstream media," they are legitimately alternative media.[63]

Similarly, the mainstream media have increasingly incorporated into their professional repertoire media practices that were thought to be exclusive to alternative media formations. Such mainstream media practices as public or civic journalism, which are becoming more and more fashionable, especially with the popularity of online media, are borrowed from alternative media practices.[64] There are also many respects in which alternative media practices borrow reportorial precepts from the mainstream media. Given the instability of the epistemological boundaries of "alternative" and "mainstream" media practices, it has been suggested that critical scholars should embrace Antonio Gramsci's notion of hegemony to gain a more theoretically sophisticated understanding of media practices. According to Atton, "[M]edia practices may be viewed as movable; they may articulate to bourgeois (mainstream) values in one instance, but become joined with radical views in another. A hegemonic approach suggests a complexity of relations between radical and mainstream that previous binary models have not been able to identify."[65] Nick Couldry,[66] for his part, argues that the insistence on a rigid distinction between "alternative" media and "mainstream" media has the effect of perpetually consigning progressive, activist media to the margins and thereby robbing them not only of what Pierre Bourdieu calls "symbolic power"[67] but also contributing to their exclusion from what the Italian political sociologist Alberto Melucci has called "the power of naming."[68] Bourdieu noted that

> Durkheim has the merit of designating the *social function* . . . of symbolism in an explicit way: it is an authentic political function which cannot be reduced

> to the structuralists' function of communication. Symbols are the instruments of knowledge and communication. . . . [T]hey make it possible for there to be a consensus on the meaning of the social world, a *consensus* which contributes fundamentally to the reproduction of social order [emphasis in the original].[69]

By accepting the label "alternative," and conceding that the bourgeois media are the "mainstream," progressive and independent media practitioners legitimize the consensus that reproduces narratives of their alterity and therefore unwittingly participate in their own rhetorical marginalization. Couldry avers that precisely because, in comparative terms, alternative media organizations lack symbolic resources and the power of naming, their activities tend to be largely invisible,[70] circumscribed, and reduced to being no more than what James Scott called "weapons of the weak."[71] The issue, then, is for the media of the oppressed not only to challenge the status quo but to also seek the symbolic capital that will empower them to contest meanings and the politics of naming. This is perhaps why many alternative-media practitioners now prefer to call their media "independent" media, with the implication that the corporate, legacy media are "dependent" on external forces—advertisers, big business, the state, and so on—for their existence and are therefore by implication compromised, unreliable, and self-interested.

The utility of this distinction, however, is limited to pre-Internet, social-movement alternative media, which were usually supported, by and large, by voluntary contributions from political activists who subscribed to the points of views of those various alternative media formations. In the age of the Internet, this has become complicated. Although activist-supported, advertisement-averse, social movement media still exist, in the new platforms enabled by the Internet, various kinds of alternative media have emerged whose practices are increasingly difficult to differentiate from the corporate, commercialized media. Has the Internet qualitatively altered the form and content of alternative media? Or are the changes brought about by the Internet on the character and practices of alternative media merely cosmetic? The next section provides insights into these questions.

Alternative Media in the Age of the Internet

Although scholars have acknowledged how the Internet has radically altered the content and character of alternative media, not all have come to terms with the ways in which the Internet has done epistemological violence to erstwhile conceptions of alternative journalism. In fact, some scholars are reluctant to admit that the Internet has inaugurated wholly new modes of practices. For instance, Atton cites the prominent new-media scholar Dorothy Kidd as finding striking parallels between "contemporary, Internet-based alternative media formations such as Indymedia and its precursors in previous decades of social movement media" and insists that the Internet is not unique in any radical way.[72] However, insistence that the Internet is no more than the migration of erstwhile forms of alternative media formations in virtual forms does a disservice to efforts to come to grips with the ways in which the Internet complicates our understanding of contemporary alternative media forms. It ignores the substantially wider reach, structural singularities, and evolving form and content of Internet-supported alternative media. In so doing, it ignores its capacity for unique patterns of publicity.

There are currently literally millions of blogs on the Internet, with over seventy thousand new blogs added every single day.[73] Although most of these blogs are owned by private citizens (which makes them potentially "alternative" or at least "citizen" media, since they are not "mainstream"), not all of them are motivated by progressive, emancipatory political agendas. Furthermore, many of them have "capitulated to capital" by allowing Internet ads to be placed on their sites.[74] As Kim and Hamilton observe in reference to a huge network of commercially successful Internet-based "alternative" media in South Korea, "The charge of hypocrisy can be levelled against a media organization ostensibly committed to progressive social change (which often includes as part of this the reform, or even the abolition, of exploitative capitalist relations) but still sells its audience as a commodity to advertisers. Similarly, critics of commercialization argue that courting advertising revenue leads to depoliticization."[75] This dilemma confronts many self-confessed progressive web-based alternative media. So if, as Atton argues, one of the abiding stylemarks of progressive alternative media is their freedom from market forces, do ad-supported but nonetheless oppositional web-based media qualify as alternative media?[76] How do Google Adsense's depoliticized, algorithmic, content-inspired ad placements on websites that sign up for their services detract from the liberatory potential and progressive politics of ad-funded progressive alternative media? Or is Rodney Benson right in arguing that the commercialization of progressive, counterhegemonic alternative media is not a sufficient basis to conclude that they have been compromised?[77] What of Internet-based "alternative" media that are not associated with, or the product of, any organized social movement?

And what about the phenomenon of mainstream media organizations maintaining and supporting vibrant, uncensored online citizen media that, in fact, provide more unrestricted avenues to ventilate strong opinions against the hegemonic order than many forms of alternative media? For instance, a 2008 "State of the News Media" report by the Project for Excellence in Journalism found that, paradoxically, the mainstream media provide greater mechanisms for feedback and critiques than most citizen media.[78] What is more, it is becoming increasingly obvious that the relationship between alternative media and the mainstream media in the age of the Internet is symbiotic rather than mutually exclusive. Most online alternative media liberally use material from the mainstream media, just as the mainstream media now increasingly utilize information from citizen media (of which alternative media are a part) for its profit-driven broadcasts.[79]

All this calls for more self-reflexive theoretical exploration of the phenomenon of alternative media in the age of the Internet, or what has more broadly been labeled citizen journalism. Of course, as pointed out earlier, there are significant differences between alternative journalism and citizen journalism. Although most alternative journalism is citizen journalism (that is, not produced by institutional and corporate media elites), not all citizen journalism is alternative journalism (that is, consciously political and counterhegemonic). So what is citizen journalism, and how is it different from other models of journalism? The next section explains citizen journalism and situates it within the context of other models of journalism.

Citizen Journalism and Resistance to Traditional Journalism

In online journalism scholarship, it is customary for scholars to deploy a variety of terms to describe the same online media formations and practices. For instance, the terms "participatory journalism," "civic or public journalism," and "citizen journalism" are often used interchangeably. However, these terms have not only distinct meanings but also different histories. Since they are used liberally in this book to refer to different genres of journalism, it is useful to distinguish them clearly.

Joyce Nip identified five broad categories of journalism: (1) traditional journalism; (2) public or civic journalism; (3) interactive journalism; (4) participatory journalism; and (5) citizen journalism.[80] Although these terms have widely different significations for different scholars and do, in fact, overlap at different conceptual levels, there appears to be sufficient agreement among journalism scholars on their distinguishing features to merit delineating them as distinct journalistic models.

Traditional journalism, according to Nip, is the kind of journalism where "professional journalists are the gatekeepers who filter through the happenings of the world, select the significant events, and report them for their audience."[81] This model has limited participatory content, except for "letters to the editor," phone-ins, and other kinds of delayed traditional audience feedback, which are sometimes no more than indecipherable crackles of background noise because they are merely reactive and neither significantly inform the content of news nor the process of news gathering. In this model, professional journalists determine what constitutes news using frames of reference internalized from their professional training and associations. In most cases, news is little more than the actions of the primary definers of news: politicians, accredited sources in government and other people and institutions that have access to the media almost as a matter of right. In this sense, as Janet Woollacott points out, the media serve "to reinforce a consensual viewpoint by using public idioms and by claiming to voice public opinion."[82] This has been the dominant model of journalism as practiced by the mainstream media for many years. In Nigeria and elsewhere, this journalist-centered, tightly controlled, few-to-many model of journalism is under tremendous professional stress and is buckling.

Public journalism, also called civic journalism, emerged as a response to the perceived inadequacies of traditional journalism.[83] According to Jay Rosen, the concept of "public journalism" first appeared in the United States in 1993 as a reaction to the deepening chasm between journalism and the citizens it professes to serve on the one hand and between the quotidian concerns of ordinary people and public life in general on the other.[84] Lewis Friedland cited the *Wichita Eagle* as the first notable newspaper to experiment with this model of journalism.[85] Public journalism, in essence, invests itself with the task of actively seeking the input of local communities both in the choice of what constitutes news and in how the news is presented. As Nip points out, "Town hall meetings, citizen panels, and polls are common techniques used to tap the concerns of the community, which would then form the reporting agenda for the journalists. During the news-gathering process, professional journalists often report back to the citizens what they have found for generating discussion in search of solutions to the problems. . . . There have been cases where the citizens even partnered with the professionals in gathering the news."[86]

Although this model represents a greater connection with the people than traditional journalism does, it still retains the professional journalist as the gatekeeper. Therefore, civic journalism, though pretending to be an improvement on mainstream news practices, is mere cosmetic reformism that leaves intact the fundamental essence of professional, mainstream media practices. For one thing, it is market driven and is constrained by the institutional and organizational structures of the dominant mainstream news practices from which it purports to depart.[87] As Louise Woodstock observes, "traditional and public journalisms adopt similar narrative strategies to effect essentially the same ends: placing the power of telling society's stories in the hands of journalists."[88] The Nigerian media landscape never experienced public journalism before the emergence of the Internet, which caused a major professional rupture in mainstream news practices. Nigerian media professionals had never developed a self-conscious awareness of the gap between their journalistic output and the needs of their consumers, so no attempt was ever made to cover it.

The interactive journalism model is not radically different from public journalism, although it seeks to improve on some of the shortcomings of public journalism by taking advantage of the improved technical capabilities of media organizations in the last couple of years since the Internet became a demotic medium. But precisely what interactive journalism actually entails is still imprecise.[89] Following Wolfang Iser, however, we can construe it as consisting in a "network of response-inviting structures, which impel the reader to grasp the text"[90] and in which the reader "is less massified and more open."[91] Jaana Hujanen and Sari Peitikainen define interactive journalism as the "increasing opportunity to communicate across 'old' boundaries of time and place, and between journalists and citizens."[92] According to Brian Massey and Mark Levy, there are two important dimensions to interactivity: content interactivity and interpersonal interactivity.[93] Content interactivity is made possible not only by the technical capabilities that give users the latitude to liberate themselves from the one-dimensionality set by professional journalists, but also by the variety of choice of content available to users. Interpersonal interactivity occurs when users can interact with professional journalists through exchange of emails or chat sessions, or when the "comment" pages of news organizations can become a site for the push and pull of contending viewpoints in response to a news story on a news website. As Nip rightly notes, interactive journalism is little more than computer-mediated public journalism, which most traditional news operations have embraced.[94]

As chapter 3 of this book will show, all Nigerian news media now enable some form of personal and content interactivity with their reportorial output. It is ironic, however, that in the age of increased Internet-enabled interactivity, prominent Western news media such as the BBC, CNN, National Public Radio (NPR), Radio New Zealand (RNZ), Norway's *Dagbladet*, and so on have chosen to curtail consumer engagement on their sites by closing their below-the-line comment sections "because of widespread abuse and obscenity."[95]

Participatory journalism goes a step further than interactive journalism by actually engaging consumers of the news in the news-gathering process. In this model, users do not merely interact with the news and professional journalists that produce the news; they also participate in some fashion in a many-to-many collaborative form of journalism. Like interactive journalism, it is also enabled by the technology of the Internet, as it allows a new generation of Internet users to become content creators. Shayne Bowman and Chris Willis define participatory journalism as "the act of a citizen, or group of citizens, playing an active role in the process of collecting, reporting, analyzing and disseminating news and information. The intent of this participation is to provide independent, reliable, accurate, wide-ranging and relevant information that a democracy requires."[96] They add that participatory journalism uses what they call a "publish, then filter" model instead of the traditional "filter, then publish" model.[97] Some of the features of this model, according to these authors, include discussion groups, user-generated content, weblogs (blogs), collaborative publishing, peer-to-peer systems, and web syndication. Although participatory journalism allows the participation of news users in the news-making process, the process is still controlled by professional journalists within mainstream institutional journalistic structures. The OhmyNews site in South Korea is often credited with pioneering this brand of journalism. On this site, readers generate the bulk of the news stories, but these stories are edited by a full-time staff of a few dozen editors. Yeon-Jung Yu, writing in the *Japan Media Review*, said, "Most are written by housewives, schoolkids, professors and other 'citizen journalists.'"[98] The San José *Mercury News* columnist Dan Gillmor predicted that the many-to-many collaborative model of Korea's OhmyNews would define the direction of news business: "OhmyNews is transforming the 20th century's journalism-as-lecture model—where organizations tell the audience what the news is and the audience either buys it or doesn't—into something vastly more bottom-up, interactive and democratic."[99]

Among prominent news organizations that have adopted the participatory model are the BBC's "Have Your Say" (http://news.bbc.co.uk/2/hi/talking_point/default.stm), which invites news users to express their views about the news and then publishes them in a particular section of the news product, and the relatively less successful MSNBC's Citizen Journalists Report (http://www.msnbc.msn.com/id/6639760/), where an editor suggests assignments for whoever is interested in reporting on specified aspects of developing news stories, and so on. Participatory journalism has also been called "crowdsourcing."

Citizen journalism is different from the preceding four models (traditional, civic, interactive and participatory) precisely because it eliminates the authority of the professional journalist. As Nip puts it, "It can be one or a number of individuals, a citizen group, or a nonprofit organization without a paid staff running a news blog, news website, community radio station, or newspaper. To qualify as journalism, the content needs to include some original interviewing, reporting, or analysis of events or issues to which people other than the authors have access."[100] In other words, citizen journalism is the model of journalism that allows a wider range of participants, including what Jay Rosen has described as "the people formerly known as the audience,"[101] to perform what J. D. Lasica calls "random acts of journalism."[102] Terry Flew identified three elements that are critical to the rise of citizen journalism and citizen media: open-source publishing; the capacity for collaborative control of content; and the availability of democratic, web-enabled forms of content distribution.[103] The Indymedia site, a transnational multimedia news outlet that became prominent for opposing the World Trade Organization meeting in Seattle in 1999, is often cited as one of the pioneers of the citizen-journalism model. More generally, news-based weblogs can also be categorized as practicing citizen journalism, because the defining feature of citizen journalism is that it is wholly user generated and is free from the encumbrances of professional news judgment and gate keeping.

The five models of audience connection proposed above vary in the extent and form of people participation, with citizen journalism involving the people to the greatest extent, and traditional journalism the least. Interactive journalism gives the users initiative after the news is published, whereas participatory journalism gets the users to gather the news. Public journalism encompasses a wide range of experimentation in engaging citizens as advisers and partners in news gathering and writing while allowing interaction after news publication.

It is clear that none of these models is an immanent, self-sufficient container of meaning. They are not self-conscious journalistic models isolated in time and space, and they constantly overlap. It does appear, though, that citizen journalism is the only model that can be thought of as distinct, even up to the minute; the rest are mere adaptations of or improvements on traditional journalism.

Most important, however, it is the migration of news and information to the Internet that has led to the robust flowering and proliferation of citizen journalism. Over the last few years, millions of weblogs, with thematic preoccupations that encapsulate a broad spectrum of human endeavors, have emerged and have continued to redefine the practice of journalism in many fascinating ways. This development has inspired optimism in some quarters that what Herbert Schiller famously called the "corporate take-over of public expression" by the traditional media is about to be subverted, perhaps even eradicated, by the unexampled discursive democracy that web-based citizen media enable.[104]

People who are enamored of this thought process often construe consumer-created citizen media as intrinsically oppositional, as the counterpart to the entrenched, time-honored legacy-media formation. Writing in the *Buffalo News*, for instance, Anthony Violanti giddily posited that "the mainstream media met their match" in blogs, which "not only compete in a new media landscape but also answer to the competitors."[105] Implicit in this enthusiastic valorization of citizen media is the idea that they exist apart from, and in fact in opposition to, the mainstream media. As Stephen Reese and his colleagues have noted, it has become customary to point to instances where news and public affairs blogs exposed inaccurate reporting by mainstream media as evidence that "the online army of bloggers will supplant the work and value of traditional journalists."[106]

Recent research has, however, shown that rather than challenging the dominance of mainstream news media by linking to and commenting on an ideologically diverse range of alternative news providers, blog writers help strengthen mainstream media dominance by further circulating, if not amplifying, their discourse. Indeed, the "derivative"[107] if not "parasitic"[108] relationship between blogs and mainstream news media makes it more accurate to characterize the blogosphere as an "online echo chamber of mass-mediated political views"[109] than as an "alternative sphere of news and views."[110] If this is the case for citizen media in advanced democracies, what is different about the citizen media of the Nigerian diasporic public sphere that gives them the power to sometimes determine the editorial agendas of the institutional media in the homeland? Why would the online media of a far-flung diaspora challenge the authority and credibility of an established homeland media formation, mobilize the citizenry both at home and abroad for collective action and, in the process, change state policies?

These facts highlight the tricky convergence between citizen journalism and alternative citizen journalism. Citizen journalism, as we have seen, is journalism that is practiced by ordinary people, that is wholly user generated, and in which professional news judgment and gate keeping, especially of the kind popularized by the corporate media, are eliminated or minimized. It is this broad category of Internet-enabled media, which includes the millions of news blogs on the Internet, that have been described as largely derivative, parasitic, and little more than online echo chambers of the hegemonic media. Nevertheless, this broad-brush characterization ignores the fact that there are also alternative and citizen media whose characteristics mark them out as independent media formations.

Let us recapitulate some of the features of online alternative media: they are often operated by activists for progressive causes, they function as resistance to monolithic commercialized media systems, they are located outside the forces of the market economy and the state, they adopt counterhegemonic reportorial practice (such as native reporting and active witnessing) in news gathering, they serve as counter information systems and agents of development power, they act as facilitators of social communication rather than as sources of information, and they are more concerned with nurturing a mobilized citizenry than an informed citizenry. But can a media formation be deficient in some of the features of alternative media and still legitimately be oppositional (to the mainstream media and the state) and activist? Examples of Nigerian alternative media platforms show they can, demonstrating that "alternativeness" can be inflected by differential temporalities, political climates, and social geographies.

Chapter Two

The Nigerian Press: From Colonial Evangelism to Guerrilla Journalism

To understand the Nigerian diaspora media formation, which influenced the emergence of vibrant domestic online journalism, it is important to undertake a bird's-eye view of Nigerian media history. This is significant because there is a surprising interconnectedness, and even continuity, in the form, character, tone, tenor, and reportorial temperaments of the various epochs of Nigerian journalism history. Chris Ogbondah constructed a dichotomous periodization of Nigerian press history into "two major periods—the colonial, which is the period essentially marked by British imperialism, and the post-independence, the period that followed the dawn of independence essentially characterized by military rule."[1] Although this periodization has a heuristic utility, it conflates distinct temporalities in Nigerian press history and obscures many subtleties. As I show later in this chapter, the Nigerian press preceded British colonialism by many years, and postindependence Nigerian press has many discrete phases that cannot be lumped together without triggering taxonomic incongruities.

Nevertheless, irrespective of historical epochs, the Nigerian press has historically functioned as a discursive parliament for the articulation, ventilation, and circulation of transformative and politically consequential national discourses, and for the instigation of momentous social changes. That is why studies of political developments in Nigeria from the colonial to the postcolonial periods have always highlighted the roles of the Nigerian press and Nigerian journalists in energizing and galvanizing popular support for major, defining issues of the times. The Nigerian press was, for instance, the primary instrument for sustained nationalist agitation against British colonialism, a fact that inspired James Coleman to write that "there can be little doubt that nationalist newspapers and pamphlets have been among the main influences in the awakening of racial and political consciousness [in Nigeria]."[2] Nigeria's first president, Nnamdi Azikiwe, who was himself an anticolonial activist-journalist, similarly characterized the Nigerian press as "identical with the intellectual and material developments of this country," pointing out that the "galaxy of immortal journalists produced by Nigeria" played tremendous roles "in this corner of the world in the great crusade for human freedom."[3]

But before and after the dislodgement of formal colonialism, to what extent did the Nigerian press serve as a site for public sphere debates, especially in light of the rather anticlimactic emergence of a corrupt, morally bankrupt, and intolerant postcolonial Nigerian state that Terisa Turner fittingly characterizes as a "gate-keeper state"?[4] This chapter attempts to answer this question by periodizing the evolution of the press in Nigeria—from the precolonial-era press in the mid-1800s to the anti-imperialist nationalist press that lasted from the late 1800s to the late 1950s, and to the implacably adversarial antimilitary press of the late 1990s, which is often dubbed the "guerrilla press." These diverse epochs represent varying degrees of the emergence, flowering, expansion, and constriction of the Nigerian public sphere and can help to explain, connect, contextualize, and even presage the materialization of the diasporic citizen and alternative online journalism with which this book grapples.[5]

It is important to note that mapping the history of the Nigerian press is a messy affair because of strong regional differences, which are rooted in the decision of the British colonialists to govern the country as two separate regions for many years before commixing them. Southern and northern Nigeria were ruled as two separate territories until 1914, when they were arbitrarily amalgamated for colonial administrative convenience. The brief history of Nigeria below will help contextualize the differences in the form and character of the southern and northern press and the proliferation of state government presses in the 1980s.

A Brief Media-Centered Political Background of Nigeria

Nigeria is a West African country made up of thirty-six states—plus Abuja, the Federal Capital Territory—and over five hundred ethnic groups, the major ones being the Hausa, Yoruba, Igbo, Fulani, Kanuri, and Ijaws. With over 180 million people, it is the most populous country on the African continent, the eighth most populous country in the world, and the world's most populous country in which the majority of the population is black. Lagos is the economic center of the country—and its media hub—and was its capital city until 1991 when a new capital, Abuja, located in almost the dead center of the country, was created.

Nigeria's modern history is traceable to 1886, when the area was occupied by the Royal Niger Company (Chartered & Limited), a mercantile company chartered by the British government. Prior to that, the territory was an amalgamation of different ethnic-based empires and kingdoms. In 1900, the British government took over direct administration over what became known as Nigeria and divided it into the southern and northern protectorates, a decision whose consequences linger to this day. In 1914, the northern and southern protectorates were combined to form Nigeria.[6] After sustained nationalist agitation, mostly on the pages of southern Nigerian newspapers, on October 1, 1960 the country became independent from Britain. It, however, retained many holdovers of British colonial rule. For instance, because of the difficulty of adopting any of the over five hundred languages in the country as the lingua franca, English was adopted as the official language.[7] Thus English emerged as the language of government, the media, the judiciary, and education. And although there are many indigenous-language newspapers in the country, the English-language newspapers are by far the most widely circulated and the most influential.

Nevertheless, there is an almost one-hundred-year gap between the British presence in Nigeria and the introduction of formal institutions of learning. By the accounts of many educational historians, it was only after the end of the First World War that the British Colonial Office began to take a systematic interest in education not only in Nigeria but also in all of the African colonies under the British sphere of influence.[8] There is ample literature on the justifications offered for this policy by British colonialists—and counterarguments from an evolving nationalist elite group that was initially educated by the British to become a buffer zone between the colonizers and the colonized.[9] Because the British Colonial Office was not interested in the education of the "natives," Christian missionaries filled the void. Thus early education in most of the former British colonies in Africa was not secular. Protestant Christian missionaries were so involved in British colonial education policy that it was customary to refer to them as Britain's "unofficial partner" in the colonial project.[10] This fact had deep implications for education, nationalist struggles, and newspaper journalism in Nigeria. Because of the Christian missionary influence on early education in Nigeria, it was stoutly resisted by the Muslim north. This opposition accounts for the wide disparity in educational attainment between the north and the south, for the unequal media presence in the two regions, and for the difference in the tone and tenor of nationalist agitations between the elites of the regions.

In fact, by the late 1950s, when Western-educated nationalists in the south were agitating for independence from British colonial rule, their counterparts in the north protested that they did not yet have the indigenous, Western-educated workforce to take advantage of the benefits of self-governance. So they replaced the 1956 date proposed by southern Nigerian nationalists for Nigeria's independence from Britain with the intentionally imprecise phrase "as soon as practicable."[11] Generally, the colonial authorities were more comfortable with elites from the north than they were with the elites from the south. There were at least two reasons for this. The Muslim north was easier to govern because it had had a preexisting centralized system of governance that stressed respect for inherited authority. The British colonialists exploited this structure to administer the vast region with little or no resistance. The second reason was that the colonial authorities made good their pledge never to Christianize the region, so the feudal elite willingly cooperated in the colonial project and were not in a hurry to achieve independence. As would be expected, when the British departed in 1960, they handed over power to northern Muslims—to the chagrin of southerners who felt their superior access to Western education made them worthier of inheriting from the departing colonizers than northerners. The resentment of the southern elites over northern political dominance in spite of the north's educational disadvantage was vigorously ventilated in southern newspapers.

Thus, from its very founding, Nigeria has been plagued by regional rivalries, which also are reflected in the character of the country's media system. After only six years of northern-dominated postindependence democratic rule, the country was engulfed in bitter internecine regional rivalries that escalated into a southern, Igbo-led Christian military coup against the northern Muslim central government. After a northern countercoup that wrested back power from the south, the Igbo ethnic group fought to secede from Nigeria and proclaimed its own country, called Biafra. This secessionist bid precipitated a bitter and bloody civil war between 1967 and 1970. Some accounts put the death toll at over thirty thousand.[12]

The division of Nigeria from three regions at independence to thirty-six American-style states in the mid-1990s was informed by the desire of successive military governments to minimize the importance of regional identification and to suppress the eruption of what Adiele Afigbo calls "Nigeria's sleeping volcano," which he defines as "the primordial federal features of Nigerian society (geographic and ethnic plurality)."[13] At independence, the three regions were the Northern Region, the Eastern Region, and the Western Region. The west and the east were part of the Southern Protectorate. In 1966, the Mid-Western Region was carved out of the Western Region. In the wake of the civil war, this regional structure was dissolved by the northern-led military government. In its place, twelve states were created, which later increased to nineteen and finally to thirty-six. State creation, however, came with its peculiar problems, which were exacerbated by the proliferation of state newspapers, each championing the points of views of its people and government, as we will see shortly.

Another important fact of Nigeria's political history is that it has been ruled by a succession of brutal, corrupt military dictatorships since 1966, with only spasmodic periods of democratic rule. Sustained democratic governance was restored in May 1999 with the election of President Olusegun Obasanjo, who had been a military ruler between 1975 and 1979 and who had been imprisoned by the previous military government for his caustic criticism of the lawlessness and venality of the government of the day.[14] After leaving office in 2007, Mr. Obasanjo, a southern born-again Christian, handed over power to a northern Muslim successor by the name of Umaru Musa Yar'Adua, who died in office in 2010. His vice president, Goodluck Jonathan, completed his term, stood for election on his own, and won a fresh four-year mandate. In 2015, he lost his bid for a second term and went in the annals as the first incumbent Nigerian president to lose election to a challenger from the opposition party.[15] Nevertheless, Muhammadu Buhari, who succeeded Goodluck Jonathan in 2015, was widely believed to have lost his reelection bid to his closest challenger, Atiku Abubakar, in 2019 but compelled the election agency to manipulate the result of the election and announce him the winner.

The Nigerian Press and the Colonial Public Sphere of Debate

Peter Golding captured a fundamental fact of the history and development of the mass media systems in the developing countries of Africa, Asia, and Latin American in general when he observed that the media are not the products of the natural, spontaneous social evolutions of these societies, but little more than cultural and professional transplants from the media systems of the "metropolitan centers" of the West.[16] But his famous assertion that the "Nigerian press was born out of anti-colonial protest, baptized in the flood of nationalist propaganda, and nurtured in party politics," while providing a good starting point to analyze and understand the history and dynamics of the Nigerian press, does not give the accurate historical context of the birth and maturation of the Nigerian media system.[17]

It is more correct to assert, as Frank Ugboajah did, that the introduction of the press in Nigeria was a consequence of the efforts of Christian missionaries who were tangentially associated with the British colonial project at the time. As he put it, "The newspaper press thus arrived to our shores . . . accompanied by its concepts and prejudices which were completely exogenous."[18] In this statement, Ugboajah reclaimed a germinal element in the birth of the Nigerian media system that was absent from Golding's account: the unequivocally missionary and colonial character of its heritage. Although British claims to a West African sphere of influence received international recognition in 1885, the territory known today as Nigeria did not formally come under the control of the British government until January 1, 1901.[19] This means that what we call the Nigerian press today, as Adigun Agbaje correctly notes, actually "predated formal colonial annexation of any part of the area now known as Nigeria."[20] In other words, the press in Nigeria is more than a quarter of a century older than the Nigerian state.

Nigeria's first newspaper, established in 1859—thirty years before the formal colonization of Nigeria by the British Empire—was founded by the Reverend Henry Townsend of the English Church Missionary Society.[21] The paper, named *Iwe Irohin fun awon Egba ati Yoruba*, which is Yoruba for "newspaper for the Egba and Yoruba people," was published in the Yoruba language. (The Egba are a subgroup of the Yoruba, Nigeria's second largest ethnic group, found in the western region of the country.) In a letter to the Church Missionary Society, the Reverend Townsend wrote: "I have set on foot a Yoruba newspaper. . . . My objective is to get the people to read . . . to beget the habit of getting information by reading."[22] Nigeria media historians have posited that this missionary paper was the first indigenous-language newspaper in the whole of Africa.[23] It is also said to be the continent's oldest surviving newspaper, although it has had hiccups in its publication and has undergone several changes in ownership and management.[24] However, Abiodun Salawu has found these claims to have no basis in historical evidence.[25] He has shown that at least three indigenous-language newspapers in South Africa preceded *Iwe Irohin* by decades. For instance, *Umshumayeli*

Wendaba, which means "The Preacher of the News" in the Xhosa language, was first published in 1837, more than two decades before *Iwe Irohin*. *Isitunywa Senyanga*, Xosa for "Monthly Messenger," was first published in 1850. In fact, two indigenous-language South African newspapers predated *Isitunywa Senyanga*: *Isibuto Samavo*, which was first published in 1843, and *Ikwezi*, which was first published in 1844.[26] Like *Iwe Irohin*, these indigenous-language South African newspapers were owned by Christian missionary societies.

Nonetheless, the significance of *Iwe Irohin* is broad. It inaugurated the first modern means of constructing a Nigerian national identity, and thus a public sphere, analogous in many ways to Benedict Anderson's account of how "print capitalism" in Europe helped create "imagined communities" that transformed hitherto diverse communities into nations.[27] It was also arguably the first modern means of mass communication to supplant talking drums and other forms of precolonial, informal, and interpersonal rural communication in Nigeria,[28] although Akinfeleye asserts that "evidence exists of irregular 'newspaper' publishing ventures before 1859 [in Nigeria]."[29] What Akinfeleye is perhaps referring to is the tradition of religious periodical publishing in the Hausa language of northern Nigeria from about the fourteenth century.

Contested Provenance: The Rise of the Press in Northern Nigeria

Northern Nigerian media historians often contest the accuracy of the claim that *Iwe Irohin* was Nigeria's first newspaper. They claim that a newspaper had been published in their part of the country through an improvised Arabic orthography called Ajami many centuries before the Reverend Henry Townsend set foot in Nigeria.[30] As Abdullah Uba Adamu notes:

> Of the three largest ethnic groups in Nigeria, the Muslim Hausa have, arguably, the most extensive and well-established literary tradition. This was made possible by [the people's] contact with Islam as far back as 1320 . . . which exposed the area to literary polemics and activities of the Muslim world at large. Thus, while most Nigerian communities glorified their literary antecedents through extensive collections of oral traditions and folklores, the Muslim Hausa, in addition to extensive collections of similar oral traditions, had the instrument to write down their literature through the medium of the Arabic language earlier than all the [other] groups.[31]

Although religious pamphlets and texts had been produced in northern Nigeria for ages, northern Nigerian media historians contend that the first publication that comes close to being a newspaper was the *Kano Chronicle*, published monthly in Hausa and Arabic around 1503, a fact that led Gausu Ahmad to argue that "the *Kano Chronicle* could be rightly regarded as the first newspaper in the territory that was later to be known as Nigeria, contrary to popular [claims] among Nigerian media historians."[32]

However, this claim is problematic on many levels. Even though media scholars have not yet reached a definitive consensus on what kinds of publications qualify to be called newspapers, Otto Groth's time-honored criteria for defining a newspaper are generally used. According to this German scholar, the criteria for adjudging whether a print publication qualifies to be called a newspaper are: (1) the paper must be published periodically, "at intervals not less than once a week"; (2) everyone who has the means to buy the paper should have access to it; (3) it must have some appeal for large, diverse segments of the society by varying its content; and (4) it must be "timely with some continuity of organization."[33] The *Kano Chronicle* did not meet most of these conditions. Although it was a monthly publication, which means it had some frequency of appearance, "its circulation was restricted within the circles of the ruling class of [the] Kano city-state."[34] Besides, its editorial content was not about news or quotidian concerns of society. Historians say its thematic preoccupations were myths of origin, genealogies of rulers, methods of succession of kings, Islamic rites, accounts of battles, and news about immigration to the city-state of Kano.[35] These subject matters were clearly not intended for a popular audience, a critical element in the conception of a newspaper. The paper's palace-centered editorial content and its exclusivity of access to the ruling circles contrast sharply with the demotic appeal of the Reverend Henry Townsend's *Iwe Irohin*. It is therefore contentious to assert that *Kano Chronicle* was the first newspaper in Nigeria.

The first attempt at publishing a truly modern, mass-market newspaper in northern Nigeria, if we accept Groth's categories for classifying print publications as newspapers, is Samuel Cole-Edwards' *Nigerian Protectorate Ram*, which was first published in September 1930.[36] During the Great Depression, the paper's unrelentingly vocal animadversions against the colonial government's belt-tightening economic policies in Northern Nigeria invited the ire of the government, which preferred charges against it in court. Cole-Edwards, a Sierra Leonean who came to northern Nigeria as a colonial staffer but who was later compelled to become "an accidental and circumstantial critic of colonialism," escaped to Onitsha, where he started the *Nigerian Weekly Despatch*.[37]

Two years later, a short-lived newspaper called *Jaridar Nigeriya Ta Arewa*, which literally translates as "the newspaper of northern Nigeria," arrived. It was published in 1932 simultaneously in Hausa, Arabic, and English.[38] Unlike that of the *Kano Chronicle*, its editorial content reflected the routine concerns of the average northern Nigerian. As Ahmad notes, "Its main contents were social news such as retirements, government policies, security matters, trade, agriculture and other development news."[39] In an interesting way, this echoes Habermas's account of the content of eighteenth-century European newspapers in coffeehouses.

In January 1939, six years after *Jaridar Nigeria Ta Arewa* ceased publishing, the colonial government in northern Nigeria decided to establish an exclusively Hausa-language newspaper called *Gaskiya Ta Fi Kwabo* (which translates as "the truth is worth more than money"), ostensibly to counter unsettling Nazi propaganda at the time, which suggested that northern Nigeria was going to be ceded to the neighboring central African nation of Cameroun, then within the German sphere of influence.[40] Dr. Rupert M. East, a high-ranking colonial officer in northern Nigeria and the brains behind the establishment of the paper, informed Abubakar Imam, who would be the paper's first editor, that the colonial administration would like to "establish a Hausa language newspaper in order to counter the German propaganda on Hitler's activities and plans for Africa."[41] He identified the propaganda as the insidious rumor being systematically spread in northern Nigeria by the German secret service that Britain and Hitler had reached "an understanding" that northern Nigeria would now fall under German colonial occupation. This propaganda was said to have created panic in northern Nigeria, and the "need was therefore strongly felt for a more effective local language newspaper to counter such adverse propaganda, hence the establishment of *Gakiya*."[42]

Although the well-known, westernized Hausa writer Abubakar Imam was chosen as the paper's editor, the colonial administration insisted that a colonial officer by the name of L. C. Giles be the deputy editor, "apparently to ensure conformity of the paper with the set colonial objectives."[43] In addition, every correspondent for the paper also had to be adjudged trustworthy by northern Nigeria's traditional rulers, who usually worked with the British colonial administration in northern Nigeria through what is known as "indirect rule."[44]

According to northern Nigerian media historians, there were other reasons for the setting up of *Gaskiya* by the colonial government that were not explicitly stated. I. A. Yahya identified at least three other reasons for the establishment of the paper. The first was to serve as a propaganda instrument to encourage northern Nigerian males to enlist in the British colonial army to fight in World War II. The second was to counter the fierce opposition to colonialism by the emergent nationalist press in southern Nigeria. And the third was to integrate the predominantly Muslim north into Western ways of life in ways that did not threaten the colonial project.[45] As Mora notes, the editorial content of the early editions of the paper consisted largely of colonial government propaganda, propaganda against Hitler's Germany and Mussolini's Italy, and mobilization of the locals for war.[46] If we were to employ Habermas's categories, *Gaskiya* would not qualify as helping to establish a public sphere because it was owned and operated by the state—and a repressive, gatekeeper colonial state at that. However, even though the paper was distrusted by the masses and by critical elements of the emergent northern Nigerian educated elite, some of them "fully availed themselves of the opportunity the paper offered in their fight against some of the colonial policies."[47] After the departure of the British in 1960, the paper was handed over to the northern Nigerian government and is still a state-run newspaper as of 2019. This makes it the oldest surviving newspaper that has been published continuously under the same ownership in Nigeria.[48] Let us now return to the *Iwe Irohin* and show how its establishment and editorial choices conduced to the emergence of a different type of public sphere in southern Nigeria.

Iwe Irohin and the First Southern Nigerian Public Sphere

Unlike in northern Nigeria, the first modern means of mass communication in southern Nigeria was not directly affiliated with the colonial government, although, as was shown earlier and will be shown in subsequent sections of this chapter, missionary activities in the colonized parts of the world were often inextricably linked with the colonial project. What is important, though, is that because of the invisibility of the role of the colonial state in the setting up of *Iwe Irohin*, the paper initially enjoyed tremendous credibility among the emergent southern Nigerian elites. Nigerian media historians note that in its reader catchment area, *Iwe Irohin* was regarded as second only to the Bible in inerrancy.[49] Akinfeleye, quoting the media historian Esuakema Uton, points out that "Nigerians looked at the news items in *Iwe Irohin* in just the same manner that they would comprehend their preacher's first sermon on the first Sunday of the New Year."[50] It must be the novelty of the printed word in a predominantly oral culture that contributed to this excessive faith in the newspaper.

The American media historian Frank Luther Mott recorded parallels in the early period of American newspapers. The origins of the American press, he said, are shrouded in claims to divinity. According to Mott, Benjamin Harris, the first person to publish a newspaper in the United States, gave three principal reasons for the establishment of America's first newspaper: (1) to record "memorable occurents [sic] of Divine Providence"; (2) to aid the understanding of public affairs at home and abroad; and (3) and to work "towards the curing, or at least the charming of that spirit of lying, which prevails among us."[51] Writing in the *North American Review* in 1866, James Parton stated: "The skilled and faithful journalist recording with exactness and power the thing that has come to pass, is Providence addressing men."[52] In fact, Mott relayed an instructive anecdote of a Baptist clergyman: "[A] newspaper having been brought into the room, he held out his hand to receive it, saying, 'Be kind enough to let me have it for a few minutes, till I see how the Supreme Being is governing the world.'"[53] It was this milieu that inaugurated what Mott calls the dogma of journalistic inerrancy in nineteenth-century America.

Perhaps because of the enormous goodwill that the *Iwe Irohin* enjoyed, Nigeria's early media historians appear to discount any suggestion that there was a connection between the nascent British colonial project in Nigeria and the setting up of the indigenous-language newspaper by missionaries. They narrativize the introduction of the press in Nigeria in the same benign and humanitarian terms as the missionary gentlemen who set it up. For instance, the eminent press historian Fred Omu asserted that missionaries

> embarked upon programmes of Western education and general enlightenment in Sierra Leone and subsequently in what became the colonies of Nigeria, Gold Coast and Gambia. Their most enduring weapon was the school but journalism played an important role. The newspaper had been established as an essential instrument of mission work outside Britain as a result of the effective use which the British humanitarian movement made of it in mobilizing support for their programmes.[54]

Similarly, the notable Nigerian press historian Dayo Duyile gave the following account of the processes that led to the establishment of Nigeria's first newspaper:

> On 17 December 1842, [Reverend Townsend] arrived at Badagry and worked with many Sierra Leonean freed slaves and natives of Badagry. . . . Rev. Townsend left for Abeokuta where he lived the rest of his missionary life, and there in 1854 he established a small printing press. Five years after, he set up an African Christian newspaper, the *Iwe Irohin*. . . . His motive, among others, was to excite the intelligence of the people in his area of operation and to get them to read.[55]

It is obvious that the laudatory accounts of the motivations behind the emergence and activities of the newspaper are no more than minor variations of the perspectives of the originator of the paper. The newspaper has been presented as the product of the humanitarian endeavor of a missionary gentleman who wanted to "excite the intelligence" of the natives and "beget the habit of getting information by reading." However, more critical analyses of the paper found that its editorial focus was broader than that. According to Jibrin Ibrahim, it covered "commercial news about local produce prices of palm oil, etc; announcements from local chiefs and from the Government of Lagos Colony; news of the movement of government and commercial representatives . . . agricultural and craft exhibitions, and progress made by mission schools. . . . The *Iwe Irohin* even carried advertisements from local firms and government agencies. . . . It was a faithful reporter and commentator of the political development of the times."[56] This catalogue of the editorial content of the paper demonstrates the inaccuracy of what Mohammed Musa and Jibril Mohammed call the "ecumenical theory of the origin of the [Nigerian] press,"[57] which historicizes the establishment of *Iwe Irohin* in terms of its preoccupation with Christian evangelization and humanitarianism while ignoring the "the extraordinary connection between Christian missions and the goals of colonialism."[58] Musa and Mohammed are not alone in calling into question the delinking of missionary activities from colonialism. Many scholars have demonstrated that Christian evangelical activists in colonized parts of the world were often working in tandem with the colonial administrators of their home countries. As Bob White notes, Protestant Christian missionaries were so involved with the British colonial enterprise that it was customary to refer to them as Britain's "unofficial partner" in the colonial project.[59]

Certainly, news about product prices, reporting on the progress of the colonial enterprise and other metropolitan business enterprises, advertising the goods of local firms or the services of colonial governments are outside the purview of pure Christian evangelical activities; they are, according

Ibrahim, "the direct requirements of capitalism moving and transforming from its phase of primitive accumulation into competitive capitalism."[60] Encouraged by the success of his Yoruba-language newspaper experiment, the Reverend Townsend, who "had some connections with newspaper work in Exeter where his brother was a newspaper publisher," introduced an English edition, called the *Early Dawn*, one year later.[61]

His experiment in newspapering was fairly successful because the southwestern Nigerian city of Abeokuta, where the paper was located, had a sizable number of natives who were literate in both English and Yoruba.[62] Prior to the arrival of Townsend in the city, there had been a steady stream of immigration of freed slaves from England and the West Indies by way of the West African nation of Sierra Leone. Freetown, Sierra Leone's capital city, was founded through a resettlement program of London's "black poor" who had joined the British army on the promise of freedom from slavery.[63] Most of these literate ex-slaves traced their ancestry to western Nigeria and chose the cities of Abeokuta and Lagos as their new homes. It is these returnees who worked to invent, systematize, and popularize Roman orthography for the Yoruba language and spread literacy both in Yoruba and in English.

However, two major events caused a hiatus (1859–97) in the operations of *Iwe Irohin* after eight years of continuous publishing.[64] First, its relative discursive inclusivity had become a source of worry for the colonial government. Southern Nigerian elites increasingly deployed the medium to oppose colonial policies. *Iwe Irohin* was in the newsstands for only three years when the colonial officer in charge of Nigeria, Governor H. S. Freeman, filed a complaint against the newspaper with the Colonial Office in London, although no formal action was taken against the paper and its owner. But on many occasions, Reverend Townsend was reprimanded by his own Christian Missionary Society "at the prompting of the Colonial Office."[65]

In 1867, the offices of the paper were burned by irate Abeokuta natives ostensibly because the paper took sides in local political disputes.[66] When the paper returned to the newsstands many years later, it was not under the same management. The birth, death, and rebirth of this missionary, indigenous paper are significant in the formation of the Nigerian public sphere and in the evolution of its media system. As Omu correctly notes, "The missionary newspapers may not have exerted a very wide influence on West African society but there can be no doubt that they introduced the first generation of educated Africans to what had become an intrinsic part of enlightened society in Europe and other lands. Their example gave inspiration to African people who inherited the idea of the newspaper and came to employ it as the chief weapon by which they were to exercise their power of participation in the government of their land."[67] This poignant observation captures the spirit behind the emergence of the nationalist press in Nigeria. As we have seen, the public sphere in the period under review was very limited and still hampered by a severe "deliberation deficit," as evidenced in the burning down of the newspaper as a consequence of disagreements with its editorial policies.[68] During the flowering of the nationalist press, however, we see a more engaged and discursive public sphere that took on the colonial administration in sustained rhetorical battles without recourse to violence.

The Emergence of the Nationalist Press

As pointed out earlier, indigenous newspapering in Nigeria and, in fact, in the whole of anglophone West Africa, was animated largely by nationalist sentiments. As William Hatchten observed, "To study either nationalism or the press in British West Africa is to study the other."[69] The first attempt to publish an independent English-language newspaper that was not owned by Christian missionaries or the colonial government began in 1863 with the founding of the *Anglo African* by a mixed-raced Jamaican émigré named Robert Campbell who humorously described himself as "one-quarter Negro, one-quarter English and half Scotch."[70] Significantly, the emergence of the *Anglo African* is a direct consequence of the growing dissatisfaction with the hypocrisy and double standards in the editorial direction of Townsend's *Iwe Irohin* and *Early Dawn*. Campbell was said to be the first to publicly proclaim that "Townsend's reputation for forthrightness and sagacity was a myth."[71] His opinions gained wide popularity when it later emerged that there was indeed a disconnect between the principles of Christian humanism that the missionaries preached and their endorsement of racist colonial policies. This, coupled, with the expansion of literacy in Lagos and other western Nigerian cities and the growth of the printing industry, encouraged the emergence of the *Anglo African*. Although the paper lasted only two years, it laid the groundwork for the growth and flourishing of the nationalist press fifteen years later.

On November 10, 1880, a prosperous half-Nigerian, half-Sierra Leonean by the name of Richard Beale Blaize, who had worked as an apprentice in *Anglo African*, founded the bi-monthly *Lagos Times*. Blaize made it clear that his venture into newspapering was not actuated by "the hope of large pecuniary returns."[72] In its inaugural editorial, the *Lagos Times* declared: "We are not clamoring for immediate independence . . . but it should always be borne in mind that the present order of things will not last forever. A time will come when the West Coast will be left to regulate their [sic] own internal and external affairs."[73] This declaration set the tone for the nationalist, anti-imperialist fervor of Nigerian newspapers.[74] It inspired the emergence of the more radical *Lagos Observer*, recognized as "one of the symbols of the intellectual aggression which characterized political developments in the two decades of the nineteenth century."[75] Many more indigenous nationalist newspapers, such as the *Lagos Weekly Record*, the *Lagos Daily News*, the *Nigerian Chronicle*, the *West African Pilot*, and so on sprang up in the 1900s and committed themselves to "raising consciousness to a high level in editorials and special columns devoted to anti-colonial issues."[76]

The colonial administration was predictably discomfited, but given its public pretenses to democracy, rule of law, and "civilizing the natives," it initially chose to take the line of least resistance by ignoring the nationalist press. In time, however, it responded to the challenges the oppositional, nationalist papers posed in four ways. Initially, it sponsored a column to publicize government notices and to counter nationalist propaganda in selected radical newspapers. When that did not work, it sponsored Nigerian citizens to set up progovernment newspapers to counter the propaganda of the nationalist, anti-imperialist press. For instance, in 1914, the year Nigeria was formally named, a newspaper called the *Nigerian Pioneer* was formed by a certain Kitoyi Ajasa. The paper consistently supported the colonial government and sought to undermine the nationalist press. However, following concerted attacks on the paper by nationalists, it soon lost credibility. The nationalist *Weekly Record*, for instance, dismissed the *Nigerian Pioneer* as "a thorough-going lickspittle journal—sworn to the blind defense of governmental policy whether right or wrong, good or bad—the greatest enemy and traitor of its race."[77]

In light of the loss of credibility of the *Nigerian Pioneer*, the colonial administration devised a different strategy: in 1925, it encouraged private English businessmen from Britain to team up with a group of Nigerian businessmen under the aegis of the Lagos Chamber of Commerce to start a new, professionally run, well-edited daily newspaper called the *Daily Times*. However, as Omu points out, "from the point of view of political development, the paper was not of much importance."[78] The colonial government complemented its encouragement of the *Daily Times* with its total control of the broadcast industry. As Uche points out, the "colonial government controlled the broadcasting medium (radio) . . . to refute the charges that the nationalists and their press were leveling against it."[79]

Finally, the government turned to overt repression. In response to the unremitting nationalist attacks on the colonial government, it not only withdrew advertising patronage from the nationalist press but also passed a whole host of draconian press laws. The government, for instance, criminalized the publication of any news that pilloried or embarrassed the government or its officials.[80] It also appointed a press censor, whose job was to "seize printing presses, confiscate newspapers and impose a bond of 250 pounds on 'undesirable' publishers."[81] When this did not work, it serially arrested, charged, and convicted journalists of sedition and tortured others. But this repressive clampdown on the nationalist press did little to daunt the resolve of its practitioners; it instead compelled them to go underground to continue their nationalist agitations.[82]

This history is worth recounting because, as subsequent sections will show, it not only set the template for subsequent government-press relations in Nigeria but also defined the contours of the tenor and nature of public-sphere debates in the country. Most important, as Philippa Hall points out, it "could be argued that this [nationalist] press constituted an emerging public sphere, in so far as it mediated the interests of Nigerian[s] . . . within the colonial state and was organized to express public opinion . . . albeit among a small section of the population."[83] It needs to be pointed out, though, that not all the nationalist agitation in the press was triggered by a patriotic zeal to dislodge colonialism. A lot of it was self-interested, and some of it was inspired and circumscribed by commercial interests. Hall has shown, for instance, that "editors and owners of the Nigerian private press had a primary interest in expanding indigenous trade, and editorials resisted or supported colonial policy as means to this end."[84] She also calls attention to the fact that the dependence of the Nigerian nationalist press on European advertising revenues for their sustenance meant that "criticism of British policy was often muted by the need for commercial presses to retain European advertising revenues."[85]

In the same vein, Mohammed Musa and Jibril Mohammed point out that the burgeoning colonial-era Nigerian elite were attracted to journalism only because of the injustices they personally suffered at the hands of British colonial administrators. "As for anti-racism, scores of skilled Africans resigned their appointments in the colonial service in favor of journalism, now seen as a thriving alternative occupation. But most importantly, journalism became the latest avenue, after the schools and churches, for decisive 'counter-hegemonic' campaigns within the colonial order."[86] However, native Nigerian journalists still suffered a colonially engineered cultural-capital deficit. In the words of Obafemi Awolowo, a foremost Nigerian nationalist and the premier of Nigeria's Western Region in the 1960s who also took to journalism to ventilate nationalist angst against colonial oppression, Nigerian journalists "were regarded as the flotsam and jetsam of the growing community of Nigerian intelligentsia."[87]

Whatever the case, the important thing was that, in many significant respects, the nationalist press, for all its structural defects, led to the development of a vigorous, if limited, public sphere of debate in which Nigerians, as colonial subjects disallowed from participating in the electoral process, could repugn the legitimacy of colonial policy by counterpointing the European rhetoric of "freedom, democracy and Christianity" with "the hypocrisy of an authoritarian colonial state based upon race superiority."[88] The next section shows, however, that the postindependence press, which replaced the nationalist press, did not necessarily expand the public sphere in any demonstrably qualitative way.

The Postindependence Press: From Nationalism to Regionalism

After independence from British colonial rule in 1960, Nigeria's press tradition changed radically. The mostly adversarial reportorial temperament of the nationalist press disappeared.[89] The emergent postindependence national media, no longer faced with a common colonial enemy, took a different form: they now reflected the divisive, regionalist, and ethnic-based character of the emergent ruling elite. Particular newspapers were identified with particular political parties, which were invariably formed along the ethnic and religious fault lines that were exploited, exacerbated, and in some cases created, by the departing colonizers. This tradition started in the late 1950s, when the British colonizers allowed some form of self-governance in the three regions they had created—the Northern Region, the Western Region, and the Eastern Region—prior to the granting of full independence, and peaked in the 1970s.

An important characteristic of the regionalist press era was that newspaper ownership shifted from private hands to regional governments.[90] This was not surprising: many of the nationalist crusaders who used the press to fight colonialism became the political leaders of the new nation. For instance, Nnamdi Azikiwe, publisher of the implacably anti-imperialist *West African*

Pilot, became the Eastern Region's premier and later Nigeria's first ceremonial president. Obafemi Awolowo, the publisher of the hitherto fiercely nationalistic *Nigerian Tribune*, became the Western Region's first premier. Unfortunately, these activist-journalists-turned-politicians used their presses to cultivate the social basis of their legitimacy through appeals to the prevalent primordial fissures in the society: ethnic differences, regional rivalries, and Muslim-Christian religious divides.

The government of the Eastern Region opened the floodgates to the emergence of regionalist newspapers when, shortly after independence, it established the *Eastern Outlook* (which it later renamed *Nigerian Outlook* to give it the semblance of a pan-Nigerian point of view). In 1961, the central government, which was dominated by northerners, established the *Morning Post* to counter the propaganda of the *Outlook*. In 1964, the government of the Western Region established the *Daily Sketch*, which, along with the privately owned *Nigerian Tribune*, defended the interest and sentiments of the people of the Western Region, who are predominantly Yoruba. (The *Nigerian Tribune*, established in 1949, was and is still owned by the Awolowo family, and is the oldest surviving, continuously published private newspaper in Nigeria). Although the *Morning Post* propagated northern Hausa Muslim viewpoints in national debates, the Northern Regional Government still went ahead and set up the *New Nigerian* in 1966. According to the British journalist Charles Sharp, who helped set it up, its purpose was to "reflect the dignity and aspirations of the north."[91]

It is significant that although the press during this period (between 1960 and 1966) discarded all pretenses to nationalism and engaged in tediously protracted partisan fights, the central government did not enact any laws to curtail the freedom of the press. No newspaper was shut down for expressing censorious opinions against the government, and no journalists were jailed. This fact inspired Frederick Schwartz to assert that the press "was probably the most potent institution supporting democratic freedom in Nigeria."[92] But this freedom lasted for only about six years.

In 1966, the military overthrew the abrasive and feuding politicians of what Nigerians like to call the First Republic and suspended the constitution, but the regional newspapers continued to exist nonetheless. The Mid-Western Region, which was carved out from the Western Region in 1963, also set up its own regional newspaper, the *Observer*, in 1968. The regionalist newspapers continued to be deeply and unabashedly partisan, but still retained what Minabere Ibelema calls the "advocatorial press tradition" of the nationalist years.[93] In a fitting observation of the character and performance of the Nigerian press during this era, Rosalynde Ainslie noted that the regionalist press, for the most part, produced polemical journalism that was highly personalized, unsparingly abusive of political opponents, and deficient in rational public-sphere debates.[94] That was scarcely surprising because, as Luke Uche points out, any newspaper that didn't take explicitly regionalist and ethnic perspectives on the issues of the day risked being "labeled a saboteur and an unpatriotic element."[95]

The second phase of the regionalist era began when Nigeria's four regions were further subdivided into twelve states. This gave rise to what Ibelema characterizes as "the state-oriented press," where "each state sought to establish its own news media."[96] The South Eastern State established the *Chronicle*, the Western State continued to own the *Daily Sketch*, Kwara State came up with the *Nigerian Herald*, the Benue-Plateau State set up the *Nigerian Standard*, the East Central State established the *Renaissance*, and Rivers State set up the *Nigerian Tide*. In 1976, the Federal Military Government took over the *New Nigerian*, previously owned by the Northern Region, which had been further subdivided into many states. The military also bought a 60 percent share in the *Daily Times*, the most influential, nationally circulated, and only privately owned newspaper at the time. Minabere Ibelema points out that "the acquisitions were made the same year that the federal government-owned daily *Morning Post* and *Sunday Post* ceased publication after years of falling circulation and revenue losses."[97] The federal government bought the papers precisely to undercut the influence of the regional newspapers, which were very critical of the center. In truth, though, the federal government was little more than the aggregation of the interests of the predominantly Muslim north, which had always been disadvantaged in media ownership owing to the low literacy rates in the region. Had the north had nearly as much of a vibrant media presence as the other regions, the northern-controlled federal government might not have needed to have its own newspapers.

The regionalist phase of the Nigerian press was characterized by two contradictory editorial impulses. It was simultaneously adulatory and critical of people in authority. Philip Elliot and Peter Golding, for instance, made this observation of the Nigerian press between the late 1960s and the early 1970s, "[I]n the Nigerian media, the largest number of stories was devoted to the action of political leaders, endlessly recording their minor speeches and airport statements, meetings and ceremonial activities. Thus, as in the West, political action is defined and portrayed by activities of incumbent elites. . . . Conflict and drama are provided by the familiar concentration on events and personalities."[98]

However accurate the observations were, they did not capture the sometimes adversarial nature of even the state-owned press. As Uche observes, one of the main reasons for the relative vitality and staying power of the state newspapers was "their policy to even bite the fingers that fed them; at times their anti-government stance on certain issues even embarrasse[d] the governments."[99] Frank Ugboajah singles out the *New Nigerian* in this regard. He notes that "of Nigerian newspapers, one of the most critical is *New Nigerian*. Its anti-government opinion on some volatile issues of development in the Nigerian society is noticeable."[100]

The military governments reacted to the occasional independence of the state-owned press by borrowing the tactics that the colonial administrations used to suppress the nationalist press. Shortly after the military took over power in 1966, it promulgated the Defamatory and Offensive Publication Decree, which conferred unlimited powers on government to arrest any journalist whose news reporting or analysis was deemed to constitute a threat to national security.[101] The next military regime that succeeded the first one (which lasted only six months) came up with an even more draconian law. It enacted the Newspaper (Prohibition of Circulation) Decree, known more popularly as Decree 17. This decree "authorized the government to ban and prohibit the circulation of newspapers" whenever such newspapers carried editorial content that compromised national security or embarrassed the government.[102] Newspapers were also required to sign every edition of their publication and to submit it to the government for vetting after publication.[103]

In a particularly dramatic case in 1973, Minere Amakiri, a journalist for the Rivers State–owned newspaper, was arrested, stripped naked, whipped, and jailed, and had his beard and head shaven with a pocket knife for writing a true story that teachers in the state had not been paid their salary for months. The military governor was particularly irked and embarrassed because the story appeared on his birthday.[104] In light of these crude repressions of the media and the self-censorship, coupled with the severely limited reach of the existing state newspapers, a need arose for the emergence of newspapers that were not state run.

The Birth of the Independent Press

The emergence of the independent press coincided with, if it was not inspired by, the restoration of democratic rule in 1979.[105] This era was characterized by the growth and flowering of what one might broadly describe as a commercial press that sought to rise above the prevalent divisions in the polity, however unsuccessfully, for profit. It was reminiscent, in some ways, of the context of the emergence of the penny press and the decline of the partisan press in the nineteenth-century United States.[106] With the military government's arbitrary takeover of the *Daily Times*, the erstwhile nationally circulating daily newspaper, and its usurpation of the *New Nigerian*, northern Nigeria's only daily newspaper and one of the nation's most influential newspapers, a vacuum resulted.

This vacuum was filled by wealthy Nigerians who, in partnership with professional journalists, established advertiser-funded, profit-driven newspapers. The *National Concord*, established by the multibillionaire Moshood Abiola in 1980, blazed the trail in independent, commercial newspaper publishing. Its success spawned another independent newspaper, the *Guardian*, which was formed in 1983 by the millionaire Alex Ibru in partnership with Dr. Stanley Macebuh, a seasoned and well-regarded American-educated journalist. These papers effectively displaced the state-run newspapers, especially the nationally circulating *Daily Times* and *New Nigerian*.

The fact that they were commercial did not, however, preclude the emergent privately owned press from being implicated in the partisan politics of the Second Republic, as the civilian rule between 1979 and 1983 is called in Nigerian political parlance.[107] The *National Concord*, for instance, came to be known as the unofficial mouthpiece of the ruling party of the time, the National Party of Nigeria. As in the First Republic (that is, the period of civilian rule between 1960 and 1966), the press was profoundly partisan and clamorous. This fact led the London-based international human rights organization called Article 19 to observe that the "period of multi-party civilian rule (1979–1983) was not a high point in Nigerian press history because all but a few newspapers aligned themselves with fiercely competing and often corrupt political parties."[108] However, it is also the case that during this brief restoration of constitutional rule, the press was relatively free and the public sphere significantly healthier than during the military era. Governments responded to criticisms either by setting up their own newspapers or by influencing news coverage and punditry in the independent media. Public debates in the media were robust, if raucous, and journalists were never arrested for their often hard-hitting philippics against political opponents.

That ended in late 1983, when the military struck again, ending five years of constitutional rule.[109] However, rather paradoxically, the return of the military, with all its notorious high-handedness against the press, inspired the evolution and flourishing of a new phase of vibrant, independent, commercial newspaper publishing the like of which had never been seen before. For instance, a corps of rebellious journalists who were uncomfortable with the editorial direction of the *National Concord* decided to resign from the paper and found Nigeria's first weekly news magazine, *Newswatch*, in 1984. According to Ray Ekpu, one of the magazine's pioneer editors, *Newswatch* was conceived by a "gang of disgruntled journalists who were far from satisfied with the exciting state of things in the Nigerian press and who hoped through their new, independent magazine, they could contribute to the practice and growth of journalism in Nigeria."[110] This trailblazing initiative came to define the contours of the independent press era. Professional journalists henceforth did not depend on wealthy businessmen to set up newspapers and magazines for them; they set them up themselves and sought social and editorial distance from the prevailing partisanships in the polity. Notable national newspapers established by professional journalists were *Vanguard* (1984); *This Day* (1995); *Weekly Trust*, which later became *Daily Trust* (1998); *Tell* (a breakaway from *Newswatch* in 1991); and *TheNews* (another breakaway from *Concord* in 1993).

This era, which endures to this day, is characterized by three fundamental features. First, it has witnessed the dramatic diminution of the presence and influence of government-owned newspapers and the rise and popularity of the privately owned commercial press, which, though not immune from the political, regional, and ethnic rivalries in the country, is not necessarily defined by them. Second, this era has seen the phenomenal incursion into journalism of what Dapo Olorunyomi, a former editor with one of the emergent radical news magazines, called "a well-educated and politically committed crop of reporters." He notes, "Not only were these young men and women prowling their beats with the confidence of brilliant college graduates, they had also undergone an activist baptism of fire from the anti-apartheid and student movements."[111] This fact is congruent with Richard Flacks's findings on how the entry of young graduates who were animated by the radicalism on U.S. campuses in the 1960s significantly transformed the profession.[112] Third, this period witnessed an extreme radicalization of the editorial temperaments of significant portions of the independent press in ways that are reminiscent of the era of the nationalist press, though this also brought with it an unprecedented government repression of the press.

For instance, in 1984, shortly after the military overthrew a democratically elected government, it arrested and imprisoned two journalists with the *Guardian* newspaper, Tunde Thompson and Nduka Irabor, for allegedly publishing incorrect information about staff deployment in the external affairs ministry of the government. In a particularly bizarre case, in 1986, the military government murdered the American-trained, aggressively muckraking editor in chief of *Newswatch*, Dele Giwa, via a letter bomb.[113] A year later, the magazine he edited was proscribed for six months and its editors jailed for "publishing reports of a government commission before it was made public."[114] In 1990, twenty-five journalists were arrested in a single day for reporting on an unsuccessful coup attempt. The *National Concord* was closed in 1992 for publishing a story that embarrassed Nigeria's then self-styled military president, Ibrahim Babangida. Several other independent papers were also proscribed when they launched virulent attacks on the military for voiding a presidential election it conducted in 1993, which Moshood Abiola, the publisher of the *National Concord*, won in a landslide.

But it was not just the press that was subjected to brutal suppression. Readers of the radical media were punished as well. For instance, in 1993, a group of Nigerians was arrested for reading photocopies of an edition of the *TheNews*. The military government's agents had thought they had seized and burned every copy of the newsmagazine. In 1995, the military government's security forces arrested and detained a news vendor for transporting several thousand copies of *TheNews*, *Tell*, and *Tempo*—three of the most adversarial newsweeklies in Nigeria at the time. When the news vendor was formally charged in court, the presiding judge asked the prosecutor if the news magazines the vendor was caught transporting to other parts of the country had been formally banned by government. He said the magazines were "simply not patriotic."[115] In another incident, a newspaper vendor was arrested for selling the radical weekly tabloid *Tempo*, which the government said contained "seditious materials" that had the capacity to cause "disaffection among members of the public and make them rebel against the authority of the Federal Government."[116] At other times, "security forces harassed, arrested and beat anyone found in a medium's premises, or anyone related to wanted journalists."[117]

The military government also invoked the antipress laws that had been on the books since colonial times, and came up with newer, crueler, more insidious ones. For instance, in 1993, the government enacted the Treasonable Offenses Decree, which imposed the death penalty on anyone who was found guilty of writing or speaking of Nigeria in ways that compromised its territorial integrity and internal cohesion. This was obviously a trap for the independent press since, in any case, a government prosecutor could go after a news vendor for merely transporting newsmagazines that the government deemed "unpatriotic." As if that was not harsh enough, the same year, the government also enacted what it called Newspaper Decree 43, which required all publications in the country to register with the military government's ministry of information for the sum of $1,000. This move appeared to be borrowed from the colonial era, when the colonial government made it mandatory for the nationalist newspapers to register with the government before they could legitimately publish their newspapers. However, these measures obviously did not work because the independent press continued to flourish, so in the late 1990s the government imposed a hefty valued-added tax on newsprint. This dramatically drove up the cost of newspapers and magazines and made them exclusive to the people at the upper end of the social scale.

These repressive measures, however, made the press even more vibrant and more adversarial, and gave rise to the blossoming of what has been called guerrilla journalism in Nigeria, which "involved a hit-and-run in which journalists operating from hideouts continued to publish oppositional and critical journals in defiance of the state."[118] As Ibelema notes, this extraordinary robustness of the Nigerian press in the face of atrociously brutal military dictatorships "demonstrates that under certain circumstances a vibrant press can co-exist with harsh censorship, albeit at high human cost. Similarly, whereas the military government's despotism and the country's economic difficulties would have predicted substantial reduction in the number of media outlets, there was actually a major expansion in both print and broadcast outlets."[119]

The Rise of Guerrilla Journalism

The government-engineered rise in the cost of newspaper and magazine production, the mass proscriptions of radical newspapers and magazines, and the arrests of their reporters and editors provided the locomotive force for the emergence of a vibrant underground press in the late 1990s and contributed significantly to the dislodgement of military totalitarianism in 1999, considered by some to be the "most significant democratic struggle in Nigeria since colonialism ended."[120] Interestingly, the inspiration for this kind of journalism derives in large part from the adversarial anticolonial journalism of the nationalist era. Nosa Igiebor, *Tell*'s executive editor, told a Nigerian researcher that he found motivation for the kind of insurgent journalism he practiced from "Nnamdi Azikiwe, Obafemi Awolowo, and other nationalists of the colonial era."[121]

What particularly redounded to the success and wild popularity of the underground press was the fact that the insurgent press was practically the sole arena for the ventilation of popular sentiments, especially in light of the fact that the broadcast industry was controlled by the government, and there was no popularly elected parliament. As Chris Ogbondah puts it, in the absence of a popularly elected parliament, the press became "the people's parliament" and the "most effective channel to express their wishes and grievances."[122]

The major publications associated with this phase of Nigerian journalism were *Tell*, *TheNews*, *Tempo*, and *Razor*—all newsweeklies. There were many other episodic, underground newspapers that perpetually changed their names, mastheads, and locations in response to the repression from the military. There was an underground radio station called Radio Kudirat, named for the wife of Moshood Abiola, who was shot in cold blood by agents of the military for leading the fight for the restoration of her husband's voided electoral mandate. Given the increasing precariousness of radical publishing and the ever more vicious desperation of the military junta, these newsmagazines decided to invent unconventional means to put out their news. Nosa Igiebor, editor in chief of *Tell*, told Ayo Olukotun, how they did it:

> We sat down and assessed the situation. Their [the military government's] business was to ensure that we didn't publish. Ours was to ensure that we came out without fail. This meant reorganizing our approach to producing. Rather than stay on one spot and become sitting ducks for state security [operatives], we had to be several steps ahead of them, by spreading out and operating in several centers or cells. If we use [one] house this week, we change the next week and use another house. We of course had to preserve the anonymity of the owners and venues of our cells.[123]

The perpetually migratory, unorthodox news practices that Igiebor outlined became the modus operandi of all the insurgent news magazines. The core of their strategy, according to Ayo Akinkuotu, another *Tell* editor, was the "duplication of offices. . . . At critical times in Abacha's five-year tenure, the magazine was forced to operate over seven 'bush offices.' Some were procured in extreme emergencies while others were evacuated without notice."[124] They abandoned the comfort of their newsrooms and held editorial meetings during soccer games or in sports facilities, theaters, hotel lobbies, taxicabs, or other places that could guarantee reasonable concealment of their identities. To avoid arrest by the military government's security agents, the guerrilla journalists "sometimes distributed their publication using a hired ambulance or water truck."[125] Babafemi Ojudu, an editor with *TheNews* and *Tempo*, recalled that he basically lived a nomadic life; his briefcase was his office, he avoided his home, and from time to time he even donned camouflage to escape the notice of security agents.[126] But the guerrilla journalists also sometimes depended on the protection of government security agents who secretly sympathized with their crusade and from whom they got sensitive government secrets. As Tokunbo Ojo put it:

> Sometimes the methods used by the underground media bordered on the unethical, but they seemed justified in the interests of public service and liberation of the country from the shackles of military dictatorship. Much of the information published underground was obtained by clandestine methods, including secret tape-recording of government meetings and gaining access to classified or confidential documents through disguised identities or through the cooperation of insiders. The stories also made use of documents leaked by whistleblowers and pro-democracy activists, as well as interviews with victims of government abuses.[127]

This insurgent, narrativistic, personalized, and explicitly partisan journalism of the military-era underground press in Nigeria ended in 1999, when the military government was compelled to organize elections and hand over power to civilians again. The 1999 military-organized elections saw many prodemocracy activists and friends of the guerrilla journalists in elective and appointive positions. The enemy was defeated and replaced by friends. This effectively led to not only the death of guerrilla journalism but also the cooptation of its practitioners in the new democratic epoch. So from 1999 to the mid-2000s, the Nigerian media landscape was overcome by an unprecedented quietude and complacency. The critical gaze that the media had fixed on people in positions of authority was averted. The disappearance of the critical press and the co-optation of many of its strongest advocates led to the untrammeled blossoming of high-profile corruption in high places.

Nevertheless, as we will see in chapters 4 and 5, the tradition of guerrilla journalism was reincarnated in the online alternative journalism of the Nigerian digital diaspora. In a way, the guerrilla press in Nigeria was the precursor to the kind of diasporic online journalism this book investigates. It is important for now to state that, along with sustained civil society agitation, guerrilla journalism contributed to the defeat of military totalitarianism and to the restoration of democratic rule in 1999. But the triumphalism and self-congratulation that this feat inspired also led to a premature abandonment of the struggle. Ayo Olukotun notes that the guerrilla journalists' "relative closeness to the political establishment has diluted their focus and mission," arguing, however, that "the precedent of an underground media system makes it easier for one to rise again."[128] And that was precisely what has happened between 2005 and 2018. The main difference is that the underground media rose again in electronic form and from citizen journalists in the Nigerian diaspora.

Although the press has been relatively free since the return of civilian rule in 1999, it has, for the most part, engaged in self-censorship.[129] This is probably a consequence of the need to escape the time-honored accusation that strident criticisms by the press of the failings of the political elites during civilian rule have often provided the alibi for the military to stage a comeback. Commenting on this, Mercy Ette remarks that the "adversarial attitude of the press toward politicians also weakened press support for democracy. This was a manifestation of an attempt by Nigerian journalists to emulate the antagonistic and cynical attitude that journalists in the West tend to adopt for the coverage of politics."[130] Given the immense sacrifices that the independent press made for the overthrow of military totalitarianism, this kind of criticism can have a restraining effect on its investigative editorial temperaments.

It could also be that the independent press was overcome by the smug self-satisfaction that came from the shifting of political power to Nigeria's southwest, which is home to the guerrilla press and many of Nigeria's independent media. Although the attacks by the press were mostly against the military as an institution, these attacks often assumed ethno-religious dimensions. This was because the military dictators who had ruled Nigeria since 1966 were mostly northern Muslims. One exception was the first military coup in 1966, led by Christians from the south, which was crushed after only six months. Another exception was between 1975 and 1978, when a southern Christian became head of state after a Muslim military head of state (to whom the southern Christian was a deputy) was assassinated. So it is entirely possible that the comfort inspired by the election of a southern, born-again Christian in 1999 induced a crippling, unaccustomed complacency.[131]

However, behind the façade of the new democratic government hid many issues that needed to be investigated. Although some sections of the independent media indeed rose to the challenge of calling attention to governmental indiscretions, their efforts were not sufficiently robust.[132] This is also perhaps because since 1999 many wealthy politicians, some them elected state governors, have set up influential newspapers that compete with the independent media. For instance, one of Nigeria's most widely circulated newspaper, the *Sun*, is owned by Orji Kalu, the former governor of the southeastern state of Abia. Other influential papers published by former and current state governors are the *Daily Independent* (owned by James Ibori, a former governor of the oil-rich southern state of Delta who was imprisoned in London for corruption), the *Nation* (owned by Bola Tinubu, the former governor of Lagos State, Nigeria's commercial nerve center and most populous state). The crowding of the media landscape with these mouthpieces of often corrupt politicians further contributes to demoting investigative journalism to the back burner, even more so since the core of the editorial staff of these newspapers is drawn from the independent, commercial, including the previously guerrilla, press. Furthermore, the void this situation has created provided the entry point for the diasporic online media I examine in subsequent chapters.

In light of this review of the history of the Nigerian press, it seems fair to say that the Nigerian press was born out of missionary evangelism and the necessity for colonial propaganda, remade by the contingent nationalism of an emergent marginalized local elite, matured in party politics, radicalized in advocacy antimilitary journalism, and weakened by the smug self-satisfaction that resulted from its role in the restoration of constitutional rule. But a new, transnational dimension has emerged in the history of Nigeria media: the birth and flowering of online journalism by Nigeria's expanding diaspora in the West, especially in the United States. In order to properly contextualize the emergence of this diasporic online journalism, the next chapter introduces the history and character of the Nigerian diaspora in America, which is at the vanguard of the nascent transnational online journalism that this book explores.

Chapter Three

The Nigerian Digital Diasporic Public Sphere

Diasporas are ethnoscapes formed by people who voluntarily or involuntarily deterritorialize from their homelands and reterritorialize in new environments. They conceive of themselves as being "outside the state but inside the people."[1] The fact of this emotional investment in the homeland in spite of geographic distance from it displaces the importance of territorial boundedness in the constructions of notions of citizenship and political participation. Although diasporas have traditionally been historicized as congeries of people who exist on the fringes of the societies in which they have reterritorialized,[2] there is significant research that point to the central roles diasporas play in influencing domestic and global politics, shaping identities, reconfiguring notions of community and peoplehood, and navigating the contours of the global economy.[3] In other words, in the age of globalization and the death of distance that the Internet has enabled, territorial displacement does not necessarily sentence ethnoscapes to what Adbelmalek Sayad has called "double absence."[4] Instead, it can activate manifold manifestations of presence, especially with the unceasingly dizzying proliferation of the "technologies of presence"[5] and the logic of "connected presence"[6] this reality enhances. Although diasporas have inspired changes in the domestic policies and politics of their homelands[7] and instigated change of government, they can also be agents of instability.[8] Nonetheless, the increasingly central roles that diasporas play in homeland politics has caused Robin Cohen to observe that they have moved "from victims to challengers."[9]

Digital diasporas, which are not delimited by national boundaries, have also emerged as core constituents of the structures and processes of the contemporary phase of globalization. Exilic elites of several countries have transformed the Internet into electronic agoras for transformative dialogic encounters with their homeland and with their current places of residence. Marshall McLuhan and Bruce Powers unwittingly foretold digital diasporas in their book *The Global Village: Transformations in World Life and Media in the 21st Century*, when they pointed out that "electronic technologies have begun to shake the distinction between inner and outer space, by blurring the difference between being here or there."[10] Although they were celebrating the nascence of visual technologies that dissolved the limitations of time and space, their insights are relevant to the conception of digital diasporic public spheres, which dissolve, or at least complexify, the differences between home and abroad in deliberative encounters. In order to properly situate my conception of a public sphere and show how the Nigerian diasporic digital public sphere emerged and matured, the next section explicates the notion of the public sphere that undergirds this book.

Understanding the Public Sphere

The notion of the public sphere is at the core of the reconstruction of deliberative democracy[11] and, increasingly, of the conception of digital diasporas. In the age of the Internet, deliberative democracy among members of digital diasporas and between diasporas and homelands is increasingly instrumentalized through spatially dispersed but nonetheless organic online communities, what Mary Chayko calls "the portability of social connectedness."[12] These have been mushrooming exponentially even in hitherto digital backwaters of the world such as Africa, which Manuel Castells had gloomily characterized as the "black hole of informational capitalism."[13] Thanks to the ubiquity of Internet-ready mobile devices, several African countries, including Nigeria, the continent's most populous nation and biggest economy, are active participants in participatory, many-to-many, user-led online communities. As I will argue in chapter 6, several of the deliberative practices in some Nigerian online diasporic communities resonate with, or at least consciously seek to abide by, some features of Jürgen Habermas's characterization of the seventeenth- and eighteenth-century public spheres in Britain, France, and Germany.

In this chapter, I give an overview of the literature on the public sphere, with special reference to the conception of the public sphere popularized by Habermas. Next, I review and interrogate the contending theoretical constructions on the deliberative potential and practices, or lack thereof, of the

Internet. I also dissect the internal categories of the Habermasian "ideal speech situation" and review the trajectory of scholarship that affirms or repudiates the symbolic nexus between the traditional, normative conception of the public sphere that Habermas theorizes and the phenomenal, dizzying democratic marketplace of ideas that, in my opinion, the Internet enables. The Internet, though sometimes falling short of the requirements of a normative Habermasian conception of the public sphere, in many respects also creates the opportunity for the robust blossoming of a variety of "public spheres," especially transnational, diasporic spheres of public discourse.

Jürgen Habermas, arguably the most notable of the second-generation members of the influential Frankfurt School of critical theory,[14] popularized the concept of the public sphere in the English-speaking world when his book, *The Structural Transformation of the Public Sphere*, first published in 1962 in German, was translated into English in 1989.[15] He conceives of the public sphere as an open, inclusive, dialogic arena of rational-critical discourse that is unhindered by either the state or the private sector and that acts as a check on state power. It is important to note, however, that although Habermas's theory of the public sphere may be the most influential today, it is by no means the only one; there is a multiplicity of competing conceptions of what constitutes the public sphere.

For instance, an influential conception of the public sphere that is coeval with but radically different from Habermas's is Reinhart Koselleck's. Koselleck's concept of the public sphere is located in his historicization of the role that secret societies such as the Freemasons played in challenging totalitarian authority in Europe.[16] By countervailing the totalitarianism prevalent in Europe in the eighteenth century, he argued, these secret societies created moral alternatives that expanded the range of discourse in much the same way that the bourgeois public sphere that Habermas famously historicized served as a counterweight to feudal absolutism. For John Dewey, an influential American theorist, the public is called into being by the concatenation of "indirect, extensive, enduring and serious consequences of conjoint and interacting behavior" of individuals and groups in society.[17] For Walter Lippmann, the public sphere resides in a core of people with specialist knowledge and skills who serve as a buffer between the government and the masses of the people.[18] In Mikhail Bakhtin's conception,[19] the public inheres in moments of wildly funny and grotesque inversion of the social hierarchies in the society, what M. Lane Bruner calls "progressive public transgression."[20] Because publics are constituted in those moments in history when the ruling classes allow for the temporary upending of social hierarchies through the carnivalesque, Bakhtin dispenses with the necessity for communicative and procedural rationality, or for the bracketing of subjectivities. What is common to all these conceptions is that the public is constituted outside the home and the state, except in Dewey's conception.[21]

The notion of the public sphere that forms the theoretical bedrock of this book is the one propounded by Jürgen Habermas because, as Nancy Fraser puts it, "no attempt to understand the limits of actually existing late-capitalist democracy can succeed without in some way or another making use of [Habermas's early conception of the public sphere]."[22] Additionally, since this book is concerned with investigating how the media of public expression can serve—and have served—as centers for discursive resistance to totalitarian state powers, Habermas's conception of the public sphere seems particularly appropriate. According to Habermas:

> By "public sphere" we mean first of all a domain of our social life in which such a thing as public opinion can be formed. Access to the public sphere is open to all citizens. A portion of the public sphere is constituted in every conversation in which private persons come together to form a public. When the public is large, this kind of communication requires certain means of dissemination and influence; today newspapers and periodicals, radio and television are the media of the public sphere. We speak of a political public sphere when the public discussions concern objects connected with the practice of the state.[23]

Habermas's theory derives inspirational strength from a historical juncture during the seventeenth and eighteenth centuries in western Europe—particularly in England, France, and Germany—when coffeehouses, salons, societies, the town hall, the village church, the tavern, the public square, convenient barns, guild halls, parks, shops, and even street corners became the arenas of debate, political discussion, and action. Habermas extends this to a normative model of popular involvement in the public sphere for contemporary times. He explains that in these venues, everyone had an equal right to speak *as if* they were equals. In England, for example, the coffeehouse conferred discursive sanctuary not only on the nobility but also on "the wider strata of the middle class, including craftsmen and shopkeepers."[24] This dialogue, he posited, transpired in a profoundly democratic forum where the status differentials and positional hierarchies of participants were bracketed and issues were discussed without external coercion.

According to Habermas, the public sphere was governed by a moral-practical discourse, and the apparatus for the mediation of this discourse was rational, critical argumentation. Habermas's analysis of communication in the archetypal bourgeois public sphere reveals that every participant who engaged in the moral-practical discourse of the time made recourse to a number of normative conditions, which he later called the "ideal speech situation" in his extension of his theory.[25] The requirements to qualify for the Habermasian ideal speech situation are as follows: the discourse should be independent from state and corporate interferences; the exchange of points of views during a discourse should be amenable to criticism and review; dogmatism should be eschewed; participants in the discourse should demonstrate reflexivity and a willingness to question both their individual assumptions and those of the social milieu in which they live; participants should show a capacity for tolerance, sympathy, and even a vicarious identification with points of views that are at variance with theirs and also avoid the use of emotive and insulting language; participants must make an effort to be sincere in their search for the truth; and there must be discursive inclusivity and equality.[26]

It is significant that Habermas himself has recognized that these are counterfactual ideals that have never been fully realized, even in the classical bourgeois public sphere. That is why in Habermasian, discursive public sphere theory it is traditional to differentiate between the ideal-normative concept of the public sphere and the empirical-descriptive concept.[27] The ideal-normative model has never materialized anywhere; it is merely derived from the prototype of the possibilities presented by seventeenth- and eighteenth-century European public spheres. This approach takes the public sphere as nonnormative, having no special "origin" but presenting itself to us just in its empirically observable form. The empirical-descriptive concept of the public sphere sees society in terms of the functioning of public institutions that act in the public domain, "such as the mass media, cultural establishments, educational institutions etc.—and of the representations that the institutions convey, such as the acts of politicians and celebrities, news and reports, advertisements, etc.—i.e. public 'images.'"[28] Most researchers deploy the empirical-descriptive concept of the public sphere to ask questions about how and why notions of reasonable deliberations work in some societies but not in others, what influences public debates, how public opinions form and influence state policies, and so on.

Interestingly, in an important extension of his theory of the public sphere, Habermas argues that if democracy is to be implemented in today's diverse and complex world, society has to learn to adjust to the reality of the impracticability of a spatially bound agglomeration of mutually consenting members in the public sphere. Instead, he proposes that citizens who are not necessarily physically copresent can develop forms of communication that dispense with the necessity for corporeal presence.[29] This extension takes into account, or even prognosticates, the centrality of mass media systems—and the Internet—in public deliberations. In this book, I explore the mass-media system and Internet-based journalistic activism of the Nigerian public sphere. However, in spite of the popularity of Habermas's theory and the immense utility it has had and continues to have for the analysis of deliberative practice and state-civil society relations, it has attracted criticism from a variety of quarters.

Criticism of Habermas's Public Sphere

Critics from different theoretical and ideological orientations have interrogated the limitations of Habermas's lofty, idyllic construction of the public sphere that most theorists of democracy and popular participation invoke to evaluate the performance of both the traditional media of mass communication and the new media in terms of meeting the conditions to qualify as public spheres. Habermas's conception of the public sphere has been criticized as Eurocentric, as biased in favor of the bourgeoisie and against the working class, as patriarchal, and as logocentric.[30]

Poststructuralists such as Jean François Lyotard even question the functional relevance of Habermas's model of consensus through rational-critical discourse.[31] Lyotard specifically queried the emancipatory and social utility of excessive rationalism in the conduct of discourse for the wider strata of society. This concept is also criticized for instituting a linear, evolutionary, progressive history of the world that ignores the differential sociohistorical experiences of non-Western or, to be sure, non-European societies. It is accused of falsely conferring on the idiosyncrasies of Enlightenment Europe a universality that age never possessed, and of consigning the differential temporalities of other societies to the discursive fringes.[32]

Feminist theorists such as Nancy Fraser also call attention to the exclusion of women from Habermas's public sphere.[33] As Neil McLaughlin observes, a typical participant in the European public sphere that Habermas historicized was usually male, educated, and propertied, and had the means and leisure to take part in public discourse.[34] Economically disaffiliated segments of society that had a need, indeed an obligation, to work hard to survive the vicissitudes and cruelties of the incipient capitalist socioeconomic order did not have the luxury of energy and time to participate in the public sphere discussions of the day. And certainly women at that time were either too ensnared by the drudgery of domestic engagements or the suffocating stranglehold of male tyranny and oppression to participate in the discursive indulgence of the public sphere. Several feminist theorists such as Anne Fernald[35] also point out that the putative discursive openness of Habermas's public sphere is premised on practices of deliberative omission not only of women but also of children and other marginal and subordinate groups in society.[36] Jodi Dean cites critics who allege that Habermas's account of the bourgeois public sphere is historically suspect, or "never existed."[37] She also characterizes it as the "utopian imaginings of democracy" that have been co-opted by "communicative capitalism."[38]

Aside from poststructuralist, postcolonial, and feminist critics, other critics such as Oskar Negt and Alexander Kluge,[39] Nancy Fraser, and Michael Warner[40] also instructively call attention to Habermas's privileging of a hegemonic public sphere, which they argue was structured to be congenial only to the preferences and prejudices of people in the upper levels of society. In place of one overarching, dominant public sphere, they postulate the concept of multiple public spheres that are not only oppositional to the hegemonic public sphere but that also incorporate the aspirations of marginal groups in society such as the working class, women, and racial and sexual minorities.

The symbolic utility of their argument in terms of contemporary scholarship in non-Western parts of the world and, in fact, in computer-mediated communication is that the landscape of the public sphere has shifted from a historico-transcendental veneration of Europe during the Enlightenment to a multiplicity of transhistorical loci of discourses. This crucial change in the notion of the public sphere assumes its full consequence when it is seen in relation to the Internet, which in many ways defies simplistic spatial and temporal categorizations and encompasses a robust array of spheres of discourses in ways that are probably unparalleled in human history.

For this study, it also allows us to conceive of the public sphere in ways that differ significantly from notions of the public sphere in non-Western societies. In Nigeria, for instance, the state is organically linked with the quotidian existence of the citizens of the country. To give just one example, a government-funded newspaper in northern Nigeria called the *New Nigerian* (see chapter 2), while largely supportive of the colonial government and subsequently northern Nigerian regional governments, also served as the arena for anticolonial protests and for searing critiques of postcolonial northern Nigerian governments. So Habermas's insistence that the absence of state interference in public discourse is crucial to the notion of a public sphere is limiting. It does not adequately capture the lived realities of people in a gatekeeper state. The Nigerian public sphere has multiple origins and a diverse character and is often called into being in relation to or within the constraints of the state—from the colonial state to the postindependence state. Most important, the emergence and centrality of the Internet in the last few years have recomposed and enlarged the structure of the public sphere. There is an increasing convergence between the public spheres of digital diasporas and the public sphere of the homeland. But can the Internet serve as a public sphere?

The Internet and the Public Sphere

Although it is obvious that Habermas did not envision the Internet when he formulated his theory of the public sphere, his caution against "Athens envy" in his subsequent work no doubt anticipates the debates about the deliberative capacities of the Internet. In an important extension of his theory of the public sphere, Habermas argued that if democracy is to be implemented in today's diverse and complex world, society has to learn to adjust to the reality of the unworkability of a spatially bound agglomeration of mutually consenting members in the public sphere. Instead, he proposes that citizens who are not necessarily physically copresent can develop forms of communication that dispense with the necessity for physical presence.[41] Although Habermas did not specifically refer to the Internet when he said this, many communication scholars have interpreted him as affirming the deliberative potential of the Internet. As Heinz Brandenburg instructively observed, "[I]t is not the case that Habermas himself or deliberative theorists went on the search to discover an effective and inclusive forum of public deliberation on a mass scale and came across the Internet. It is rather the other way around: namely that early cyber-enthusiasts quickly embraced Habermas's notion of the public sphere and the theory of deliberative democracy and began to claim that the Internet provides just that: a virtual public sphere."[42]

One of the most notable early cyber theorists who rhapsodized over the emancipatory and deliberative potential of the Internet was Howard Rheingold, who popularized a cyber-enthusiastic vision of the electronic agora,[43] or what Kevin Robins and Frank Webster have characterized as the vision of an "Athens without slaves."[44] Rheingold believes that Internet technology, "if properly understood and defended by enough citizens, does have democratizing potential in the way that alphabets and printing presses had democratizing potential."[45] He postulates that the formation of virtual communities on the Internet provides the chance to revitalize the public sphere, and that the chance to do this has been put back in the hands of the public in a manner that is unparalleled in the records of human democratic progress. One of the main benefits of the Internet, he said, is the wide latitude it gives its users to find others who share similar interests, concerns, and worries with them. He made the point that although one cannot, for instance, simply pick up a phone and ask to be connected with someone who wants to talk about Islamic art or Californian wine, one can join a newsgroup on any of those topics and converse with the people there, either privately or publicly.

In spite of his faith in the strengths and promises of the Internet, Rheingold was careful not to draw a mechanical link between the normative public sphere and the Internet, preferring to use the word "potential." Hubertus Buchstein was less restrained. He was certain that the Internet is the Habermasian public sphere, reincarnated in an electronic form. He contends that it "looks like the most ideal speech situation."[46] Douglas Kellner also states that the Internet has "produced new public spheres and spaces for information, debate, and participation that contain the potential to invigorate democracy and to increase the dissemination of critical and progressive ideas."[47] Similarly, Michael and Rhonda Hauben conclude, from their empirical inquiry into the discursive practices of Usenet groups and other forms of deliberation on the web, that the Internet expands the range and diversity of communication and viewpoints "through the freewheeling and rambling discussion" that it enables.[48]

However, several other scholars do not share in the optimism of these cyber enthusiasts. For instance, on the basis of empirical research, Lincoln Dahlberg concludes that the gains of Internet discussion groups in terms of opening up new vistas for advancing the concept of the public sphere are vitiated by the growing commercialization and commoditization of cyberspace by state and corporate concerns.[49] He also notes that the Internet as presently constituted is undermined by a dearth of reflexivity, a deficit of mutual tolerance, difficulty in authenticating identity claims and information put forward by participants in Internet discussion groups, the disaffiliation of large sections of people from online political forums, and the monopolization of cyber discourse by a few individuals and groups. He contends that this reality detracts from the ascription of the status of public sphere to the Internet.

In their introduction to *Resisting the Virtual Life*, James Brook and Iain Boal are even harsher in their critique of the Internet. They say it is "pernicious" when it is deployed as a "substitute . . . for face-to-face interactions."[50]

However, scholars such as Susan O'Donnell strike a happy balance between the cyber enthusiasts and the cyber skeptics. O'Donnell's research applies the public-sphere concept to the Internet and argues that although the Internet does have democratizing potential, it often fails as a public sphere in practice.[51] How do these views relate to an actual, extant site of discourse on the Internet?

The Nigerian Diaspora in America

The last few decades have witnessed phenomenal migratory flows of Africans to the West, especially to the United States, at a proportion outpaced only by the transatlantic slave trade.[52] In the case of Nigeria, which leads all African countries in migratory flows to the United States, this deterritorialization has had and continues to have a profound impact on the politics of the domestic public sphere.[53] Many scholars have studied how Nigerians in the diaspora, using the transnational cultural and political capital that their privileged territorial displacement has conferred on them, established strategic linkages with domestic activist-civil-society groups to form the National Democratic Coalition (NADECO), which became a central and symbolic locus of political mobilization in the long and arduous struggle to dislodge totalitarian military regimes in Nigeria in the 1990s.[54] As would be expected, when democratic rule was restored in 1999, the newly elected government acknowledged the struggles of Nigerians in the diaspora by formalizing associative relations with them. The government inaugurated the group Nigerians in Diaspora Organization (NIDO) and even created liaison offices for diasporic Nigerians in major Western embassies.[55]

However, whereas the political and economic consequences of the migratory flows of Nigerians to the United States have been captured fairly robustly in the scholarly literature on globalization,[56] there is scant attention to the transnational online journalistic practices of Nigerians in the diaspora and what impacts these practices have had and continue to have on not just the form and content of journalistic practices in Nigeria but also on the national postmilitary politics of the country.

The first noticeable wave of numerically significant Nigerian migratory flow to the United States began in the 1960s.[57] However, the United States did not become attractive to Nigerians for permanent residence until the late 1980s. In the past, most Nigerians who came to the United States on student visas went back to the homeland on completion of their studies. There were valid reasons for this. The Nigerian economy was vibrant then and could comfortably accommodate and sustain the middle-class aspirations that foreign qualifications and exposure to life in the United States inspired. Sakah Mahmud, for instance, points out that in the early years of independence, Nigeria actually attained "self-sufficiency in agricultural production, enough for both domestic consumption as well as for export."[58] In addition to achieving self-sufficiency in food production, Nigeria also witnessed what has been characterized as "bonanza development,"[59] which Richard Joseph insightfully defined as "earnings from petroleum exports considerably above the country's actual expenditure."[60]

This rosy picture changed in the 1980s with the collapse of the economy, in part because of IMF/World Bank–inspired structural adjustment programs[61] and the unprecedented institutionalization of venality at the highest levels of government by the totalitarian, unaccountable military regimes that seized power from the democratically elected government in 1983. Thus, from the late 1980s, a steady stream of Nigerians began to migrate to the United States and other parts of the Western world. According to U.S. Immigration and Naturalization Service figures, only 112 immigrants admitted for legal permanent residence in 1986 identified Nigeria as their country of birth. By 2000, this figure rose to 4,355. The 2001 figures from the U.S. Bureau of Citizenship and Immigration Services indicated that 134,940 legal permanent residents in the United States were born in Nigeria.[62] Since 2001, statistics on the number of Nigerians living in the United States have been widely variable. For instance, although Pew Research said the number of Nigerian Americans increased to 280,000 as of 2017,[63] the Voice of America put the number of Nigerian-born Americans at 327,000 as of 2015.[64] The American Community Survey, a US Census Bureau initiative, estimated that there were 380,785 Nigerians in the United States as of 2016.

Regardless of the actual number, it is important to note that these figures are extrapolated from the thousands of Nigerians who immigrated to the United States through the Diversity Visa (green card) Program[65] and from other formal immigration records. It excludes a large number of Nigerians who fall outside the category of permanent legal residents. For instance, it excludes thousands of undocumented people who have overstayed their student, tourist, or professional exchange visas; people who came to the United States illegally; and people who are studying in various colleges and universities in the United States and who are unlikely to return to the homeland in the immediate future on completion of their studies. It probably also excludes second- or third-generation Nigerians who were born and socialized in the United States and who are now indistinguishable from native-born African Americans but who, in spite of being born in the United States, have deep emotional investments in Nigeria. If these people are taken into account, there are probably up to 2 million Nigerians living in the United States. If the present trend continues, it seems reasonable to expect that the United States will surpass Britain as the second home of Nigerians. But what kinds of Nigerian immigrants live in the United States? And how do their cultural assets enable them to influence the domestic public sphere through their citizen media?

The demographic characteristics of Nigerian immigrants in the United States especially conduce to the cultural capital they wield in the homeland. Scholars who have studied Nigerian immigrants point out that they are usually middle-class professionals with at least a college degree and are often significantly more educated than most other immigrant groups in the United States.[66] The most recent statistics from the US Census Bureau show that 43.8 percent of African immigrants (of whom Nigerians have an overwhelming numerical dominion) have obtained a college degree, compared with 42.5 of Asian Americans, 28.9 percent of immigrants from Europe, Russia and Canada, and 23.1 percent of the US population as a whole.[67] A 2009 study also found that "among high school graduates, 'immigrant blacks'—defined as those who immigrated to the United States or their children—are significantly more likely than other black Americans to attend selective colleges. In fact, immigrant black Americans are more likely than white students to attend such colleges."[68] In his syndicated column of January 16, 2018, Tyler Cowen added: "Or consider Nigerian-Americans, Nigeria being Africa's most populous nation: Their education levels are among the very highest in the U.S., above those of Asians, with 17 percent having a master's degree."[69]

According to the Migration Policy Institute, "29 percent of Nigerian-Americans over the age of 25 hold a graduate degree, compared to 11 percent of the overall U.S. population."[70] The US Census Bureau's 2016 American Community Survey also found that 45 percent of Nigerian American professionals work in education services, and scores are well regarded professors and researchers at elite colleges and universities, "all while confidently emerging as one of the country's most successful immigrant communities, with a median household income of $62,351, compared to $57,617 nationally, as of 2015."[71] As a *Chicago Tribune* columnist noted in a March 18, 2007 article, "That defies the usual stereotypes of Asian-Americans as the only 'model minority.' Yet the traditional American narrative has rendered the high academic achievements of black immigrants from Africa . . . invisible, as if that were a taboo topic."[72] In an interesting parallel, London's *Daily Times* noted, "Black Africans have emerged as the most highly educated members of British society, surpassing even the Chinese as the most academically successful ethnic minority."[73]

The high academic achievements of Nigerians in the United States were noted as early as the 1960s. In his study of the academic performance of Nigerian students in American colleges in the early 1960s, Gordon D. Morgan noted, "It is a matter of record that Nigerian students do as well as American students in their college work here. Whether this is due to equal prior training is open to dispute. Perhaps an explanation can be found in the Nigerian's superior motivation to achieve, the immediate benefits of academic success back home, or his desire to avoid the stigma of failure among friends in Nigeria."[74] Like most immigrants in most places, Nigerian immigrants are a self-selected group who are not always representative of the populations from which they emerge. They tend to be highly motivated, self-driven, and obsessed with success in more ways than the host population or the population from where they emigrated. Since most Nigerian immigrants come to the United States first in search of educational opportunities before they make the transition to the workforce, their superior educational attainment is not surprising. They must first take rigorous entry exams (such as the Test of English as a Foreign Language, the Graduate Record Examinations, the Scholastic Aptitude Test, etc.) and get high grades before they are considered for admission and visa issuance. It is therefore predictable that they will be more educated than the general population. They are also likely to transfer the work ethic that brought them to America to their children. But more often than not, by the third or fourth generation, descendants of immigrants fully assimilate and become indistinguishable from the general population.

A distinctive feature of Nigerian immigrants in the United States, according to Rachel Reynolds and Scott Youngstedt, is that although their ancestral provenance is spatially located in a postcolonial periphery, they are usually "structurally integrated into communities at the core . . . working in finance, engineering, sales and management."[75] This fact, which is in many respects congruent with the experiences of many highly skilled third-world immigrants who are "dislocated" to the first world, gives rise to a situation where "the familiar lines between 'here' and 'there,' center and periphery, West and non-West have to some extent become blurred."[76] Like most deterritorialized communities and displaced populations, the Nigerian diaspora in the United States has a strong nationalist attachment to the homeland.[77] Even though the homeland is usually polarized along ethnic and religious fault-lines, the reality of their shared experience of displacement in a strange cultural habitus has forced Nigerians to cultivate and nurture a diasporic romantic nationalism, often lubricated by the instrumentality of hometown associations, the print media, and lately the World Wide Web[78]—what Arjun Appadurai would call the "paradox of constructed primordialism."[79]

Barbara O'Connor and Carol Mackeogh have pointed out that the media are indispensable instruments for the construction of a sense of belonging[80]—or what Benedict Anderson called "imagined communities"[81]—among otherwise disparate people. Anderson argues that "all communities larger than primordial villages of face-to-face contact (and perhaps even these) are imagined."[82] This imagination is increasingly materialized through the communicative spaces of the Internet. In defining a nation as "an imagined political community – and imagined as both inherently limited and sovereign,"[83] Anderson prognosticated online communities and engaged digital diasporas such as Nigeria's US digital diaspora. Digital diasporas and the conglomeration of online communities they spawn are "imagined" because, as Anderson points out, "the members of even the smallest nation will never know most of their fellow-members, meet them, or even hear of them, yet in the minds of each lives the image of their communion." The community this imagination creates "is always conceived as a deep, horizontal comradeship," although this "deep comradeship" varies in depth, breadth, degrees of involvement, and access to power and privileges.[84] The Internet has enabled many Nigerian immigrants in the United States to transcend their previous diasporic nationalism, which was disaffiliated from the politics of the homeland, to one that actively engages with the domestic public sphere through transnational, diaspora-generated online media outlets.

As a consequence of these demographic characteristics of the Nigerian diaspora in the United States, members of the community have historically been media savvy and among the first to embrace the opportunities that the digital space provides for social interaction and the cultivation and nurturing of an idealistic diaspora nationalism. Misty Bastian's research on the Nigerian diaspora community in the United States shows that even in the early 1990s, the community already had its newspapers, magazines, television, and a Listserv called Naijanet that were used to foster a sense of community and to familiarize members with "news from home."[85] The first steps "toward developing a Nigerian online network took place in 1991" when a Nigerian at Dartmouth College began forwarding to select friends email news about the home country.[86] From this modest beginning emerged Naijanet, which Anna Everett described as "one of the Internet's most robust and enduring Afrocentric virtual communities."[87]

Bastian reported that since 1992 "Naijanet has spun off at least six related online networks," and that at its height of influence and popularity in 1995, "Naijanetters" numbered approximately 750. During this period, too, Mary Ebeling informs us, the Nigerian diaspora of the Ogoni ethnic minority from Nigeria's Niger Delta region "used the Internet as a political mobilizing resource very effectively" to call international attention to the exploitation of their resources and the degradation of their environment by Shell Oil Company and the military regime of General Sani Abacha.[88]

The late 2000s saw the migration of most of the print media outlets of the Nigerian diaspora to the Internet and the emergence of new online-native newspapers with no offline antecedents. The dissolution of spatial and temporal boundaries that the Internet facilitates has conferred a hitherto unthought-of transnational social capital on diasporic media in ways that fulfill Bastian's 1999 vision of a convergence of Nigeria's everyday realities, the concerns and content of the diaspora's online media, and the domestic politics of the homeland. Writing in 1999, Bastian prognosticated:

> The wiring of Nigeria itself is probably inevitable, especially under the climate of political transparency developing in the new Nigerian republic, and is awaited with great impatience by Nigerian academics and businesspeople alike. At the moment when virtual Nigeria becomes open to real Nigeria, there is the possibility of a new synthesis, a drawing closer of the electronic world of the brain drain diaspora and the real worlds of both material diasporic experience and Nigerian quotidian life.[89]

The emergence of popular diasporic online newspapers that now engage in perpetual political and cultural dialogues with the homeland would seem to have bestowed an uncannily accurate materiality to Bastian's vision. There is now a robust synthesis between the digital media of the Nigerian diaspora in the United States and the "quotidian life" of Nigerians in the homeland. This is giving rise to a literal and metaphoric double presence—that is, territorial presence in the diaspora and a sociopolitical cum symbolic presence in the homeland—through such technologies of presence as the Internet, mobile telephony, and travel. With the progressive expansion of Internet facilities in

Nigeria and other technologies of connected presence, this reality is expanding at a pace that probably exceeds Bastian's expectations.

The death of critical journalism in the Nigeria public sphere as a result of the defeat of military absolutism and the co-option of journalists into the circuit of governmental malfeasance fertilized the emergence and expansion of diasporic citizen online journalism. The "brain drain" digital diaspora, as the next chapter shows, chose to deploy its exilic cultural capital to fill a void that emerged in the media landscape of the homeland. It went from being a distant, aloof, disempowered, and dispersed collective to an active, transformational one.

Chapter Four

Profiles of Diasporic Citizen Media Sites

The upsurge of diasporic Nigerian citizen journalism in the United States in the mid-2000s is almost coextensive with the mass migration of Nigeria's print newspapers to the Internet. On the surface, this development seems incongruous, even counterintuitive. The migration of news content from homeland legacy newspapers to the Internet, which frees it from the constraints of time and space, should have satisfied the yearning for domestic news by diasporic Nigerians in the United States and therefore obviated the need for the emergence of diasporic news outlets that publish news about the homeland. Nevertheless, diasporic citizen news outlets not only compete with but also vigorously undermine the credibility of homeland newspapers. As this and the next chapter will show, two fundamental factors account for this situation.

The first reason, as chapter 3 hinted, is the dearth—in fact, the outright death—of the brand of investigative and advocacy journalism that characterized the anticolonial and antimilitary eras, which found an especially concentrated expression in the guerrilla press of the 1990s. The absence of a robust, uncompromised domestic watchdog media system committed to comforting the afflicted and afflicting the comfortable in the face of the enormous venality that has accompanied Nigeria's return to democratic rule needed to be corrected.[1] Homeland newspapers have proved either unwilling or unable to take up this challenge. The second reason for the rise and popularity of Nigerian diasporic online media was the technical deficiency of the websites of homeland newspapers. Their websites were neither updated in real time nor sufficiently interactive and multiplatform in the fashion of contemporary legacy media websites in the West with which diasporic Nigerians have become familiar.[2] So whereas the mainstream media in the West ventured into online journalism out of anxieties about the potentially disruptive effects that emergent citizen online journalism might have on their professional authority,[3] in an interesting reversal, the Nigerian mainstream media's lack of sophisticated web presence partly inspired the emergence of Nigerian citizen online journalism, which now potentially disrupts the authority and dominant journalistic practices of the homeland mainstream media.

Mark Deuze identifies three features that are fundamental to the possibility and vitality of online journalism: interactivity (the ability for readers or audiences of online content to react to or interact with and even adapt news content presented to them), multimediality (the technical potential for news content to be presented on multiple platforms such as text, video, audio, and animated graphics), and hypertextuality (the ability "to connect the story to other stories, archives, resources and so forth through hyperlinks").[4] Deuze explores these three broad characteristics in terms of four types of online journalism: "mainstream" news sites, "index and category" sites, "meta and comment" sites, and "share and discussion" sites. "Mainstream" and "index and category" sites, he points out, are characterized by "moderated participatory communication," whereas "meta and comment" and "share and discussion" sites are characterized by "unmoderated participatory communication."[5] In reality, though, most online news sites are hybridized; they have a bit of all of these dimensions of online journalism.

John Pavlik, for his part, identifies three stages in the evolution of online journalism.[6] In the first stage, mainstream newspapers merely recycled their print content to their new online platforms This is often derisively called "shovelware" in the industry vernacular.[7] The second stage in online journalism improved on the first and involved some interactivity with news content posted on news websites. Content was regularly updated on websites as news broke. So news appeared on news websites first before it appeared in the print editions. The third and current stage is convergent; it features dynamic content that is not necessarily the same as the print content and that has a lot of multimediality. This is the contemporary phase of online journalism, where lengthy interviews that cannot be published in whole due to the traditional constraints of newspaper space are posted online, where the audio and video files of interviews published in print can be uploaded onto news sites, and where exclusively video- and audio-based or photographic reports that cannot possibly be captured by the print medium are featured on the web. The next stage is shaping up to be a fusion of social media streams into convergent journalistic practices. In other words, online journalism has evolved

Table 4.1. Three stages of online journalism

Stage 1	Stage 2	Stage 3	Next stages
• Print on web • Content not dynamic or updated	• Text • Picture • Hyperlink • Content regularly updated	• Audio • Video • Animation • Content regularly updated • User feedback	• The future: • Fusion of social media and journalism
Shovelware	Hypertextuality	Multimediality	Social networked journalism

Source: adapted from Dimitrova and Neznanski, "Online Journalism and the War in Cyberspace."

from textuality to hypertextuality, and finally to multimediality. Although some people prognosticate that the next stage might witness the death of the traditional media, others caution against such gloomy, apocalyptic projections, insisting instead that "newspapers can coexist with the Internet while surrendering some tasks, such as archiving factual background, becoming instead more analytical advocates."[8]

For a long time, the websites of Nigerian homeland newspapers failed the requirements of Deuze's multimediality and hypertextuality and seemed to be stuck in Pavlik's second stage in the evolution of online journalism. The defunct *Post Express*, the first Nigerian newspaper to migrate its content to the Internet in 1996 under the direction of the late Stanley Macebuh,[9] merely recycled its print content to the web. Since then, for the most part, subsequent Nigerian newspapers that appeared on the web also repurposed static shovelware from their print versions. There were exceptions, though. The Nigerian *Guardian*, which prides itself on being the "flagship of Nigerian journalism,"[10] used to be interactive. The online forums and chat rooms it created for discussing its news content were so popular between the late 1990s and the early 2000s that it was the first port of call for homesick Nigerians living in the West. A participant in the chat-room discussions who lived in the United Kingdom at the time called it the "rallying point for Nigerians at home and abroad to meet and discuss common issues of national importance."[11] However, realizing that its forums had become wildly popular, the paper decided to commercialize participation. It required people to pay upfront before being allowed to participate in the online discussion forums. The paper lost nearly all of its participants. Nobody was prepared to pay a fee in order to be able to discuss across spatial and temporal boundaries. Instead, this move to commercialize participation in the *Guardian*'s chatrooms inspired diasporic Nigerians to set up their own discussion groups.

To require people to pay a fee before interacting with a newspaper's content was a thoughtless and unimaginative business strategy. The *Guardian* could have used one of the many strategies the DailyMail.co.uk deployed to earn money from its message boards, including advertising overlays and sponsorship, use of "intelligent hyperlinks" within postings, etc.[12] As of 2019, the below-the-line comment section of *Guardian*'s website, which had been closed to the public for years, does not generate vibrant online commentary. For the most part, the content of the site consists of mostly shovelware versions of its print edition, its search feature is not intuitive, and it does not have an online archive of its content—all features that are basic and integral to the architecture of the websites of almost all mainstream Western news media. However, it does have occasional video.

A Nigerian newspaper that became one of the first legacy media outfits to transition to the second stage of Pavlik's periodization of online journalism is the Abuja-based *Leadership* newspaper. The paper's website provided a robust platform for readers to react to and interact with its stories. Reader comments were uncensored and unfiltered. However, in time it attracted Internet trolls who turned the forum into avenues for throwing caustic vitriol not only at the writers, editors, and reporters of the paper but also at other Nigerian ethnic groups. The site was also hacked through the message boards.[13] The paper took a decision, after about one year of uncensored comments, to require that readers must register before they can post comments on the site. The policy drove most readers away.

As of 2019, almost all Nigerian newspapers have some form of interactivity on their websites. Papers such as the *Daily Trust* (based in Abuja, Nigeria's federal capital), *P.M. News*, *Vanguard*, *Punch*, and the *Nation* (all based in Lagos) update breaking news stories on their sites first and incorporate occasional video news reporting. There are almost no Nigerian newspapers with an online presence that are stuck in the first stage of online journalism as of 2019, but many have not quite made the leap to the second stage. In many ways, the majority of Nigeria's mainstream newspapers are guilty of the criticisms that media critic Jon Katz leveled against the US media in the late 1990s. He criticized US newspapers for remaining "insanely stagnant in an interactive age."[14] Donald Matheson attributed this to the mainstream media's tendency to have a "rather static core set of news practices" and to place "other journalistic practices at its margins."[15] The business and technology columnist Dan Gillmor, for his part, attributed the slow adoption of the blog by the mainstream media to their "innate conservatism" and asserted further that "when big media companies consider having a conversation with their audience, they tend not to push many boundaries."[16] These criticisms now seem dated in reference to the mainstream media in the West, but they are still partly applicable to the mainstream media in Nigeria. In the case of Nigeria, however, it seems more plausible to implicate low technological development and print journalists' unease with Internet technology for this state of affairs than the "static core of news practices" or an "innate conservatism."

It is precisely this structural and functional deficiency of traditional homeland newspapers that provided the spur for the emergence, popularity, and acceptance of citizen media by Nigerians who reside beyond the shores of their native country. Diasporic citizen online newspapers merely took advantage of the weak online presence of Nigerian newspapers to establish their relevance. Most of the websites that will be profiled in the next section clearly belong in the third stage of Pavlik's mapping of online journalism. Their content is active and updated in real time. They are hypertextual, interactive, and multimedia. Because of these qualities, they have beaten homeland newspapers—except the emergent, online-only homeland newspapers discussed in chapter 6—in breaking regular, routine news stories. Typically, in moments of political crisis, the most popular diasporic websites used to shut down because of high traffic. Before the websites of homeland newspapers caught on, diasporic online media outlets used to be the only sites that provided video and audio clips of newsworthy events, such as video of a Muslim governor caught dancing with Arab prostitutes and spraying money at a Dubai night club[17] and an audiotape of a serving Nigerian governor detailing plans to rig elections by using thugs dressed in fake military attire to intimidate voters. This quality—that is, accompanying stories with multimedia features—redounded to the popularity and credibility of diasporic online news sites. Until the last few years, mainstream Nigerian newspapers did not have the technical capability, expertise, or willingness to report on the kinds of news stories that involved video and audio components and animated graphics, and this was precisely why the institutional media in the homeland were such poor competitors to their diasporic online counterparts. So even the traditional homeland media that embraced online journalism out of reactive and pragmatic imperatives were stuck in the twilight zone between tradition and change, and many still are in 2019.

Online Media of the Nigerian Diaspora

As chapter 3 illustrates, members of the Nigerian diaspora, especially in the United States, were early adopters of the discursive facility of the Internet. They have used it for debates and for sharing information about the homeland and their immigrant/exilic conditions. However, only from 2005 onward that this technology has been deployed in a transnational fashion to engage with, and even influence, the politics of the homeland while being physically displaced from it. Some of the earliest diaspora online newspapers that set the stage for the online news revolution in Nigeria are Elendu Reports,[18] Sahara Reporters,[19] the Times of Nigeria,[20] the Nigerian Village Square,[21] Huhuonline,[22] and PointBlankNews.[23] There were many others such as Empowered Newswire,[24] USAfricaonline.com,[25] IReports-NG.com,[26] and TheWill,[27] but in the main, their influence in the Nigerian domestic public sphere was peripheral at best and nonexistent at worst.

Since their forceful emergence in 2005 and beyond, they have continued to break sensitive news stories that have radically altered the journalistic practices and politics of Nigeria, as the case studies in this and the next chapter will show. These diasporic news outlets have gone beyond being instruments for the construction of subjectivities in the migratory settings of their owners and consumers to being active change agents in the domestic politics of the homeland. The next section profiles these sites and highlights some of their major news stories.

Elendu Reports

Elendu Reports is published from Lansing, Michigan, and is associated with Jonathan Elendu, a former newspaper journalist with the Nigerian *Daily Times*. The fact of his being a previous newspaper journalist who got involved with citizen and alternative journalism brings to mind Tony Harcup's caution (see chapter 1) against the "binarism" so often evident in the conceptualizations of alternative and mainstream media formations. Harcup's research suggests that "there may be some crossover of ideas, content, style, and, not least, people between what may be termed the alternative and what may be termed the mainstream; that some of the alternative media's 'hybridized voices' . . . may on occasions resonate within the mainstream."[28] This is certainly the case with Elendu Reports, and it was especially true in the early period of its emergence. Although the site is owned by Elendu, who is now a legal permanent resident in the United States, some of the most momentous news reports and investigations on the site were contributed by diverse citizen reporters who had no previous journalistic training or experience.[29] This illustrates "the existence of what might be termed a continuum, with people, ideas and practices moving along this continuum, in both directions."[30]

It is not only in the professional profile of its key personnel that Elendu Reports can be said to represent a continuum between mainstream and alternative journalism practices; even the structural configuration of the site, at least in its first iteration, maintains a kinship with the websites of homeland newspapers. For instance, unlike other diasporic citizen media sites, it does not post video or audio content. Nor does it have a mechanism for readers to interact with its stories in the form of reader comments. However, its content is updated in real time, making it a resource for domestic newspapers in Nigeria and a resource for Nigerians in search of up-to-date news about the homeland.

Elendu Reports was established on May 20, 2005.[31] In its heyday, it conducted hundreds of investigative stories and hundreds of interviews. It used to solicit questions from readers for its interviews—its most interactive and participatory feature. The first major story the site broke, titled "Carlton Masters: Obasanjo's Multi-Million-Dollar Lobbyist," was an investigative story on the shady dealings between Nigeria's former president Olusegun Obasanjo and the Atlanta-based GoodWorks International, which was founded by Andrew Young, the former US ambassador to the United Nations. Elendu Reports alleged that Carlton Masters, a cofounder of GoodWorks, helped launch a presidential library campaign for Nigeria's president, Olusegun Obasanjo, who then blackmailed Nigerian public and private enterprises to contribute millions of dollars for the project in violation of Nigeria's laws. Wole Soyinka, Africa's first Nobel Prize winner for literature, described this as an act of "executive extortion."[32] The story also alleged that oil contracts running into several millions of dollars were awarded to GoodWorks without due process.[33] One of Nigeria's most widely read newsmagazines, *The News*, picked up the story and reproduced it verbatim.[34] Other daily newspapers followed suit. The story was significant because it ruptured the image of transparency and honesty that the president had managed to build around his public persona over the years.[35] Elendu Reports took advantage of the US Freedom of Information Act to check the records of GoodWorks and exposed many shocking details about the morally questionable relationship between Nigeria's president and his lobbyists in America. This became grist for the editorial mills of local Nigerian newspapers. In fact, the *Atlanta Journal-Constitution*, Andrew Young's hometown newspaper, also picked up the story from Elendu Reports.[36]

Similarly, when Louisiana Congressman William Jefferson was embroiled in a bribery controversy that also implicated Nigeria's then vice president, Atiku Abubakar, local Nigerian newspapers depended on Elendu Reports for updates on the story. Before Elendu Reports' emergence, Nigerian newspapers would have had to depend on Western news agency reports; if the news agencies did not show an interest in the story it would never be reported on in the local media. But a distinctly Nigerian journalistic reporting and interpretation of the Jefferson bribery case, using the journalistic resources of the United States, altered the nature and character of reportage on the issue in the Nigerian domestic press. An evaluation of the archives of major Nigerian newspapers at the time of the incident showed that the reporting and interpretive frameworks of Elendu Reports, not US news agencies or newspapers, informed the local reporting of the issue.

Another major story that the citizen media site broke in 2005 was the involvement of former President Olusegun Obasanjo's twenty-eight-year-old son in the acquisition of multimillion-dollar property in New York. The site published credible, verifiable documents to substantiate its claims. The news became so widespread in Nigeria that the government was forced to respond to the allegations in the domestic press, even though most domestic newspapers initially ignored the story for fear of falling afoul of Nigeria's notoriously slippery libel laws. The government's spokesperson claimed that the son of the president acquired the property with a mortgage from a US bank. This turned out to be false. Unfamiliar with the nature of record keeping in the United States, the government did not realize that citizen reporters at Elendu Reports could easily disavow their claims by investigating the lending history of the president's son. The site's investigation showed that the president's son did not get a mortgage to buy the property.[37] The local media got interested in the story and picked it up. It became a major embarrassment for the government.

The site also broke sensational stories about the US investments and bank accounts of serving Nigerian governors and other important government officials. The Nigerian constitution forbids elected officials to keep foreign bank accounts. Violation of this policy, according to the Nigerian constitution, is sufficient grounds for the impeachment and removal of elected officials and for other kinds of stern disciplinary measures against appointed government officials.[38] It also published pictures of the insanely expensive homes purchased by Nigerian governors and ministers in Potomac, Maryland, and in London.[39]

In time, however, Elendu Reports began to soften its criticism of Attahiru Bafarawa, then the governor of the northwestern state of Sokoto, about whom it had done a series muckraking reports. Its reports had been picked up almost entirely by *TheNews* and the *Nigerian Tribune* and became the basis for a motion to probe the governor by the Sokoto State House of Assembly, the legislative arm of the state government. The legislative committee that investigated the governor "tendered in evidence to the Committee . . . copies of *TheNews* magazine, the *Nigerian Tribune*, excerpts from Elendureports.com and other newspaper publications."[40] Curiously, shortly after he was exculpated by a pliant, rubber-stamp committee that putatively investigated him, Bafarawa called Jonathan Elendu to tell him that "the State Assembly has cleared me from the trouble you started for me. . . . I am obviously very happy as you can tell."[41] Subsequent stories published on the site whitewashed the governor.[42] Advertorials from the governor began to appear on the website with a regularity that many observers found curious. It later emerged that Jonathan Elendu had struck a deal with the governor to become his "media consultant."[43] Omoyele Sowore, Elendu's main partner, was disillusioned and scandalized. He subsequently stopped any professional association with Elendu Reports.[44] In 2006, after leaving Elendu Report, he set up SaharaReporters.com.

Elendu Reports, as has been shown above, exposed corruption and challenged abuse of power in radical ways, although its credibility has been tainted over the course of its existence. Perhaps it is not surprising that the site turned out to be not the alternative news site that people assumed it was—or that it started out as. The site indicatively described itself as a "for-profit company" but solicited contributions from members of the public and insisted that "your contributions to the sustenance of Elendureports.com does [sic] not entitle you to anything or create any obligations between you, the publisher, editors, and staff of Elendureports.com."[45]

Although Elendu Reports' credibility has been badly besmirched by its questionable association with a governor it had reported to be corrupt, the Nigerian federal government still found Elendu himself a sufficient source of concern to arrest and detain him when he traveled to Nigeria. (Details of this incident are discussed in chapter 6.) Elendu Reports exemplifies the difficulties of identifying what constitutes alternative journalism. As mentioned earlier, the main personality associated with the site is a former mainstream newspaper journalist who chose to expose corruption in his homeland in ways that ruffled the composure of the elite. Additionally, by not having ads, the site gave the impression that its politics and editorial choices were motivated by lofty, progressive ideals. In time, however, it became profoundly implicated in the ills it fulminated against. Thus, it ultimately became no different from the homeland legacy media, whose loss of critical, investigative reporting tradition was the basis for the popularity of the site. This shows the fluidity and hybridity of journalistic genres and the inappropriateness of the binaries between alternative journalism and mainstream journalism. It also illustrates that overt aversion to advertising is not necessarily an indication of principled editorial independence.

Sahara Reporters

Sowore Omoyele, a New York-based activist and permanent US resident who had no previous mainstream journalistic training or experience, broke away from Elendu Reports to set up the Sahara Reporters. The name "Sahara," he told the *New York Times*, was inspired less by geography than by an aspiration to "kick up a storm across Nigeria" from his exilic location in New York.[46] Sowore, a former radical president of the University of Lagos student-union government, drew national and international media attention in 1992 when he led thousands of students to protest against military rule. Police opened fire on the student protesters and killed seven of them. Sowore inexplicably survived the bloodbath and became a media sensation. Before he relocated to the United States in 1999, he had been illegally imprisoned and tortured by the law-enforcement agents of Nigeria's military regimes at least eight times. The journalistic practices of the site he founded are consciously modeled on the tradition of "guerrilla journalism" in Nigeria—unconventional, uncompromising, adversarial advocacy journalism that was used by certain weekly newsmagazines to confront brutal military dictatorships in Nigeria in the 1990s.[47] The site's "About Us" page sums up its founding philosophy and identity thus:

> Sahara Reporters is an online community of international reporters and social advocates dedicated to bringing you commentaries, features, news reports

> from a Nigerian-African perspective. A unique organization, founded in the spirit of Article 19 of the Universal Declaration of Human Rights, comprising of [sic] ordinary people with an overriding commitment to seeking the truth and publishing it without fear or favor. Because *its core members are unapologetic practitioners of advocacy journalism* [emphasis mine], Sahara Reporters also serves as an umbrella outlet for objective reporting of verifiable and accurate news and untainted social commentaries for anyone wishing to exercise their freedom of speech in the public interest and common good.[48]

Of all the Nigerian diasporic online media currently in existence, Sahara Reporters was, until 2018, the closest approximation to the previously adversarial but now mainstream Nigerian guerrilla newsmagazines. In fact, it has turned out to be more influential and more adversarial than these erstwhile alternative media platforms. Amory Starr has pointed out that the web has now become a veritable extension of the alternative press.[49] But in the Nigerian case, it is not an extension but a reincarnation and intensification of the alternative press. The site's explicit revolutionary inclinations and almost compulsive opposition to all governments in Nigeria mark it out as the most "alternative" of all the Nigerian diasporic media. Evidence of its revolutionary commitments came to light in the story of a young Nigerian who applied to work for the site as a citizen reporter from Nigeria. The young Nigerian who described himself as a faithful reader of the site recalled his experience: "I wanted to be a Sahara reporter. I scribbled down an application letter and sent by email, in a minute I got a reply to my mail." The response he received, which he reproduced in his article, graphically captures the uncompromisingly adversarial editorial philosophy of the site. It reads:

> Dear you,
>
> This is to acknowledge receipt of your application to the organization.
>
> As part of [our] company policy, eligible candidates must possess the following: A penchant for government dirty news, ownership of a covert camera, ownership of dual passports, ownership of a face mask, ability to pick up arms and revolt, ability to incite the public against the government, [and] guerrilla warfare experience will be an added advantage.
>
> If you meet the above mentioned qualifications, please feel free to give us a call.
>
> Regards,
> The Sahara team[50]

The writer said he was perplexed. He expected to read about educational qualifications and years of journalism experience as yardsticks to measure his suitability for "admission into an enviable organization like Sahara Reporters." He ended his rumination by criticizing the Sahara Reporters brand of journalism. "My fellow Nigerians, yes we know all is not well with our nation [but] Sahara reporters is not doing us any good. We need to focus and re-strategize not with the likes of Sahara reporters exposing our weaknesses like a cancerous growth. Corruption and bad leadership [are] not exclusively Nigerian."[51]

In an interview with *Tell*, one of the erstwhile "guerrilla" newsmagazines, Omoyele Sowore was asked if he thought "Sahara Reporters does what Nigerian journalism is not doing? How well is SR doing?" His response was as insightful as it was viciously censorious of mainstream news practices at home:

> Saharareporters is not a journalistic endeavor. It is a reportorial platform for Nigerian citizens. It is a place where citizens report news—where they report themselves. We do not lay claim to the practice of journalism. We do not write or keep journals. We report events, news and write reports of real time issues. *It is our response to the failure—the refusal or lack of will on the part of professional journalists—to report real news to the people* [emphasis mine]. The goal of Saharareporters is like asking citizens to prepare their own food instead of eating junk food. SR is doing well in that regard. We have broken the sound and speed barriers of reporting authentic, evidence-based news.[52]

In the same interview, he told the magazine that "Nigerian journalism . . . is going through its worst moments today. There is a difference between journalism and the circulation of press releases written by state governors and their media aides." When he was asked what message he had for Nigerian journalists, he said, "The message for them is on Saharareporters. They know how to get it." And in response to a question about what awards he had won since starting Sahara Reporters, he said he did not venture into adversarial citizen journalism to garner awards:

> I have received lots of threats: those are my awards for what I do. It comes with the territory. The threats and harassment, just like awards, are the inspiration that push this work. Each time I am threatened, I interpret it to mean that we must necessarily create a society where no one is threatened for expressing his or her opinion and for using his or her talents.[53]

Similarly, in an appeal for financial assistance on its site in 2008, Sahara Reporters announced, "We want to remain true to our dream of providing average readers with the tools that can help them make informed decisions about how their nations are run in the Sub-Saharan African region" and vowed to "remain the authentic, independent, and investigative citizen reporters who unearth what has remained hidden from the public eye."[54] Later that year, according to the *New York Times*, Sahara Reporters got funding from the "Ford Foundation and the Global Information Network, an independent, nonprofit organization focused on news from the developing world."[55]

Sahara Reporters was, for many years, far and away the most popular and the most politically consequential web-based newspaper with Nigerians both at home and in the diaspora. It got millions of hits a month, and its news stories generated hundreds of reader comments. Until the emergence of homeland web-only news sites (discussed in chapter 7), no other Nigerian website came even close to this. The site was interactive, hypertextual, and multimedia—all the elements of the third stage of online journalism identified by Pavlik. It used to have a devastatingly effective photo-essay section that graphically chronicled corruption among Nigerian elites and an extensive "E-library" that contained incriminating documents—such as convictions—against prominent government officials. More than any Nigerian media outlet—whether mainstream or citizen—it had a huge, fanatical online community of readers and commenters that also supported it financially through voluntary contributions. In moments of political uncertainty in Nigeria, the site literally would shut down due to exceptionally high traffic. For instance, when news from the grapevine filtered through that Nigeria's then ailing president, the late Umar Musa Yar'adua, had been flown back from Saudi Arabia (where he was receiving treatment) to Nigeria in an air ambulance in order to stop his vice president from assuming acting presidential duties, millions of people turned to Sahara Reporters. The site crashed but posted this message on its site: "Please accept SR's apologies. As expected we were hit with high traffic leading our server resources to max out. We are gradually back online and should be fully back later today, check out www.saharareporters.com for the latest information on Yar'adua's mysterious and highly secretive return to Abuja early today!" No other Nigerian news site ever witnessed this volume and intensity of web traffic in moments of national uncertainty. Editors and reporters of local Nigerian newspapers monitored it closely for scoops and breaking stories that they considered "safe" to republish.[56] Although the site's reportorial practices sometimes verged on premeditatedly extravagant exaggeration in its bid to run down corrupt governments, its credibility had not been called into question in any serious way. It used to expose incumbents as much as it hit opposition politicians.

Increasingly, it attracted the attention of international news organizations such as CNN and the BBC, and international wire services such as the Associated Press, Reuters, and Agence France-Presse. For instance, when news of the Nigerian underwear bomber broke on December 25, 2009, American and other international news media, including wire services, turned to Sahara Reporters for the background of the would-be suicide bomber. In fact, the first photos of the would-be bomber published in the Western news media were obtained from Sahara Reporters.[57] This gave the site more international visibility and an added importance at home. Many Nigerians wrote articles to celebrate this feat.[58]

Until it mellowed in 2018, the site's biggest draws were its uncanny capacity to exploit the discontent and intraclass bickering of the Nigerian ruling elite to get sensitive scoops and its ability to "on several occasions . . . [report on] stories months before they [broke] in the local Nigerian media."[59] In an interview with another major Nigerian newspaper called the *Sun*, Sowore said, "When Obasanjo was president, I had people among those who travel[led] with him that gave me information. And when I report[ed] it, everybody would be wondering where we got the information from. I have moles inside the closet of Obasanjo when he was president of this country. But we don't have to reveal such people."[60]

Sahara Reporters' first major story that shook the Nigerian state was an interview it had with the first son of Nigeria's president in 2006, Olusegun Obasanjo. The president's son made many shocking revelations about his father, the country's vice president, and corruption in high places. He said, for instance, that his father had a "libido problem," that his father's close lieutenants desired to extend his stay in power beyond the two terms of four years allowed by the Nigerian constitution, and that the vice president of Nigeria at the time was corrupt and greedy.[61] The interview was reproduced in its entirety by almost all Nigerian newspapers and magazines. The presidency panicked and sought to control the damage of the allegations in the interview. The president's son later denied ever granting any interview to Omoyele Sowore and sued Sahara Reporters, as well as select Nigerian newspapers and editors that republished the interview.[62] In retrospect, however, almost all the issues revealed in that interview were verified. The president and his vice president later fell out acrimoniously and publicly. It later emerged that top officials of the president were indeed trying to manipulate the Nigerian National Assembly into amending the constitutional provision that imposed presidential terms limits. More sensational, the president's son divorced his wife and told the court that his putative children were actually sired by his father, the former president.[63]

Some of the site's other major stories that called attention to it were the publishing of the pictures of a governorship candidate in morally compromising circumstances. Although the pictures were not reprinted in Nigerian newspapers because of their lurid nature, they were viewed widely by Nigerians at home. The pictures were printed off the Internet and widely distributed to people who had no Internet access. This scandal outraged the moral sensibilities of the establishment and caused the political party of the governorship candidate to withdraw his nomination for election.[64]

In 2007, the site also broke stories of allegations of certificate falsification against a governorship candidate and even the chair of the Independent National Electoral Commission, the organ of government charged with the responsibility of conducting federal and state elections. Both the governorship candidate, identified as Andy Uba, and the chief electoral officer, Maurice Iwu, indicated in their resumes that they were educated in US and British institutions, respectively. But inquiries to these institutions by Sahara Reporters showed that the governorship candidate and the electoral umpire either fabricated some certificates outright or exaggerated their educational attainments. The story captured the imaginations of the local media and the Nigerian public.

In spite of Sahara Reporters' uncompromisingly adversarial stance against government officials, it received attention from official circles. For instance, Nigeria's then vice president Atiku Abubakar, who was at loggerheads with his boss over political differences, granted Sahara Reporters a full-length interview in which he made stunning allegations against the president. A day after the interview was posted on Sahara Reporters' website, Nigerian newspapers picked it up and splashed it on their front pages. A measure of the importance of the site could be gleaned from the fact that government representatives habitually responded to negative stories written about them on the site. To its credit, Sahara Reporters published all responses that disagreed with its stories.

Sahara Reporters was initially sustained mostly through donations from its readers. Then it welcomed advertising on its site from different sources: Google Ads; US-based for-profit online universities such as Capella University, University of Phoenix, and so on; ads from Nigerian businesses such as banks and oil companies; and Nigerian politicians, including corrupt politicians. Interestingly, however, throughout the thirteen-year period that I observed this site, there was no evidence of reciprocal editorial acknowledgment of the advertising patronage of corrupt politicians who advertised on the site. In fact, there were instances when politicians placed ads on the site, and the following day an unflattering story about them appeared. A powerful instance of this concerned Emmanuel Uduaghan, the governor of the oil-rich Delta State in Nigeria's deep south. The governor's ads promoting his bid for a second term in office appeared on Sahara Reporters regularly for much of the year 2010. Nevertheless, in May of the same year, Sahara Reporters broke a story that implicated the governor in a corrupt transaction involving his predecessor, James Ibori.[65] But Uduaghan's ads continued to appear on the site nonetheless. Many Nigerian print newspapers and magazines also advertised on the site. This was particularly true of emerging publications seeking to be noticed and also of older publications that wanted to attract potential readers' attention about scoops they uncovered.

It is noteworthy that coming to terms with Sahara Reporters' brand of "insurgent journalism," as James Curran and Jean Seaton call alternative journalism,[66] did not occur as smoothly as my analysis might seem to suggest. It was first resisted by the mainstream domestic media; however, when the resistance had the effect of vitiating the credibility of the local newspapers because news-hungry Nigerians either rushed to Internet cafes to read the stories directly from the site or printed out the stories in bulk for sharing with people who could not afford to read a paper online, the newspapers were forced to reprint and occasionally add more local color to some of the stories published on the site. This was true for some of the other diasporic citizen media. In a bid to undermine their authority, however, the diasporic media were not usually given credit for the stories lifted from their websites; they were often just nebulously referred to as "agency reports" or "offshore news sites."

So the relationship between the "insurgent" Sahara Reporters and the local press was at best ambivalent. It was sometimes mutually beneficial, as when the local press utilized the investigative resources of the diaspora press to expose certain governmental corruption—and in the process give the diaspora press more "mainstream" national visibility. At other times it was adversarial, as when the domestic media ignored the exposés by the diasporic media of politicians connected to the owners of some Nigerian newspapers. Such a stance usually imposed strains on the credibility of the domestic press. Often, opposition politicians who benefited politically from investigative stories against politicians that the domestic press ignored would recruit young men to make large printouts of the online stories and distribute to people free of charge. But Sahara Reporters has now become such a fixture in Nigeria's public sphere that it can't be ignored either by the legacy media formation or by the political class, although its latter-day editorial tepidity and unexpectedly progovernment temperaments may render it irrelevant.

What the profile of Sahara Reporters tells us is that commercialism and critique are not mutually exclusive. The fact that the site accepted ads from corrupt politicians (which it stopped doing as of 2018) did not stop it from exposing their sordid corruption. This fact is a challenge to the dominant strand in alternative media scholarship that insists that freedom from commercial pressure is the sine qua non of alternative journalism. Although advertising does indeed subtly (and in some cases overtly) control editorial content in media organizations, Sahara Reporters' example, when it was a truly alternative news outlet, has shown that it is possible to resist this control. The contrast between Elendu Reports and Sahara Reporters is particularly noteworthy: although Elendu Reports did not accept advertising from any source, its editorial output was found to be thoroughly compromised, whereas Sahara Reporters showed remarkable editorial independence in spite of the fact that it accepted ads even from the people it tormented through its formerly adversarial journalism.

Nonetheless, in 2018 the Sahara Reporters founder, Omoyele Sowore, signified his intention to run for president of Nigeria to, as he said, "disrupt" the political landscape as he did the media landscape, but he won only a few hundred thousand votes. Most important, as I will show in chapter 7, his foray into partisan politics has diminished Sahara Reporters significantly. As of 2019, the site no longer does the sort of investigative, adversarial journalism that made it stand out, and was indistinguishable from homeland newspapers.

The Times of Nigeria

Another notable diasporic citizen media outlet that exerted some influence on politics and journalistic practices in the homeland was the Times of Nigeria (TON), which ceased publication after its founder, Sunny Ofili, died in a car crash in Nigeria on August 9, 2014.[67] Unlike Elendu Reports and Sahara Reporters, TON was not a muckraking news outlet. It was more mainstream and traditional in its reportorial temperament than all the other diasporic citizen media examined in this book. Its strongest point from its inception to the time it died in 2014 was its ability to break exclusive news stories about Nigeria. Started in 2005, it was owned by Sunny Ofili, a Maryland-based Nigerian journalist who was a former reporter with the defunct *African Guardian*. He immigrated to the United States in 1993 "with the resolve to become successful in that country."[68] The TON described itself as "an African initiative by journalists with significant experience in Africa and international coverage," and said its goal was to "break news as it happens. We will provide an authoritative, comprehensive, authentic and analytical coverage of the political process as well as other facets of life in Nigeria and the African continent."[69] Elsewhere, it described itself thus: "TheTimesOfNigeria.com is Nigeria's first independent online newspaper committed to providing real time, dynamic and dispassionate news from Nigeria and Africa. We recognize that, often, news about Nigeria and indeed Africa lack[s] depth and balance. We intend to remedy this anomaly. TheTimesOfNigeria.com will report Nigerian and African news events from an African perspective."[70] The site's strength, especially in its early days, was the richness and reliability of its news sources. Local newspapers looked up to it for breaking news and for scoops. A measure of its acceptability in the political mainstream in the homeland was that all the major candidates in the 2007 presidential elections in Nigeria advertised on its website. In fact, when Nigeria's ruling-party presidential candidate, Umara Musa Yar'Adua, physically collapsed during one of his campaign events prior to the elections and was rushed to a German hospital for medical attention, it was TON that broke the story before the local or other diasporic citizen media reported on it. In time, rumors spread that Yar'Adua had died in the German hospital where he was admitted. Even the normally authoritative Elendu Reporters reported that Yar'Adua had died.[71] Interestingly, when Yar'Adua himself heard the news of his death while in the hospital, the first news medium he called to confirm that he was alive was the Times of Nigeria.[72] A day after TON published the interview on its home page, the local media picked it up.[73] The paper also had the distinction of having interviewed a serving Nigerian vice president, former presidents and military heads of state, and several other top political figures, indicating its acceptance in the mainstream of Nigerian politics.

Perhaps TON's strongest point was that it was the medium of choice for propaganda by Niger Delta militants protesting the desperate poverty in their communities amid vast oil wealth and the unconscionable environmental despoliation of their farming communities by oil companies. The Movement for the Emancipation of the Niger Delta (MEND), the most prominent group in the Niger Delta, often released scoops to the TON before any other media organization. For instance, in 2007, CNN asked its African correspondent Jeff Koinange to do a story on Niger Delta militancy, which often involved the kidnapping of Western oil workers for ransom.[74] But Koinange and leaders of MEND could not agree on a time for them to take him around their base of operation. Nevertheless, because he had to meet his deadline, he arranged for a group of youths to pose as members of MEND. He then interviewed them and sent a staged, inauthentic news report to CNN.

In the video of the made-up CNN report, the viewer sees menacing, hooded "militants" dancing themselves to a state of "trance," aiming their guns at purportedly kidnapped Filipino oil workers, and insisting that they would grant CNN an interview only in the middle of the river for "spiritual" reasons—all ploys to make the report seem authentic and to make it conform to the prevalent fantasies about Africa in the West. The wild gyrations and exaggerated, even theatrical, show of militancy and bloodthirstiness of the people in the video were simply out of step with the image of a people who were angry. Naturally, the Nigerian government protested and charged that the report was staged. MEND also dismissed the report as staged. This created a strange positional confluence between the Nigerian government, which did not like the report because it portrayed the government in a bad light, and members of MEND, who had hoped that CNN would tarry a little while, speak to the real MEND, and give wider publicity to their case against the Nigerian state.

CNN stood its ground, insisting that the report was real.[75] For a while, it seemed that both the Nigerian government and MEND were unfairly accusing CNN of reportorial fraud. Then MEND contacted the TimesofNigeria.com and gave them the log of the email correspondence between Koinange and their leader, Jomo Gbomo. As noted above, Koinange got a group of Niger Delta youths, paid them some money, and told them how to act and what to say for the report.

In the email correspondence published by TimesofNigeria.com, Koinange told MEND's spokesman Jomo Gbomo that "CNN [has] been given the GREEN LIGHT to come into the Delta" and that he wanted to "check with you first and make sure this is a legitimate 'invitation' from you and that [you're] aware of it." Gbomo responded: "Hi Jeff, do not waste your time with those criminals . . . misleading the Nigerian government and oil companies into believing they have a relationship with us. They can arrange a few boys who will take you on stage trips through Delta State alone. They do not represent MEND or the people of the Niger Delta." He advised CNN's

Koinange to "kindly wait till I give you the green light to come down here" and then added that the "Nigerian government has been working through such traitors to infiltrate and destroy our group." Koinange appeared to be convinced. He wrote: "In that case, my Brother, I shall wait for your WORD and will only come when you are ready for us," adding that he was getting "a lot of pressure from my headquarters in Atlanta to come and do this story."[76]

Koinange apparently could not wait for the legitimate MEND. Perhaps because he was "getting a lot of pressure from [his] headquarters in Atlanta to come and do this story," he dispensed with the real MEND and preferred to "arrange" a "stage trip" with "criminals." The result was histrionic journalism on CNN that earned the condemnation of both the Nigerian government and MEND. But when Koinange was interviewed on CNN, he claimed that he had no reason to believe that he was not talking to the real MEND. The leakage of the email correspondence between him and MEND spokesman on TimesofNigeria.com put the lie to his claim. He was later fired by CNN as a result of the report.[77] It is instructive that MEND did not choose a domestic Nigerian newspaper to leak the email correspondence to. Nor did it send the incriminating emails to CNN or any international news organization.

The Times of Nigeria had rich, colorful graphics, was interactive, and also streamed video at a time when these features were almost absent in domestic legacy newspapers. It had citizen correspondents in Nigeria, especially in southern Nigeria, who competed with local newspapers for routine news stories. However, TON's editorial temperament, for the most part, seemed like those of traditional newspapers. It also seemed to have many connections with state governments in Nigeria's oil-rich Niger Delta, from which the owner of the site hailed. Many state governments from that part of Nigeria, especially Delta State, advertised copiously on the site. This was perhaps not altogether unexpected. Many of the stories the site carried about the often-corrupt state governments in the area were mostly uncritical at best and gushingly laudatory at worst. The advertising on the site by the state governments was clearly a reciprocal acknowledgment of the site's compliant reporting. In fact, TON's Facebook page "liked" many pro-government groups such as Deltans Want Uduaghan Again, a Facebook group that championed the reelection of the governor of the Delta State; Youth Alliance for Emmanuel Eweta Uduaghan, another propaganda group for the Delta State governor; Atiku for President 2011, a Facebook group for the promotion of the presidential aspirations of Atiku Abubakar, Nigeria's corrupt former vice president; and so on. In fact, on the site's front page, Ofili proudly proclaimed himself the "Coordinator—Delta Professionals for Uduaghan." It was no surprise that he ended up as a media adviser to a Niger Delta governor before his death in 2014.

Interestingly, since the site's founding in 2005, it never exposed any act of corruption by any government. On the contrary, it often refuted unflattering stories published against certain government officers, especially anticorruption stories by Sahara Reporters and other muckraking citizen media sites. A sample of stories published on the site from 2005 to 2009 proves this.[78] Perhaps because the site survived through direct advertising patronage from state governments in the Niger Delta, it did not solicit voluntary contributions from its readers as other diasporic citizen media did. It also did not have Google ads but had a lot of advertising from Nigerian banks.

TimesofNigeria.com, clearly, was not an alternative-media site in the sense that Sahara Reporters was. It could, however, be said to be a site of resistance for Niger Delta struggles, a site for exclusive news about Nigeria's political intrigues, and a site of cynical official propaganda, although there was no evidence that it was bankrolled by any government body. Its greatest significance in the media politics of Nigeria was that it helped to broaden the availability of news. It obviously had access to top politicians in the country and to Niger Delta militants, and the advantage of its online platform made it desirable. In this sense, it qualified only as a citizen media site.

Nigeria Village Square

NigeriaVillageSquare.com was founded in 2003 by a group of immigrant Nigerians based in the United States. The main person associated with it is Philip Adekunle, a Chicago-based computer information systems specialist. The site was set up as a locus for the unimpeded exchange of ideas and opinions about the homeland by Nigerians both at home and in the diaspora.[79] It is the reinvention, in an electronic form, of the deliberative content of the "village square" in the precolonial African social formation where "people from all corners [met] at the Village Square after a hard day's work to sip unadulterated palm-wine, share news, gossip, jokes, music, dance, events and opinions."[80] In many respects, the precolonial African village square that the owners of this website refer to has many resonances with the early European bourgeois public sphere that Habermas historicized; but the African village square was premodern and prebourgeois. It did not function as a counterweight to the ruling class, nor did it have any purposive, codified normative ideals that guided its deliberative practices. But it was a core cultural institution that was crucial to the intergenerational perpetuation of traditions, customs and mores that were shattered with the advent of colonialism.

The reincarnated village square in electronic form, however, both replicates and transcends the structures and discursive practices of its predecessor. Although NigeriaVillageSquare.com has guidelines on the forms of articles to be posted on its front pages and on its discussion forums, the site is largely unmoderated. It accepts opinion articles, news commentaries, trivia, and even fictional creative writing from all Nigerians and non-Nigerians interested in Nigerian affairs. Contributors to the site do not have to be subscribers or registered users to submit articles, although they need to be registered to participate in online discussions of materials posted on the site. This reflects the site's inclusivity.

Although this site is not primarily a news site, it publishes breaking news stories, has a citizen media project called "iWitness,"[81] which collates reports from citizen reporters from all over Nigeria especially during periods of conflict, and is often the interim medium for many diasporic citizen media projects. For instance, after breaking with Elendu Reports, Sahara Reporters' reports were first published at Nigerian Village Square for months before an independent website was secured for it. Huhuonline.com also first published its stories on Nigerian Village Square before getting its own independent site. Many of the strictly news-oriented citizen media sites still share their news stories on the Village Square's message boards as of 2019, and a great number of politically consequential citizen initiatives that went on to change state policy started on the site.

The site also has links to the web addresses of major Nigerian newspapers that have an online presence, periodically posts high-impact and controversial news stories from both domestic newspapers and diasporic online newspapers on its front page, and invites discussion from subscribers. This feature made it one of the most popular Internet sites for Nigerians at home and in the diaspora, although the emergence of social media and the rise of websites such as Sahara Reporters have affected the Village Square's visibility and weakened its influence. The debates in the site's forums, at the peak of its influence from the early 2000s to the early 2010s, were not only robust, sometimes frenzied, and even emotional but also evinced a studious concern for civility in public discourse. Aware that Internet deliberation is easily susceptible to degenerate into ad hominem attacks, the site has what it calls the "Nigerian Village Square Publishing Guide," which gives not only instructions on how commentaries should be posted on the site but also the ground rules for deliberation. It stresses the importance of eschewing emotive language and embracing what Habermas would call rational-critical debate. One of the mechanisms established to ensure that this rule is observed is the formation of what is called the "village dumpster" where articles, comments, and discussions that are deemed irreverent or overly personal and insulting are consigned.[82] The decision about what posts should be pushed to the "village dumpster" is often arrived at through the votes of registered members of the site. This structural check has imposed self-moderation on many discussions in the forum, but it also occasionally raises allegations of majoritarian tyranny.

It is instructive that over the years the site has metamorphosed from being a mere cyber salon for quotidian dialogic disputations to a close-knit cyber community where deliberations and decisions about national politics take place. For instance, in 2006, when the Nigerian president wanted to manipulate the national legislature to amend the constitution to allow him to run for a third term, "villagers," as members of the discussion forums on the site call themselves, started an Internet petition drive to stop the move. They generated petitions from thousands of Nigerians in the diaspora and contributed money to send a representative to deliver the petition to the president of the Nigerian Senate and to the speaker of the House of Representatives. It was also delivered to the president when he visited the United States.[83] This move generated publicity in the national media and contributed to the defeat of the president's third-term bid. Similarly, in the same year, when Osamuyia Aikpitanhi, a Nigerian immigrant, was murdered by Spanish immigration officers, the "villagers" not only vigorously deliberated on the issue but also contributed money and sent a delegation to Spain to demand an explanation on the circumstances of the death of their compatriot. The delegation also met with the parents of the deceased Nigerian and gave them a $1,200 check that the "villagers" contributed. The incident was robustly covered by Nigeria's biggest, state-run television network, the Nigerian Television Authority, more popularly known by its acronym, NTA.[84] Similarly, they had a meeting with Nigerian government officials and got the president and the Nigerian legislature to request that Spanish authorities explain the circumstances surrounding the death of the Nigerian and to pay compensation to the family if need be. Weeks after this visit, what would have been an ignored issue was elevated to a major diplomatic row between Nigeria and Spain.[85] The Spanish government set up a commission to investigate the murder of Aikpitanhi and issued an interim apology to the Nigerian government while the investigation was in progress.[86]

The "villagers," many of whom had never met physically but only through the virtual village square, directly intervened in many other domestic political issues. Another prominent example is the petition drive that was started in the village square in the midpoint of 2007 to force the Nigerian vice president to declare his assets. Although the Nigerian constitution does not require public officials to declare their assets publicly, Nigeria's newly elected president, in a bid to show his seriousness in fighting corruption, publicly declared his assets for the first time in the country's history.[87] This singular act earned him praise, but it also paved the way for citizens to demand the same forthrightness from other elected representatives. The vice president insisted that because he was under no constitutional obligation to declare his assets publicly, he would not be railroaded into doing so. Again, members of the Nigerian Village Square started a petition drive to which hundreds of Nigerians in the diaspora appended their signatures. A representative physically went to Nigeria not only to deliver the petition but also to attract wide media attention to this event.[88] This pressure contributed to forcing the vice president to publicly declare his assets.[89] Efforts were redoubled to shame other well-placed public officers into publicly declaring their assets.

The media attention that the interventionist activities of members of NigeriaVillageSquare.com generated gave it tremendous visibility and clout in government circles, and many well-known personalities in government were known to be registered members of the forum either anonymously or by their full names. A case in point is that of Olusegun Adeniyi, the former spokesperson for the late Nigerian president Umara Musa Yar'Adua. In the wake of withering attacks against Adeniyi over a frivolous trip he undertook to the United States,[90] he appeared in the forum under his own name to defend himself.[91] In no way, however, could this be construed as an infiltration of the forum by the government. On the contrary, it represented a dialogue with citizens who would ordinarily not have had the privilege of this deliberative exchange had they sought traditional means of communication with the government.

As most scholars argue, at the heart of most conceptions of the public sphere, especially the Habermasian one, is the idea of conversation, which this Internet forum seemed to enhance in more ways than spatially bounded notions of deliberation can. Indeed, many scholars contend that conversation in the public sphere is a precondition for democracy. Michael Schudson, for instance, notes, "Democracy is government by discussion."[92] Bruce Ackerman also states, "Dialogue is the first obligation of citizenship."[93] This

Internet discussion group did certainly make possible the types of categories necessary for most, if not all, of Habermas's "ideal speech situation" to occur.

The communicative acts that took place in this Nigerian virtual village square confirm, to a large degree, that the Internet is capable of facilitating discourse that replicates the central construction of rational-critical debate and that, in a variety of ways, approximates the prerequisites of the Habermasian public sphere. It is discursively inclusive, as evidenced in its policy of not moderating its discussions and in not requiring potential contributors of articles to the site to be registered members. Participation was also entirely voluntary and not the product of coercion by government or corporate interests, and the site's deliberative practices had impacts on governance in the homeland. What is more, although members of the forum came from different social backgrounds—professors in American, British, and Nigerian universities, engineers, doctors, students, Nigeria-based working-class people, and so on—there had not been any record of open social discrimination in the discursive enterprise. However, although the main preoccupation of the forum was politics in the homeland, it also featured short-story fiction and trivia and could sometimes get bogged down by petty personality disputes.

James Bohman notes that a crucial deficiency of Internet public spaces is that they have no linkages with structures of power—a condition, he says, that divests them of the capacity to "secure the conditions of publicity but also in order to promote the interaction among publics that is required for deliberative democracy."[94] Bohman's arguments are difficult to sustain when applied to the Nigerian Village Square, since the activities of this Internet site generated a lot of media attention in Nigeria. Nancy Fraser's exposition of what constitutes a transnational public sphere also strengthens the case for the Nigerian Village Square to be ascribed the status of a transnational online public sphere. According to Fraser, "a public sphere is supposed to be a vehicle for mobilizing public opinion as a political force. It should empower the citizenry vis-à-vis private powers and permit it to exercise influence over the state."[95] This website's continually productive engagements with the Nigerian state on domestic policy issues certainly elevated it to a politically consequential public sphere.

It must still be admitted, though, that the relative numerical inferiority of this Internet-based public sphere, and its inability to sustain its activities, potentially detract from its potency. Similarly, although many contributors to the forum were identifiable by their names, several others used anonymous handles. Scholars have debated whether the incidence of anonymity on the Internet invalidates the notion of conversation in news groups and chat rooms in the real sense of the word. This concern is perfectly legitimate, but, as Jodi Dean reminds us, "anxieties around authenticity on the Net function primarily to reassure our trust in the authenticity of other sorts of mediated interactions, indeed, to pathologize our justifiable paranoia."[96] The point, therefore, is that although some of the Internet's shortcomings significantly detract from the Habermasian status of the public sphere that many scholars ascribe to it, there are certainly important respects in which it fulfils this requirement, as the analysis of the Nigerian Village Square suggests.

The foregoing discussion, though, does not seek to institute the relative discursive openness of the Nigerian Village Square as representative of the sort of interaction that takes place on all Nigerian online media forums. Although such examples abound on the Internet, there is also a multiplicity of websites that do not have deliberative democracy—or anything remotely related to that—as their raison d'être. Although it is incontestable that the Internet meshes with existing, even preexisting, social functions and extends them in many fresh, sometimes up-to-the-minute, ways, it does not fit easily in comparison to characteristically modern organizations or stereotypically idyllic early modern social and cultural institutions such as the Habermasian public sphere. The new peculiarities and idiosyncrasies of the Internet can only become intelligible if a conceptual frame of reference is adopted that does not limit the discussion of the Internet from the outset to predetermined and preordained patterns of interpretation. More important, the Nigerian Village Square has shown the possibility for the coexistence of online communities and citizen journalism. The site provided the platform for citizen reports, for discussions about politics in the homeland, and for direct action. This fits the outlines of the traditional conceptions of alternative journalism. However, the Village Square is a loose collection of disparate people and interests that are not all united by notions of progressive ideology, as Sahara Reporters was in its heyday. In more ways than one, it problematizes the boundaries between alternative and citizen journalism in that it provides an arena for both forms of journalism.

PointBlankNews

PointBlankNews was launched on January 20, 2007 by Jackson Ude, a Nigerian immigrant in the United States. Other people associated with the site were Oladimeji Abitogun and Churchill Umoren, who were also based in the United States at the time of the site's founding.[97] This restlessly muckraking but sometimes over-the-top site is published in New York. It describes itself as "an independent online news magazine created to bring about more professionalism in online [j]ournalism. It has no affiliation with any political party, ethnic groups; religious or social groups within the United States or [anywhere] in the world. PointBlankNews is primarily committed to the freedom of speech . . . fundamental human rights and the journalism ethical responsibility of balance[d] reporting."[98] PointBlankNews adds that it is inspired by the desire to "promote developmental Journalism" and foster a platform "for people to be able to interact, share opinions and proffer solutions to the many political, social and economic problems facing Nigeria and Africa at large."[99] It is curious, though, that an implacably antigovernment, investigative online news outlet like PointBlankNews would choose a label like "development journalism" to describe itself. Development journalism has been conceived as a counterpoint to Western conceptions of news, which are said to stress displacement of routine, oddity, and conflict supposedly at the expense of "development," of which third world countries are said to be sorely in need. But this concept has been ridiculed as a cover-up for "government-say-so journalism."[100] In fact, some scholars have pointed out that many repressive African governments have exploited the press to "consolidate and perpetuate power in the name of development journalism."[101] It is entirely possible that the site used the phrase "development journalism" out of ignorance of the term's conceptual subtleties, historical trajectory, and ideological underpinnings.

The site is multimedia, allows for interaction with its content, and liberally lifts stories from the websites of Nigeria's domestic papers on its homepage. But it also has an "exclusive news" section that contains only stories that the site's citizen reporters have posted. Before venturing into online publishing, PointBlankNews's editor in chief had edited the *African Post*, a periodic publication that catered to the Nigerian immigrant community in the borough of the Bronx, New York. Prior to this, he had no journalistic experience. The major story that brought PointBlankNews to the attention of Nigerians at home and abroad was its exposé of a former Nigerian state governor, Orji Uzor Kalu, who was standing trial for corruption and who forged a letter from the Brigham and Women's Hospital in Massachusetts as a ploy to run away from the country. The letter, purportedly written by a Dr. Black to Orji Kalu, requested the former governor's presence in the United States for his wife's surgery. The letter read in part:

Dear Kalu,

> The Brain Tumour Programme at Brigham and Women's Hospital and Dana Farber Cancer Institute provides a multi-disciplinary brain tumour clinics in radiation therapy, chemotherapy and neurosurgery, a tumour board and radio surgery evaluation and is a closely-coordinated effort between Dana Farber Cancer Institute and Brigham and Women's Hospital.
>
> A comprehensive evaluation and long-time management of your spouse's present health condition . . . necessitates a repeat of neurosurgery of the nervous system. . . . This decision was reached at our board meeting on Friday, July 27, 2007.
>
> At present, based on our evaluation, Ifeoma's basic cognition is inadequate to offer consent for this surgery to proceed. We, therefore, as required by Massachusetts General Law, request your presence to offer your consent as next-of-kin for this immediate needed care to proceed.
>
> Please be advised that your immediate attention is required as the surgery is scheduled for Wednesday, August 8, 2007 at 6.30 a.m.

On the basis of this fraudulent letter, Kalu asked the Federal High Court in Abuja to grant him permission to travel to the United States. "I have just received information through Victor Onochie (by fax) to the effect that my wife is due for a major surgery on 8th August in Brigham and Women's Hospital in Massachusetts, USA," he said in a sworn affidavit. But PointBlankNews found out that the letter from Brigham and Women's Hospital was, in fact, a forgery. "When PointBlankNews confronted the Hospital with the letter," the online news outlet reported, "Dr. Kwan said, 'That is not Dr. Peter Black's signature. It is obviously forged. This hospital does not issue such letters.'" It further quoted the doctor as saying, "This is strange and we are not taking it lightly. We are looking into it and we might require the police to come in."[102]

Many mainstream and diasporic Nigerian newspapers, apparently spurred on by the PointBlankNews scoop, did a follow-up and found exactly the same information: the letter was forged.[103] As a result, the former governor was denied permission to travel. The site also exposed Saminu Turaki, another corrupt former governor of Jigawa State in Nigeria's far north, who also forged a letter from a Singaporean hospital in an attempt to escape trial for corruption.[104] From its very nascence, the entire mission of PointBlankNews appeared to be to expose corruption in high places, especially corruption with international dimensions. Of the 358 stories in the site's "exclusive news archive" between its founding and 2011, 320 unmasked corruption in government at all levels.[105] It was no surprise that of all the diasporic online media outlets, it was on PointBlankNews that the Economic and Financial Crimes Commission (EFCC), Nigeria's anticorruption agency, chose to advertise its services for many years. The most prominent ad on the site's front page for much of the first quarter of 2010 was from the EFCC. It also had context-specific text, image, and video ads from Google AdSense and other web-based ad-serving applications.

However, the site's reports were not always accurate or responsible. Many of its sensational reports turned out to be mendacious, scurrilous attacks on innocent people. The most outrageous of this was the site's allegations that Oyindamola Sam-Amuka, the wife of the *Vanguard* newspaper's publisher, had murdered a fourteen-year-old boy for a ritual sacrifice. "According to PointBlankNews extensive investigations, during the rituals, Oyindamola, a native of Owo in Ondo State, held onto the already hypnotized boy's head and chanted incantations before the helpless boy was eventually beheaded," the site alleged.[106] It said its citizen crime reporter in Nigeria "stumbled on the scene and surreptitiously captured everything with his lens. He also put a call across to police detectives who arrived at the scene, unfortunately at a time the boy had been beheaded. Four police detectives soon arrived from the Crime Investigation Department (CID), Panti, Lagos."[107] According to the story, the newspaper publisher's wife's motivation for the crime was that "her husband was dating another woman whom she wanted the ritualists to kill through supernatural means. Besides, she took along names of some *Vanguard* directors and editors whom she believed were obstacles to her gaining financial control over the newspaper."[108] It further alleged that the woman, on being apprehended, bribed the police with the sum of 4 million naira (equivalent to about fifty thousand dollars at the time). The story was complete with pictures, which made it seem credible.[109]

Shortly after the story broke, the PointBlankNews citizen reporter was arrested by the police and charged with extortion and blackmail.[110] But the site vouched for its story. While insisting that "PointBlankNews is owned and operated by a team of seasoned Nigerian Journalists based in the United States who have practiced both in Nigeria and in the United States with strict professional ethics and integrity," it defended its decision "to publish the story of the alleged involvement of Mrs. Oyindamola Amuka-Pemu, wife of the Publisher of Vanguard Newspapers in the alleged killing of a 14 old year boy for ritual purposes . . . out of our responsibilities as journalists who owe it a duty to the public to inform and educate."[111] It added matter-of-factly:

> Since we live and work in the United States, we know the seriousness of corruption and we operate by the highest ethical standard possible. It is preposterous for Vanguard Newspaper, [and] the Amuka family to think or even imagine that we would blackmail anyone for any reason. It is on record that we have exposed several corrupt public officers, (in and out of service), involved in cocktails [sic] of graft. We have never for once been accused of blackmail.[112]

However, while the back-and-forth exchanges and court case between the Vanguard and PointBlankNews raged, the boy whom PointBlankNews alleged had been beheaded by the wife of the *Vanguard* publisher appeared in court.[113] PointBlankNews was forced to eat humble pie and apologize for misleading its readers.[114] It was a high-impact story that kept the whole country on edge. It later came to light that PointBlankNews's citizen reporter in Nigeria (who also freelanced for local print publications) actually attempted to extort and blackmail the wife of the *Vanguard* publisher through a devious digital image modification that made it seem as if the woman was actually beheading the boy for ritual purposes.

Although it is entirely possible that the United States–based owners of PointBlankNews were not part of the extortion, this case dramatizes the negative uses to which diasporic online publications can be put. Their geographic distance from Nigeria and the insulation this affords them make them attractive media for blackmail, extortion, and mendacious reporting. This is particularly possible because the diasporic online media do not suffer any legal consequences for libelous publication, although as I show in chapter 6, there have been several attempts by Nigerian governments to sue many of the radical diasporic online media in US courts. In 2013, PointBlankNews changed it editorial focus from an alternative, anticorruption diasporic website to a mundane news source for routine political events in Nigeria. It also purged it all its content from 2007 to 2012.

Huhuonline.com

Huhuonline.com, published from Arlington, Massachusetts, by Emmanuel Emeke Asiwe, a former Nigerian newspaper journalist, is the least editorially impactful of the six diasporic online media profiled in this book. This multimedia, interactive, graphically rich medium started publication in 2007. Its editor in chief, Asiwe, was a reporter with *ThisDay* newspaper, one of

Nigeria's notable newspapers that is nonetheless also notorious for gross ethical infractions and progovernment reporting.[115] He was also a media assistant to two government ministers.

The site describes itself as "an independent e-news medium established for the purpose of presenting objective and impartial reporting of events" and boasts that it is the "first news site to engage in the ground breaking idea of publishing wholly captioned pictures."[116] Declaring that it is "[r]enowned for hard truth," the site claims, "[W]e owe allegiance to no political party, ethnic community, religious or other interest groups. Our primary goal is to fiercely promote justice, constitutionalism and free enterprise."[117] This goal of fierce promotion of, among other things, "free enterprise," perhaps, has roots in Asiwe's background as a former World Bank consultant. He describes himself as "an alumni [sic] of Harvard Business School . . . [who] had a brief stint with the World Bank, before he veered into Journalism in 1998."[118]

Apart from its multimedia, interactive, and graphic features, Huhuonline.com also utilizes "thin-media," like Sahara Reporters, to disseminate its stories. But its thin-media updates are more frequent than those of Sahara Reporters. It has an extensive database of email addresses of Nigerians at home and abroad, which it uses to alert readers each time it updates its homepage with news and opinion articles. The site's editorial temperament is a mix of radical and routine reporting. Although it is not known for independently digging up dirt on corrupt Nigerian politicians, it republished anti-corruption stories first posted at SaharaReporters.com and PointBlankNews. A good portion of its content is also made up of stories culled from homeland newspapers. What it did best, however, was to break routine news stories before domestic newspapers and sometimes before other diasporic online media outlets.

Huhuonline.com first got noticed on an international scale when it exposed a series of corruption scandals in Christ Embassy Church, a Nigerian megachurch based in South Africa. Huhuonline.com reported on the church's "stage-managed miracles"; its brazen embezzlement of church funds contributed by unsuspecting South Africans who believed in the "miracles" of its Nigerian pastor, Chris Oyakhilome; the profligate and debauched lifestyles of its Nigerian pastors; and the impoverishment of its South African victims. In a particularly dramatic example, it reported the case of:

> a lady that had been sitting on a wheel chair in the healing line . . . for hours while waiting for the man of God to come and minister to her. When nature called, she forgot she was supposed to act paralyzed. And there she

> was standing and running to the toilet. Minutes after that, she received serious tongue-lashing from the Healing School pastors for the great embarrassment she caused. No one really understood this because she was not allowed to return to the wheel chair as people had seen her dash off to the toilet. Her empty wheel chair was wheeled out of the room.[119]

In more than ten investigative reports, the site revealed other scandalous doings of the church. Many newspapers in Nigeria, South Africa, and Ghana reproduced the stories, which became the basis for the investigation of the activities of the church by the South African government. But the site has also been known to be unashamedly partisan in its support for—and viciously scurrilous in its attacks against—certain personalities in Nigeria's corporate battles for supremacy. For instance, when a crisis broke out between two Nigerian billionaires and former business associates, Aliko Dangote and Michael Otedola, over mutual allegations of share manipulation in the Nigerian Stock Exchange, Huhuonline.com consistently carried stories that demonized Dangote and exculpated Otedola. It never made even the vaguest pretense of balance and fairness. Curiously, however, many Nigerian newspapers' coverage of the controversy was shaped by Huhuonline.com's reporting.[120] The site always had exclusive reports that no other Nigerian media had, suggesting that the publisher of the site had a close relationship with one of the parties in dispute.

Whatever the case, the Nigerian diasporic Internet-based media have transformed both the form and content of Nigerian journalism in ways that at once enrich and complicate the dynamics of informational flow from the core—in this case, a privileged diasporic "peripheral core"—to the periphery where the ancestral roots of the migratory elite that are now spatially situated at the core are located. As we have seen, the Internet-based diaspora news outlets have become so influential that, in many cases, opposition politicians fed up with the domestic media's double standard and timidity—and even government officials hoping to fly kites, that is, expose government secrets for personal gain—bypass the mainstream print domestic Nigerian media and go straight to territorially displaced citizen journalists in the diaspora. Once a story gets prominence in the diaspora online press, it almost always eventually becomes the editorial staple of the traditional domestic press at some point, even if there is initial reluctance from the domestic media to give such stories prominence.

Diasporic online citizen media have become part of Nigeria's institutional fabric. Whether this will be permanent is a legitimate subject for debate, but it seems reasonable to suppose that the citizen media of the Nigerian diaspora will continue to make incursions into the mainstream of the Nigerian political arena in light of the restoration of constitutional rule in the country in 1999. In a significant respect, the profiles and activities of the diasporic online media examined here represent a rejection of the binarism between notions of the "diasporic public sphere" and the "domestic public sphere." Here, we are witnessing a progressive hybridization that dissolves the barrier between diasporic media and domestic media and ruptures the distinction between alternative journalism and mainstream journalism. The citizen media sites have annihilated the barriers of space and time and welded the home and the diaspora.

Similarly, many of the websites profiled here defy easy definition. Although a few can be safely described as citizen, nonalternative media sites, others straddle the categories. One website that started out as an unrelentingly adversarial, anticorruption platform, and therefore deserving of being characterized as an alternative media site, became enmeshed in the moral putrefaction it called attention to. We have also seen websites that occasionally evinced flashes of radicalism but that relapsed to the tepidity and safe editorial formulas of much of the homeland traditional media. But we have seen a website that was almost exclusively defined by its compulsively—and consistently—uncompromising opposition to governmental corruption. However, all of these websites, in a sense, collectively constitute a challenge to homeland media formation and to the political power structure. The fact that their emergence brings a novel dimension to the political economy of news flow in Nigeria is itself "alternative." Yet it is not "alternative" in the traditional conception of the term: it is not anticapitalist, does not employ "native reporting" in the sense in which that term is generally understood, and is not always a purposively counterinformational storehouse. But as the case studies in the next chapter reveal, the critical sections of the Nigerian diasporic citizen media formation not only expose corruption in government but also bring to light the unreported corruption in the domestic mainstream media with the kind of effectiveness that alternative media in the West do not seem to have. As I point out in the concluding chapter, these realities call for an expansion of the epistemological boundaries in the conceptions of alternative journalism.

Chapter Five

From the Diaspora to the Homeland: Role Reversal in News Flows

The online media of the Nigerian diaspora, as has been adverted to in previous chapters, have competed favorably with, and in some cases actually superseded, the homeland media in charting the course of far-reaching national discourses and in confronting and exposing corruption both in government and in the media. Chapter 4 illustrated some of the ways in which the diasporic news media exposed high-level corruption among the Nigerian domestic ruling elite, although some of the diasporic media are themselves not always immune from the ills they have railed against. This chapter highlights and discusses more case studies that instantiate the ever-rising significance of the Nigerian diasporic online citizen media formation. It shows that in addition to being consequential enough to cause governmental policy changes, the diasporic citizen media have also exposed corruption in the Nigerian press and thereby weakened the legitimacy of a hitherto vibrant but now thoroughly compromised traditional national media establishment.

The case studies in this chapter are organized and thematized as follows: cases where diasporic online citizen media stories led to homeland governmental policy changes and cases where the diasporic online media exposed high-level corruption in the local media. All case studies selected for this chapter have had momentous consequences in the domestic public sphere and are likely to define the form and substance of the relational dynamics between the Nigerian diasporic online citizen media formation and the traditional media and politics of the domestic public sphere in the foreseeable future. How the diasporic citizen media chose to report on the cases highlighted in this chapter will enrich and complicate the extant literature on the modalities and singularities of citizen reporting and illustrate how what Deborah Chung and her colleagues called a "form of amateur journalism" is challenging the role of traditional journalism in a transnational setting.[1]

How Diasporic Citizen Media Reporting Caused Governmental Policy Reversals

One dramatic case that exemplifies the power of the Nigerian diasporic online media to compel homeland government to reverse policy decisions was the controversy over a proposed "capacity-building" training for Nigeria's state governors at Harvard University. On May 25, 2009, Bukola Saraki, the governor of the north-central state of Kwara and chairman of the Nigerian Governors' Forum—the ad hoc but nonetheless politically powerful association of all elected governors in Nigeria—announced, through his press secretary, that the governors' forum had signed a memorandum of understanding with Harvard University "on [the] provision of academic support for the governors on capacity building, best practices and good governance."[2] The agreement, which the statement said had been signed on behalf of Harvard University by a Professor Robert Rotberg, identified as the director of Harvard's Kennedy School of Government, would have all of Nigeria's thirty-six governors attend the training in batches.

This news scandalized many Nigerians at home and abroad.[3] For many Nigerians, the purported training was no more than a convenient official cover for the governors not only to waste public resources but to invest their stolen wealth in America.[4] In a searing piece, for instance, Sam Amadi, an alumnus of Harvard and at the time a human rights lawyer, captured the widespread sentiments of many Nigerians about the vain, profligate Harvard adventure of Nigeria's notoriously corrupt governors:

> It is irresponsible for a governor elected on the guarantee that he possesses the expertise and virtues to provide public good to abandon his responsibility to attend a non-descript capacity building program in Kennedy School or in Cambridge University. Such a governor treats his or her responsibility flippantly and is in breach of the ethic of responsibility. It is even worse when the academic misadventure involves all the 36 state Governors.[5]

Amadi was calling attention to an emerging trend in Nigerian elite circles of acquiring a Harvard education, however trivial and inconsequential, and advertise it as a badge of honor, as a basis for legitimizing their continued exploitation of ordinary Nigerians. But to have all thirty-six Nigeria governors attend a crash course at Harvard was the height of absurdity. One of Nigeria's most influential newspapers, the *Guardian*, was even more withering in its censure of the governors' "capacity training" agreement with Harvard. It described it as "offensive, self-demeaning, wasteful and most unacceptable. The MOU [memorandum of understanding] should be thrown into the dustbin where it rightly belongs."[6] In spite of the upsurge of opposition against the governors' proposed Harvard training, however, the governors insisted they would go ahead with it. They said it would be "funded by donor agencies and not from the states' coffers as wrongly reported [in the media]."[7] They even enlisted the support of U.S.-based Nigerians[8] and top Nigerian newspaper columnists[9] to help justify the training. A cornucopia of articles on the Internet and in Nigerian newspapers began to appear in support of the governors' extravagantly wasteful and dubious training agreement. It is reasonable to assume that the write-ups were sponsored by the governors' forum, given the way Nigerian governors have become adept at manipulating journalists to doctor opinions in their favor through pecuniary gratification.

However, the conversation changed when Majek Adega, a Canada-based Nigerian attorney, conducted what he called a "citizen investigation" about the supposed memorandum of understanding. The citizen investigation was a simple email. Adega first sent an email to Harvard University's Communications Office seeking clarification on the nature and compass of the agreement the school signed with the Nigerian governors. The office denied the existence of any agreement with then governors and directed him to contact the Kennedy School of Government's director, Robert Rotberg. The lengthy, angry email he sent to the school's director is worth quoting at some length because it gave expression to the feelings of a lot Nigerians about the purported training agreement:

> You may be surprised to know that the trip to Harvard University may have cost the Nigerian taxpayers millions of dollars in airline tickets for the governors and their retinue of assistants/girlfriends, payment of bloated official allowances and hotel accommodation. [And] the trip may actually have been used as a cover for the primary purpose of squirreling looted funds out of Nigeria and into American bank accounts. . . .

> The real victims of the Harvard University jamboree are the ordinary Nigerian people who could have had several boreholes installed for them but for the jamboree. The real victims are the newborn babies and mothers dyeing [sic] because of lack of basic medical supplies, including incubators. The victims may not be in front of you, you may never meet them, your knowledge of them maybe [sic] limited to figures/statistics, but they are real human beings. They are people's children, parents, brothers, sisters, uncles, aunts, husbands and wives. Think about them when you deal with these politicians. There is a groundswell of anger against your esteemed university. The perception is that your university is conniving with notorious Nigerian politicians to further deplete an already depleted treasury.[10]

The email was designed not only to prick the moral conscience of Harvard University but also to play on the heartstrings of university officials who signed the agreement. It achieved this by calling attention to the real material consequences of their actions. The strategy worked. Less than one hour after he sent the email, Professor Rotberg responded. He said his school did not sign an agreement to train Nigerian governors and that "there will never be an agreement."[11] What had happened, he said, was that after four Nigerian governors visited Harvard University, the governors and the school's Kennedy School of Government drafted a memorandum of understanding to cooperate on good governance. Rotberg stated further:

> The MOU was meant to be the first step in the exploration of a possible training program and as a means of signifying the intent on both sides to work together to craft such a program. Neither that document nor even the possibility of developing a joint Forum–Harvard Kennedy School training project had as yet been brought before the Kennedy School for consideration or approval, so it was premature for an announcement to have been made in Nigeria.[12]

The citizen reporter Adega shared his findings with all the major U.S.-based Nigerian diasporic online citizen media.[13] The following day, all the major newspapers in Nigeria republished it.[14] For more than a week, this was the grist in the editorial mills of most Nigerian newspapers. It is interesting that until an untrained citizen journalist conducted a random act of inquiry, it did not occur to Nigerian journalists to find out more information about the Harvard "capacity training" for governors, which had attracted a whirlwind of criticism back home. All that the local media did was to provide a platform for the push and pull of arguments in favor of and against the issue, which did nothing to cause a policy shift. It took the casual act of journalism of one geographically displaced Nigerian to avert what would have amounted to a colossal waste of national resources. Of course, the governors did devise more inventive ways to corruptly enrich themselves and waste public resources, but it was significant that this stratagem to divert public resources for a pointless, self-serving venture was prevented by an individual through the instrumentality of a previously inconsequential diasporic citizen media formation.

It is apparent that Harvard was indeed interested in exploiting the greed and vanity of the Nigerian governors to make a quick buck. The director of the Kennedy School of Government admitted that there was indeed a memorandum of understanding with the governors. His only problem was that it was announced before it was concretized with the appropriate authorities. It is entirely conceivable that had the Nigerian diasporic "citizen investigator" not shamed Harvard University through his guilt-inducing emails, which he shared widely with the Nigerian diasporic online media and which were subsequently picked up by the domestic media, the school would not have disowned the governors. Although Harvard denied ever having signed an agreement for a one-time training of the Nigerian governors, the governors showed documentary proofs that such an agreement had indeed been signed.[15]

In the aftermath of the heat and embarrassment that the controversy generated, especially after Harvard disowned the governors, dissension ensued between the governors. One of the four governors who had widely been identified as the person who signed the agreement with Harvard on behalf of the governors' forum repudiated it. He said he did not need a Harvard education to govern his state.[16] The governors' forum fired back and accused him of duplicity. In the end, the governors collectively decided to cancel the program, both because Harvard University had earlier hinted that it was no longer interested in the partnership and because the intensity of the opposition to the training had heightened considerably after the results of the citizen investigation became more widely dispersed in the domestic public sphere.[17] This act of citizen inquiry achieved three things simultaneously: it shamed Harvard University into repudiating a questionable agreement with corrupt Nigerian governors, it deprived the governors of the opportunity to waste public funds and stash even more in US banks, and it exposed the laziness and reportorial incompetence of the Nigerian national media, which could not perform the simple act of sending inquiries to Harvard University to confirm or disconfirm the claims of the governors.

In another respect, the simultaneous shaming of Harvard University and the Nigerian governors introduces a novel dimension to the theory of the "boomerang effect," which traditionally accounts for how local and international NGOs can cause dictatorial, unaccountable governments to change their policies through shaming them and provoking mass outrage against their policies in the global court of public opinion. In *Activists Beyond Borders,* Margaret Keck and Kathryn Sikkink observe that transnational advocacy networks have become core instruments for tilting the balance of power between states and individuals and for the "redistribution of knowledge":

> [I]n a world where the voices of states have predominated, networks open channels for bringing alternative visions and information into international debate. Political scientists have tended to ignore such nongovernmental actors because they are not "powerful" in the classic sense of the term. At the core of the network activity is the production, exchange, and strategic use of information. . . . When they succeed, advocacy networks are among the most important sources of new ideas, norms, and identities in the international system.[18]

Here the authors are concerned primarily with how organized advocacy networks deploy the power of information to shame recalcitrant and dictatorial regimes into reversing their constriction of the discursive space. They point out that "voices that are suppressed in their own societies may find that networks can project and amplify their concerns into an international arena, which in turn can echo back into their own countries."[19] The authors characterize this strategic deployment of informational resources to effect policy changes in erring nation-states as "leverage politics" and argue that, "by leveraging more powerful institutions, weak groups gain influence far beyond their ability to influence state practices directly."[20] For them, this phenomenon is illustrative of the waning power of the nation-state because the increasing capacity of nonstate actors to compel states to change policies undermines modern states' "absolute claims to sovereignty."[21]

But it is also often said that only weak, peripheral states are subject to the boomerang effect of transnational NGO activism and that, more often than not, it almost always requires the overt and subtle threats of strong nation-states in the West for weak, erring, dictatorial nations in the developing world to give in to international pressures. As Chetan Kumar observes, the "right circumstances" that can enable transnational activism to effect the dislodgement of "nasty dictatorships" necessarily incorporate "a specific interest on the part of a major power capable of using force."[22] And as Martin Shaw points out, "the activists of globalist organizations, such as human rights, humanitarian and development agencies, make a reality of global civil society, by bringing the most exposed victims among the world's population into contact with more resourceful groups in the West."[23]

Well, here a powerful educational institution like Harvard University, which is not only located in the West but is, in fact, one of the West's most recognized intellectual powerhouses, has been shamed into reversing an agreement it entered into with corrupt governors of a third-world country, not through whipping up international public opinion against it but by merely creating an online citizen media buzz, which then reverberated to the local Nigerian media, with a potential to go beyond that. It is entirely conceivable that Harvard University quickly rescinded its agreement with the Nigerian governors because it did not want the story to be picked up by the US media and/or the US blogosphere, which would have likely created a massive public relations disaster for the institution. Whatever the case, the lone, random act of "citizen investigation" by a marginal diasporic Nigerian had the effect of shaming a corrupt local elite and a powerful institution in the West in ways that the Nigerian domestic media would have been incapable of doing, challenging Thomas Hargrove and Guido Stempel III's conclusions that citizen media "present . . . little threat to mainline news media."[24] This shows that the online citizen media of a politically consequential third world diaspora can both instigate a conventional boomerang effect against their homeland governments and a reverse boomerang effect against powerful nonstate actors in the West.

Another instructive, paradigmatic case of how diasporic citizen media reporting shamed the Nigerian government into reversing a governmental policy occurred in late 2009. Nasiru El-Rufai, the former Federal Capital Territory minister and later governor of the northwestern state of Kaduna in 2015; and Nuhu Ribadu, the former chairman of the anticorruption agency, the Economic and Financial Crimes Commission (EFCC), emerged as prominent opposition figures against the government of Nigeria's president, Umaru Musa Yar'Adua, whom the duo had helped to install. El-Rufai and Ribadu bitterly fell out with the Yar'Adua government after a short honeymoon. They launched broadsides against the government in local and international media, which provoked counterblasts from the government, including threats to their lives. Both fled to the United States, where they continued their campaigns against the government using Nigerian diasporic citizen media platforms in the United States.

In retaliation, the government indicted El-Rufai in absentia over "abuse of office" and misappropriation of public funds. The new leadership of the EFCC issued a "wanted" notice for him and enlisted the support of Interpol to have him arrested and deported back to Nigeria.[25] A "wanted" notice was also issued for Nuhu Ribadu, a former police officer and as well as the head of the EFCC. He was, in addition, demoted and dismissed from the police. He fled to the United States after agents of the federal government nearly assassinated him.[26]

Matters came to a head when the government gave a furtive directive that the two opposition figures should never be allowed to renew their passports at any Nigerian consular office in the United States or Europe. The point of this directive was to get them stranded and unable to move around the world. El-Rufai went to the Nigerian High Commission in London to renew his passport, oblivious of the fact that he could not. Officers at the High Commission told him his passport could not be renewed. "On further enquiries in the High Commission and Abuja," El-Rufai said, "I confirmed that President Umaru Yar'Adua gave the order through the National Security Adviser, Abdullahi Sarki Mukhtar, and then to the Director General of the Nigeria Intelligence Agency, NIA, Mr. Imohe."[27] Interestingly, news of the denial of his passport renewal request was carried only by the diasporic online news outlets and by *NEXT*, a now-defunct newspaper in which the former minister had substantial investments. All the domestic media organizations blacked it out. However, when the government was compelled to deny El-Rufai's claims that he was forbidden to renew his passport at the instance of the president, all the local newspapers published the denial. The government said El-Rufai had never been denied passport renewal, nor had any directive been given that he or any other Nigerian be denied one. It said the former minister merely wanted to whip up public sentiment against the government.

The back-and-forth exchange between the spokespersons for the government and the self-exiled opposition politicians would have lost steam had Sahara Reporters not stumbled on the original memo instructing all Nigerian embassies and high commissions in Europe and America to refuse the reissuance or renewal of the passports of El-Rufai and Ribadu. The online citizen media outlet said it was in possession of original documents to that effect. "Referring to a 'continuous and unyielding campaign of calumny against the Federal Government abroad' by the two men, it said a decision had been taken 'at the highest level' to deny them 'consular assistance of any form.'"[28] The site later published scanned copies of the original memos. Almost immediately, local newspapers in Nigeria, which had ignored the story, picked it up.[29] In no time, harsh criticisms of the directive filled Nigerian newspaper pages. Nigerians in the diaspora also initiated an online petition drive to compel the government to reverse its directive. The petition, which had hundreds of signatories, declared that based on reporting by Sahara Reporters, it had "incontrovertible evidence" that the federal government of Nigeria had instructed its missions abroad not to renew the passports of certain citizens of Nigeria, saying it was a "tragic reminder of the dark days of brutal military dictatorship when the confiscation of the passports of political opponents, human rights activists and pro-democracy campaigners was the order of the day." It concluded by saying:

> We shudder at the thought that those of us in the Diaspora who criticize the government of the day for any reason may suddenly become passport-less and hence be unable either to carry out our jobs that require international travel, visit our families back at home, or worse still be subject to deportation by our host governments. We shudder at the thought of our Nigerian compatriots inside the country who can become shut in and hence cannot travel to visit their families abroad or carry out official or professional duties simply because their passports have been preemptively seized due to non-renewal.[30]

The Nigerian federal government was embarrassed by the exposé of its secret memo and by the flurry of condemnation that followed. President Yar'Adua quickly disowned the memo and fired the director general of the Nigerian National Intelligence Agency, who purportedly originated it.[31] To save face, the president even ordered a probe into the activities of the NIA boss.[32] He then directed the foreign affairs minister to send a cable to all Nigerian consular services worldwide to ignore the previous memos mandating them to deny consular services to the two opposition politicians. In a cable message—also intercepted and reproduced verbatim by Sahara Reporters—the government said that "all Nigerian missions should give requisite consular assistance to *any Nigerian repeat any Nigerian* [emphasis original] that requests for [sic] such assistance in any Nigerian mission abroad."[33] But Nigeria's *Guardian* reported that the director general of the Nigerian National Intelligence Agency was merely "sacrificed" to save the president from an "international embarrassment."[34] Not surprisingly, after the resolution of the passport renewal controversy in his favor, El-Rufai singled out diasporic Nigerian citizen journalists for commendation. In an interview with the *Daily Trust*, he said, "I am particularly grateful to the patriotic Nigerians that got those documents out and published them. Without those documents, the government would never have back-tracked on its decision. Clearly you can see from the contents of the documents that this decision came from Yar'Adua himself, in spite of his lame attempts to deny it."[35] Although he gave the credit to diasporic Nigerian citizen reporters for exposing the government memos that caused a reversal of the government policy against him, it was obvious that he was the source of the authentic copies of the memos published on Sahara Reporters. He revealed as much in his own ruminations after the incident. In a blog post in the Nigerian Village Square, he wrote:

> After I was branded a liar by the authorities when I told the world of my ordeal (a lie which a lot of Nigerians unwittingly bought into) I determined to expose my tormentors. With the help of well wishers and men of conscience right at the heart of the government in Abuja, I was able to get documentary evidence to prove that what I had said was true and that what the administration said was a blatant lie. Thus exposed, the administration chose to sacrifice the Director General of the National Intelligence Agency, a man that I know and respect for his sterling gentlemanly qualities.[36]

By admitting that he was "able to get documentary evidence to prove that what I said was true," he clearly implied that he was the source of the documents that Sahara Reporters published. However, it is remarkable that he chose to give these exclusive documents to a diasporic online citizen medium and not homeland newspapers, not even *NEXT*, his own newspaper, which had the same multimedia and hypertextual capabilities as Sahara Reporters. This fact underscored the increasingly preeminent position of diasporic online citizen media outlets in charting national discourses. Had he given the documents to homeland newspapers, the story would not have had the same effect. The papers probably would not have touched the documents with a barge pole for fear of running afoul of the laws of sedition, which forbid and criminalize the unauthorized publication of classified government documents.[37]

Here, the lesson is that alternative online newspapers do not necessarily have to adopt "native reporting" or such other subversive reportorial practices discussed in chapter 1 to upset the power structure. They can exploit the internal dissensions of the ruling elite to subvert the system. This is a system of reporting that Sahara Reporters perfected when it was intentionally oppositional in its reporting. It accepted confidential documents exposing the dirt of various ruling-class factions; it assured sources of confidentiality but did not spare these sources if competing elites exposed dirt about them. The geographical distance of the diasporic citizen media especially makes this possible. I call this alternative media practice "strategic reportorial entrism." By strategic reportorial entrism I mean a system of reporting by which alternative reporters, particularly in developing countries, infiltrate the inner recesses of the power structure by pretending to share in their intrapower grief only so that they may get muck against competing elites who themselves can become sources of muck against their opponents. I draw from the Trotskyist infiltration strategy called entrism, which has been defined as "infiltration into a political organisation to change or subvert its policies or objectives," to propound notions of strategic reportorial entrism, which Sahara Reporters practiced and perfected.[38]

But more important, what redounds to the formidability and effectiveness of the diasporic online media is the greater capacity they have to shame governments and politicians at home than do the domestic media, especially because the diasporic media have now become such an important fixture of the Nigerian media landscape that they have attracted the attention of the US government and of Western international news organizations. In a report about Sahara Reporters titled "Africa's WikiLeaks," the *Daily Beast*'s Philip Shenon reported that Sahara Reporters' "impressive muckraking has drawn the support of that most august of American philanthropies—the Ford Foundation, which has given Sahara Reporters $175,000 over the last two years." He quoted Calvin Sims, a former *New York Times* foreign correspondent who now works for the foundation and is overseeing the grant, as saying, "I hadn't seen anything like this. The impact it's having—holding political leaders to account—is very impressive," pointing out that Sahara Reporters could be a model for similar sites throughout the developing world.[39]

It is precisely because of the increased international exposure of the Nigerian diasporic citizen media outlets that governments back home are so opposed to them. It is noteworthy that part of the reason the government quickly rescinded its decision to deny consular services to opposition politicians after the memo was exposed was the fear of being exposed to "international embarrassment." In other words, the diasporic media have an enormous capacity to bring a boomerang effect to bear on the governments in ways the homeland can only dream of. Their location in the West, particularly in the United States, whose goodwill Nigerian governments always actively court and cherish, give them added symbolic capital. It needs to be pointed out, nonetheless, that the traditional domestic media help to amplify, even if initially reluctantly, some of the transformational stories that emanate from diasporic citizen media sites.

Watching the Watchdogs: Exposing Corruption in Homeland News Media

The diasporic citizen media are not only a thorn in the flesh of governments and corrupt politicians; they also expose corruption in homeland newspapers and, in the process, contribute to eroding the credibility and legitimacy of the traditional domestic media. In the run-up to the 2011 president elections, for example, the diasporic online media, especially Sahara Reporters, were particularly hard on the traditional media. Sahara Reporters, for instance, reported that the editorial board chairman of the widely circulated national newspaper *Punch* had attended a "nocturnal meeting" with the former corrupt military dictator Ibrahim Badamasi Babangida (IBB) who campaigned to be elected president again. Sahara Reporters alleged that the *Punch* journalist, along with other top media executives, collected huge sums of money from the former dictator to launder his image in the media. It published photographs of the meeting to support its reporting.[40] The management of *Punch* was embarrassed and fired the editorial board chairman named in the Sahara Reporters story.[41] The unmasking of this secret meeting by Sahara Reporters, which had been kept from public knowledge, led to a huge media firestorm and debate.[42]

The site also published a secret text message that the editor of the same paper sent to its reporters and section editors, instructing them never to write any negative stories about President Goodluck Jonathan, who was also a contestant in the presidential race.[43] The publication of the text message on Sahara Reporters caused a hurried policy reversal and the deliberate publication of a rash of negative stories against the president to prove the story wrong. But in this chapter I focus on only two dramatic, far-reaching stories that shook the roots of traditional media practice in Nigeria: exposure of land allocations to top Nigerian editors to stop them from writing about a corrupt government minister and the practice of editors and reporters serving as "consultants" to corrupt politicians and shady businesses.

In early 2009, Sahara Reporters exposed the ugly underbelly of Nigerian journalism when it revealed that a former minister of Nigeria's Federal Capital Territory (FCT), Aliyu Moddibo, had bribed top Nigerian editors and chairs of newspaper editorial boards with juicy land allocations

For instance, it was revealed that the chairman of the company actually conspired with Ishiekwene to protect politicians who paid huge sums of money to ward off negative stories about them. A particularly dramatic case involved the wife of Vice President Goodluck Jonathan (who became president from 2010 to 2015), who was caught by the Economic and Financial Crimes Commission while trying to launder millions of dollars. The story had already been written and was being printed for the next day's edition when Ishiekwene, the director of publication, called the vice president's press secretary and informed him about it. The press secretary requested that the story be "killed" in exchange for favors. As the source put it:

> No sooner had printing started than the editor ran down to the press to order that printing should stop and that all that had been produced be condemned. He had received a call from the Chairman, Chief Ajibola Ogunshola, that anything relating to the VP and his wife in the paper for the next day and subsequently be suspended. . . . We later learnt the VP paid the bill for the next day's total print and the adverts to get the chairman to order the destruction of the copies already printed. That was the end of the report. So, in trying to nail the ED, we should not forget the involvement of the Chairman in this whole thing.[53]

This revelation further inflamed and outraged the Nigerian cyber community. Paying for the entire print run of Nigeria's largest circulating newspaper, including paying for all the advertisements that were contained in the edition, must have added up to millions of dollars. This is what makes the corruption in the media a double-edged tragedy: it not only involves journalists who corruptly enrich themselves by protecting corrupt government officials; it also involves government officials embezzling massive public resources to bribe the news media on a sustained basis. In time, the story percolated into the pages of the domestic media; it could no longer be ignored. A well-known New York–based columnist for the influential *Guardian* newspaper, Sonala Olumhense, was the first to bring the discussion into the mainstream. In his popular column in the *Guardian*, he wrote an article titled, "The Nigerian Mass Media on Trial." He argued that what the news of the scandal at *Punch* had done was to give a face to the well-known journalistic perversions that have become endemic in mass-media practice in Nigeria in general. In a witty yet blistering critique, he wrote:

> In retrospect, the Ayorinde story is not about *The Punch* at all, but about journalism in Nigeria. One cannot read Mr. Ayorinde's protest without coming

> away with the frightening impression that many senior journalists have now adopted a loose lifestyle of selling their influence to government officials and businessmen in exchange for cash and gifts without the slightest concern for any conflict of interest. This is a terrible burden because the power of the press lies in its credibility. If stories are being paid for, or editors bought in order to ensure specific kinds of coverage, a newspaper is, in effect, a doctored and worthless document.[54]

Olumhense's incisive commentary activated a flurry of condemnations of the Nigerian legacy press in Nigerian cyberspace and in the traditional domestic media. One commentator, for instance, characterized the Nigeria press as the "fourth estate of graft,"[55] an apparent witty inversion of the popular characterization of the press as the "the fourth estate of the realm," a phrase first coined by Thomas Babington to describe the coffeehouses of Restoration England,[56] but which the rhetoric of nineteenth-century liberalism ascribed to the modern mass media.[57]

A Nigerian media NGO reported that the scandal at *Punch* had "become the talk of the town in most newsrooms with many journalists of the view that the allegations would damage a profession that is already suffering from a credibility crisis."[58] But the consequences of the damning revelations against Azubuike Ishiewene reverberated beyond Nigeria and its digital diaspora. The CNN MultiChoice African Journalist Award, the prestigious organization that rewards excellence in African journalism and on whose panel of judges Ishiekwene served, dismissed and replaced him with another Nigerian editor.[59] This effectively dimmed his rising international profile. On April 16, Ishiekwene voluntarily retired from *Punch*, obviously as a consequence of all the heat that was generated by the unmasking of his unscrupulousness. But in a widely circulated statement, he said, contrary to stories in the papers and on the web, he was not forced to resign his job, and that he voluntarily recused himself from serving on the CNN award panel in light of the weighty allegations against him, pointing out that the committee set up to investigate him found him innocent.[60]

This story has far-reaching significance. It brought into bold relief the complicity of the Nigerian traditional media in the institutional corruption that plagues the country, which the news media are supposed to expose and fight. The editor who called attention to this media corruption was clearly not innocent, either. Several comments, including Ishiekwene's rebuttal, pointed to his own entanglements in corrupt deals and in the "killing" of unfavorable stories for his clients. The second petition against Ishiekwene actually mentioned him as acting in conjunction with the director of publications to prevent stories that were unfavorable to certain government officials from being published. In fact, Ishiekwene was forced to resign his position as editor because he was caught planting a story for the political rival of his "client."

The heat that this exposé on corruption in the media generated brought to renewed limelight the report that Sahara Reporters had done earlier, but which did not pick up much steam outside the Nigerian cyber sphere. Many commenters on the series of stories about the scandals at *Punch* did make the connection between the Sahara Reporters story on the land bribery of top editors and editorial board chairmen and what now became public knowledge about the coziness of certain top journalists with government officials. One commenter remarked thus:

> I'm surprised that this is the first time a corruption allegation against media executives is receiving serious attention. I could remember that sometimes [sic] last year, SaharaReporters wrote about some senior editors of different newspapers involved in a land allocation scam in Abuja. Nothing came out of this revelation. Nobody followed it up. I think all sections of Nigerian Media should be investigated, especially the print media, not just *The Punch*, in order to restore people's confidence in their info.[61]

Unfortunately, there is no consensus among top Nigerian journalists on the need to cleanse their craft of graft—or whether, in fact, an ethical crisis exists. Lasisi Olagunju, editor of *Saturday Tribune*, the weekend edition of the *Nigerian Tribune*, dismissed these examples as isolated and as deviations from the norm:

> For instance, I was news editor for the *Nigerian Tribune* between 1999 and 2003 and I have been a title editor since September 2012. I can say that I have not been faced once with such a demand from inside or outside the newsroom. Many of us also read about journalists acting as consultants for politicians but this, again, remains very speculative. There are no hard evidences to pin this on identifiable persons.[62]

The editorial page editor of *Punch*, Joel Nwokeoma, lent support to Olagunju's position. He insisted that outside of the ethical journalistic scandals in the public domain, "there's not been any reported incident." He admitted, however, that "the practice of journos acting as media go-betweens for organizations appears impactful even though it isn't widespread in the industry. Impactful in the sense that organizations seem to relish on [sic] it."[63] Nevertheless, not all journalists share the notion that the ethical infractions among Nigerian journalists that diasporic citizen media outlets exposed are isolated aberrations. For instance, Nuruddeen M. Abdallah, *Daily Trust*'s assistant editor of investigations, said journalists cozying up to the politicians they are supposed to hold accountable is a "widespread syndrome." He asserted:

> This menace is perfected mostly by the various "associations" inside the media industry. For instance, we have the Guild of Editors, the Forum of News Editors, as well as beat associations. At their various levels, these groups determine which story to be published or not to be published, and at what time. All for pecuniary interests. The phenomenon is already eroding public confidence in the media. The situation is so bad that members of the public can say which newspaper or editor services which political party, agency of government, or even private corporations. They also know which media houses won't do certain stories no matter what. This development is further eating away the remnants of credibility the media possesses. The public now resorts to the online media, which they believe are more independent to get stories they think can never make it to the newspapers.[64]

As *Daily Trust*'s point man on investigative reporting, Abdallah has uncovered and reported on corruption in government for years and has intimate familiarity with the soft underbelly of his profession. His self-critical assessment of the performance of his profession found concordance with other editors. For instance, Ajibola Amzat, former features editor of the *Guardian* and current editor of the International Center for Investigative Reporting (ICIR), said "cases of editors and reporters working as 'consultants' for politicians and agencies of government are frequent and widespread." Drawing on his years of professional practice, Amzat confirmed the ethical misconduct diasporic citizen media reported, and disagreed with Olagunju and Nwokeoma, who insisted that these misconducts are not mainstream:

> As an insider, I am privy to information about how governors put some editors on payroll in order to help them "kill" unfavorable stories, or to publish stories that promote their administration.
>
> Some federal ministers also offer gratification to editors and reporters to launder their image in the media so that they can retain their office.

> More frequently, reporters are provided with transport fares aka Brown Envelope at functions organized by government agencies or private companies. The objective is mainly to get positive media reports. And journalists who dared publish a report critical of the hosting agencies or corporate organizations will not get invitation to attend another event.[65]

Martins Oloja, a former editor of the *Guardian* who is now the paper's executive head of editorial board, agreed with Amzat, but attributed the rampant ethical rot in the industry to poor, irregular, or nonexistent salaries for journalists. His insight is worth quoting at length:

> If you don't pay your journalists, some news sources will pay them to do some unethical things. Here is the deal: some dubious reporters thus will become "consultants" to state governors, bank chiefs and chief executives of oil and gas firms. As most media organs have been failing in their financial responsibility to their state correspondents (they fail to send running costs to the stations outside head offices), state actors begin to even furnish offices for some organs in the states. So, instead of monitoring governance and holding state actors, state executives to account, correspondents report malfeasance and oddities to the state actors (they are to cover) who most times pay to spike such stories. Then some unethical editors have to survive too: they also monitor developments in the states with a view to telling the corrupt chief executives that they are aware of some unusual developments in their domains and bureaucracies. Others (editors) even file some of their reporters' negative stories back to the chief executives of states who will in turn pay to kill such stories.[66]

The cumulative, although as yet unconfirmed, effect of the series of corruption in the traditional media in Nigeria, according to Abdallah, Amzat, and Oloja, is that that the general public is progressively losing faith in them and are now turning to the plethora of diasporic and domestic online citizen media for their informational needs. This could very well be the single most important factor that will cause the death of traditional newspapers in Nigeria, although digital-native newspapers, even in the diaspora, are not immune from ethical compromises and pay-to-play journalism. However, Nigerian news readers are, for the most part, perceptive and critical, and tend to withdraw loyalty from explicitly compromised news outlets. With progressively deepening Internet penetration in Nigeria and the lowering of the barriers to entry, more credible online news sites will emerge to satisfy the yearning for credible and reliable information.

According to the International Telecommunications Union's 2010 report, 40 percent of all Internet traffic from the whole of Africa came from Nigeria.[67] With growing Internet penetration in other African countries, Nigeria's dominance of the Internet space in the country has fallen to 27.4 percent of the continent's total usage as of December 2017, which is still significant.[68] But according to Internet World Stats, there were 98,391,456 Internet users in Nigeria as of December 2017, which represents 50.2 percent of the country's population. That number increased to more than 100 million by 2019. Advertisers whose patronage sustains newspapers are taking notice. The crisis of the Nigerian domestic newspaper market will deepen once advertisers migrate in large numbers to citizen online media. Nevertheless, not all citizen online media are immune from the malaise that plagues the media in Nigeria. In fact, as the example of Elendu Reports in chapter 4 shows, being exclusively online—or being located in the diaspora—is not a safeguard against corruption and compromise.

It is not yet clear where this will all lead. What is clear, however, is that the legion of diasporic online citizen media that have sprouted in the Nigerian diaspora have reversed the unidirectionality that hitherto characterized news flows between the homeland and the diaspora. They have increased and enriched access to Nigerian news for Nigerians everywhere. Most important, by taking over the watchdog role that the homeland media had traditionally performed in addition to being the watchdog of the watchdog-turned-lapdog, they could potentially supplant the homeland news media. What implications do these realities have for the way we theorize news flows, citizen and alternative journalism, and emerging forms of journalism? Chapter 7 answers these questions.

Chapter Six

The Nigerian Government's Response to the Diasporic Citizen Media

Intolerance of and unease with dissent is an abiding feature of the Nigerian state since its founding, as chapter 2 illustrates. As the later part of this chapter will show, the reactions of Nigerian governments from 2005 to 2019 to the critical searchlights beamed on them by the diasporic citizen media appear to be adopted from the germinal ideas initiated and executed by British colonialists against the critical gaze of the nationalist press. During Nigeria's colonial occupation by British imperialists, the critical journalism of the independent nationalist press was aggressively countermined through a three-pronged strategy. The colonial government sponsored rival, acquiescent, Nigerian-owned newspapers that endorsed and authorized colonialism. When that strategy was not successful, the colonial government chose to starve the independent nationalist press of advertising patronage, and encouraged British-owned private businesses to withhold advertising from the papers in hopes that they would wither and die. The continued vibrancy and stridency of the press in spite of these measures compelled the colonial government to enact repressive press laws, which gave a legal imprimatur to its all-out assault on the press. Nigerian military regimes borrowed from the colonial template in their dealings with the Nigerian press.

However, as shown in chapter 3, the brief periods of constitutional rule from 1960 to 1963 and from 1979 to 1983 saw a radically healthier and more tolerant attitude of governments toward critical journalism. Instead of the repressive suppression of dissent that we saw in colonial and military regimes, the civilian governments of the 1960s and the 1980s responded to oppositional, watchdog journalism by setting up their own newspapers to counter the scrutiny and attacks of the press, particularly of the political-party press, which dominated the media landscape in 1980s Nigeria. They also used spin doctors to influence news coverage and punditry, in common with many liberal democracies. There were no records of arrests and torture of journalists or the forceful seizure of newspapers.

In a curious twist, nevertheless, the reaction of supposedly democratic governments to critical diasporic citizen online journalism since 2005 is uncannily reminiscent of previous totalitarian colonial and military governments. The reaction of the Nigerian governments, and of corrupt politicians who are not formally inserted in the structures of government but who are nonetheless part of the orbit of power, to the piercing scrutiny of their activities has ranged from blackmail, smears, arrest, and detention of diasporic bloggers; to blockage of diasporic citizen media sites from being viewed in Nigeria; to well-funded web counteroffensives; to hacking diasporic citizen media websites; to co-optation of oppositional bloggers; and to the initiation of expensive libel suits against particularly radical online media outlets such as Sahara Reporters and Elendu Reports in its earliest uncompromisingly contrarian incarnation.

For example, Sahara Reporters' Sowore Omoyele revealed in a media interview that the Nigerian government made several overtures to him to "join them" in government.[1] "Joining" here does not necessarily mean employment with the government; it can mean partaking in the prevailing corrupt practices in the country. Containment of adversarial journalists through financial inducement is a well-known strategy in Nigeria, as chapter 5 shows. Compliant reporting is traditionally secured through "brown envelopes," a euphemism for bribes given to journalists to induce favorable coverage and to suppress negative stories. The bribes used to be concealed in brown envelopes (thus the name) to mask them but, but they are no longer given in that form. Terje S. Skjerdal expounded on the brown-envelope phenomenon:

> The term "brown envelope journalism" is applied to denote journalistic activity which involves transfer of various types of rewards from sources to the reporter. Although the usage of the term varies somewhat from context to context, it is safe to say that the following three characteristics are usually involved if we speak about the original "little" brown envelope": the practice occurs on the *personal level*, it has some degree of *confidentiality*, and it denotes an *informal contract* [emphasis in original] between the source and the reporter whereby both parties have certain obligations. These three characteristics are

> visualized through the image of a brown envelope containing cash physically handed over from a source to a reporter.[2]

The brown-envelope culture is lubricated and sustained by Nigeria's patronage culture and by the poor remuneration of journalists. Chinwe Akabogu pointed out that many Nigerian journalists rationalize accepting brown envelopes from government officials and politicians "on the basis that [they are] not well paid and [are] faced with a lot of financial problems within and outside [their] work environment."[3] Senior Nigerian journalists no longer collect brown envelopes; they now style themselves "media consultants" and are placed on hefty monthly retainers by corrupt government officials and politicians, as we saw in chapter 5 in the matter of the top editors of *Punch*. As the Nigerian journalist and media critic Lanre Arogundade observed, "Some journalists also work as paid consultants to politicians and businesses thus threatening professionalism."[4] It was the carrot of "joining" the government in the form of offering "media consultancy" to government officials that Jonathan Elendu, who pioneered the diasporic citizen online journalism genre, could not resist and that irretrievably destroyed his credibility, as chapter 4 chronicles. When Nigerian governments invited Sahara Reporters' Sowore to come and "join" them, they meant that he could work as their "media consultant" and earn handsome financial rewards. He also said in an interview that government officials

> have tried to compromise him or get him to at least be less critical. Some government agencies, such as the Nigeria National Petroleum Corporation, have offered him advertisements. He saw the gesture as a way of courting him, so he rejected it and announced on his site that SaharaReporters won't accept advertisements from government officials and agencies. Administration officials visiting New York often seek meetings with him. Some have sent emissaries. But he has remained elusive and unmoved. "As a rule, I avoid private meetings with government officials," he explained. "I just tell them that there is no discussion we can't have by telephone or email. Physical meetings are unnecessary."[5]

When invitations to "join" the government failed to contain the adversarial journalism of the diasporic media formation, the government changed tactics. In 2007, President Olusegun Obasanjo sent a secret bill to the National Assembly (as the Nigerian congress is called) to give legal endorsement to the blocking of certain Internet sites from being viewed in Nigeria.[6] The bill was targeted at the critical diasporic media, which had become an unendurable thorn in the flesh of the government. The exposé of this secret bill by diasporic online news sites, which was also published in the domestic press, thoroughly embarrassed the government, which abandoned the bill. Censoring or outright blocking of websites is associated with totalitarian regimes such as those of China, North Korea, and Saudi Arabia, where governments make no pretense of being democratic. Nigerian civilian governments often strain not to be tagged totalitarian by Western governments and institutions. But it is unclear how the government intended to block popular Nigerian diasporic websites secretly in Nigeria in ways that would escape the notice of Nigerians and the international community. More than anything, the government's move signaled the depth of its frustration with the adversarial diasporic media.

In response to the blistering criticism of government and the divulgence of acts of corruption in high places by Sahara Reporters, the Nigerian presidency in 2008, as we saw in chapter 1, took the unprecedented step of requiring staff members in the presidency to swear an oath of secrecy. This oath was designed to prevent damaging leaks from getting out to the online diasporic media. Ironically, news of the confidentiality oath was leaked to the domestic press.[7] The leak about the unusual steps government took to stop leaks to diasporic online news outlets, particularly Sahara Reporters, proved the futility of the efforts. The government decided to launch an all-out attack on the credibility of critical diasporic journalists. It sponsored an ad hoc organization with the paradoxical name "Network for Good Governance" to attack the integrity of Sahara Reporters in Nigerian newspapers. In paid advertorials titled "Who Is Behind Sahara Reporters?" that were published in major Nigerian newspapers, the group alleged

> [t]hat the Editor of SaharaReporters Mr. Omoyele Sowore who has no visible means of livelihood in New Jersey USA has over four properties in the United States is an indication that there are people funding him. And the question is who are they, what is their interest and why are they interested in bringing the government down? . . . The ideal thing would have been to ignore their puerile ranting and negative journalism, but greater wisdom demands that such tissues of lies be exposed to avoid unsuspecting public attaching weight to their lies.[8]

The advertorial went on to list the properties Sowore supposedly owned in New York and New Jersey and charged, "It is a shame that a man like

Omoyele Sowore who cannot shun illicit acquisition of wealth in favour of reputation is masquerading as an apostle of accountability and good governance. We must be vigilant!"[9] The problem was that the list of properties Sowore allegedly owned was actually only a list of his past rented apartments. The first house listed in the advertorial "was the first apartment that [Sowore] was put in as a 'pro-democracy refugee' when he first arrived in this country. . . . He was sharing it with three other co-refugees."[10] The second property listed on the advertorial was a rented one-bedroom apartment he moved into after his initial stay at the "pro-democracy refugee" apartment. The third house, amusingly, was the Columbia University student housing where Sowore stayed when he was a graduate student. And the fourth property was his current rented apartment.[11] It turned out that the agents of the government merely entered his name on sites that offer a variety of people-search tools and public records data. To their discredit, the government agents were not perceptive enough to interpret the information they got from their searches.

The inaccuracy of the charges against Sowore soon became public knowledge, and the Nigerian government and its agents became the butt of jokes. A Nigerian professor of African history at Vanderbilt University wrote:

> In a sense, then, the high-ranking Nigerian officials who commissioned such a shoddy inquiry are the second biggest suckers in all of this, next to Nigerian taxpayers whose monies were probably used to finance this charade. The smart crook at the dirty core of this mischief swindled the sponsoring officials by playing on their ignorance of advanced public record-keeping and of the banality of the information marketed to them as a product of painstaking, esoteric inquiry. Given the desperate irrationality of guilt-ridden Nigerian officials, it is plausible that they even paid the opportunistic crook to travel to the US on a mission to uncover Sowore's purported property ownership only for him to simply steal into one of Nigeria's Internet cafes to do a simple people search on one of the search engines. A fancy printout from some foreign-managed search engine would have blown the desperate minds of his IT-challenged sponsors.[12]

The unintended effect of these mendacious charges against Sahara Reporters was to increase the site's popularity in Nigeria and galvanize its supporters in the diaspora to give it more financial support. Several commenters on the story said they donated to the site in protest. Sahara Reporters itself not only exposed the government agents, the amount of money voted by government to fund the character assassination campaign, and the search engines used to carry out the "investigation" (which it famously called the use of "simple data websites that offer 'fast-food' type information on individuals who live in the West—especially the US and the UK"). The website also used the moment to solicit financial support to do more investigative reporting on government corruption.[13] It showed, for instance, that all that the government agents did was to pay Intelius, a controversial Washington-based public-record business, the sum of $1.50 and to enter the name of Sahara Reporter's editor in chief, Omoyele Sowore. Sahara Reporters illustrated this by paying $1.50 to Intelius and entering the name "Omoyele Sowore." It turned out that the list of Sowore's supposed choice properties that was published in Nigerian newspapers was "in the exact order provided by INTELIUS. One of the buildings, 547 Riverside Drive, New York, is a Columbia University student hostel."[14]

When these attempts to diminish Sowore's credibility, the government made several attempts to hack the site, "but [it] survived owing to the foresight of its managers."[15] Not done, the government mandated its lawyers to threaten the US web host of Sahara Reporters with a lawsuit if it did not shut down the site. In a letter to the web host, written in all caps, the government agents, claiming to be "solicitors and advocates" with Reardenilson and Associates, wrote:

> We are aware that Domains by Proxy is a reputable company. We are worried that a Web site http://www.saharareporters.com/ hosted with Domains by Proxy is being used for subversive dissemination of information against the president and people of the Federal Republic of Nigeria. We have read the terms of registration of Websites which say that any Website used for illegal purposes, morally objectionable/defamatory and libelous articles will be closed down. Please note that http://saharareporters.com/> has violated the laws by writing articles that are treasonable offence [sic] in Nigeria. We therefore request that as a responsible company that you are to shut down http://saharareporters.com/ immediately to avoid any legal proceedings which may affect your company and affect your business."[16]

Although the law firm was apparently based in Nigeria, it nonetheless scared the US-based web-hosting company enough to warn Sahara Reporters to desist from publishing libelous materials. It subsequently shut Sahara Reporters down.[17] In a widely distributed press release, Sahara Reporters said, "[O]ur Webhosting company complained to us that our Website was 'abusing their server and using their cpu at 100%' and as such had to shut down SAHARAREPORTERS because it was rendering others sites on their server 'inoperable.'" It, however, dismissed this technical explanation for shutting down the site as mere obfuscation, saying, "There is a conspiracy to put our site out of existence. However, this will not happen, as such we will be working round the clock to resume our activities online ASAP."[18] It also asked for suggestions on how Sahara Reporters could get its own server and avoid having to go through third parties. The response was overwhelming: readers contributed funds to buy an independent server for the site.

Having failed in taking Sahara Reporters off the Internet, the government shifted its battleground. Several law firms in Nigeria and in the United States wrote to threaten legal action against Sahara Reporters and Elendu Reports. In fact, early in the life of Sahara Reporters, President Olusegun Obasanjo's "personal legal counsel on international matters" wrote a well-publicized press release asking the site to withdraw a "malicious defamation of President Olusegun Obasanjo."[19] A month after, the same "personal legal counsel" to the president wrote a "cease and desist" letter to Sahara Reporters regarding what the lawyer called the invasion of the privacy of a woman that Sahara Reporters had identified as the president's mistress, whom it also said had been a beneficiary of many corrupt deals.[20]

In 2008, Dr. Paul Orhii, the director general of the National Food and Drug Law Administration, sued Sahara Reporters in a Texas court and asked for $25 million in punitive damages. The Media Legal Defense Initiative, the London-based NGO that provides "legal support to journalists and media outlets who seek to protect their right to freedom of expression" said Dr. Orhii's case was handled by "the high-powered Cook law firm in Houston."[21] The NGO linked up with the US-based Media Law Resource Center, which provided Julie Ford, an experienced Texas-based media lawyer, to defend Sahara Reporters for free. "She defended Mr Omoyele on grounds of personal jurisdiction, arguing that since the publication was clearly aimed at a Nigerian readership and the defendant had no links with Texas, the Houston courts had no jurisdiction."[22] The judge was persuaded and the case was dismissed on March 31, 2009.[23] But this was not the end of the legal challenges that Sahara Reporters has had to contend with. The same month that the Texas judge dismissed the suit against the site, another US-based lawyer for the Nigerian federal government sued Sahara Reporters for libel in a Maryland court.[24] Again, in April 2010, Joy Ogwu, Nigeria's ambassador to the United Nations at the time, notified Sahara Reporters that she would begin a multimillion-dollar lawsuit against the website over "exposure of improper contracts awarded by her at the nation's Permanent Mission."[25] The case was dismissed on November 27, 2012, for failure to pass the "actual malice" test and for the inability to "make a showing sufficient to establish the elements essential to the party's claim and on which the party will bear the burden of proof at trial."[26]

Nevertheless, a libel suit against Sahara Reporters in Nigeria by Bukola Saraki, Nigeria's senate president from 2015 to 2019, inflicted considerable financial damage on the online platform. On June 28, 2017, a lower court in Nigeria found Sahara Reporters guilty of libel against Saraki and awarded a 4-billion-naira fine against it. A month later, Saraki's lawyers got a garnishee order to freeze the bank accounts of Sahara Reporters Media Foundation, a "Lagos-based 'civic media laboratory' project" funded from a $600,000 MacArthur Foundation grant.[27] During a political stump speech in the southeastern city of Owerri in April 2018, Sowore revealed that as a consequence of the court judgment against Sahara Reporters, the entire $240,000 in the Sahara Media Foundation's Nigerian bank account had been seized. An appeal court overturned the judgment of the lower court on December 8, 2018 and ordered a retrial at a different lower court.[28]

Sonala Olumhense, a respected Nigerian journalist and syndicated columnist, summed up the strategies of the Nigerian government against Sahara Reporters: "So that is the line-up: technological warfare designed to make SR unpublishable; a scorched-earth campaign to discredit Mr. Sowore personally; a gigantic lawsuit by an interested party; and a political appeal to Internet hosts to take the site off the air."[29] These actions were scripts created out of an elaborate $5 million budget by the Nigerian government to dilute the growing influence of diasporic online citizen media and to "ensure that Websites like Saharareporters.com and others are stopped from taking root in Nigeria."[30] Part of the plan included sponsoring rival diasporic citizen media outfits and unleashing an army of progovernment commenters on the discussion boards of radical and popular sites such as SaharaReporters.com to subvert the growth of "critical blogging culture that is taking the Nigerian nation by storm and effectively replacing the mainstream local media."[31] But this did not work. Like the compliant newspapers that colonial governments sponsored to weaken the power and influence of the independent nationalist press, the progovernment diasporic citizen media sites the government sponsored were shunned by the Nigerian reading public, which caused them to fade away and fizzle out.

It is obvious why explicitly progovernment diasporic websites would lack even the vaguest scintilla of credibility. For one thing, the progovernment sites erupted in the immediate aftermath of government's public show of anger and frustration with critical diasporic media sites, which made their appearance suspicious for discerning readers. Similarly, the sites were overzealously laudatory of government in ways that were indistinguishable from the domestic state-run media with which Nigerians were already fed up. Most important, for good reason, most Nigerians have already been primed to be suspicious of any journalism that is not critical of bad governance and corruption in high places. The irrecoverable diminution of the reputational capital of Elendu Reports after it deviated from the critical, anticorruption alternative online journalism it pioneered and started "media consultancy" for elected politicians clearly indicated that websites that explicitly opposed the adversarial journalism of the diasporic media sites and promoted a progovernment editorial slant would not survive. Given the scale of graft that defines governance in Nigeria, only what Matthew Ehrlich calls "journalism of outrageousness"[32] tends to resonate with the Nigerian reading public.

When progovernment websites that purported to be based in the Nigerian diaspora failed to take hold, the government decided to feed off the credibility of critical diasporic websites by cloning them. From January 2015 to April 2016, government officials created at least three websites that stole the logo, style, "About Us" page, and design of Sahara Reporters. One of Nigeria's most notable domestic online-only newspapers, Premium Times, reported, "The publisher, Omoyele Sowore, said his team had so far blocked three fake websites since January 2015. He said the faking [sic] websites were blocked from Google, Web4Africa and Twitter."[33] The site's publisher determined that Bukola Saraki, Nigeria's Senate president from 2015 to 2019, was responsible for the cloning of Sahara Reporters. The site had published a rash of critical reports about his corruption as governor and as Senate president. But as Premium Times noted, Saraki was not alone. "Identity theft is an emerging fraud in the Nigerian cyberspace, mainly used by politicians to clone digital identities of critical media houses with the aim of using the clone to pass down propagandist inform[ation] [and] fak[e] endorsements."[34]

The government later experimented with a more desperate measure: the arrest of diasporic citizen journalists who traveled to Nigeria. This was calculated to contain their growing influence in the domestic public sphere. The first diasporic citizen reporter to be arrested by Nigeria's security forces was Jonathan Elendu, the owner of Elendu Reports, discussed in chapter 4. He was arrested when he traveled to Nigeria from his base in the United States in October 2008. Elendu's arrest was both symbolic and curious. It was symbolic because he is the progenitor of insurgent diasporic citizen media activism, but it is curious because at the time he was arrested he had lost his credibility, popularity, and critical bite due to his dalliance with the same corrupt politicians his website had exposed. His website had lost its luster and he had stopped making even the faintest pretense of being an anticorruption citizen media activist.

He was accused of being the sponsor of a "guerrilla news agency"[35] and was "tortured to . . . disclose the sources of the several embarrassing news reports on prominent political leaders in Nigeria," according to the Human Rights Writers Association (HURIWA).[36] The charge against him was later amended to include "money laundering and sedition."[37] It later emerged that the Nigerian government had arrested him because he was thought to be aligned with Sahara Reporters.[38] Elendu also confirmed that during his twelve-day detention by Nigerian security forces, he was tortured to share information with the government about Omoyele Sowore.[39] Sahara Reporters' Sowore, who had severed all professional ties with Elendu at the time, issued a press statement to say that he had "no financial, professional or other ties to Elendu."[40]

Oddly, the arrest of Elendu generated more buzz among Western media NGOs than it did in Nigeria. It was virtually blacked out in the Nigerian domestic media. A Nigerian writer wrote: "Although the incident took place within their vicinity at the Nnamdi Azikiwe airport Abuja, it was the online publications—PointBlankNews and Sahara Reporters—that broke the news." He added: "Even when the publisher was charged with sedition by the State Security Service (SSS) [the Nigerian secret police], only *Punch* gave it wide coverage."[41] He attributed the indifference to, or inadequate coverage of, Elendu's arrest by Nigerian traditional journalists to the fact that journalists in Nigeria did not regard diasporic online journalists as colleagues. However, it was not just the traditional Nigerian media that failed to show sufficient outrage in publicizing Elendu's arrest and detention; even diasporic Nigerians did not. For instance, a Facebook group set up to secure his release, "Free Nigerian Blogger Jonathan Elendu," had only fifty-nine members.[42] In fact, the discussions on many Nigerian online discussion boards were dismissive of Elendu's brand of journalism. The following is a sample of comments on Nairaland.com, one of the most popular Nigerian online discussion forums:

> I prefer to call it imaginative journalism, because the standards of that publication are so low! Their stuffs [sic] sometimes reflect publicity stunts, they also churn out unsubstantiated facts, which is sometimes caused by Jonathan Elendu's hallucination, what one of my role model [sic] Edgar Hoover calls mental halitosis.

> I think these guys are just 'sensational gangster-style' journalists. I thought I was over critical of the quality of Elendu's reportings [sic] until I read the views of other people. I can't substantiate this fact, but I believe Elendu is making money from the sensationalism. . . . If you read his story about the Sokoto State government before and after his visit to the state (God knows what transpired during the visit, I hear journalists too collect brown envelopes) you will wonder where his objectivity lies. He also seems to be partisan in his views of the Nigerian politics. I suspect he might be on some politician's payroll going by his write ups.[43]

This dismissive attitude toward Elendu was broadly representative of the opinions that many Nigerians expressed about his brand of journalism. Many critical readers recalled the mercurial twists in his site's editorial temperament and attributed this to his decision to ingratiate himself with corrupt politicians whose muck he pretended to rake for the public good. It was no surprise that the credibility of his site went down the drain. In more ways than one, this illustrates the agential power of readers and of their capacity to discern and make judgments about the hidden messages encoded in news stories. For any online news outlet to survive and enjoy respect, it must continually win the trust and confidence of its readers. As Seungahn Nah and Deborah S. Chung have found out, "[O]nline community news readers may perceive that, regardless of the type of journalists, both professional and citizen journalists should be critical and adversarial to community power holders, such as political and business elites."[44]

Emmanuel Asiwe, the editor in chief of Huhuonline, was the second diasporic online journalist to be arrested by Nigerian security forces. He was arrested and detained when he traveled to Nigeria in 2009. Nigeria's national security agency said he was being "questioned over matters of national security."[45] After pressure from human-rights groups worldwide and from the United States government (Asiwe is a dual citizen of Nigeria and the United States), Nigerian courts declared his arrest illegal.[46] On January 1, 2018, government security forces also arrested and detained Daniel Elombah, the publisher of Elombah.com, a UK-based citizen media site, and his brother, Tim Elombah, over critical commentaries and news stories that appeared on the site against President Muhammadu Buhari's government.[47] Daniel Elombah said he was never told why he was arrested, but it was speculated that his arrest was triggered by a series of critical opinion articles written against the inspector general of police on Elombah.com.[48] But Elombah insisted that the article that incensed the inspector general, "IGP Ibrahim Idris's

Unending Baggage of Controversies," for which he was arrested, actually appeared on an obscure site known as opinionnigeria.com and was written by Ebiowei Dickson.[49] The inspector general of police could not articulate a coherent reason to justify detaining the journalist and his brother. When journalists pressed him to give a reason for arresting the brothers, he said that they "committed an offence," adding, "whenever you commit an offence it is our duty to ensure that we respond."[50] In the wake of sustained social media and international NGO pressures, the government released the blogger and his brother after twenty-five days in police detention. On realizing that they could not justify the detention of the journalists for nearly a month on grounds of defamation, the police charged them with "Cybercrime, cyber stalking, cyber bullying and for 'championing Biafra terrorism,'" which the Elombah brothers denied.[51]

Consequent on the widening influence of diasporic online citizen journalism and the online journalistic activism it inspired in Nigeria, on May 15, 2015, President Goodluck Jonathan signed into law the Cybercrime Act which, among other provisions, prescribes a three-year jail term or a fine of 7 million naira (approximately $19,500) or both for anyone convicted of "causing annoyance, inconvenience, danger, obstruction, insult, injury, criminal intimidation, enmity, hatred, ill will or needless anxiety to another."[52] Nigerian governments and institutions now invoke this law to muzzle free speech and to silence critical voices in Nigeria's vibrant online public sphere. In a special report, Premium Times found that between May 2015, when the law came into effect, and October 2017, there were "no fewer than 15 cases in which Nigerians have been detained for alleged violation of the Cybercrime Act," pointing out that its findings "likely represent only a fraction of arrests linked to Cybercrime Act, because few of such matters ever make it to court or become public knowledge."[53] When they were arrested, the Elombah brothers were charged with violating the amorphous and vague Cybercrime Act. One of the charges against them was that they published an opinion article on their site titled "Roadmap to Biafra," which the Nigerian police said constituted a "crime against humanity."[54] The Elombah brothers, for their part, sued the Nigerian government and won 5 million naira (approximately $13,855) in damages.[55]

The law has also been used to crack down on domestic online news outlets that republish diasporic citizen online journalistic investigative reports that embarrass the government. For example, Jones Abiri, a hyperlocal journalist in Nigeria's deep south, was detained without trial for more than two years for republishing two investigative reports from the US-based

PointBlankNews. In the July 10, 2016 edition of his weekly newspaper, the *Weekly Source*, he republished a Pointblank.com report titled "Rumble in the Military: Inside the Coup Plot Story . . . Militants' Warning Alters Plot," which exposed "an alleged conspiracy that top military officers working with politicians had approached the Joint Niger Delta Liberation Force (JNDLF) militant group to intensify bombing pipelines as a justification to overthrow President Buhari."[56] It also republished a PointBlankNews investigation alleging that President Muhammadu Buhari's powerful cronies and close aides had undermined investigations by Nigeria's Economic and Financial Crimes Commission (EFCC) into the corrupt deals of an oil company that donated to the president's 2015 presidential campaign. Premium Times reported that "Jackson Ude, the publisher of PointBlankNews based in the U.S., in an interview in 2016 said he had received threats, from proxies of the SSS, asking him to pull down stories from his website that locally based journalists like Mr Abiri were re-publishing in their newspapers and tabloids. He said he had been warned of possible arrest whenever he came to Nigeria."[57] Under pressure from international media NGOs such as the International Press Institute and the Committee to Protect Journalists to release Abiri, the presidential spokesperson Garba Shehu said Abiri was not a journalist but "a guest of the security agency because of his alleged involvement in militant and criminal activities."[58] The argument the Nigerian president's spokesperson made to delegitimize Abiri's professional identity was strange. He said Abiri was not a member of the Nigerian Union of Journalists (NUJ), although being a member of the NUJ is not a requirement for practicing journalism in Nigeria. In fact, unlike in many developing countries, Nigerian journalists are not required to be registered. The vice president of the NUJ in the deep southern state of Bayelsa, where Abiri worked, told Nigeria's *Daily Independent* that Abiri's weekly magazine was well known locally and that, because he was a publisher rather than a reporter, there was no expectation that he should be a member of the NUJ.[59] Newspaper and magazine publishers in Nigeria typically belong to the Newspaper Proprietors' Association of Nigeria (NPAN) instead of the NUJ.

It is obvious that the Nigerian government was being intentionally duplicitous when it claimed that Abiri was not a journalist. The Nigerian president's spokesperson was himself a one-time president of the Nigerian Guild of Editors and has an intimate familiarity with the contours of the Nigerian journalism landscape. As the Bayelsa NUJ vice president pointed out, "As a publisher, they have their own body, and [Abiri's] group has made a representation to NUJ. [Abiri] also has people working for him. They have expressed their concern and we had put out a statement in this regard."[60] The government elected to undermine Abiri's professional identity in order to deflect attention from the reason he was detained. In the wake of international and domestic social media pressure, he was charged to court, but one court dismissed the case and another asked the government to pay him compensatory damages for wrongful detention and violation of his human rights. He was released in August 2018. However, in March 2019, Nigeria's secret police rearrested him at gunpoint.[61]

By June 2019, the Buhari regime expanded its repression of free speech to include social media users. In an ironic twist, on June 12, 2019, which the Buhari regime has declared as Nigeria's new "Democracy Day," the country's secret police "announced a nationwide crackdown on individuals allegedly caught posting inciting materials on the Internet."[62] The clampdown on free speech on the Internet was inspired by the snowballing exuberance and influence of Nigeria's frenetic social media scene, which increasingly sets the agenda for the news media and drives national conversations. Indiscriminate and often secretive arrests and detention of social media critics of the Buhari regime had been rife, particularly before and in the immediate aftermath of the contentious 2019 general election, but publicizing the mass arrests of unnamed social-media users for alleged incitement had no precedent in Nigeria. As this example shows, the squelching of dissent by Nigeria's civilian administrations is becoming increasingly multilayered. It encompasses the traditional domestic media, online-only news media, and critical online voices that have no affiliations with the media. The progressive melding of virtual Nigeria with "real" Nigeria will blur the nature and complexion of governmental repression of free speech.

Repression of Critical Journalism at Home

Why have civilian, and supposedly constitutional, governments since 2005 shown less tolerance for dissent than their counterparts in the 1960s and 1980s? Why are they only marginally better than totalitarian military regimes? On the surface, it seems sensible to argue that civilian governments reacted to the diasporic online media the way they did because they had no template for engaging with the instability and unfamiliarity of deterritorialized, diasporic online journalism. Nevertheless, it is difficult to sustain that argument in light of evidence that civilian governments from 2005 to 2019 exercised military-style brutal repression of the press.

For instance, in December 2006, Godwin Agbroko, a gutsy *ThisDay* columnist who, as editor of *The Week* magazine, was imprisoned by military authorities in 1997 for reporting "disagreements within the ruling military Government,"[63] was brutally murdered in circumstances that suggested that it was a consequence of his biting critiques of the politics of Nigeria. In September 2009, Bayo Ohu, the Nigerian *Guardian*'s assistant news editor, was murdered in mysterious circumstances. In 2010, several journalists also were murdered under mysterious circumstances. Edo Sule Ugbagwu, a journalist with the *Nation*, was similarly murdered by assassins in April 2010. This string of deaths of journalists prompted the Committee to Protect Journalists to note that, "Reporting in Nigeria has become an increasingly hazardous profession as the list of unsolved journalist murders in the country continues to grow."[64]

Governments also repressed the news media through the arbitrary enforcement of legislation designed to rein in critical journalism. For instance, in September 2008, President Umaru Musa Yar'Adua's government revoked the broadcast license of Channels Television, one of Nigeria's foremost private TV stations, because it aired a speculative report that the president was considering resigning on account of his failing health.[65] (He died in office two years later.) But the Nigerian Broadcasting Corporation, the agency that regulates broadcasting in Nigeria, said at the time that broadcasting this speculation was "detrimental to national interest."[66] The story was considered so "detrimental to national interest" that Remi Oyo, the managing director of the state-run News Agency of Nigeria (NAN), and her deputy, John Ndukuba, were arrested for republishing it in the agency's news feed. Although Remi Oyo was in China on official business when the story was published on NAN's news feed, operatives of the Nigerian state police arrested her as soon as she set foot in the corporate headquarters of the news agency in Abuja.[67] The Abuja-based *Leadership* newspaper also had several run-ins with officials the Yar'Adua administration. The government was so incensed by the paper's reporting on the president's health that it ordered its secret police to invade the paper's head office, forcefully seize the paper's computers, and arrest some its reporters and editors. It later sued the paper over its "reprehensible efforts to embarrass the President and destabilise his administration."[68]

The Goodluck Jonathan administration, which succeeded the Yar'Adua administration, was no less intolerant of dissent and critical investigative journalism. From June 6 through June 10, 2014, the government mandated military operatives to confiscate thousands of printed copies of Nigeria's top newspapers, reputedly on "security" grounds. The military's spokesperson,

Chris Olukolade, told the news media that the seizure of the newspapers was no more than a "routine security action" in the wake of "intelligence reports indicating movement of materials with grave security implications across the country using the channel of newsprint-related consignments."[69] At the end of the "routine security action," the military did not find any "materials with grave security implications" in any newspaper, but the government did not apologize to newspapers for disrupting their business and for causing them loss of revenue. The presidential spokesman Doyin Okupe removed all doubt that the clampdown had the imprimatur of the president when he told journalists that it was just a little temporary discomfort that Nigerians should learn to live with in the fight against terrorism.[70]

The first sign that the reason given for the seizure of thousands of copies of newspapers was merely a cover emerged when it came to light that soldiers continually harassed and brutalized newspaper distributors, vendors, and even readers across the country, suggesting that even reading newspapers had "grave security implications." It turned out that the "materials with grave security implications" were also written on newspaper pages; they were not merely concealed in "newsprint-related consignments." That was why newspaper readers were beaten during that period for merely reading a newspaper. A Nigerian newspaper editor told Reporters without Borders that soldiers "flipped through the pages [of newspapers] to be sure that there is no major stories [sic] on Boko Haram."[71] So the "materials with grave security implications" were the uncomfortable stories newspapers wrote about the military. One of those uncomfortable stories was the *Daily Trust*'s exclusive June 4, 2014, story about top generals who illegally shared a plot of land that the government had designated as the site for a barracks.[72] Another was *Leadership*'s story about the alleged court-martial of several serving generals who actively aided and abetted Boko Haram terrorists.[73] The story was picked up by many international news outlets.

Confiscating newspapers in hopes of suppressing the uncomfortable stories they published only amplified the stories, however. In addition, the seizure of print copies of newspapers was ineffective because, as I pointed out in chapter 4, all major Nigerian newspapers now have a dual presence in both hard copies and online. Nigerian newspapers are actually much more popular online than they are offline. All of the newspapers that the military seized get more daily hits on their websites than the combined annual hard-copy circulation of all newspapers and magazines in the country. Stories that are suppressed in physical form almost always become "social stories," that is, they go viral because they are voluntarily shared by users on social media platforms, and that was precisely what happened to the stories the Nigerian government wanted to suppress: they went viral.

The Muhammadu Buhari administration has been even more vicious in its suppression of media freedoms and free speech than previous civilian administrations. This is perhaps not altogether unexpected because Buhari was a military dictator who subverted Nigeria's democracy from 1983 to 1985. Critics of the government are routinely fired without recourse to due process. For example, Bolouere Opukiri, who worked for a government agency called the Presidential Amnesty Office, was dismissed from her job because she called the vice president a "novice" and described the president's wife as "not classy" on Twitter.[74] As I pointed out earlier, critical voices on social media are arbitrarily arrested and jailed on trumped-up charges, and the traditional news media are forced to self-censor and squelch critical voices in their opinion pages. Websites critical of governments are also routine blocked, mostly quietly, but it occasionally attracts international attention. For instance, the Office of the United Nations High Commission for Refugees (UNHCR) called attention to the blockage of twenty-one websites by the government in its country report on Nigeria:

> In November 2017, it was revealed that service providers blocked 21 websites, including the popular Naij.com online news outlet, at the request of the [National Communication Commission]. Though the blocking order lacked transparency, . . . [m]any of the blocked sites promote the independence of Biafra, the region that attempted to secede from Nigeria in 1967 and fought against the federal government in the Biafran War. Although access to Naij.com was eventually restored, as of April 2018, at least 15 of the websites remained blocked. The NCC's actions have raised concerns that the websites of opposition parties and critical NGOs could be blocked during the 2019 election campaign period.[75]

Similarly, a fearless, enterprising Premium Times reporter by the name of Samuel Ogundipe was arrested, detained for three days, and charged with "violating official secrets" for writing a factual news story using nonclassified government documents, which nonetheless embarrassed the government.[76] More than a year earlier, the Buhari government had raided the head office of Premium Times in Abuja and arrested its publisher and its judiciary correspondent in protest against critical stories the online newspaper had published about the military.[77] Similarly, on January 6, 2019, a team of military officers invaded the head office of the *Daily Trust* in Abuja and its regional offices in Maiduguri, Lagos, and Kaduna, arrested and detained its reporters and editors, seized its computers, and shut down its operations for hours over an unfavorable news report the paper published about the military.[78]

As the Yar'Adua administration had done in 2008, in June 2019 the Buhari government also withdrew the broadcast license of Daar Communications, which owns Africa Independent Television (AIT) and RayPower FM.[79] The National Broadcasting Commission (NBC), the government agency that regulates the broadcast industry in Nigeria, said it withdrew the broadcast licenses of the TV and radio station because they "embarked on use of inflammatory, divisive, inciting broadcasts and media propaganda against the government and the NBC for performing its statutory functions of regulating the broadcast industry in Nigeria."[80] The reasons given for withdrawing the licenses of the TV and radio stations were a cover. The real reason the government clamped down on them was that they provided an outlet for the ventilation of the anxieties of the opposition about how the country was being governed.

One of AIT's professional infractions, according to a leaked NBC memo to AIT that trended online, was that on January 18, 2019, its presenter for a program called "Kakaaki Social," which highlights trending tweets, "Read out a tweet from @Gold Rush: '. . . Aticulated [sic] FC consolidated its position at the top of the table with a huge away win in America . . . while lifeless FC is battling with relegation at Ogboru Presidential Stadium, Warri. Presenter just laughed." It is important to unpack the political humor of the tweet to appreciate why it discomfited government officials. The tweet was sent in the heat of the 2019 presidential election that pitted the All Progressives' Congress's Muhammadu Buhari against the People's Democratic Party's Atiku Abubakar. Drawing on a popular play on Atiku Abubakar's first name, supporters of his candidature referred to themselves as the "Aticulated Football Club" (or "Aticulated FC" for short). They also referred to Muhammadu Buhari and his supporters as the "Lifeless Football Club" (or "Lifeless FC" for short), which was derived from *Financial Times*'s reporting that President Donald Trump described Muhammadu Buhari as "lifeless" after meeting with him in the White House in April 2018.[81]

The tweet suggested that Abubakar gained enormous political prestige by traveling to the United States in January 2019, even though Buhari's propagandists had said he could not travel there because he would be arrested and prosecuted for an alleged transnational money-laundering crime. The tweet contrasted the political capital that the US visit conferred on Abubakar with the political downward spiral Buhari suffered in Delta State during the same time, when he mistakenly declared Delta State's APC governorship candidate Great Ogboru to be APC's presidential candidate. The government and its agent were aroused to irritation not only because the tweet was read out on the air on a popular TV station, thereby merging new and traditional media, but also because the presenter laughed when he read it out. Guy Debord has argued that repressive states have no capacity to appreciate humor, "since the state is always the ultimately unjust institutional site of 'law and order' in the service of the corruptly wealthy and powerful."[82] In tyrannical regimes, humor, especially transgressive humor, is a threat that must be eliminated. Nevertheless, transgressive humor is crucial to critical democratic citizenship and to the sustenance of a healthy state. There is probably no greater evidence of Nigeria's descent into the atrocious pits of totalitarian suffocation of the discursive space than the fact that even oppositional political humor constitutes a basis for official censure and sanction. As Michael Bruner notes, "[A] state's sense of humor is proportionate to the strength of citizens' rights and freedoms against the state, the general openness of government deliberations, the breadth and depth of political dialogue, and the degree to which state officials are legally constrained to tolerate public criticism. Rebellious citizenship, in fact, has often been valorized by political theorists and practitioners as something essential for state health."[83] Although the emergence of civilian rule is supposed to birth democracy and deepen democratic ethos, deliberative inclusivity, and the toleration for humor and dissent by the state, Nigeria has witnessed quite the opposite since 1999, as this chapter has illustrated. The restoration of constitutional rule in Nigeria is coextensive with the emergence of mobile technology and the massification of the Internet. This has meant that since 1999, governments have had to deal with more complexity and uncertainty in the informational and journalistic spheres than previous civilian governments in the 1960s and the 1980s had. Add to that the broadening and deepening of Nigeria's public sphere and deliberative practices, and the result can be overwhelming for a stagnant government structure that is still stuck in the 1980s. The inability of governments to come to terms with the frenzied pace of growth and development in the perpetually evolving informational universe, made even more complicated by the emergence of a critical diasporic online media formation, has obviously bred a sense of insecurity in governments. It is probably this abiding sense of insecurity that drives the government's repressive, military-style response to not just online journalists but also to citizen bloggers and traditional journalists. Perhaps Bertrand Russell was right when he said, "Freedom of opinion can only exist when the government thinks itself secure."[84]

Security springs forth from legitimacy, prosperity, and self-assurance, which the Buhari government—and the governments that preceded it—lack. The processes that brought the Buhari regime back to power in 2019 were fraught with manifest fraud. In their final report on the 2019 election, even the European Union observer mission noted, "The elections became increasingly marred by violence and intimidation, with the role of the security agencies becoming more contentious as the process progressed. This damaged the integrity of the electoral process and may deter future participation."[85] Amid the political illegitimacy of the government, Nigeria had also earned the dubious honor of being the poverty capital of the world, as a direct result of government's incompetence in managing the economy, which saw "an estimated 87 million Nigerians, or around half of the country's population, thought to be living on less than $1.90 a day."[86]

The government's self-construal of its illegitimacy amid biting poverty and the restlessness that this will instigate will heighten its insecurity and deepen its intolerance of adversarial journalism, critical online discourse, rebellious citizenship, and even transgressive political humor. Not even the judiciary, a supposedly independent arm of government that administers justice, is inoculated against the government's widening and deepening tyranny. The government, for instance, once raided the homes of judges in the dead of the night on suspicion that they had received bribes, but the government agents who carried out the raids later said they found no evidence for their suspicion. The chief justice of Nigeria, Walter Onnoghen, was arbitrarily removed by the president without recourse to the Constitution and replaced with a pliant alternative from the president's geoethnic zone without the approval of Nigeria's Judicial Council, which is constitutionally mandated to discipline and remove erring judicial officers.

Paul Usoro, president of the Nigerian Bar Association (NBA) also disclosed on June 21, 2019 that judges no longer felt safe in performing their constitutional duties of interpreting the laws of the country and delivering fair judgments because of the constant "intimidation of judges by members of the executive arm and security operatives."[87] This came as no surprise because the president had told the Nigerian Bar Association on August 27, 2018, that he had no use for the rule of law and due process wherever and whenever these precepts are in conflict with Nigeria's "national interest." "The rule of law, he said, "must be subject to the supremacy of the nation's security and national interest."[88] Invocation of the "national interest" is a well-worn rhetorical strategy by dictators to contract personal freedoms. That is why it is always willfully characterized by definitional vagueness, conceptual imprecision, and variable interpretive renditions. In other words, it is a floating signifier, which, as Jeffrey Mehlman points out, "may mean whatever their interpreters want them to mean."[89] The Buhari regime also legitimizes its strangulation of basic democratic liberties through appeals to an anticorruption crusade that has been intentionally designed to ensnare only its opponents and spare its supporters.

Chapter Seven

Domestic Online Media, Social Networked Journalism, and Participation

Misty Bastian's 1999 prescient prediction of the "possibility of a new synthesis, a drawing closer of the electronic world of the brain drain diaspora and the real worlds of both material diasporic experience and Nigerian quotidian life"[1] materialized not just in the emergence of the diasporic citizen media formation that arose from where the guerrilla journalism of the 1990s left off. It also emerged in the vibrant domestic, digital-native media formation it spawned during the early 2010s. Inspired by the success, popularity, impact, and promise of the diasporic citizen online media, an abundance of home-based online news sites emerged starting in 2011. Many of them mimic Sahara Reporters' erstwhile editorial template. At least one of these online-only domestic news sites matches, and sometimes outmatches, Sahara Reporters in its earliest form. Most of them, nevertheless, have not been able to replicate Sahara Reporters' success and seem condemned to linger on the margins of the Nigerian journalistic landscape. However, a measure of their rootedness in the Nigerian news media landscape can be gleaned from the fact that a visible professional association, the Online Publishers Association of Nigeria, now exists for Nigerian digital-native journalists at home and in the diaspora.

Premium Times is a home-based online news site that shook the foundations of Nigerian journalism and that rivaled the earlier incarnation of Sahara Reporters in impact and hard-hitting investigative reporting. It was established in 2011 by home-based, professional, award-winning investigative journalists, some of whom were associated with the guerrilla journalism of the 1990s. According to Alexa Rank, from 2017 through 2019, Premium Times was among the top 40 most visited websites in Nigeria and the country's fourth most visited news site, topped only by *Punch*, *Vanguard*, and the Daily Post. It had edged out Sahara Reporters from the fourth spot in news traffic by 2018, in large part because Omoyele Sowore, Sahara Reporters' editor in chief, devoted more time to his presidential campaign than he did to his website. Further, as a consequence of Sowore's relocation to Nigeria and his obsession with his presidential run, the site ceased to be the trove of sensational muckraking journalism that it had become famous for. For a long time, as will be shown in subsequent sections of this chapter, Premium Times was the unrivaled go-to site for exposés of malfeasance in government, although by 2019 it had lost its investigative vibrancy.

Premium Times is based in Abuja, Nigeria's federal capital, and has offices in Lagos and Washington, DC. Its publisher and chief executive officer, Dapo Olorunyomi, is a well-regarded, gutsy, award-winning investigative journalist who cofounded *The News* magazine, one of the iconic guerrilla news outlets that fought military totalitarianism (see chapter 2). Its editor in chief, Musikilu Mojeed, is also an esteemed, multiple-award-winning muckraker who reported for most of the prominent 1990s guerrilla news outlets: *The News*, *Tempo*, and *TELL*. Premium Times creatively combines the sober professionalism of traditional journalism and the uncompromisingly plucky editorial temperament of alternative news media. These characteristics conferred on it both credibility and enthusiastic patronage.

It was no surprise that in its first seven years of publishing, Premium Times won more international journalism awards than most Nigerian news platforms at home or abroad. For instance, it won One World Media's Special Award in 2014;[2] Africa Check's Best Fact-checking Report in Africa award in 2015;[3] CNN/MultiChoice's News Impact Award in 2015;[4] Rotary International's Humanitarian Reporting Award in 2016;[5] CNN/MultiChoice's Sports Category Award in 2016;[6] Global Editors Network's Data Journalism Award (jointly with the International Consortium of Investigative Journalists);[7] the Global Shining Light Award in 2017;[8] and the Pulitzer Prize for Explanatory Reporting (also jointly with ICIJ) in 2017.[9] It also won several domestic awards, such as the Wole Soyinka Prize for Investigative Reporting, which it won four times between 2012 and 2017. Phil Harding, the vice chair of One World Media's board of trustees, which gave Premium Times its Special Award in 2014, described the paper thus:

> This Nigerian investigative newspaper and website has, in the three years of its existence, established a fast-growing reputation for brave and courageous journalism with real impact. With an impressive string of hard-hitting exposés, it has acted as a powerful reminder that, in a modern democracy, the media is crucial in holding those in power to account. PREMIUM TIMES shows that in the face of misrule and suppression, the media can act as a beacon for those who wish to create a better society.[10]

The nascence and flourishing of Premium Times is a testimony to a creative, mutually reinforcing cycle of influences. Alternative online diasporic media sites such as Sahara Reporters derived inspirational strength for their brand of journalism from the uncompromisingly adversarial reportorial template of the guerrilla press of the 1999s, but their success with real-time, multimedia online publishing from their exilic locations inspired the reincarnation of a version of the guerrilla press in Premium Times. Although Premium Times lacked the advocatorial temperament of the earlier incarnation of Sahara Reporters and of the guerrilla press, its capacity for uncovering corruption in government using traditional journalistic reporting styles and cross-border collaborative resources set it apart from the rest before it mellowed.[11] In its profiles of fifteen prominent news organizations in the world, the Open Society Foundations (OSF) found that the core inspiration for the emergence of Premium Times was "the goal of renewing Nigerian journalism," with "a new kind of Nigerian media organization: one that is 'professional, fact-based, independent' and focused above all on 'accuracy in reporting and verification of claims.'"[12] The most important guarantee of the site's editorial independence, perhaps, was its source of funding. Like Sahara Reporters, it started as a self-funded journalistic project, then became an advertiser-supported news outlet, and later a philanthro-journalism project. The decline of its fearless, hard-hitting investigative reporting in 2019 coincided with the drying up of its grant funding and its reliance on advertising from government to survive.

Philanthro-journalism is the sort of journalism that is not dependent on advertising revenue for sustenance but is instead funded partly or entirely by donations and grants from foundations such as the Ford Foundation, the John D. and Catherine T. MacArthur Foundation, the Bill and Melinda Gates Foundation, and so on.[13] America's Pulitzer Prize–winning online-only ProPublica news site is an example of a philanthro-journalism project. According to the Open Society Foundations, "Advertising makes up 35 percent of Premium Times revenue, and another 15 percent comes from events, data sales and due diligence work. The remaining 50 percent is supplied by foundation funding, including from the Bill and Melinda Gates Foundation, the Natural Resources Governance Institute, the OSF's Open Society Initiative for West Africa, MacArthur Foundation, Ford Foundation and the Free Press Unlimited."[14] Premium Times nourished its independence not only through its philanthro-journalistic sources of funding but also through paying its reporters and editors "very competitive" salaries, including putting in place "pension and insurance schemes" for its all its workers.[15] It is not clear if the paper's competitive salaries have immunized its reporters and editors against the lure of financial inducement (the "brown envelopes" of African journalism, in chapter 6), but its consistently intrepid reporting on high-profile corruption in government, at least until 2018, bespoke an uncommon independence, unusual in the Nigerian traditional media space since the restoration of constitutional rule in 1999. The paper reported spurning financial enticements from government officials hoping to inveigle it into abandoning potentially embarrassing stories. For instance, in July 2018, when the paper uncovered that Nigeria's minister of finance, Kemi Adeosun, had forged a National Youth Corps (NYSC) exemption certificate—a criminal offense punishable by imprisonment—it said its "staff came under undue pressure over the story, including attempts at compromising those thought to be working on the report and the management."[16]

Nevertheless, it appears that Premium Times has realized that philanthro-journalism is not a sustainable model of financing. By 2018, it had ventured into a donation-based crowdfunding initiative, which solicits voluntary financial contributions from readers who value its journalism. It must have been inspired by the success of the British *Guardian*, which reported in July 2018 that it "now earns more money from its digital operations than from its print newspapers for the first time in its history, aided by increased support from readers making online contributions."[17] This caused the paper's editor in chief, Katherine Viner, to enthuse, "The *Guardian*'s reader funding model is working."[18] From 2018 until the mid-point of 2019, when this study was concluded, Premium Times posted the following solicitation at the end of every news story on its site:

> Good journalism costs a lot of money. Yet only good journalism can ensure the possibility of a good society, an accountable democracy, and a transparent government.
>
> For continued free access to the best investigative journalism in the country we ask you to consider making a modest support to this noble endeavour.

> By contributing to PREMIUM TIMES, you are helping to sustain a journalism of relevance and ensuring it remains free and available to all.

It is uncertain how effective and enduring this model of financing will be in a country like Nigeria, where the middle class is progressively shrinking and where the masses of the people are too wracked by endemic poverty to be able to afford donating to a news organization. The political and financial elites who have the means to donate are not impressed by investigative journalism because they are often its target. Starting in 2018, the paper also showed evidence of reciprocal positive coverage and concealment of untoward dealings in government, perhaps in return for advertising patronage from government. Critical citizens are unlikely to be persuaded to donate to such a news organization.

Another domestic digital-native news outlet that has emerged as a fixture in the Nigerian media landscape is TheCable. It was established on April 29, 2014 by former traditional newspaper journalists "to deliver knowledge-driven journalism in the pursuit of Nigeria's progress."[19] The paper's founder and CEO, Simon Kolawole, was a long-term editor of *ThisDay*, one of Nigeria's most influential but compromised newspapers, from which he resigned in protest after he was unceremoniously "reassigned" as an "editorial director" in June 2012. TheCable's strength does not lie in exposing corruption in government but in breaking news in real time and in using the closeness of its editors to Nigeria's power brokers to report on exclusive stories, such as getting the scoop on the names of top government appointees weeks, sometimes months, before their formal announcement. Unlike Premium Times, the paper's comment section does not attract reader participation, nor are its social media streams particularly vibrant, but its reporters and editors have successfully parlayed their reputational capital and name recognition from *ThisDay* into the online medium. This has ensured that TheCable's reports sometimes have instigated changes in government policies. For instance, its July 24, 2017 enterprise reporting on the dreadful state of elementary education in the northwestern state of Zamfara caused the state government to award contracts for the rehabilitation of primary schools in the state one week later.[20] Although several ads from Nigeria's private sector appear on TheCable's front page, its Policy Radar Initiative (PRIN), a three-year project whose goal is to "support investigative journalism in Nigeria and to educate the public and other important audiences about issues related to corruption, with a focus on the electricity and education sectors," is funded by the MacArthur Foundation.[21]

Other notable and influential, if comparatively marginal, online-only news media that complement existing traditional hybrid newspapers are the Daily Nigerian and the Daily Post. The Daily Nigerian was founded in Abuja in March 2016 by the tautonymous Jaafar Jaafar, who had worked as a reporter and editor at the *Daily Trust* and Premium Times and as a spokesperson for the governor of the northwestern state of Kano from 2011 to 2015. The paper became famous in 2017 after it revealed, with remarkably irrefutable documentary proof, evidence of shocking financial indiscretion against the vocal and reformist emir of Kano, Muhammadu Sanusi II.[22] The report led the Kano State House of Assembly to instruct the state's Public Complaints and Anti-Corruption Commission to investigate the emir.[23] The emir was in danger of being dethroned but for the intervention of prominent Nigerian political leaders.[24] Reporting on corruption in traditional institutions is unusual in modern Nigerian journalism. It is even more unusual for a report on corruption against an emir published in an online news medium to form the basis for a probe of the emir preparatory to his dethronement. It was apparent that the emir's troubles stemmed from his strident criticisms of both the governor of his state and of the president of Nigeria, which was unprecedented in Nigeria's history. Traditional rulers, who have no constitutional role and who are appointees of state governors, typically support every reigning administration and hardly offer critical counsel to governments publicly. It seems plausible that government officials or people sympathetic to them gave the scoop on the emir's financial indiscretions to the Daily Nigerian. Nevertheless, it was remarkable that *Daily Trust*, northern Nigeria's preeminent newspaper and winner of Nigeria's Newspaper of the Year Award in 2016, was bypassed for an up-and-coming online-only newspaper.

Perhaps the Daily Nigerian's most impactful reporting, which riveted sustained national attention for months, was its series of videographic stories in late 2018 showing Abdullahi Ganduje, the governor of Kano, collecting millions of dollars in kickbacks from contractors. The reportorial strategy the paper deployed to unmask the governor's corruption was the first of its kind in Nigeria. The paper's editor in chief recounted it this way:

> The sting operation to capture the governor on camera began two years ago when one of the contractors agreed with DAILY NIGERIAN request to plant a spy camera on his kaftan lapel while offering the bribe. During about 10 months efforts to capture the bribe giving/taking scenes, the governor's face and body were clearly captured in nine clips, while six others did not clearly

> reveal the governor's face. About $5m dollars were delivered to the governor during the sting operation.[25]

The editor in chief of the paper and writer of the story spurned entreaties and resisted enormous financial inducements from people in the corridors of power to release the videos. When entreaties and financial inducements failed, the publication's editor in chief was threatened with death, which compelled him to relocate his family to Lagos. The Daily Nigerian's reporting on the governor's corruption defined the tenor of conversations not only about the 2019 gubernatorial election in Kano but also about the presidential election in the same year. President Buhari's impolitic response to questions about the governor's behavior in the videos became fodder for his political opponents and helped to dramatize his insincerity about fighting corruption.

The Daily Post straddles the twilight zone between a news aggregator and a news site. Most of its content is republished from traditional Nigerian online news sites, including nondescript sites from the fringes of the web, but it also has original news content. Its most important strength isn't the accuracy, immediacy, or pungency of its reporting, since it has hardly any original content; it is the effectiveness of its search engine optimization (SEO) strategies, which ensures that it ranks at the top of search results even for stories and key words that are not original to it. As Dimitrios Giomelakis and Andreas Veglis point out, although the emergence of news websites is coextensive with the rise of search engines, news websites were late to recognize the importance of search engine optimization in news writing.[26] This was still true of Nigerian online newspapers as of 2018. Most of them do not appreciate the importance of investing in the training of SEO experts whose exclusive job is, as Giomelakis and Veglis describe, to "customize a headline, a lede or the text of an article to improve the placement in Google's search results and have a better chance of being read."[27] As of the midpoint of 2018, the Daily Post was the fourteenth most visited website in Nigeria and the third most visited news site.

All the domestic online-only news websites can be located in John Pavlik's third stage of online journalism (see chapter 4). They are published in real time; they are multimedia, interactive, and hypertextual; they have searchable databases, and they are mobile friendly. Since at least 2015, domestic online-only newspapers such as Premium Times, TheCable, Daily Nigerian, and others have not only become mainstream and key actors in the political, social, and cultural life of Nigeria, they are also the main agenda setters for the national news media and for the nation.[28] As Ibraheem Musa, the editor of the Abuja-based *Weekend Blueprint*, said, "The online guys in Premium Times, TheCable, and Daily Nigerian have reduced us to writing history and reviews. They now break the news and regular newspapers do follow-ups."[29]

Coterminous with the growth of home-based online journalistic sites has been the rise of social media networks as independent sources of news, as cocreators of news for the traditional media, and as amplifiers of news from traditional sources. This development has been made possible by the exponential growth of Internet usage in Nigeria over the last decade. According to the Nigerian Communications Commission (NCC), as of February 2018, there were over 100 million Internet users in Nigeria.[30] This means that there are more Internet users in Nigeria than the population of the United Kingdom or France. Internet penetration went from a tiny 0.06 percent in 2000 to nearly 40 percent in 2014.

Nigeria has not only the largest population of Internet users in Africa and the seventh largest in the whole world; it also has one of the world's fastest growing Internet usage rates. For instance, between 2011 and 2012 over 9 million new Internet users were added in the country; between 2013 and 2014, a whopping 10 million news users were added, a 16 percent increase, fueled largely by the proliferation of Internet-enabled mobile devices in the country. The explosion of Internet usage via mobile devices isn't exclusive to Nigeria. It is happening all over the African continent, prompting Erik Hersman, the cofounder of the open-source, crowdsourcing platform Ushahidi, to characterize Africa as the "mobile continent."[31] Similarly, a 2014 report in the (UK) *Guardian* quoted researchers as predicting that Internet usage on mobile phones in Africa "will increase 20-fold in the next five years—double the rate of growth in the rest of the world," while pointing out, "People in Africa use mobiles for online activities that others normally perform on laptops or desktop computers as the technology overcomes weak or non-existent landline infrastructure in large swaths of the world's poorest continent."[32] A 2015 Pew Research Center study also showed that "cell phones are as common in South Africa and Nigeria as they are in the United States."[33]

This unprecedented mobile-enabled Internet penetration has afforded Nigeria the opportunity to digitally leapfrog from what Manuel Castells once called the "black hole of informational capitalism"[34] to the emergent, horizontal, self-directed, socially networked information age that Castells calls the "network society." At the symbolic core of the social morphology of the network society are such social media sites as Facebook and Twitter, in which Nigerians now increasingly participate. As Statcounter's Global Stats shows, more than 85 percent of Nigerian social-media users have accounts on Facebook, while about 12 percent use Twitter. Predictably, Facebook has emerged as the biggest site for online sociability, discursive engagement, and social-media journalism. Nevertheless, although "Nigeria is among the top ten countries with the fastest increase in Facebook membership" in the world,[35] with more than 26 million subscribers as of January 2018,[36] Nigeria's traditional media are only just now taking central roles in guiding and influencing community conversations on this platform. However, h Facebook's changes to its algorithms in 2018 saw steep drops in referral traffic to most news sites, causing them to look for alternatives beyond Facebook.[37]

As of May 2019, the *Vanguard* had 3,147,975 likes on Facebook; Sahara Reporters, the New York–based citizen media platform, outpaced it slightly with 3,153,854 likes. *Punch*, Nigeria's most widely circulated newspaper, had 1,562,811 likes; the *Nation* had 1,747,768 likes; *ThisDay* had 977,274 likes; *Daily Trust*, northern Nigeria's preeminent newspaper, had 1,199,041 likes; Premium Times had 1,241,357 likes; the *Nigerian Tribune*, Nigeria's oldest surviving privately owned newspaper, had 993,191 likes; the *Sun* had 944,429 likes; the *Daily Independent* had 800,252 likes; *Leadership* had 1,311,322 likes; the *Guardian*, Nigeria's self-described newspaper of record, had 755,449 likes; *Daily Times*, Nigeria's oldest surviving newspaper, had 652,374 likes; TheCable had 431,499 likes; and the Daily Nigerian had 216,848 likes. Given that there were up to 16 million active Facebook users in Nigeria as of 2019, it is obvious that the Nigerian news media have not maximally connected with Nigerians on social media.

The Nigerian news media's Twitter following isn't any better. As of May 2019, *Punch* had 2.43 million followers, *Vanguard* 2.05 million followers, Sahara Reporters 2.31 million followers, the *Guardian* 1.32 million followers, *ThisDay* 1.07 million followers, *Daily Trust* 728,000 followers, *Premium Times* 952,000 followers, the *Nation* 686,000 followers, *Leadership* 680,000 followers, Daily Post 615,000, TheCable 247,000, the *Nigerian Tribune* 1800,000 followers, the *Daily Times* 43,000 followers, and the *Daily Independent* 27,000 followers and the Sun 22,000 followers.

But it is not the modest numerical strength of Nigeria's traditional news media's social media presence that vitiates their influence; the social ecology of the Nigerian social media space vests more power and authority in trendsetters, digital influencers, and other everyday users with vast and engaged followers than it does in legacy media institutions and their journalists. There are scores of individuals who are not pop-culture celebrities but who have vastly more Facebook and Twitter followers than news media platforms. In other words, social media give more editorial power to the crowd than they do to the mass media. That is why most defining national conversations on social media now take place outside the spaces of the Nigerian traditional news media or their social media streams. For example, in more ways than the traditional news media, social media networks, particularly Facebook and Twitter users, played central roles in Nigeria's elections in 2011, 2015, and 2019.

The first illustration of the diminishing importance of the industrial homeland media formation in Nigeria in shaping the course of a momentous national event occurred in 2011 when microbloggers (on Facebook and Twitter) and citizen journalists played roles in the general election that year. Following the renewed enthusiasm and faith in electoral politics that the appointment of the respected academic Attahiru Jega as chairman of the Independent National Electoral Commission generated in the country, scores of citizen media initiatives were set up to monitor and safeguard the integrity of the electoral process. Many young people and civil-society activists chose to deploy the instrumentality of the Internet and mobile technology to influence the course of the election. They resolved to share with the world textual updates of the election on Twitter and Facebook, and to video blog about it on YouTube and Facebook with their phone cameras. The Nigerian power structure was alarmed at this prospect, and so Nigeria's inspector general of police issued a directive that forbade voters to take cameras to the polling units. As would be expected, the directive outraged Nigerians. It met with so much stiff resistance from civil-society groups, media pundits, and citizen reporters that the authorities were compelled to withdraw it forthwith.[38] The Independent National Electoral Commission, the agency that conducts elections in Nigeria, also dissociated itself from the directive. "INEC has said anyone can bring their phone or camera to the polling unit. Anything to the contrary is not the position of INEC," the agency declared in a widely publicized press statement.[39]

This set the stage for robust citizen participation in the election. Dozens of web-based citizen initiatives quickly sprouted. At least eight such initiatives had widespread followings and popularity across Nigeria. Perhaps the most popular such initiative was ReclaimNaija: Election Incident Report System, an activist citizen initiative that was formed to ensure transparency in the conduct of the 2011 general elections through citizen reporting. Its membership was drawn from a vast array of grassroots, peasant, working-class, and civil-society organizations across the country. It provided phone lines for election observers to reach it and open-source mapping software known as Ushahidi for people to report their observations in real time, and it encouraged members and nonmembers alike to send tweets about the election with the hashtags #reclaimnaija and #NigeriaDecides. "Project 2011 Swift Count" was another hugely successful project that stood out not only because of the efficacy of its citizen reporters but also because of its capacity to unite many elements in Nigeria's traditional primordial fissures. It brought together the Federation of Muslim Women's Associations in Nigeria (FOMWAN); Justice, Development and Peace/Caritas Nigeria (JDPC); the Nigerian Bar Association (NBA); and the Transition Monitoring Group (TMG). It persuaded members of the public to announce results of election in their polling units as soon as they were available, to subvert the possibility of official manipulation of results. The Police Service Commission was set up to monitor the conduct of police officers posted to polling units. In the past, the police were often accused of colluding with politicians to intimidate voters and to change election results. This group encouraged citizen reporters to chronicle, if possible through phone cameras, instances where police officers were complicit in electoral fraud. It provided dedicated phone numbers where citizens could report the conduct of the police in real time.

"Vote or Quench" (Nigerian pidgin English for "vote or be damned") was also active in monitoring the conduct of the election through its pack of youthful citizen journalists who shared updates on its site. So were many Facebook groups, such as the Nigeria 2011 Election Center, which attracted vigorous debates and status updates on the election. There were also many "video-your-vote" channels on YouTube. These initiatives complemented the efforts of such well-known diasporic citizen media sites as Sahara Reporter, the Nigerian Village Square, The Will, the African Examiner, Eagle Eye Report, and so on. Although citizen reporters did not influence the outcome of the election, they shaped and guided its processes, conduct, and discourse. For instance, the first set of the three-tier election that was scheduled for April 2, 2011, was postponed a week, partly because of the irregularities uploaded by citizen reporters at the ClaimNaija project. As a Slate.com reporter observed:

> I saw dozens of voters transformed into informal election monitors—snapping photos on their mobile phones and alerting friends when the lines were shortest. A local newspaper took note: "The tweets, Facebook updates, Skype messages, text messages and pictures that voters exchanged via email and mobile phones gave the addresses of the polling booths, the locations, the number of people accredited, those who voted and the votes that each party got." Within

> 12 hours of the polls closing, a charming YouTube video documented the group count at one polling unit. If thugs tried to snatch that ballot box, they might have seen their face on the evening news.[40]

The consequences of citizen media reports on the elections extended beyond the conduct of the elections. Many citizen reporters captured video evidence of election rigging in many parts of the country, and aggrieved politicians who were at the receiving end of electoral fraud used these videos as testimonial evidence to ask for the invalidation of the electoral victories of their opponents. The unprecedentedly enthusiastic participation of citizen reporters in the electoral process eclipsed the traditional role of the Nigerian mass media as the first source of information. Alarmed by their diminishing role, the mainstream media felt compelled to invest more effort in their online delivery. The *Daily Trust*, for instance, started live, real-time updates of the elections from all parts of the country. For the first time also, it instructed its reporters to record video news of the election, which it uploaded on its site. The *Vanguard*, *Guardian*, *Punch* and many other legacy newspapers not only started live updates on the election but also created online communities on their sites and invited citizen participation. These efforts did not, however, gain much traction because they were not sufficiently robust and because they could not rival the sheer ebullience of citizen bloggers on Twitter, Facebook, diasporic media sites, and the lively discursive arenas created by sundry citizen initiatives.

Social media were also central in shaping the contours of the 2015 presidential elections, which saw an opposition candidate, Muhammadu Buhari, defeat the incumbent president, Goodluck Jonathan. That marked the first time in Nigeria's electoral history that an opposition candidate trounced a sitting president handily. Whereas the People's Democratic Party, the political party in power, exploited and relied on its control of state-run broadcast stations to appeal to the hearts and minds of the Nigerian electorate, the opposition party took to social media to solicit support for its candidate, since it was denied airtime in the state-run broadcast media, which typically have a wider reach than newspapers. Although there is no firm empirical proof to make the case that the opposition party won the election because it deployed social media more artfully than the president's party (which also robustly used social media in addition to its monopoly over the broadcast media), all observers agreed that such social media platforms as Facebook and Twitter did play remarkable roles in ensuring transparency in the electoral process. As a Quartz report noted, "The consensus from all sides is that while social media didn't decide the vote it had a significant influence on perception, expectations and a demand for transparency. All in all it seemed that social media was a winner with the #NigeriaDecides hashtag resulting in citizens proclaiming that Democracy is alive and well in Africa's most populous nation."[41] Hours before the Independent National Electoral Commission announced the official results of the presidential poll, Nigerian social media users had accurately predicted them, and the Nigerian traditional media's reporting of the election was almost entirely reliant on social media feeds from ordinary citizens. This was possible because millions of Nigerians with smartphones not only shared the results of the elections from their polling units in real time on Twitter and Facebook but also took pictures of the official results and videotaped instances of electoral malpractices, which they shared on Facebook, Twitter, and YouTube.

The 2019 general election, which was widely believed to have been massively and brazenly rigged by the ruling party, was also fought on social media. In spite of enormous investment in putative technological safeguards against electoral manipulation, the Independent National Electoral Commission "conducted about the worst election in the history of the country."[42] The results the electoral umpire announced as the product of the election were, in many cases, inconsistent with the figures officially declared at polling units and shared on social media platforms. Citizens used their cell phones to capture instances where ballot boxes in polling units won by opposition candidates were seized, burned, or dumped in sewers by government-sponsored thugs. Instances of massive thumb-printing of ballot papers in the strongholds of the ruling party were captured and shared on social media. The troves of evidence of enormous electoral malpractice, including intercepted phone conversations and video recordings, captured by citizens on their cell phones and shared on social media, formed the core evidentiary base in the legal challenge to the declaration of Muhammadu Buhari as the winner of the 2019 election.

The ubiquity of smartphones and the unceasing flow of social media updates on the processes and immediate aftermath of Nigerian elections since 2011 disprove Scott Campbell's notion of cell-phone-induced "network privatism," which he conceptualized as "the proposition that intensive mobile communication in the intimate realm of social life can be detrimental for being connected to others more broadly."[43] That notion has no ontological utility in Nigeria, where cell phones have had unimaginably liberatory power in Nigerian citizen participation and discursive democracy. Cellphone usage during elections also had the effect of what Michel Foucault called the panoptic gaze on government-appointed superintendents of the election and forestalled, or at least provided irrefutable documentary proof of, the scale and kinds of voter fraud that were typical of past elections in Nigeria. Foucault described the panoptic gaze in the following way: "There is no need for arms, physical violence, material constraints. Just a gaze. An inspecting gaze, a gaze which each individual under its weight will end by internalizing to the point that he is his own overseer, each individual thus exercising this surveillance over, and against, himself. A superb formula: power exercised continuously and for what turns out to be a minimal cost."[44] But while traditional scholarship on the mass surveillance industry customarily talks of the panoptic gaze in Orwellian terms, where big brother's ever-present and intrusive gaze over citizens constrains them, in the Nigerian case, it was an inverse, contradirectional, many-to-many, collaborative panoptic gaze on the state and its institutions by politically conscious, smartphone-wielding Nigerian citizens. In other words, big brother wasn't watching the citizens; the citizens were watching big brother with their hand-held devices and social-media status updates. The traditional news media didn't have such powers; their reach was limited, since they couldn't be at every polling station. They didn't have the collective intelligence of the social media crowd and came to depend on it for their own reportage. A *Daily Trust* survey of Nigerian journalists in 2012 brought this point to the forefront of national consciousness. The paper said, "More than ever, many journalists who spoke to *Sunday Trust* claimed they can reach their news sources, gather stories and make verifications on the authenticity of the stories with less difficulties through the social networks."[45] This phenomenon is known as the "backdraft," which, according Seol Jin-ah, occurs "when the traditional media such as newspapers or television news receive and use such things as Twitter feeds or individually created content in their reporting."[46]

Backdraft in Nigerian journalism is not limited to the coverage of elections. On many other issues of national importance, the news media have on several instances lifted stories directly from social-media feeds and run them on their pages and websites, sometimes without verification. For instance, *Saturday Vanguard*'s May 10, 2014, cover story was "Chibok: American Marines Locate Abducted Girls in Sambisa Forest," with a rider that read, "Joint Operation with Nigerian Military Leads to Arrest of Leader of Abductors," complete with a photo of the alleged chief abductor. It was sourced entirely from unverified social-media chatter. The story, which alleged that the whereabouts of more than 200 schoolgirls abducted by Boko Haram in 2014 had been found by American marines and that the brain behind the abduction had been arrested, turned out to be completely fictitious. Nonetheless, it went viral in Nigerian social-media circles before it was picked up by *Saturday Vanguard* (the weekend edition of *Vanguard*). The paper was forced to apologize and eat humble pie when it emerged that a Nigerian social media user with a large, engaged audience had made up the story, and that the photo the paper used to illustrate the story was an old photo of a man who had been arrested by French soldiers in the Central African Republic.[47]

Similarly, on May 27, 2014, many Nigerian newspapers, including the *Vanguard* and *Daily Trust*, reported a transparently fictional story about how women in the northeastern state of Borno invoked a magical spell to subdue Boko Haram terrorists who had reputedly come to attack them. *Vanguard* quoted a nameless eyewitness of this putative supernatural encounter as saying that Boko Haram "attackers invaded the village yesterday on motorcycles but met some women, adding 'they wanted to hit the women with sticks but when they raised the sticks, their hands refused to descend.'"[48] The *Daily Trust*'s reporting on this same alleged event was even more dramatic and fantastical than *Vanguard*'s. Like *Vanguard*, *Daily Trust* also quoted an unnamed eyewitness who said, "The insurgents wanted to attack the women but their guns did not work. They tried hitting them with the boot of their guns but mysteriously, all the hands of the insurgents hung until youth and vigilantes in the area mobilized and killed them."[49]

It later emerged that the story of the "mystical" Borno women was started by influential, rumor-peddling social media users who based it on a 2012 stock photo of gun-toting Malian women "bent on revenge against Tuareg rebels," as *The Times* (of London), from whose website the picture was downloaded, put it.[50] An intentional fabrication was spun around the photo: that the women in the photo were Borno women who repelled Boko Haram attacks with the instrumentality of magic spells. The photo and the mendacious caption that accompanied it went viral, and many Nigerian newspapers published it without verification—and based solely on the secondhand account of an unnamed source.

These social-media-induced journalistic misadventures are not an exception; they are increasingly becoming normalized in Nigerian journalism. Typically, news now starts from social media chatter, percolates into online news networks, and then migrates to the mainstream news media, from which it is further shared by social media users to create social stories. It sometimes takes a different route: it may start as social-media gossip, get picked up by the traditional media, get republished on a host of fringe Nigerian online news sites, and be amplified even further by social-media sharing. At other times the propaganda and chatter of individual Nigerian digital trendsetters, some of whom have more social media following than the traditional media, define the news agenda. This role reversal, whereby what used to be the traditional audience for news now functions both as the source for news and the audience for news, is inflicting tremendous violence on the professional authority of Nigeria's institutional media. However, what the traditional media still have going for them, at least for now, is their symbolic power to give a professional imprimatur to social-media chatter, which the social-media chatterers then quote to support their positions. But when mendacious social-media rumors find their way into the traditional media and their accuracy is called into question, as happened to *Saturday Vanguard*, the traditional media's credibility is eroded. In the long term, this will vitiate the professional authority and symbolic capital of the media.

In this fast-paced, discursively robust era of social media, the traditional media in Nigeria, more than ever before, need to stand out from the crowd by sticking to the time-honored journalistic ethos of skepticism and verification before publication if they are to remain relevant. Most important, as the realm of social news is becoming more salient and central to journalism, and as social media sites are becoming the landing pages for news, the media must understand their role not merely as reporters of the news but as managers and guides of news conversations. This requires them to increase their presence on social media, provide robust platforms for citizen social-media conversations on their media platforms, and not be mere echoes of citizen social-media chatter. Although the media in Nigeria seem to be immune to the financial hemorrhaging and uncertain future that the Western media are confronted by, going forward, they will need to justify their existence by living up to the demands of twenty-first-century journalism, which is increasingly networked, multimedia, interactive, archival, interactive, and driven by social media trends. The only reprieve for Nigeria's corporatized media is that advertisers are still leery of the efficacy of advertising in online platforms. This reluctance is unlikely to last forever. The gradual decoupling of the traditional media in the United States from advertising, which we have witnessed in the past few years, will sooner or later creep into Nigeria, especially as Internet penetration deepens and the Internet becomes demotic. The crisis of the Nigerian domestic newspaper market will deepen once advertisers migrate in large numbers to the online Nigerian citizen media.

Deliberative Democracy and Online Civility in Nigerian Cyberspace

For at least the past decade, Nigerian discourses have been rapidly migrating to what one might call the cyberian public sphere. Spirited and occasionally transformative discourses about Nigerian politics, economics, and culture are now increasingly taking place on Facebook and Twitter, and in the comment sections of Sahara Reporters, the Nigerian Village Square, Premium Times, *Punch*, *Vanguard*, and a whole host of other digital discursive arenas. Discursive democracy, which had been sorely lacking in Nigerian political culture, appears to be taking root. This is especially helped by the impersonality and anonymity of the Internet, which conduce to the bracketing of social status, so that people at the lower end of the social scale can converse on equal terms with people at the upper end of the scale. This all bodes well for deliberative democracy, which Stephen Coleman and Jay Blumler describe as "talking with other citizens about political questions in an honest and open-minded way,"[51] except that the nature, tenor, and compass of most of the discussions that take place in cyber Nigeria (or Cyberia) give cause for a little worry.

A casual visit to the comments page of a typical article in, say, Sahara Reporters or Premium Times on any issue would cause one to be petrified by the unnervingly savage profusion of unspeakably raw, undiluted ethnic and religious chauvinism that passes for "comments." On news stories that involve people of the northwestern Fulani ethnic group, for instance, it is typical for commenters from the south to deride them as "Foolani," a vituperative blend of the English "fool" and Fulani. Members of the Yoruba people are also habitually called "Yorobbers," a portmanteau of "Yoruba" and "robbers." The Igbo are called "IBO = I Before Others," suggesting that they are a disobliging, self-centered lot. It is also typical for commenters from the north to insult southern commenters as "products of baby factories" and for southern commenters to describe northern Muslims as "almajiris," "terrorists," "Boko Haram" maniacs or "killer herdsmen." Every region in Nigeria has its stereotypical vulnerabilities. From religious extremism to endemic child abandonment to 419 email scams, from child trafficking and prostitution in foreign lands, to disabling alcoholism, to kidnapping, and so on, Nigerians can, and often do, easily territorialize these crimes, moral infractions, and cultural vulnerabilities within their national space. These stereotypes are often the stuff of online comments even when the subject matter of the stories has not the remotest connection to the insults.

Similarly, in the opinions of much of the Nigerian Internet commentariat, no opinion is ever the product of any individual's independent analytical or discursive choice; it is always already inspired either by primordial loyalties or by pecuniary gratification—or by both. Commenters are routinely attacked as the paid poodles of politicians or the champions of ethno-religious causes. Often, the only "objective" and "balanced" opinions are those that reinforce and give comfort to the commenters' prejudices and biases. Although there are the occasional sane, measured, and thoughtful comments on articles and news stories, they are usually, for the most part, drowned out by a cacophony of rank bigotry. Every issue is gazed at through the prism of Nigeria's primordial fault lines, which unfortunately have been actively promoted, and even sanctified, by the country's ruling elite since Nigeria's founding. Calls for the dissolution of the country or for the excision of certain parts of the country from the union, or the stereotypical belittling of whole peoples and cultures, almost always accompany any Nigerian online discussion. In short, the quality of online discourse is often so terrifyingly crude, so rhetorically violent, so destitute in basic conversational decorum that one would think one was in a godforsaken cyber jungle where wild, blood-thirsty animals are tearing each other apart with maniacal glee. If Archon Fung and Erik Olin Wright are right that the structural core of deliberative democracy consists in "facilitating active political involvement of the citizenry, forging political consensus through dialogue, devising and implementing public policies that ground a productive economy and healthy society, and, in more radical egalitarian versions of the democratic ideal, ensuring that all citizens benefit from the nation's wealth,"[52] one might argue that deliberative democracy is yet to take root in cyber Nigeria.

It is also tempting to conclude that the hate and bile that online comments exude in the comment sections of Nigeria's online newspapers and on social media platforms where Nigerians congregate are a repudiation of the fascinating ethnic and religious tapestry that is Nigeria. However, this may be an inaccurate assessment for a number of reasons. First, there is something about anonymity that just brings out what Bill Reader calls "unfiltered honesty from people."[53] Carolyn E. Nielsen argues that the "reduced social cues model" imbues online commenters with "a sense of equalized participation and status because their identities were concealed, protecting them from social judgments based [on] gender, age, race, class, etc."[54] People write mean-spirited and unmentionably vile things about other people that they cannot say about them or to them if they were to meet physically. Anonymity frees people from the burdens of responsibility, accountability, and restraint.

This fact, to be fair, is true of most anonymous online discourses; it is not exclusive to Nigeria, although a certain class of Nigerians would seem to be patenting hate and irresponsibility in online comments, the kind that John Suler calls "toxic disinhibition."[55] It can be therapeutic but also dissociative. As Suller puts it, "The online self becomes a compartmentalized self. In the case of expressed hostilities or other deviant actions, the person can avert responsibility for those behaviors, almost as if superego restrictions and moral cognitive processes have been temporarily suspended from the online psyche. In fact, people might even convince themselves that those online behaviors 'aren't me at all.'"[56] Second, for most of its life as a nation, Nigeria has been ruled by totalitarian military governments whose major characteristic have been the cruel, ironclad strangulation of dissent and honest national conversation. The brief periods of civilian administrations have not been qualitatively different from the totalitarian military regimes they succeeded, with the possible exception of the Second Republic from 1979 to 1983 (see chapters 3 and 6). Moreover, Nigeria's national media formation is, for the most part, corrupt, compromised, closed, and obsessed with the petty squabbles of the ruling elite. This has ensured that Nigerians have not had avenues to give expression to the pent-up anger, angst, and anxieties that have built up in their systems over the years. The Internet is now providing the platform for them to ventilate their suppressed frustrations. Perhaps, after a while, the undisguised rawness and vulgarity that characterize online comments on popular Nigerian online discussion forums may wane, and rational, reasoned conversations and logical disputations will take place. As Marcin Lewinski found out, although discussions in online forums tend to be characterized by coarseness, conversational incivility, ad hominem arguments, unprovoked insults, and diversionary irrelevancies, they still have deliberative utility.[57]

Third, it appears that the poor and low taste of the comments in Nigerian online platforms is a reflection of the low quality of the minds of the people who participate in them. If mastery of basic English grammar is a reliable measure of educational attainment (it not always is), then most of the commenters sound barely educated; they come across as ignorant, angry, ill-mannered little terrors. It appears that mature, well-educated Nigerians have withdrawn from participating in online forums and just watch in amusement and bemusement from the sidelines. As Misty Bastian's study of early Nigerian Internet discussion forums[58] and the analysis of the deliberative practices in the Nigerian Village Square in chapter 4 show, this was not always the case. The breathtakingly staggering ignorance and viciousness that now pass for discussion on Nigerian online discussion boards are relatively recent. Many newspapers have shut down their online comments; others require registration with real names and email addresses before commenting, which discourages a substantial number of potential commenters. Several writers and journalists have also chosen to ignore online comments on their news reports and commentaries, which is a loss because there are the occasional insightful comments, contestations, additions, suggestions, and so on, from a few thoughtful readers. But most have said the benefit of freedom from the torment of reading hate-filled, scorn-worthy, malicious ignorance trumps the occasional intelligent comment.

Several people, particularly those in government and government apologists, have seized on the indecorous quality of online comments to advocate the muzzling of online speech. The Nigerian government deploys the nebulous Cyber Crime Act (see chapter 6) to censor and silence critical voices. A 2015 bill that would have fined Nigerians up to $25,000 or seven years in prison for writing "abusive statements" on the Internet or posting "anti-government messages on platforms such as Twitter and Facebook" was dropped after massive social media protests.[59] The Nigerian Senate said the bill was unnecessary because it was a "duplication of other existing laws and [is] counter-productive."[60] But in March 2018 a senator again introduced a "hate speech bill" that would have imposed the death penalty on any Nigerian "who uses, publishes, presents, produces, plays, provides, distributes and/or directs the performance of any material, written and/or visual, which is threatening, abusive or insulting or involves the use of threatening, abusive or insulting words or behavior," particularly against ethnic and religious groups.[61] Governments in Uganda, Tanzania, and Zambia also curtail free speech on the Internet, particularly on social media, through an obnoxious "social media tax."[62] The egregiousness and bad taste of online speech is no justification for a clampdown on free speech. Plain, unvarnished censorship or the suffocation of the discursive space through social media taxation are not only counterproductive but form what Shannon Sindorf calls "symbolic violence."[63]

Although discussions on online forums routinely get animated, cause passions to be inflamed, and push conversational civilities to the back seat, there is no justification to constrict the deliberative space because of this. Kaigo and Watanabe have found that online forums, in spite of their proneness to vulgarity, irreverence, and rhetorical violence, can self-regulate through robust counterarguments and social ostracism of vile and untoward posts, which ensures that "the user community functioned pro-socially in an uncontrolled, anonymous Internet forum."[64] In addition, as scholars of online sociality know, the invisibility, asynchronicity, dissociative anonymity, deindividuation, disinhibition, and pseudonymic cover that online interaction enables can cause otherwise rational and polite people to throw off their inhibitions. Communicative and procedural rationality in discourse, of the kind Habermas theorized (see chapter 3), is problematic in online discursive arenas. Although there is wisdom in civility and restraint in online and offline discursive engagements, the reification of "rational-critical" debate (as Habermas calls it) and the vilification of expressive spontaneity as the sole basis for dialogic engagements is misplaced. Bakhtin is right that, contrary to Habermas's deadpan, ossified valorization of "formal unities" in the discursive enterprise, divorced from the lived experiences of people, it is inevitable that we will sometimes inscribe our personal signatures and "emotional-volitional" tones in our everyday dialogic encounters.[65] In discursive terms, Ken Hirshkop says, this translates to "a different style of discourse, in which the narrative of our social history emerges out of the various languages we use rather than serving as their mute, but all-powerful background."[66] As Michael Gardener points out, the Habermasian conception of the public sphere, with its undue emphasis on civility and agreeableness, is disaffiliated from the quotidian, experiential realities of real, living human beings. It is long on normatively prescribed discursive templates and short on engagement with the actual, extant, material discursive practices of contemporary society.[67] Conversational cordiality is not the most important driver of discursive democracy and is, in fact, structurally biased against subordinate social classes in society. As Toby Miller and George Yudice remind us, "Social harmony is bought at the expense of those whose tastes are not only aesthetically unacceptable but, more importantly, potentially contestatory."[68]

But more than anything, the Miltonian market place of ideas, where truth and falsehood compete, is relevant here. In his *Areopagitica*, John Milton says the "truth" needs no protection from self-appointed moral custodians. We inflict injury on truth, he said, by doubting its capacity to rise superior to falsehood. "Let her and Falsehood grapple; who ever knew Truth put to the worse, in a free and open encounter," he wrote.[69] This is one of the philosophical foundations of Wikipedia, the most thoroughgoing, consistently user-generated, mass-intelligence-driven system on the Internet. It repudiates elite-centered censorship and gatekeeping, and allows the "truth" to emerge through the unremitting push and pull of contending discursive forces. Nigerians can learn a lesson from the success of free, uninhibited discursive arenas on the Internet.

Chapter Eight

Mainstreaming of Diasporic Citizen Journalism and Implications for Nigerian Journalism

This chapter distills and coalesces the data presented in the preceding chapters of this book. It draws conclusions about the future of online journalism and discursive democracy and makes recommendations for future research based on the ruminative and perspectival synthesis of the data in previous chapters.

The emergence, popularity, and progressively soaring impact of the Nigerian diasporic citizen media examined in the previous chapters were actuated and propelled by six underlying factors. The first was the death or dearth of a critical press tradition in Nigeria—especially the adversarial guerrilla press tradition that reigned in the 1990s—in the face of the profound moral putrescence that the restoration of democratic rule has paradoxically inculcated since 1999. At a time when billions of dollars were brazenly stolen and salted away in foreign bank accounts by political officeholders and when bald-faced cronyism and avarice had overtaken the public sphere, the national media, for the most part, either looked the other way or were actively complicit. This state of affairs was inconsistent with the progressive, agitational, and inquiring disposition that had defined the character, disposition, and performance of much of the Nigerian press since its founding in the mid-1800s. As was shown in chapter 2, the Nigerian press has historically been vigorously critical of the powers that be. It almost single-handedly dislodged colonialism and helped fight against military dictatorship. The guerrilla press of the 1990s especially had a powerful impact on the media practice and politics of Nigeria. One of its enduring legacies is that it has predisposed Nigerians to expect their press to be robustly fearless, critical, and uncompromisingly adversarial. Nevertheless, after winning the fight against military dictatorship, much of the national press lost its critical bite; the press appeared to have been anesthetized into a false sense of triumphalism at a time when corruption by the emergent political elite it helped to bring to the forefront took newer, more insidious forms. In many cases, the traditional Nigerian press was co-opted into the mindless looting of the national treasury that has attended the restoration of democracy, as the case studies in chapters 4 and 5 illustrate. Top editors and reporters of influential newspapers and magazines are now "political consultants" to corrupt politicians and dodgy businesses. They censor unfavorable stories about their "clients" and punish idealistic reporters and editors who still innocently cherish the virtues of good old investigative journalism. This widespread assault on basic journalistic norms has given birth to drab, pliant, colorless, and boringly predictable national media.

The absence of watchdog media, therefore, has created a yawning void that many of the diasporic citizen media filled. Although not all the online diasporic citizen media were critical of the hydra-headed corruption in the homeland during the period this study was conducted, many of them exposed it in more vigorous and effective ways than the homeland media. The most popular of them, predictably, were those that fearlessly and evenhandedly called attention to acts of corruption and abuse of power in the domestic public sphere. Thus, for an extended period, it was only in the online media of the Nigerian digital diaspora—and the emergent digital-native domestic media formation it inspired, such as Premium Times, TheCable, Daily Nigerian, and the International Center for Investigative Reporting (ICIR)—that critical journalism was practiced. And this critical journalism, more often than not, also involved the uncloaking of corruption in the traditional homeland media themselves, as the case studies in chapters 4 and 5 demonstrate. For instance, the diasporic media divulged the sordid dalliance between top editors and editorial board chairmen of major Nigerian newspapers and corrupt governors of states and thereby brought to the forefront of public awareness the depth of the compromised nature of news reports and analyses in the national press.

The complicity of the homeland traditional media formation in sky-high venality, which had been known to the discerning reading public for a long time, eroded the credibility of the domestic media. An indication of Nigerians' loss of confidence in the local media, even before the emergence of the diasporic online media, was evident in the fact that such global news media outlets as CNN, BBC, and the Voice of America had outcompeted the domestic media as sources of credible news. As Ayo Olukotun notes, Western international news media have for long dictated and influenced the editorial direction of the Nigerian news media.[1] With the rise in the credibility and reputational capital of the Nigerian diasporic online media, however, the influence of the global news media in Nigeria has receded considerably. Similarly, with the rise, acceptance, and popularity of diasporic media outlets, government-owned media that had wrestled with credibility problems right from their very founding may be forced out of existence in the foreseeable future. A Nigerian researcher who investigated the impact of the diasporic citizen media on government-owned media concluded that "more people are increasingly relying on citizen media for news, information and entertainment than [on] government-owned media. This gives a negative signal about the survival of government-owned media."[2]

The second reason for the ascendance in the popularity and acceptance of Nigerian diasporic citizen online journalism was the backward state of the web presence of the traditional homeland news media. Until fairly recently, most of Nigeria's traditional newspapers lacked basic multimedia and hypertextual capabilities and were therefore incapable of telling twenty-first-century stories, which are increasingly not only video- and audio-based but also "networked" and interactive.[3] For instance, the story about a northern Nigerian "Sharia" governor who furtively danced with prostitutes at a nightclub outside Nigeria while harshly punishing similar activities in the state he governed could only be told with a video post. Sahara Reporters told that story videographically to maximum effect. Few, if any, traditional Nigerian newspapers were technically equipped to do that. Similarly, a secret audio recording of a Nigerian state governor conspiring to rig elections for his friend using fake military personnel to intimidate voters that was published on Sahara Reporters and other diasporic citizen media sites would have lost its punch, vitality, and even credibility if it were merely transcribed and published in traditional newsprint. Since the Nigerian traditional media had neither the technical ability nor the inclination to report on such multimedia stories, several such stories passed them by and caused diasporic online news outlets and their online-only domestic counterparts to become popular for being the exclusive purveyors of such stories.

However, it was not only the capacity to report stories with multimedia and interactive corroborations that gave the diasporic media an edge; it was also their ability to report them in real time. The traditional domestic media have now caught up with their diasporic and domestic online competitors in updating their sites in real time. Nonetheless, the majority of Nigeria's homeland newspapers' websites are still no more than "shovelware" versions of their print editions. They are in the main aesthetically unappealing, unintuitive, noninteractive, and lacking in such basic technical capabilities as archiving. Although they have transcended the infancy of the evolution of online journalism that Pavlik perceptively periodized,[4] they still have not quite evolved to its last stages. For young, web-savvy Nigerians, including Nigerians in the diaspora whose privileged geographic location exposes them to cutting-edge industry trends in the media, the Nigerian traditional media became woefully inadequate. It was only natural that when alternatives or complements were introduced, they enthusiastically embraced them.

The third reason for the emergence of the diasporic online media is related to the second: the technical incompetence and lack of initiative of Nigeria's traditional print newspapers, which ensured that their websites were often stagnant, lifeless, and slow to respond to breaking news. In fact, until 2016, Nigerian newspapers never updated their websites, even if a politically consequential news event occurred. Before the profusion of web-based diasporic citizen news media, news-hungry Nigerians always had to wait until the following day to get updates on evolving news events. Evidence that the citizen media chosen for this study are partly popular because of their capacity to update news stories in real time can be seen in the number of times the previously wildly popular Sahara Reporters crashed due to the massive traffic it received in moments of breaking news and national uncertainty. For instance, in early 2010 when Nigeria was enveloped in a cloud of political uncertainty as a result of the sickness of the late President Umaru Yar'Adua, Nigerians in their millions turned to Sahara Reporters for updates. On the day the late president was flown back to Nigeria in the dead of the night from Saudi Arabia, where he had been receiving treatment, to avoid having to hand over power to his deputy, no traditional Nigerian newspapers had the story on their site. It was Sahara Reporters that broke the story; because millions of people logged on to it simultaneously for updates, the site crashed.

In this age of dizzyingly fast-paced informational flows across the bounds of time and space, it was hardly surprising that Nigerians increasingly turned to news media that could give them the news as it occurred, even if the sources of the news were located thousands of miles away from the physical scene of events that they covered. For the traditional media in Nigeria to reclaim their authority and readership, they need not only to catch up with the digital-native media in reporting news in real time and with rich, multimedia complements but also to outrival them in these emergent multiplatform news-delivery mechanisms. Although there is ample evidence to suggest that this is changing, most traditional journalists in Nigeria are technophobic, disaffiliated from contemporary technological advances in the media world.[5] The newspaper organizations they work for are themselves hampered by excessive red tape of the kind that stifles creativity and imagination. But going forward, the very survival of the traditional media in Nigeria will depend almost entirely on how they navigate and come to terms with the reality of the new demands of real-time, multiplatform, networked news delivery, especially with Internet service increasing in Nigeria and other parts of the developing world through mobile phones,[6] all the more because news-thirsty diasporic Nigerians, who number in their millions, have easy access to the Internet.

Another factor that has contributed to the vigor and attractiveness of the Nigerian diasporic citizen media is the comparative richness and reliability of their sources of information, made possible by the willingness of privileged but disgruntled or conscientious Nigeria-based sources to confide in these citizen reporters. The diasporic citizen media built its credibility by publishing seemingly improbable stories about corruption and influence peddling in high places in Nigeria that readers either initially doubted or scoffed at but which turned out to be mostly true, as the case studies in chapters 4 and 5 show. In many cases, otherwise improbable stories are accompanied by vividly telling pictorial and documentary corroborations. Perhaps the biggest gain in the credibility of the online diasporic news media happened in December 2010, when cables released by the whistleblowing, secret-spouting WikiLeaks confirmed most of the stories that the diasporic online media had published. Sahara Reporters, for instance, ran a series of articles comparing its previous stories about corruption in the Nigerian presidency with new revelations that came out in WikiLeaks cables. Nevertheless, starting in 2018, Sahara Reporters appears to have lost this advantage after its owner and editor in chief, Omoyele Sowore, decided to run for president, leaving the site to be no more than a predictable chronicle of quotidian, run-of-the-mill political events in Nigeria, which are mostly pro-regime propaganda. Interestingly, the void Sahara Reporter's mainstreaming has created is being filled by such home-based digital-native publications as the International

Center for Investigative Reporting (ICIR), which has yet to gain traction in the Nigerian public sphere.

The geographical distance of the practitioners of diaspora citizen online journalism conferred many advantages on them. First, it assured would-be whistleblowers in Nigeria that their identities would be concealed and protected, since U.S.-based citizen reporters were unlikely to be under pressure to reveal their sources to Nigerian authorities. Nigerian traditional journalists, on the other hand, cannot give such guarantees even if they wanted to practice adversarial journalism, because they have to contend with the ever-present reality of libel and sedition laws. They can also be subpoenaed by the courts to reveal their sources.[7] Although at least three diasporic citizen journalists were arrested and detained when they traveled to Nigeria in 2008, 2009, and 2018 (see chapter 6), there was no indication that they revealed their sources, even though they were all charged with "sedition." They were ultimately released after international pressure was brought to bear on the Nigerian government.

The geographic distance of the diasporic citizen journalists also gave them the advantage of access to a wealth of information about Nigerian political elites who have huge investments in the West, especially in the United States and in the United Kingdom. Citizen journalists took advantage of the US Freedom of Information Act to ferret out embarrassing information about the shady foreign investments and indulgences of corrupt Nigerian politicians and public figures. John Campbell, a former American ambassador to Nigeria, disclosed that as a result of the intense scrutiny they have been subjected to by Western governments, aided in part by the work of certain Nigerian diasporic citizen media, corrupt Nigerian politicians were forced to move their ill-gotten wealth to China and the Middle East.[8] This was certainly a momentous setback in the efforts by critical sections of the Nigerian diasporic citizen media to fight corruption, but it nonetheless underscored the power and influence of a hitherto marginal media formation.

But, best of all, all attempts by Nigerian government officials to sue the critical sections of the Nigerian diasporic citizen media in the United States were unsuccessful: first, because it is almost impossible for governments to win libel cases against the media in the United States; and second, because the Nigerian government officials who have sued these diasporic media often have their cases dismissed for jurisdictional incompetence. Additionally, many international media-rights nongovernmental organizations (NGOs) often provided free legal defense to the diasporic citizen media practitioners who were sued by Nigerian government officials in US courts. Ultimately, the citizen media had nothing to lose for their adversarial journalistic practices as long as they confined their presence to the United States. Sahara Reporters was successfully sued—and its money frozen by a court order—in Nigeria because it chose to invest in Nigeria. When you take into account the fact that entry into citizen journalism is cheap and easy, it is not difficult to figure out why diasporic citizen media flourished. As Davis Merritt observes, a primary reason for the unstoppable growth of citizen journalism worldwide is that "it has the ability to operate from multiple platforms at minimal fiscal cost to either the creator or the consumer, unlike the revenue-driven models of traditional journalism institutions."[9] It is precisely this fact, more than any other factor, that would make it difficult for the traditional media in Nigeria to stop the rising profile of Nigeria-focused citizen journalism and, with it, the inevitable weakening of the homeland legacy media.

It is evident that the popularity of diasporic online citizen media took the Nigerian professional journalistic fraternity by surprise. As chapter 4 illustrates, the participation of diasporic Nigerians in online discussions about news in the homeland initially took place in the few online forums provided by traditional newspaper organizations that had a web presence. By the mid-2000s, however, that reality changed. The people formerly known as the diasporic Nigerian audience of domestic Nigerian newspaper content, to paraphrase Jay Rosen, decided to practice what J. D. Lasica famously called "random acts of journalism."[10] They were initially ignored, their emergence dismissed as a flash in the pan, and their journalism thought to be too amateurish to have staying power. However, when the diasporic citizen media sites began to break stories and write about issues that were beyond the reach of the domestic media and began to attract the attention of people who mattered in the Nigerian society and beyond, the traditional media redefined their attitude toward the emerging diasporic media formation from insouciance or indifference to a cautious embrace. They initially found the newborn diasporic citizen media to be useful sources of information, especially for stories about Nigeria that originated in the United States. However, the cautious embrace changed to cold hostility when the online citizen media began to compete with the local newspapers for local Nigerian stories. Because Nigeria's traditional journalists had assumed that many Nigerians at home had no access to the Internet, they had imagined that most of their readers would not have access to the diasporic citizen media. So they often lifted and republished, in many cases without the time-honored journalistic courtesy of attribution, agreeable stories, such as those that furthered the political aspirations of their sponsors and political allies. In time, Nigeria's professional journalists realized that many ordinary Nigerians increasingly had access to the Internet and could often spot—and did, in fact, point out in online comments—stories that had been lifted directly from diasporic citizen media sites. This created a crisis of credibility for the homeland industrial news media, a crisis that was exacerbated when the diasporic citizen media reported the squalid sleaze that now characterizes traditional, legacy media practice. Then the relationship turned to ambivalence.

As of 2018, the traditional media in Nigeria have come to terms with the reality that the diasporic citizen media are not the temporary success they had envisioned or hoped they would be. These geographically displaced, amateur citizen media now drive national conversations. Their exclusive stories, which have on many occasions forced governments and politicians to react through the national media, are now the grist in the editorial mills of many Nigerian newspapers. To cite just one addition to the case studies in chapters 4 and 5, in late November 2010, Sahara Reporters broke the story of an embarrassing presidential corruption scandal that became the subject of intense front-page newspaper coverage, editorial commentaries, denials, and affirmations in the Nigerian domestic public sphere for more than two weeks. The Nigerian president at the time, who was seeking to extend his tenure for another four years, invited members of the Save Nigeria Group, a prominent civil society organization and NGO, to a clandestine meeting. After the meeting, he bribed them with $50,000 in cash—in US dollars. The president of the NGO, Tunde Bakare, who also is a church minister, declined the bribe and returned it to the president through one of his close aides. Sahara Reporters broke the story of the details of the meetings and the exchange of the bribe a few minutes after the event happened, which was past midnight.

The following day, the presidential aide to whom the money was returned for onward delivery back to the president issued a tepid, mealy-mouthed denial of the story, but the church minister confirmed it to Sahara Reporters the same day, saying only that what the president had offered them was not a bribe but "transport money." Other members of the NGO who attended the meeting with the president confirmed Sahara Reporters' story in its entirety as well. The back-and-forth exchanges between members of the NGO—who swore that they did not leak the story to Sahara Reporters—and government spin doctors dominated the news cycle for days on end. Curiously, however, almost all the Nigerian newspapers never referred to Sahara Reporters by name; it was often identified as "an online news site," an "online news agency" or sometimes an "offshore news agency." And this was not an exception. Until the early 2010s, when the traditional news media lifted stories from or made reference to the diasporic citizen media, they never identified them by name, lest it would appear they helped make these competitors more popular and more formidable than they already were. This illustrated the increasing agenda-setting powers of the diasporic online media and the professional anxieties of the traditional media about this reality. This professional anxiety was reflected in the labels homeland journalists deployed to identify the diasporic citizen media. By refusing to identify them by name, the homeland journalists sought to denude them of professional legitimacy and visibility before the Nigerian domestic reading public. This was the subject of a comment by the Nigerian columnist Sonala Olumhense, who railed against Nigeria's *Guardian* for choosing the WikiLeaks founder Julia Assange as its 2010 Man of the Year while ignoring Sahara Reporter's Omoyele Sowore, who had leaked stories about graft in Nigeria that WikiLeaks confirmed months after and whose website predated Assange's by one year. Olumhense concluded: "If whistleblowing and unearthing official secrets that are of great importance to a nation is the subject, nobody has done that with greater dedication in the Information Age than SaharaReporters. Somehow, however, in the past five or six years *The Guardian*—unlike several other Nigerian newspapers—does not seem to have noticed SaharaReporters, despite the impact it has made on the nation."[11]

Although the writer mentioned only the Guardian as the legacy newspaper that ignored Sahara Reporter, the fact was that those who acknowledged it—and other diasporic citizen media—did so with hypocritical contempt. They monitored the media fervently, got stories and story ideas from them, but often failed to give them credit. Wherever they grudgingly gave them credit, they sought to undermine them, nonetheless, by referring to them with unflattering descriptive markers. In spite of the thinly veiled hostility toward the diasporic citizen media, however, an evaluation of the Facebook fans and Twitter followers of the major diasporic online media outlets showed that almost all Nigerian journalists were fans and followers of especially Sahara Reporters.[12] Interestingly, the diasporic citizen media were unfazed by the professional snub by the homeland newspapers. They took solace in the fact that the traditional homeland media had declined as the dominant force in the public sphere.

By 2018, the cold hostility of the domestic media toward the citizen news media of the Nigerian digital diaspora had thawed, for obvious reasons. The diasporic news media have now assumed the role of agenda setters for the Nigerian national media and have inspired successful copycats in the homeland. There is an interesting parallel between this development and what Ben Syre and his colleagues found in the relationship between the traditional American media and their new social media competitors over the coverage of California's Proposition 8.[13] They found that the "traditional media system may be losing some of its agenda-setting ability to emerging social media."[14] Thus, the emergence of web-based citizen journalistic forms is adding new dimensions to what has been called the agenda-setting function of the media in mass-communication research.[15] This increasingly seems to be the case in Nigeria as the diasporic media are mainstreamed into the domestic public sphere. This fact contradicts research cited in chapter 1, which concluded that rather than challenging the dominance of mainstream news media, the plethora of citizen media that the Internet has spawned does no more than strengthen the mainstream media's dominance by further circulating, if not amplifying, their discourses. The researchers who arrived at these conclusions, therefore, characterize citizen media as having "derivative"[16] and "parasitic"[17] relationships with the mainstream news media and conclude that online citizen media, therefore, are more the "online echo chamber of mass-mediated political views"[18] than "alternative spheres of news and views."[19] Contrary to the conclusions of this research, Nigerian diaspora citizen media are not only alternative spheres for the dissemination of news and views in their own right but also influence what the domestic mainstream media write about and report on, although they can also, on occasion, be online echo chambers of the discourses of the domestic, traditional media. The available evidence at the moment suggests that citizen media will continue to coexist with the traditional media and be engaged in an as-yet indeterminate push and pull of influence in the foreseeable future.

Significantly, the old model of doing journalism in Nigeria—and elsewhere—is being actively challenged, and the overwhelming power and cultural capital that the traditional media enjoyed for many years are diminishing. Hierarchical, centralized, traditional structures for news production and distribution are now being confronted by a networked, heterarchical structure typified by the robust proliferation of many-to-many information flows and amateur but technically efficient and occasionally radical citizen news sites. The traditional media in Nigeria are responding to these changes in different ways, but the majority of them have now been compelled to appreciate the importance of interactivity and reader involvement in news gathering. When the gathering of data for this study began in 2008, only two major Nigerian newspapers, *Leadership* and the *Daily Trust*, allowed reader comments on their stories. But by late 2018, many traditional newspapers not only allow reader comments but also have inaugurated participatory, "crowdsourcing" platforms on their sites.[20] For instance, the *Vanguard* came up with the Vanguard Online Community in late 2010. This platform allows users to upload pictures and videos, share news stories, post blogs, and play online games. The *Daily Trust* also created an "iReport" page that allowed readers to post unreported or underreported stories in their communities. It is conceivable that more Nigerian newspaper websites will incorporate participatory elements to their sites—that is, if they can overcome their technophobia. What appears to be slowing down this process is the fact that advertisers, the live wires of institutional media organizations, still patronize the traditional media and have yet to robustly migrate online in the same way that advertisers in the West have done.[21]

The online citizen media of the Nigerian diasporan became politically consequential precisely because they ruffled the composure of governments in the homeland. As we saw in chapters 4 and 5, the Nigerian diasporic online media caused an incumbent vice president to publicly declare his assets after initially declining to do so. They also caused the country's president to rescind a government directive denying consular services to some self-exiled opposition figures after the story that they were denied the privilege of passport renewal was leaked and published by the diasporic online media. And the publication of the pictures of the president's son bathing in loads of cash, including the leak of several troves of top-secret information, compelled the president to demand that all workers in the Nigerian presidency swear an unprecedented oath of secrecy. But more than these, the majority of the diasporic media attracted and retained the attention of the reading public through their continued unmasking of the corruption of the ruling elite in Nigeria. From the very beginning, diasporic online news outlets, such as Elendu Reports and Sahara Reporters, took advantage of their location in the United States not only to dig up information on the corruption of the Nigerian political elite but also to publish pictures, addresses, and other details of their investments. The enormous popularity of these kinds of stories forced indicted government officials to react through the local press.

This development had two effects. First, it helped popularize the diasporic media in the domestic public sphere. People who did not have a chance to read the original stories—or who were not aware that the diasporic news sites existed—looked out for them. Through recommendations and word of mouth, their popularity grew exponentially. Second, although suspicion that the new political elites spawned by the restoration of constitutional rule were thoroughly corrupt had always been part of the national psyche, there had not been any evidentiary proofs confirming these suspicions. To make matters worse, much of the local media had been either unwilling or unable to investigate allegations of corruption against politicians. Therefore, the rash of evidence-based citizen news reports in the diasporic media about transnational elite corruption in Nigeria became an instant hit. In a country where cynicism about public officials has justifiably become a national culture, the forceful denials by politicians and government officials of reports of corruption against them only confirmed the truth of the reports. Here, Claude Cockburn's perceptive, if ironic, quip that we should "never believe anything until it is officially denied" is particularly applicable.[22] The fact that government officials were concerned about stories of corruption against them to the point of issuing forceful, impassioned rebuttals in the local press conferred credibility on the purveyors of the stories. However, ignoring the stories, which were increasingly being read and shared by many people, would not have been wise either; silence could be interpreted as admission of guilt. In a way, because of the perception that they are sunk deep in corruption, the Nigerian political elite are mired in a catch-22, which made the diasporic online news media all the more popular. Premium Times, a domestic online newspaper, took off where Sahara Reporters stopped. It participated in many cross-border investigative journalistic initiatives to unmask the transnational corruption of Nigeria's political elites, the most prominent being its 2016 collaboration with the International Consortium of Investigative Journalists to report on the Panama papers, for which it won a joint Pulitzer Prize.

Another reason that the diasporic online media had the capacity to cause governments at home to change state policies in response to their sustained reportage on issues was the fact that they often inspired the formation of episodic, informal, but nonetheless cohesive activist online diasporic communities that organized to effect change back home based on stories published in the diasporic media. Online petition drives based on stories published on diasporic citizen media sites, the sending of delegations of diasporic Nigerians to appeal to governments in Nigeria to change certain decisions, and generating publicity for all these were common occurrences, as detailed in chapter 4. This fact conforms to the broad outlines of alternative media, which scholars characterize as consisting of "mobilizing information,"[23] "information for action,"[24] "action on action,"[25] or simply "useful information."[26] In other words, unlike the mainstream news media, alternative media go beyond publishing ostensibly disinterested information; they invite readers to take action based on the information they provide in their reportage. They encourage readers to initiate online petition drives or to be part of an offline, on-the-ground protest in order to cause governments to change unpopular policies or practices. The Nigerian Village Square and Sahara Reporters (which indicatively had a section called "Take Action") are the best examples of Nigerian diasporic citizen media sites that effectively put this principle into practice.

Concerns about being exposed to international ridicule, especially in the eyes of Western governments, is another reason the diasporic media were able to influence governments in Nigeria. Many of the diasporic media, as stated in previous chapters, have acquired international clout. Sahara Reporters, for instance, has been profiled and referred to by such powerful Western news organizations as the Associated Press, CNN, BBC, MSNBC, and so on. This publicity caused the site to be noticed by the US government and by donor agencies such as the Ford Foundation, Omidyar Network, and the MacArthur Foundation, which wholly funded it until 2018. More important, though, the relationship between the US government and Sahara Reporters appeared to go beyond financial assistance; the site broke many stories and leaked state secrets that embarrassed the Nigerian government, which all seemed to have emanated from US government sources. It has also quoted anonymous State Department sources for many sensitive stories that turned out to be accurate. Clearly, certain people in the State Department in possession of sensitive information against the Nigerian government leaked it to Sahara Reporters. The WikiLeaks cables about Nigeria have confirmed this. It is supremely ironic that the US government was miffed when WikiLeaks did to it what its employees do to another government in a developing country.

Since Nigerian governments have historically worked to win the approval of the US government, they are often sensitive to stories that put them in a bad light.[27] It also seems likely that Nigerian government officials interpreted leaks to Sahara Reporters from the State Department as coded diplomatic messages to them from the US government. More specifically, the diasporic citizen media often took advantage of the reality of the "boomerang effect" discussed in chapter 5 to push for changes in the homeland. The "boomerang effect" accounts for how advocacy networks, in this case diasporic citizen media, deploy the power of information to shame recalcitrant and dictatorial regimes. In their influential book *Activists Beyond Borders*, Margaret Keck and Kathryn Sikkink point out that "voices that are suppressed in their own societies may find that networks can project and amplify their concerns into an international arena, which in turn can echo back into their own countries."[28] In the Nigerian case, because of a domestic media formation that has become compromised and therefore unable to expose corruption as it should, online citizen media sprouted in the Nigerian diaspora and helped bring to light homeland corruption to both domestic and international audiences. It is entirely conceivable that had the diasporic citizen media been viewed only in Nigeria, their effect would not have been as great as it was. What appears to make them forces to be reckoned with was the fact that they were inserted in the discourse and politics of an activist international arena, which gave their stories significance and visibility beyond the bounds of Nigeria. Fear of "international embarrassment," as we saw in chapter 5 in the case of two self-exiled opposition politicians who were initially denied consular services on the orders of the president, is a powerful incentive for policy change in Nigeria. And there is no better structure to bring this about in the Nigerian situation than citizen media outlets managed by Nigerians outside the borders of Nigeria.

Traditionally, the scholarship on diaspora media studies has focused on three areas: how diasporans set up niche news media to construct and negotiate their identities and to come to terms with their new culture and environment; how the mainline media in the host countries construct exilic ethnoscapes in dominant media narratives; and how diasporans keep up with the politics, culture, and other singularities of their homelands through the consumption of their homeland news media.[29] Indeed, until 2005, the Nigerian diaspora in the West, as Misty Bastian's insightful work shows, had media that exclusively catered to their informational needs, and they looked elsewhere for news to quench their nostalgia for the homeland.[30] When Nigerian newspapers began to migrate their content to the web in the early 2000s, diasporic Nigerians flocked to their sites to read up on news about the homeland and to discuss common topics of concern. This was a radical improvement on the previous state of affairs, when expatriate Nigerians waited for the occasional newspapers from the homeland from people who traveled home or from the few Nigerian newspapers that sold print copies of their papers in such Western cities as New York and London.[31]

But beginning in the mid-2000s, all that changed. Diasporic Nigerians ceased to be mere consumers of news from the homeland; they also became producers of news and have now graduated to being editorial agenda setters for the mainline news media in the homeland. The hitherto unidirectional flow of news from the homeland to the diaspora has now given way to a new flow that is not only bidirectional but is, in fact, circuitous. News from homeland news media seep out to the diaspora through the web faster than was ever the case, but news about the homeland that has never been reported in the homeland also gets back to the domestic news media—and, ultimately, to the domestic public sphere—through the citizen media of the diaspora. In an interesting way, both media formations have become echo chambers of each other. The relational dynamics between diasporic citizen media and the established vehicles of informational flows in the homeland moved from cooperation to competition and then to thinly veiled confrontation and finally to acceptance and mutual respect. The diasporic citizen media were first regarded as additional sources of news for the homeland traditional media. As long as they were not perceived as threatening the authority and credibility of the homeland news media, Nigeria-based journalists accepted them, if halfheartedly. However, when it became obvious that they were assuming a position of centrality in the news dissemination enterprise, the homeland news media saw them as rivals, and the online citizen media themselves began to act in ways that suggested that they saw themselves as competitors of the homeland news media for the eyeballs of Nigerian readers. This fact inspired the traditional journalists in Nigeria to begin an artful patrol of the boundaries of journalistic authority. One of the ways they attempted to do this, as was hinted at earlier, was to denude citizen media practitioners of the social capital that comes with being identified as journalists or with being regarded as legitimate news sources. Stories culled from or inspired by the citizen news media of the diaspora, as pointed out before, were either never acknowledged outright or were attributed with pejorative identification labels such as "offshore guerrilla news agency" or simply "an Internet site"; they ceased to be mentioned by name. This got worse when some of the diasporic citizen media started to expose corruption in the domestic media, which had the effect of making homeland reporters lose their grip on their much-cherished journalistic authority and credibility.

The Nigerian-based journalists were being beaten at their own game by people who have neither formal journalistic training nor elaborate institutional support, and who lack the locational advantage that living in the homeland should confer on newshounds. However, the relational tension between Nigeria's traditional journalists and the US-based Nigerian citizen journalists fits a pattern that has been observed in many other contexts. Many journalism scholars have pointed out that professional journalists in the mainstream media perpetually seek to consolidate their professional legitimacy and power by appealing to their authority and by denigrating alternative sources that question their news judgment or undermine their professional confidence.[32] More specifically, Barbie Zelizer argues that journalists often tend to deploy three kinds of narrative strategies to assert their authority. She identifies them as synecdoche, omission, and personalization.[33] In the Nigerian case, journalists not only subtly invoked their professionalism as a strategy to assert their authority and undermine the diasporic citizen media but also called attention to their locational advantage by labeling the diasporic media "offshore" news sources and eliding them as mere "online sources." In a different article, Zelizer observed a similar phenomenon in American journalism, where "reporters use the authority culled from their local placement within the event to expound on its more general significance."[34] Here, she is talking about the privilege and capital that "eyewitnessing," "being there," "being on the spot," and such other signifiers of positional vantage confer on journalists in contradistinction to nonjournalists, who might have legitimate grounds to question the narrative fidelity of journalistic accounts but who would potentially be undermined by an absence of this privilege. Nigeria's traditional journalists, it would seem, discursively constitute their actual physical presence in Nigeria, as against the virtual "presence" of the diasporic citizen media, as a form of cultural capital to preserve their authority and competence. However, the growing importance and centrality of the diasporic media in the Nigerian public sphere suggests that these rhetorical strategies have not been effective.

Now, although diasporic media that exclusively report on the conditions, concerns, and anxieties of Nigerian diasporans in the West still exist, they are progressively either dying out or changing focus to report on issues that pertain to the politics of the homeland.[35] At last count, there are at least sixteen diasporic citizen media sites—all but one of which are based in the United States—with correspondents and informants in Nigeria. As noted earlier, these online diasporic citizen media break stories faster than the domestic media, leading a commentator to note, "In Nigeria, the greatest threat to traditional media seems to come from online bloggers who are more often than not based outside the country. It is interesting to note that a greater percentage of news about Nigeria is being broken by online citizen media."[36] With the proliferation of domestic online news sites and the technical improvement of homeland legacy newspapers, this is no longer entirely accurate. Nevertheless, the cartography of news flows between Nigeria and its Western diaspora has been complicated by the emergence and rising significance of diasporic online citizen media, threatening the very life of the traditional media in Nigeria. The one-dimensionality that had hitherto characterized news flows between the homeland and its diaspora has now given way to a labyrinthine multidimensionality, which in turn has profound implications for the traditional scholarly conversation about news flows between the Western core and the developing-world periphery.

As was noted earlier, the rise of diasporic online media in Nigeria has significantly dimmed the influence of Western news organizations. This presents us with a fascinating situation where indigenous ethnoscapes are now assuming the roles previously occupied by Western "media imperialists." Although Western news organizations still exert a tremendous influence in Nigeria's media landscape, their influence is being progressively diminished by the Nigerian diasporic online media. The diasporic citizen journalists have the "native credibility" that Western news sources lack, but they share in the cultural capital that being located in the West confers. This unique positional vantage has earned the diasporic citizen journalists credibility both with Western news sources seeking to find "local color" in stories they report on from their Western locations and from Nigerians at home who value them for their privileged location and uncommon access to news sources that are often unavailable to traditional journalists back home. What this means is that stories in Western news media about Nigeria that were usually uninformed or slanted because of inadequate information owing to the difficulty in getting local sources will now benefit from the input of the legion of Nigerian citizen journalists in the West. We saw that with many Nigerian stories, such as the December 25, 2009, attempted "underwear" bombing of a Delta airliner by the Nigerian Umar Farouk Abdulmutallab. All the major Western news organizations turned to the diasporic citizen media for pictures, background, and even perspectives on the story. This may very well provide a template for reversing time-honored concerns about the disproportionate flow of news from the West to the developing world. More important, this development has provided novel dimensions to the notion of contraflows, which has been theorized to point out the inadequacy of classical notions of media and cultural imperialism. The reality of the weakening of the influence of Western news organizations as a consequence of the emergence of diasporic citizen online journalism by Nigerians living in the West, and the increasing dependence by Western news organizations on these citizen media outlets for Nigeria-related stories emanating from the West, provide grounds for speculating that this may constitute the basis for an African contraflow.[37]

Although for the most part, the diasporic citizen media sites studied in this book enrich and expand Nigeria's informational space, different motivations and impulses can be isolated for their existence. Elendu Reports, for instance, started out as an uncompromising, anticorruption alternative news media site. It published pictorial proofs of the corruption by the Nigerian political elite, wrote many piercingly hard-hitting stories that discomfited government officials, brought down public officials, and caused many more to be investigated and pilloried. It was the "go-to" site for alternative news in Nigeria. The fact that the site had no advertising of any kind strengthened its progressive credentials.[38] So it seemed for a while that Elendu Reports was the ultimate insurgent, emancipatory citizen media site that had capitulated neither to capital nor to politics. But it soon emerged that the proprietor of the site, Jonathan Elendu, was in bed with the same corrupt politicians about whom his site raked muck. This discovery dented his credibility and led to the decline in the popularity and significance of his site. In retrospect, the website actually characterized itself as a "for-profit company," which nonetheless solicited donations from the public but insisted that donations to it did not entitle donors to preferential editorial treatment. What is apparent from all this is that the site was set up primarily as a commercial venture. Its initial radical and populist reportorial comportment was a mere marketing strategy to call attention to it. After the attention was secured, the proprietor turned himself into a "political consultant" to the same corrupt politicians his site railed against. It was crass, Internet-enabled journalistic mercantilism of the kind that has become prevalent in the domestic Nigerian media and that certain other diasporic sites have taken pains to unmask, as we saw in chapter 5. This reality should impose some restraint on the urge to conceive of all the diasporic citizen media as necessarily wholly distinct from their homeland counterparts. It is particularly noteworthy that Jonathan Elendu was a traditional journalist in Nigeria before migrating to the United States. But it is equally remarkable that citizen media sites that betray their readers' trust and confidence often lose credibility and patronage faster than do the homeland traditional media. This is, of course, the consequence of the amplified power and centrality of what one might call "netizen reader-participants" in the news business.[39] The practical death of Elendu Reports in the Nigerian blogosphere and in the domestic public sphere is a telling proof of this reality.

The Times of Nigeria, PointBlankNews, and Huhuonline.com are also obviously motivated by the same commercial imperatives as traditional, corporatized news media in Nigeria. Although they have published many anti-corruption stories, they also aggressively solicit advertising and have taken partisan stances in defense of certain sections of Nigeria's political and financial elites. They accept advertising from governments, corrupt politicians, and private companies in Nigeria. There is evidence from the archives of these sites that there is some reciprocal editorial acknowledgment of advertising patronage in the form of favorable coverage. For instance, corrupt governors of the oil-rich states of Nigeria's Niger Delta region who lavishly advertised on these sites were spared, for the most part, from critical scrutiny. In some cases, in fact, they were whitewashed and defended from attacks from more radical citizen media sites such as Sahara Reporters. Nevertheless, this has not hurt their credibility, first, because they did not define themselves from the beginning as muckraking, antigovernment outlets; and second, because they derive the social basis of their legitimacy and credibility from niche appeals. For instance, before its collapse, TimesofNigeria.com was the most reliable source of news about Nigeria's volatile deep south. Militants fighting for a fairer, more equitable distribution of the oil wealth in this region often reached out to this site first before any other news organization. PointBlankNews, for its part, appealed to readers who were attracted to bizarre scandals involving people in high places. But some of the site's reports are not always faithful to the facts. As we saw in chapter 4 a newspaper publisher's wife was wrongly reported to have decapitated a boy for a ritual sacrifice. Huhuonline was a "go-to" site for the unmasking of what might be called clerical corruption—that is, the scandalous financial fraud of Nigeria's mushrooming church businesses, which the domestic mainstream news media have ignored.

The sites that could reasonably be said to be animated by democratic, progressive ideals were Sahara Reporters and the Nigerian Village Square. Whereas Sahara Reporters was an unabashedly and uncompromisingly antigovernment news site, the Nigerian Village Square was a fiercely independent arena for unrestrained political discourse on Nigeria and for initiating and coordinating transformative, transaction-oriented changes in Nigeria. Both sites went beyond calling attention to what was wrong with Nigeria and actually physically did something about the problems they identified and inveighed against. An online petition drive and physical protests in Nigeria, which were initiated in the online forums of the Nigerian Village Square, led Nigeria's vice president to publicly declare his assets against his wishes. Although participants of the Nigerian Village Square were scattered all over the world and had never physically met, they often contributed money through PayPal to send delegations to Nigeria to protest government policies and to demand for change. Although Sahara Reporters always encouraged its readers to "take action" on the basis of the stories it wrote, the "actions" often took place in the Nigerian Village Square, which became a close-knit community of concerned and politically active Nigerian diasporic netizens who had cultivated mutual trust, in large part due to the leadership and organizational effectiveness of the site's founder, Philip Adekunle, an Illinois-based IT professional.

As pointed out in chapter 5, the Nigerian Village Square is not strictly a journalistic enterprise; it is a site for both citizen reporting and for news-inflected community and discursive participation. As Bill Kovach and Tom Rosenstiel have observed, since its birth in seventeenth-century Europe, the "concept of journalism" has always been wedded to the "concept of community and later democracy."[40] The Nigerian Village Square shared this preoccupation with Sahara Reporters in its first incarnation. The success of both sites showed that they provided a model for the future of journalism in transitional societies that resemble Nigeria's media and political systems, although their form and substance did devolve into stasis. By late 2018, the Nigerian Village Square had lost its luster and power to Facebook and Twitter, and Sahara Reporters was no different from a daily online newsletter from the Nigerian Ministry of Information.

Both Sahara Reporters and the Nigerian Village Square used to be sustained by online advertising from Google ads and from Nigerian businesses and politicians. Interestingly, politicians who advertised on the sites had never been able to influence the editorial and discursive directions of the sites, lending credence to the observations of some alternative media scholars that commercialism does not necessarily translate into depoliticization and compromise. But after getting its first $175,000 in funding from the Ford Foundation in 2010, Sahara Reporters discontinued accepting advertising from governments and politicians. It bears pointing out, though, that before the grant from the Ford Foundation, Sahara Reporters got the bulk of its funding from voluntary contributions by its readers. This was the case for the Nigerian Village Square as well. Both sites had a permanent "donate" button and often embarked on periodic solicitations of help from their loyal visitors when they ran into financial difficulties. By contrast, TheTimesofNigeria.com, Huhuonline, and PointBlankNews did not raise funds from their readers. By the early 2010s, these three sites started a disturbing trend of lending uncritical support to corrupt politicians seeking elective offices. But given that the people associated with these sites are, like Jonathan Elendu, former newspaper journalists in Nigeria, it would not be surprising if it comes to light that they have become paid "political consultants" to politicians.

What is evident from the foregoing is that freedom from commercial pressures and location outside corporatized, institutional media structures in and of themselves are not sufficient safeguards against editorial compromise.

Association, or lack thereof, with a higher, overarching, progressive ideal is a more reliable predictor of the performance of noncorporate, citizen media. Although Huhuoline.com, ElenduReports.com, TheTimesofNigeria.com, and PointBlankNews are located outside the orbit of mainstream media formation, they are subject to the same limitations that are denuding the traditional domestic media of their credibility. This is because their performance is not actuated by any identifiable liberatory ideal; they are mere additional, not necessarily alternative, sources of Nigerian news, a distinction that strikes at the core of the conceptual difference between alternative journalism and citizen journalism. Similarly, although Sahara Reporters and the Nigerian Village Square were subject to commercial advertising pressures in order to survive, they remained remarkably independent and were on record as offering witheringly devastating critiques of their advertisers. They reached such positions of prominence that advertisers desired them more for the eyeballs they attracted than for the politics of their news and editorial commentaries. Just as advertisers needed them for their own commercial gains, they needed the advertisers for survival. It was a relationship that was sustained by self-preservationism rather than ideological considerations.

From the foregoing, it would seem that previous association with homeland Nigerian journalism is key here. The diasporic citizen media that had difficulty rising above some of the grave limitations of Nigeria's traditional journalistic practices were those whose owners and writers were once inserted into—and who have internalized the conventions, mores, and weaknesses of—Nigeria's traditional journalistic practices. Diasporic media sites that are refreshingly different and for that reason enormously popular and influential, are run by people who were never associated with corporatized traditional journalism in Nigeria. This may be fortuitous because, as I will show shortly, Sahara Reporters is becoming indistinguishable from both the homeland legacy media and compromised diasporic citizen media sites. What is not fortuitous, however, is that it would seem the key to continued relevance in the Nigerian blogosphere and in the domestic public sphere is the capacity to be transparently different from the Nigerian traditional media formation, which is broadly held hostage by corruption, clannishness, and narrow political loyalties.

From 2005 to 2018, Sahara Reporters lived up to this expectation. As a result, its power and influence were disproportionately higher than those of other diasporic media sites. However, as I pointed out earlier, by 2018, the site stopped the sort of intrepid, adversarial journalism that had distinguished it in the Nigerian media landscape. As of 2019, the site had decidedly abandoned its editorial template of being a comforter of underdogs and a tormentor of overdogs in Nigerian political circles. Although the 2019 presidential election, in which the site's editor in chief participated as a contestant, was blatantly rigged, the site legitimized it by uncritically reproducing the propaganda of the beneficiaries of the electoral fraud. When a past president was rigged into power in 2007, the site took a decision either never to address the winner as "president" or to insert scare quotes around his title to call attention to his illegitimacy. However, in 2019, it not only uncritically accepted the results of the election, which was adjudged to be fraudulent even by international observers, it became an instrument to torment opposition candidates who challenged the results of the election. It was not certain, when this book was completed, if the site had capitulated to the temptations of government carrots as Elendu Reports had done. However, the site's relegation from Nigeria's fourth most visited news site from 2005 to 2017 to the 121st site by 2019 suggests that should it sustain its abandonment of the template that popularized it, it will suffer irrecoverable reputational diminution and go the way of other previously compromised news sites.

Citizen Journalism, Alternative Journalism, or Stand-Alone Journalism?

What journalistic conceptual frames do the diasporic citizen media studied in this book fit? Which of the diasporic online sites qualified as "alternative" media sites? Which were merely "citizen" media sites? This is important not only because the preponderance of scholarship on online journalism tends to erroneously conflate these categories but also because classifying them helps to explain their content, character, performance, and editorial temperaments. As we saw in chapter 1, the abiding characteristics of citizen media outlets are that they are run by people who are not necessarily professional journalists and who would ordinarily be classified as "audience" members in the traditional model of mass communication, people whose journalistic output is random, episodic, and unburdened by the demands of institutional journalism.

This definition concatenates the conceptions of citizen journalism separately postulated by Kristen A. Johnson and Susan Wiedenback,[41] Joseph D. Lasica,[42] Jay Rosen,[43] and Joyce Nip.[44] Jonson and Wiedenback's notion of citizen journalism as the kind of journalism that is practiced by people with no professional training, although reasonably admissible, fails to take into account the fact that many professional journalists now practice citizen journalism both within and outside the structures of traditional media formations. For instance, four of the six citizen media sites examined for this book are run by former newspaper journalists. That is why Lasica's apt description of citizen journalism as "random acts of journalism," Rosen's witty characterization of citizen journalists as "people formerly known as the audience," and Nip's insistence that the elimination of the "gatekeepers" in news flows is the central element in the definition of citizen journalism all come together to define the essential singularities of citizen media. This definitional clarification helps us to properly situate and characterize the sites that have been analyzed in this book, which were founded by a mix of people who have no professional training in journalism and those who previously were journalists in Nigeria. Jonathan Elendu, the owner of ElenduReports.com, was a journalist with the *Daily Times*, Nigeria's oldest surviving English-language newspaper. Similarly, Emmanuel Asiwe, publisher of Huhuonline.com, was a journalist with *ThisDay*, an influential if notoriously compromised daily newspaper in Nigeria. Sunny Ofili, owner of the TheTimesofNigeria.com, was a journalist with the defunct *African Guardian* newsmagazine before he relocated to the United States. And the two main founders of PointBlankNews, Jackson Ude and Churchill Umoren, were practicing journalists in Nigeria before they migrated to the United States as well.

However, Sahara Reporters' Omoyele Sowore has no previous journalistic experience. Neither has Nigerian Village Square's Philip Adekunle and the army of ordinary citizens who independently investigate news stories and publish on SaharaReporters.com and NigeriaVillageSquare.com. But all these people are regarded as citizen journalists because their journalism is not routinized and is unencumbered by the dictatorship of the multilayered editorial gatekeeping typical of institutional journalism. Axel Bruns instructively characterizes this as the transformation of journalism "from gatekeeping to gatewatching."[45] Nevertheless, the fact that these websites are becoming more or less regular sources of news from which their owners increasingly earn a living challenges us to think of more appropriate terminologies to capture their activities beyond the increasingly generic "citizen journalism" label. Sahara Reporters, for instance, has moved from the margins to the mainstream; it now publishes news stories with the same unfailing regularity and predictability as the homeland oligopolistic media formation. It seems appropriate to characterize the journalism that takes place in all the media outlets studied for this book—except the Nigerian Village Square, which is actually more of a platform for random news reports, analyses, and opinionating than a strictly news-reporting site—as "stand-alone citizen journalism." The term "stand-alone journalism" was first coined by the journalist Chris Nolan to describe citizen journalism that is fairly regular, that has a substantial reader catchment area, and that is unaffiliated with a corporate news organization. She defines a "standalone journalist" this way:

> They are people who are using blogging technology—software that allows them to quickly publish their work and broadcast it on the Internet—to find and attract users. They understand that the barrier to entry in this new business isn't getting published; anyone can do that. The barrier to entry is finding an audience. That's why their editorial product is consistent, reliable and known. Readers have expectations and stand alone journalists understand this and put that understanding into practice.[46]

According to this definition, stand-alone journalists are not random reporters for just anybody. They have a specific audience in mind and work to meet the expectations of that narrow audience. Since the diasporic online media studied in this book can no longer be described as engaging in "random acts of journalism" (their journalism is now far too regular for that description to be apt) and are not exactly "the people formerly known as the audience" (since most of them were professional journalists back in Nigeria) but are still not employed by corporate news organization, nor do they have an obligation to update their sites at regular, inviolably specific time slots as the traditional media do, they still practice citizen journalism, but it is a form of citizen journalism that defies the conventional notions of citizen media practice. It seems appropriate, therefore, to borrow Nolan's phrase and characterize this type of journalism as "stand-alone citizen journalism."

Alternative citizen media, on the other hand, are online citizen media that do not merely produce episodic, nonprofessionalized, nonroutinized journalism but that are, in addition, committed to a higher, progressive ideal of extirpating the dominant, oppressive ideology in a social formation. In the West, alternative journalism often takes an anticapitalist or at least a countercultural form. In Nigeria, however, the dominant concern of the progressive segment of the population is markedly different. There, opposition to corrupt governments—and increasingly, a close, corrupt, and compromised mainstream media formation—constitutes the core of an "alternative" praxis. In this book, therefore, I conceptualize Nigerian alternative online journalism as that type of episodic, nonroutinized citizen reportage that is implacably opposed to corrupt governments at all levels, that scrutinizes and holds accountable the domestic national media, and that is sufficiently and uncompromisingly consistent in its advocacy journalism on behalf of a transparent, democratic, and free Nigeria to cause governments to be disconcerted and to seek ways to undermine it.

Using this schema, the only Nigerian diasporic online citizen media site that qualified as an "alternative media" outlet was Sahara Reporters' earliest form. The site not only indicatively described itself as "unapologetic practitioners of advocacy journalism," it also lived up to that declaration in its reportorial temperaments and practices until 2018. This fact was acknowledged even by people outside Nigeria. For instance, as we saw in chapter 5, *The Daily Beast*'s Philip Shenon once characterized Sahara Reporters as "Africa's WikiLeaks."[47] This comparison is instructive because, like WikiLeaks, Sahara Reporters depended on whistleblowers located in the inner recesses of the Nigerian power structure to leak embarrassing information about the inner, murky workings of government and about government officials. But whereas WikiLeaks is merely a treasure trove of sensitive, hacked documents that Western governments would rather keep shrouded in secrecy, Sahara Reporters was a journalistic project that simultaneously acted as a site for hacked documents and for analyses and reportage of the documents. WikiLeaks depends entirely on citizen and traditional news media sites for the editorial analyses of the classified documents it episodically "dumps" on its site. So whereas Sahara Reporters is a citizen journalism project, WikiLeaks is not. As Joyce Nip notes in her conception of citizen journalism, "to qualify as journalism, the content needs to include some original interviewing, reporting, or analysis of events or issues to which people other than the authors have access."[48]

But Sahara Reporters certainly shared the subversive information-gathering technique of WikiLeaks. This was evident in Sahara Reporters' updated "philosophy and editorial policy," which stated in part, "We depend on the efforts of concerned citizens who act [as] whistleblowers as well as the main sources for our exposés. In a continent where much of the 'professional' media is compromised, we make a point of investigating and reporting stories that the mainstream media dare not or will not report."[49] This quotation also points to the key distinction between the reportorial practices of Western alternative media formations and Sahara Reporters. Whereas the core of the reportorial quiddities of Western alternative media formation consists of such unconventional journalistic practices as "native reporting" and "active witnessing," Sahara Reporters combined these practices with the practice of proactively tapping into the internal discontent within the Nigerian ruling class to get exclusive, often anonymously sourced, stories to expose high-profile corruption and, in the process, discomfit the ruling class and force major policy changes. The site was especially well suited to this kind of reporting, as has been pointed out earlier, because whistleblowers who exposed government muck to the site could often be assured that their identities would be concealed and, not being located in Nigeria, owners of the site could not be subpoenaed by Nigerian courts to disclose the sources of their information. This was a privilege that no Nigerian-based media organization can have. Sahara Reporters fiercely protected the anonymity, confidentiality, and safety of its sources.

Another factor that redounded to the site's "alternativeness" was that it was reasonably financially independent. When the site started, as I pointed out earlier, it was sustained primarily by self-financing, then crowdfunding, and online advertising. It also initially accepted advertising from governments but did not spare those governments from its adversarial, antigovernment advocacy journalism. However, after it won a $175,000 renewable grant from the Ford Foundation in 2010 and several other philanthrojournalistic funding, the site adopted a policy of rejecting all advertising from any government in Nigeria. What is important in all this, though, is that Sahara Reporters once demonstrated that commercial success does not necessarily preclude radical critique. The news journal *Comedia* came to this realization long ago.[50] So did Abe Peck in his insightful social history of the "underground press" in 1960s America.[51] They have shown examples of commercially viable alternative media outlets that have not abandoned progressive ideals.

However, alternative media scholars such as Gholam Khiabany[52] and Herbert Pimlott[53] caution that exposure to more advertising patronage than is sufficient to sustain the life of alternative media can compromise their editorial independence and vitality. Their warning is not entirely without merit. This was certainly the case with Elendu Reporters, which, as we saw in chapter 4, started out as a vigorous, uncompromisingly muckraking alternative online media platform but degenerated into a mouthpiece for state governors whose sordid corruption it had earlier unmasked. The editorial focus of the site began to change after it accepted advertising from the people whose misdeeds it covered and uncovered. Jonathan Elendu, the site's owner, later took jobs as a political and media consultant to many politicians whom his site had exposed as corrupt. Of course, the consequence of that misadventure was that the site degenerated from the leading Nigerian citizen media outlet between 2005 and 2006 to a peripheral, inconsequential one by late 2010, and to a virtually nonexistent one as of late 2018.

Interestingly, when security agents of the Nigerian government arrested and detained Elendu when he traveled home from his base in the United States on suspicion that he was associated with Sahara Reporters, his plight elicited minimal concern from Nigerians at home and in the diaspora. He was condemned by many as the victim of his duplicity and lack of principles. PointBlankNews showed occasional flashes of radicalism in ways that tempt one to characterize it as belonging to the alternative online media subformation. However, there is strong evidence that after accepting advertising from Nigerian federal government agencies, it has tempered the causticity of its critiques of government. Its owner also later served as director of strategy and communication under President Goodluck Jonathan. What is apparent from the foregoing is that as Tanni Hass,[54] John Downing,[55] and others have theorized, "alternative media" is not a neat, self-sufficient, and unblemished category, nor can it always be conceived in binary opposition to "mainstream" media formations. Although Sahara Reporters was decidedly an alternative media platform in the context of the politics and performance of the Nigerian media system, its reportorial practices were not always radically different from those of its mainstream, homeland counterparts. And although it was unique in publishing citizen investigations and testimony unedited, it robustly deployed anonymous sourcing, a time-honored mainstream reporting style. Although it rejected advertising from government after obtaining funding from Western foundations, it had accepted it in the past. Besides, its wild popularity and acceptance in mainstream society both in Nigeria and outside of it calls into question the appropriateness of its designation as an "alternative media" outlet. It was at best a mainstreamed alternative citizen media outlet before it became a mere conduit for the circulation of news releases and quotidian occurrences that are covered in other media outlets.

Another point that complicates the characterization of media outlets as "alternative" is the reality of intentional ideological deceit evident in many Nigerian diasporic online media outlets. Many of them started out as impassioned, hard-nosed, anticorruption media only so that they could be noticed. They then exploited the reputational capital that their momentary popularity conferred on them to seek opportunities for self-enrichment. This is now becoming a trend, with Sahara Reporters being the latest example. This reality complicates the mapping of diasporic media into ordinary citizen media and alternative media.

Some of the features of alternative online media isolated in chapter 1 include the following: they are usually run by activists who are motivated by emancipatory progressive impulses; they intentionally function as counterweights to the corporate media; they are often unfettered by the pressures of the market and free from state control; they deploy activist, unorthodox reportorial practices (such as native reporting and active witnessing) in news gathering; they serve as counterinformation systems and agents of development power; they act as facilitators of social communication rather than as sources of information; and they are more concerned with nurturing a mobilized citizenry than an informed citizenry. Even before it capitulated, Sahara Reporters did not neatly fit these categories. Although the site's politics and journalistic preoccupations were clearly motivated by liberatory impulses and were not subject to commercial and governmental pressures, it was not a social-movement platform, nor were its reportorial practices always in opposition to the conventions of corporate news media practices. However, within the context of the politics of Nigeria—and indeed, of all countries that share Nigeria's sociohistorical characteristics—its journalism could not be described as anything other than "alternative." Thus, the epistemological and ontological boundaries of the traditional concept of alternative journalism among media scholars need to be expanded to take account of the fact that alternative media can exist without being obsessed with extirpating capitalism or running against the cultural mainstream; or being led and sustained by organized social movements; or, for that matter, being both sources of information and facilitators of social communication. Such a reconsideration of the conception of alternative journalism would escape the charge of occluding the sociohistorical singularities of non-Western societies. What should matter in the conceptualization of alternative journalism is the degree to which journalism is consistently oppositional both to the mainstream media (which are by definition pro status quo and core instruments for the legitimation and naturalization of the power structure) and oppressive cultural and political practices within societies and social formations. The form and substance of this journalism will necessarily differ from society to society. Transitional, emerging democracies will have alternative media formations that are different from those of freer, more transparent societies, which will in turn be different from deeply oppressive and closed societies. In other words, the form and character of alternative media formations in the world will be inflected by their sociohistorical and cultural singularities. However, they also share a passion for extirpating inequality, instituting justice and economic liberty for all, and disrupting the comfort of oppressive power structures.

Summary and Recommendations

This book has illustrated that diasporic online citizen journalism of the kind that has been examined here has the capacity to construct loose but nonetheless vigorous media-created virtual public spheres that can influence, challenge, and alter the politics and traditional media formations of homelands in peripheral, transitional societies as well as being alternatives or complements to state-run and corporate media. This extends the conversation about how the Internet has transformed the dynamics of content creation and consumption. Although the transformation of audiences into content creators has been amply documented within the bounds of nations and states, this book has chronicled one of only a few instances of previous diasporic consumers of homeland news becoming creators of news content for and about the home from which they are permanently separated geographically and, in the process, contributing to raising the bar of domestic national discourse, media practice, and governmental policy formulations. This study is therefore important in pointing out ways that countries saddled with a compromised or strangulated domestic media system can turn to their diasporas in the West—or in any other technologically and politically advanced society—to challenge or improve homeland media formations and influence government policies.

Although instances of exilic individuals challenging homeland state policies and even changing whole governments through the instrumentality of "small media" have been well documented,[56] the kind of diasporic journalism examined in this book is unique in many respects. First, it is practiced by people who are not temporary political exiles but permanent legal residents in their host countries. Many of them were professional journalists back home who changed careers on arrival in their new countries. Others were prodemocracy and human-rights activists before they relocated to the United States. Still others are US-based IT professionals who are merely interested in expanding the discursive space in Nigeria. But most, if not all, of them practice citizen journalism as a part-time endeavor. Unlike the exilic elites of 1980s Iran, for example, who brought about changes back home while away from it by using small media and going back home thereafter, the Nigerian exiles at the vanguard of the online citizen journalism in this book have a sense of rootedness and membership in their host communities and probably have no desire to return to the homeland permanently.[57]

Similarly, over the years, their diasporic online media have been mainstreamed and are now seen as part of Nigeria's media landscape. This fact has conferred on them institutional authenticity in ways that the small media of exilic elites highlighted in previous studies did not have. So the citizen media system that the Nigerian diaspora has helped birth is not episodic, contingent, and inspired by fleeting political concerns. It emerged first as a complement and later as a competitor to the domestic media. The Nigerian diasporic media formation, located solely in virtual space but with preoccupations entirely centered on the homeland, is unique. It is even more unusual that such a media system can influence domestic government policies and threaten the professional and institutional authority of the domestic legacy media. Thus, this media system, as the Ford Foundation aptly notes, provides a model for deepening participatory democracy and serving as a foil to compromised media systems in developing societies. Of course, not all the online media highlighted for this study have democratizing potential, but it is significant that the discursive democracy the Internet enables also makes it easy for readers to desert news outlets that betray the trust of their audiences. The irrelevance of Elendu Reports and the increasing loss of traffic of Sahara Reporters since it lost its critical bite in 2018 is a testament to this.

It is obvious that that the diasporic online media in Nigeria were effective partly because of their capacity to attract the attention of government back home. And they succeeded in attracting the attention of government because the diasporic media sites are located in the United States, a country whose approval Nigerian governments traditionally seek, with a few exceptions.[58] As one of the case studies showed, fear of being exposed to "international embarrassment" (which is often shorthand for American disapproval) is often a potent motive for changing unpopular state policies in Nigeria. It is conceivable that were the diasporic citizen news media to be located anywhere outside America, they would not have been as effective as they were. This is the core of the claims of the theory of boomerang effect: its power derives from the willingness of governments of resource-rich countries in the West to compel governments in the developing world to change policies considered unpopular. This means that the relative success of the diasporic online media can be replicated only in countries where governments are sensitive to international public opinion, where governments are eager to be in the good graces of Western governments, and where the press systems are at least "partly free," to use the Freedom House's terminology for the classification of the world's freedom index.[59] Nigeria has been consistently classified as "partly free" except for one occasion when it was classified as "free." It was also once classified as "not free" during General Sani Abacha's brutal military dictatorship. The point is that the online citizen media of developing-world diasporas cannot be effective and active agents of change in their original homelands unless those homelands at least make pretensions to democracy and freedom, as Nigeria does. It would be pointless in countries such as North Korea, Cuba, Iran, China, Pakistan, the Persian Gulf states, and so on, where governments can block websites arbitrarily without reputational consequences to the governments, where governments are contemptuous of international public opinion, and where anti-Western sentiments are mainstream. In other words, countries where the press systems are "not free" are exempt from the consequences of the random acts of journalism of geographically displaced ethnoscapes in the Western core. This consideration is the major limitation in the applicability of this study. However, even in these totalitarian or authoritarian countries, the proliferation of mobile Internet access is rendering government control of the web rather slippery. In China and Hong Kong, for instance, many demonstrations have been successfully organized by otherwise widely dispersed people through cell phones.

It is important to note, too, that although the Internet is not as widely accessible in the developing world as it is in the West, potentially limiting the power and reach of online citizen media, Internet access and literacy have been growing by leaps and bounds lately, especially with the wild popularity of mobile Internet service. In Nigeria, as in most developing countries, most people get access to the Internet through their cell phones. More important, as the two-step flow theory of communication (sometimes called the multiple-step-flow theory of communication) suggests, the effects of mass communication are not often measured primarily by the number of people who have had first contact with the content of the mass media. News often percolates to the general populace through a network of interpersonal relationships led by "opinion leaders."[60] The two-step theory posits that news from the mass media usually first gets to opinion leaders, who are usually well educated and media savvy and who have access to modern communication facilities. The opinion leaders relay news to the lower strata of the society through informal channels. Most of the stories covered in the online diasporic media that had momentous consequences in Nigeria became topics of national conversation precisely because they were first exposed to a few influential people who had access to the Internet and who later diffused the information to the larger populace through a multiple-flow process. With the profusion of Internet access through cell phones, which empowers many more people to encounter news directly on the Internet, this theory and its implications may become less significant.

As a result of the success of the first set of diasporic online citizen media outlets, there has been a mushrooming of diasporic and domestic online citizen media that are actively involved in traditional news reporting. It is conceivable that they will become a permanent fixture on the Nigerian media landscape, but it is also possible that their emergence is actuated by the push and pull of electoral politics. Most of these sites are obviously politically motivated, are designed to bolster the political aspirations of certain politicians and to undermine those of others, and generally fall short of the expectations that made some of their forerunners popular and successful. Similarly, such older diasporic media sites as Sahara Reporters, Pointblanknews, and Huhuonline have become partisan in ways that suggest that they have been compromised and that they are selling their influence to politicians. The good thing, though, is that these sites seem to be losing their readers. The deliberative democracy that the Internet makes possible will ultimately allow readers to express their feelings through online comments and patronage. In the final analysis, the websites that survive will be those that are not only transparent and unaffiliated with politicians and political parties but that are seen to be so by readers.

Unfortunately, by 2019, when research for this book ended, the tradition of radical, advocatorial journalism has receded at home in Nigeria, in the diaspora, and among both online and legacy media outlets. In the face of momentous existential national crisis occasioned by President Muhammadu Buhari's creeping fascist totalitarianism, all the Nigerian news media have been curiously quiescent, even complicit. The tradition of robust dissent is dead, and wherever it manages to manifest episodically, it is criminalized and punished. What there is now is what I have called a "Hitler-level fascist conquest of the Nigerian democratic space."[61] Nonetheless, Buhari's fascist monocracy is enabled and nourished by the very people who had made it their life's calling to fight past military dictatorships. Human rights organizations, prodemocracy groups, and the legacy and citizen news media formations either are in bed with Buhari's fascist regime or are too cowed to speak up. Since at least 2018, the new media, including the previously critical online media of the Nigerian diaspora and the homeland, have basically caved in to tyranny. They have gone from being the watchdogs of society to being the lapdogs of the powerful, from being comforters of the afflicted and afflicters of the comfortable to being comforters of the comfortable and afflicters of the afflicted. The practitioners of the radical guerrilla journalism of the 1990s are now either the new oppressors or intellectual enablers of oppression. However, if the history of radical journalism in Nigeria is any guide, this is only a transitory reversal. A sustained absence of the sort of adversarial journalism that routed military totalitarianisms and put the excesses of civilian governments in check will constrict the democratic space, asphyxiate freedoms, and ultimately ignite the resurgence of critical journalism, possibly in digital-native media environments. The past successes of Sahara Reporters and Premium Times will always inspire the recrudescence of activist and emancipatory media formations.

A few diasporic online journalistic outlets that are consequential in the homeland have emerged in Africa, prominent examples being those of Ethiopia and Somalia. It would be interesting to compare them with the Nigerian example. It would also be useful to undertake comparative online media journalistic-activist studies with countries that share Nigeria's demographic and sociohistorical attributes, such as Malaysia, where bloggers once caused a major political earthquake by helping to unseat a government that had clung to power since the country's independence through an ironclad strangulation of the discursive space. In Malaysia, as in Nigeria, "people trust the Internet more than official sources." That is why Malaysian researchers found that "more than 70 percent of voters in March 8 [2008] elections were influenced by blogs."[62] Such an effect has not been systematically measured in Nigeria, but given the mass disillusionment with the mainstream media in Nigeria and the immense popularity of online media, it is entirely possible that a similar finding will be made.

Notes

Introduction

1. See Escobar, "Welcome to Cyberia: Notes on the Anthropology of Cyberculture."
2. The term was first used in reference to "cyber Nigeria" in Kperogi, "Guerrillas in Cyberia."
3. Panagakos and Heather, "Return to Cyberia," 109.
4. For a helpful discussion on the etymology and semantic evolution of the term *cyberspace*, see Holeton, *Composing Cyberspace*. See also Samoriski, *Issues in Cyberspace*.
5. Gibson, *Neuromancer*, 51.
6. Benedikt, *Cyberspace First Steps*, 1.
7. Hughes, *From Webspace to Cyberspace.*
8. Dyson et al., "Cyberspace and the American Dream."
9. See Turkle, *Life on the Screen. See also Jordan, Cyberpower. Another useful reference on this is Castells' The Internet Galaxy.*
10. Schneider grapples with this notion of the dimension of cyberspace in "Evolution in Cyberspace."
11. Castells, *The Internet Galaxy*, 203.
12. See Dodge and Kitchin, *Mapping Cyberspace*, 63.
13. See Adams, "Network Topologies and Virtual Place."
14. Dodge and Kitchin, *Mapping Cyberspace*, 63.
15. Luke, "Cybercritique," 137.
16. See Castells, *End of Millennium*, 162.
17. Panagakos and Heather, "Return to Cyber," 109.
18. It is projected that Internet users in Nigeria will increase to 187.8 million in 2023.
19. Sahara Reporters is a bit of an exception here. Although it started as a barebones, stripped-down operation, its impact caused it to be noticed and funded by Western philanthropic foundations, as chapter 5 shows.
20. Mowlana, *Global Information and World Communication*, 37.
21. Karim, "From Ethnic Media to Global Media."

22. Laguerre, "Homeland Political Crisis, the Virtual Diasporic Public Sphere, and Diasporic Politics."
23. Brinkerhoff, *Digital Diasporas.*
24. Karim (1998) notes that in postcolonial and cultural studies, the term "diaspora" exclusively refers to voluntary and involuntary migrants from the periphery and semi-periphery of the world; it seldom refers to immigrants who deterritorialize from the core nations of the world, such as the UK, the US, France, etc. to peripheral and semi-peripheral nations.
25. See Sheffer, "A New Field of Study," 3.
26. Appadurai, *Modernity at Large*, 18.
27. Appadurai, 22.
28. Fraser, "Transnationalizing the Public Sphere," 7.
29. Conway and Singh, "Is the World Social Forum a Transnational Public Sphere?" 65.
30. See, for instance, Vertovec, "Conceiving and Researching Transnationalism"; Guidry, Kennedy, and Zaid, *Globalizations and Social Movements; Becker and Wehner, "Electronic Networks and Civil Society"; and Karim, "Mapping Diasporic Mediascapes."*
31. For examples, see Cammaerts and Audenhove's study of the role of the Internet in the enabling of a transnational public sphere in a European context: Cammaerts and Audenhove, "Online Political Debate, Unbounded Citizenship, and the Problematic Nature of a Transnational Public Sphere." Also see Bernal's study of the same phenomenon in an African context: Bernal, "Diaspora, Cyberspace and Political Imagination."
32. Hannerz, *Transnational Connections*, 101.
33. Most scholars who study the media of diasporic public spheres often do no more than study the media-consumption patterns of migratory elites in their bid to reterritorialize in their host countries. See, for instance, Karim, ed., *The Media of Diaspora*; and King and Wood, eds., *Media and Migration: Constructions of Mobility and Difference.*
34. See, for instance, Rodriguez's *Fissures in the Mediascape.*
35. Johnson and Wiedenback, "Enhancing Perceived Credibility of Citizen Journalism Web Sites," 333.
36. Atton, "What is 'Alternative' Journalism?" 26.
37. Alternative media researchers traditionally evaluate the "alternativeness" of media by the extent to which those media emphasize political versus cultural news, offer critiques of capitalism, and mobilize the citizenry for action in their news reports. See Benson, "Commercialism and Critique."
38. See, for example, "News Blogger Detained in Nigeria"; Committee to Protect Journalists, "Second U.S.-based Nigerian Blogger Held." Also see Sahara Reporters, "Federal Court Declares the Arrest and Detention of US-based Blogger Emmanuel Asiwe Illegal."

39. Fraser, "Transnationalizing the Public Sphere," 7.
40. Spitulnik, "Alternative Small Media and Communicative Spaces," 179.
41. Furuholt and Kristiansen, "Internet Cafés in Asia and Africa"; Kyem and LeMaire, "Transforming Recent Gains in the Digital Divide into Digital Opportunities."
42. See, for example, Agamben, *Homo Sacer*; Hansen and Stepputat, *Sovereign Bodies*; and Mbembe, "Necropolitics."
43. Brinkerhoff, *Digital Diasporas*, 2.
44. Dirlik, "Intimate Others," 496. Ritivoi's *Yesterday's Self* also offers an interesting and incisive exploration of the intersections among nostalgia, identity, and the immigrant experience.
45. Dirlik, "Intimate Others," 495.
46. For scholarly works on the tensions between citizen journalism and the traditional media in the West, see Thurman, "Forums for Citizen Journalists?"; Matheson, "Weblogs and the Epistemology of the News"; and Thurman and Jones, "From Nexus to Newslog."
47. Frank, *New Consensus for Old*, 283; Morris, "Banality in Cultural Studies."
48. Fiske, "British Cultural Studies and Television."
49. Kellner, *Media Culture*, 39.
50. Atton, *Alternative Internet*, 25.
51. Boyd-Barrett, "Media Imperialism"; Golding, "Media Professionalism in the third world."
52. Schiller, *Communication and Cultural Domination*; see also Schiller, *Mass Communications and American Empire*, 140.
53. Schramm, *Mass Media and National Development*, 65.
54. Appadurai, *Modernity at Large*.
55. Thussu, "Introduction," 3.
56. Thussu, "Mapping Global Media Flow and Contra-Flow," 11.
57. Joseph D. Straubhaar, "Beyond Media Imperialism: Asymmetrical Interdependence and Cultural Proximity," *Critical Studies in Mass Communication* 8 (1991).
58. See Appadurai, *Modernity at Large*. For a recent insightful account of how several loci of hitherto non-hegemonic forms of cultural imperialism are emerging in places that have themselves been victims of media and cultural imperialism in the past, see Punathambekar, "Bollywood in the Indian-American Diaspora."
59. See Sreberny-Mohammadi, "Globalization, Communication and Transnational Civil Society: Introduction."
60. See Giddens, *Runaway World*.
61. Curran, "Globalization Theory."

Chapter One

1. See, for instance, Rodriguez's *Fissures in the Mediascape*. She uses the terms interchangeably.
2. Johnson and Wiedenback, "Enhancing Perceived Credibility of Citizen Journalism Web Sites," 333.
3. Atton, "What is 'Alternative' Journalism?" 26.
4. Alternative media researchers traditionally evaluate the "alternativeness" of media by the extent to which the media emphasize political versus cultural news, offer critiques of capitalism, and mobilize the citizenry for action in their news reports. See Benson, "Commercialism and Critique."
5. See Kperogi, "Clash of Civilization or Clash of Newspaper Ideologies?"137, 138.
6. Haas, "Alternative Media, Public Journalism and the Pursuit of Democratization."
7. Rauch, "Activists as Interpretive Communities."
8. See, for instance, Atton, "Alternative Media in Scotland"; Atton, *Alternative Media*; Atton, "News Cultures and New Social Movements"; Atton, "What is 'Alternative' Journalism?"; Atton and Wickenden, "Sourcing Routines and Representation in Alternative Journalism"; Downing, "Audiences and Readers of Alternative Media"; Ford and Gil, "Radical Internet Use"; Haas, "Alternative Media, Public Journalism and the Pursuit of Democratization."; Kim and Hamilton, "Capitulation to Capital?"; Platon and Deuze, "Indymedia Journalism."
9. See Atton, "News Cultures and New Social Movements."
10. Downing, *Radical Media*.
11. Atton, "News Cultures and New Social Movements," 492.
12. See Atton, *Alternative Media*; Downing, *Radical Media*; Halleck, *Hand Held Visions*; Rodriguez, *Fissures in the Mediascape*; Streitmatter, *Voices of Revolution*; Bailey, Cammaert, and Carpentier, *Understanding Alternative Media*; Atton and Hamilton, *Alternative Journalism*; Forde, *Challenging the News*; Harcup, *Alternative Journalism, Alternative Voices*; and Atton, *The Routledge Companion to Alternative and Community Media*.
13. See Atton, "What is Alternative Journalism?"; Cecil, "Alternative Media"; Gibbs and Hamilton, "Special Issue of Media History: Alternative Media"; Kidd and Barker-Plummer, "Social Justice Movements and the Internet"; Turner, Editorial; Haller, Holt, and de La Brosse, "The 'Other' Alternatives."
14. Gibbs and Hamilton, "Special Issue of Media History: Alternative Media," 117.
15. Campbell, *Information Age Journalism*, 178.
16. See Evans, "Hegemony and Discourse"; Sholle, "Access Through Activism"; Jacubowicz, "Musical Chairs?"

17. Gibbs and Hamilton, "Special Issue of Media History," 117.
18. Downing, *Radical Media*, 45.
19. Curran and Seaton, *Power Without Responsibility*, 16.
20. Harcup, "The Unspoken—Said," 372.
21. Hamilton, "Alternative Media: Conceptual Difficulties, Critical Possibilities."
22. Haas, "Alternative Media, Public Journalism and the Pursuit of Democratization," 115.
23. Downing, *Radical Media.*
24. Atton, *Alternative Media.*
25. Hochheimer, "Organizing Democratic Radio."
26. Atton, *Alternative Media.*
27. Atton, *Alternative Media.*
28. Tomaselli and Louw, "Alternative Media and Political Practice," 213.
29. Haas, "Alternative Media, Public Journalism and the Pursuit of Democratization,"116.
30. Atton, *Alternative Media*, 154.
31. Melucci, *Challenging Codes*, 379.
32. Whitaker, *News Limited*, 105.
33. Cottle, "Rethinking News Access," 433.
34. Cottle, 434–35.
35. Atton, "Ethical Issues in Alternative Journalism," 22.
36. Couldry, *The Place of Media Power.*
37. Peters, "Witnessing."
38. Bourdieu, *Language and Symbolic Power.*
39. McChesney, *Rich Media, Poor Democracy*, 49–50.
40. McChesney, 110.
41. Atton, *Alternative Media*, 11.
42. Harcup, "'I'm Doing This to Change the World,'" 362.
43. Philips, "Keep Your Mouth Shut."
44. Dare, *Guerrilla Journalism*, 91.
45. Atton, "Towards a Cultural Study of Alternative Media on the Internet," 53.
46. Atton, "Towards a Cultural Study of Alternative Media."
47. Harcup, "The Unspoken—Said," 257.
48. Rauch, "Activists as Interpretive Communities."
49. Rauch, "Activists as Interpretive Communities."
50. Hall, "Encoding/Decoding."
51. Atton, *Alternative Internet*, 25.
52. Silverstone, *Why Study the Media?* 103.
53. Silverstone, 103.
54. These news outlets usually capitalize on the internal wrangling in the Nigerian elite circles to get exclusive, sometimes incriminating, documents against

public officials, among other news-gathering strategies, as we will see in the data chapters.

55. Atton, *An Alternative Internet*, 26.
56. Atton, *An Alternative Internet*, 26.
57. See Downing, *Radical Media.*
58. Downing, *Radical Media d*, viii.
59. Downing, *Radical Media*, ix.
60. Downing, *Radical Media.*
61. Atton, "Ethical Issues in Alternative Journalism."
62. Harcup, "'I'm Doing This to Change the World,'" 362.
63. Haller, Holt, and de La Brosse, "The 'Other'Alternatives," 3.
64. Public or civic journalism, as subsequent sections will show, is the kind of journalism that actively seeks the input of the reading or viewing public in the news-gathering process. For a scholarly exploration of how mainstream corporate media organizations are co-opting alternative journalistic reportorial styles, see Kperogi, "News with Views."
65. Atton, "Towards a Cultural Study of Alternative Media on the Internet," 58.
66. Couldry, "Mediation and Alternative Media."
67. Bourdieu, *Language and Symbolic Power.*
68. Melucci, *Challenging Codes, 182.* He contends that "The real domination is today the exclusion from the power of naming."
69. Bourdieu, *Language and Symbolic Power*, 166.
70. Couldry, "Mediation and Alternative Media."
71. Scott, *Weapons of the Weak.*
72. Atton, "Towards a Cultural Study of Alternative Media on the Internet," 55.
73. Kahn and Kellner, "Technopolitics, Blogs, and Emergent Media Ecologies," 226.
74. Kim and Hamilton, "Capitulation to Capital?"
75. Kim and Hamilton, 542–43.
76. Atton, "Towards a Cultural Study of Alternative Media," 53.
77. Benson, "Commercialism and Critique."
78. See Bauder, "Web Has Unexpected Effect on Journalism."
79. For a perceptive discussion on the interdependence of citizen blogs and mainstream media, see Hass, "From 'Public Journalism' to the 'Public's Journalism'?"
80. Nip, "Exploring the Second Phase of Public Journalism."
81. Nip, 216.
82. Woollacott, "Messages and Meanings," 109.
83. See Glasser, ed., *The Idea of Public Journalism.*
84. Rosen, *What Are Journalists For?*
85. Friedland, *Public Journalism.*
86. Nip, 216.

87. Davis, "Public Journalism: The Case Against"; Glasser, "The Politics of Public Journalism."
88. Woodstock, "Public Journalism's Talking Cure," 37.
89. Matheson, "Weblogs and the Epistemology of the News."
90. Iser, *The Act of Reading*, 34.
91. Matheson, "Weblogs and the Epistemology of the News," 453.
92. Hujanen and Peitikainen, "Interactive Uses of Journalism," 383.
93. Massey and Levy, "Interactivity, Online Journalism, and English-language Web Newspapers in Asia."
94. Nip, "Exploring the Second Phase of Public Journalism."
95. See Loba, "Have Comment Sections on News Media Websites Failed?" Also see Goujard, "Why News Websites Are Closing Their Comments Sections."
96. Bowman and Willis, "We Media: How Audiences Are Shaping the Future of News and Information."
97. Bowman and Willis, "We Media."
98. Yu, "OhmyNews Makes Every Citizen a Reporter."
99. Gillmor, "A New Brand of Journalism Is Taking Root in South Korea."
100. Nip, "Exploring the Second Phase of Public Journalism," 218.
101. Rosen, "The People Formerly Known as the Audience."
102. Lasica, "Blogs and Journalism Need Each Other."
103. Flew, *New Media.*
104. Schiller, *Culture Inc.*
105. Violanti, "Alternative News Made its Mark," p. C1.
106. Reese, Rutigliano, Hyun, and Jeong, "Mapping the Blogosphere," 236.
107. See Andrews, "Is Blogging Journalism?"; Baoill, "Weblogs and the Public Sphere"; Carroll, "Culture Clash: Journalism and the Communal Ethos of the Blogosphere."
108. Halavais, "The Web as News: September 11 and New Sources of Web News."
109. Singer, "The Political J-Blogger," 23.
110. Redden, "Read the Whole Thing,"162.

Chapter Two

1. Ogbondah, "Nigerian Press under Imperialists and Dictators, 1903–1985," 4.
2. Coleman, *Nigeria*, 184.
3. Quoted in Omu, *Press and Politics in Nigeria 1800–1937*, vii.
4. Turner, "Commercial Capitalism and the 1975 Coup," 171.
5. This review of the press history of Nigeria excludes the broadcast industry for two reasons. First, as Colin Legun notes, throughout the colonial period between the late 1800s and the late 1950s, there were no television stations in all of Africa. It was not until 1958 that the first TV station on the continent

was established by the self-governing but nonetheless partly British-controlled Western Region of Nigeria. The colonial governments also had exclusive control over radio, except in the tiny Western African nation of the Gambia, where a private radio station was allowed to exist. Television, therefore, is largely only a postindependence phenomenon in Africa. Second, even after its emergence, the broadcast industry (which includes radio and television) has been "wholly owned and controlled by the government, usually under the direct authority of the Ministry of Information or a commission, corporation or board under Ministry supervision," which is a legacy from colonialism (see Legun, "The Mass Media," 27.) Conversely newspapers traditionally have been privately owned and therefore are more vigorous instruments of and avenues for public expression.

6. It is traditional to delineate the country into North and South. These demarcations are not merely cartographical; they are also political, cultural, and historical. Northern Nigeria, which is predominantly Muslim (except in the north-central states), includes 19 of Nigeria's 36 states and occupies more than three quarters of the entire landmass of the country. Southern Nigeria, on the other hand, is predominantly Christian (except in the southwest) and consists of 17 states.
7. It should be noted, however, that the Hausa language, native to northern Nigeria, is the most widely spoken language in Africa in terms of numerical strength. It is spoken by over 80 million people in Nigeria, Niger, Ghana, and some parts of Sudan. But because Hausa has been identified with a particular ethnic group, there is reluctance, indeed resistance, to adopting it as the lingua franca of Nigeria.
8. See Whitehead, "The Historiography of British Imperial Education Policy, Part II." He argues that part of the reason for the reluctance of the British to educate their African colonial subjects was the desire to avoid the grim prospect of mass-producing a troublesome "intellectual proletariat," as was the case in India.
9. See, for instance, White, "Talk about School."
10. White, 18.
11. Post and Jenkins, *The Price of Liberty*, 156.
12. de St. Jorre, *The Nigerian Civil War.*
13. Afigbo, "Background to Nigerian Federalism," 27.
14. Olusegun Obasanjo is one of only two former military heads of state from the south. The other was Johnson Thomas Aguiyi-Ironsi, Nigeria's first military head of state. The rest were northerners.
15. In chapter 7, I discuss how networked social-media journalism, which traces inspirational descent from diasporic citizen journalism, helped bring about the unparalleled electoral defeat of an incumbent president.
16. Golding, "Media Professionalism in the Third World," 291.

17. Golding, 301.
18. Ugboajah, "Four Options for Press Regulation," 130.
19. See Falola, *The History of Nigeria.*
20. Agbaje, *The Nigerian Press, Hegemony, and the Social Construction of Hegemony, 1960–1983*, 41.
21. Omu, *Press and Politics in Nigeria*, 130. The first printing press to start a newspaper was brought to the city of Calabar in Nigeria's deep south by the Reverend Hope Waddell of the Presbyterian Mission from England in 1846, a few years earlier than the Reverend Townsend, but didn't start publishing a newspaper until some years after. See Ogbondah, "Nigerian Journalism." It is also worthy of note that forms of newspapers existed in northern Nigeria earlier than 1859, calling into question the consensus in Nigerian press history that 1859 is the year the first newspaper was published. This controversy will be expanded on in subsequent sections of this chapter.
22. Uche, *Mass Media, People and Politics in Nigeria*, 93.
23. Nwankwo and Kurian, "Nigeria."
24. According to Ralph Akinfeleye, "copies of the *Iwe Irohin* . . . can still be found on sale in several Nigerian newsstands, particularly in the southwestern states of Nigeria." See Akinfeleye, "Religious Publication," 31.
25. See Salawu, "Not Iwe Irohin but Umshumayeli."
26. Salawu, "Not Iwe Irohin but Umshumayeli."
27. Anderson, *Imagined Communities*, 44–46.
28. See Eribo, "Internal and External Factors Affecting Press Freedom in Nigeria."
29. Akinfeleye, "Religious Publication," 28.
30. For a thoughtful and perceptive account of the history and use of Arabic script to write sub-Saharan African languages, see Hassane, "Ajami in Africa." Also see Ngom, *Muslims Beyond the Arab World.*
31. Adamu, "Istanci, Imamanci and Bollywoodanci."
32. Ahmad, "Gaskiya Tafi Kwabo: From Colonial Service to Community Beacon," 99.
33. Cited in Bittner, *Mass Communication*, 22.
34. Ahmad, "Gaskiya TaFi Kwabo," 98.
35. Palmer, *Sudanese Memoirs.*
36. Ochonu, *Colonial Meltdown.*
37. Ochonu, *Colonial Meltdown*, 104.
38. Yahya, *Hausa a Rubuce.*
39. Ahmad, "Gaskya Ta Fi Kwabo," 101.
40. Shehu, "The Role of Mass Media in National Development."
41. Quoted in Mora, *The Abubakar Imam Memoirs*, 31.
42. Ahmad, Gaskiya Ta Fi Kwabo," 102.
43. Ahmad, Gaskiya Ta Fi Kwabo," 102.

44. Indirect rule was the British policy of co-opting precolonial traditional power structures into colonial administration where such structures already existed and inventing them where they did not exist. British colonialists wanted the cooperation of the former ruling classes (for personal profit and safeguarding much of the dynastic heritage) of the various areas that constituted the new country in order to prevent the risk of a rebellion by both the subjects and leaders of the traditional order. For an excellent analysis of the British policy of indirect rule in Nigeria, see Nwabughuogu, "The Role of Propaganda in the Development of Indirect Rule in Nigeria."
45. Yahya, *Hausa a Rubuce.*
46. Mora, *The Abubakar Imam Memoirs.*
47. Ahmad, "Gaskiya Ta Fi Kwabo," 97.
48. Haruna, "The Life and Times of Abubakar Imam."
49. Akinfeleye, "Religious Publication," 30.
50. Akinfeleye, "Religious Publication."
51. Mott, *The News in America*, 34.
52. Mott, *The News in America*, 33.
53. Mott, *The News in America.*
54. Omu, *Press and Politics in Nigeria*, 6.
55. Duyile, *Makers of the Nigerian Press*, 6.
56. Ibrahim, "Towards a Political Economy of Mass Communication in Nigeria."
57. Musa and Mohammed, "The Political Economy of Media Ownership in Nigeria," 232.
58. Musa and Mohammed, 231.
59. White, "Talk about School," 18.
60. Ibrahim, "Towards a Political Economy of Mass Communication," 8.
61. Omu, *Press and Politics in Nigeria*, 7.
62. See Aluede, "Regional Demands and Contemporary Educational Disparities."
63. Killson, *Political Change in a West African State.*
64. Salawu, "Paradox of a Milieu."
65. Omu, *Press and Politics in Nigeria*, 8.
66. Akinfeleye, "Religious Publications."
67. Omu, *Press and Politics in Nigeria*, 8.
68. "Deliberation deficit" is often theorized as the absence of the culture of consequential democratic discussions without threats of violence, cynicism, and name-calling. Although this term has traditionally been applied to societies that are thought to lack a history of the Habermasian public sphere, it is not unusual to apply it to the decline of communicative rationality in modern societies that promote themselves as democratic. In his *Civility and Subversion*, Goldfarb, for instance, uses the term to denote the progressive decline of the culture of rational debate in the United States and eastern Europe.
69. Hatchten, *Muffled Drums*, 144.

70. Omu, *Press and Politics in Nigeria*, 20.
71. Omu, 21.
72. Omu, 31.
73. Uche, *Mass Media, People and Politics in Nigeria*, 93.
74. Uche.
75. Omu, 30.
76. Falola, *History of Nigeria*, 83.
77. Omu, *Press and Politics in Nigeria*, 42.
78. Omu, 62. The *Daily Times* is published to this day. It was taken over by Nigeria's central government between 1975 and 1999. It has now been privatized and is operated by private citizens. Interestingly, all through its history, the paper has been aloof from popular agitations and supportive of the government even when it has not been owned by the government.
79. Uche, *Mass Media*, 97.
80. Ogbondah and Onyedike, "Origins and Interpretations of Nigerian Press Laws."
81. Agbese, *The Roles of the Press and Communication Technology*, 47.
82. Nwankwo and Kurian, "Nigeria."
83. Hall, "'Think Imperially,'" 249.
84. Hall, "'Think Imperially,'" 249.
85. Hall, "'Think Imperially,'" 250.
86. Musa and Mohammed, "Political Economy," 237.
87. Chick, "The Nigerian Press and National Integration," 125.
88. Omu, *Press and Politics in Nigeria*, 128.
89. Sobowale, "The Historical Development of the Nigerian Press."
90. Uche, *Mass Media, People and Politics in Nigeria.*
91. Sharp, "Gaskiya Corporation and the Establishment of the Ahmadu Bello University Press, Creation of a Daily Newspaper to Serve Northern Nigeria and the Possible Amalgamation of *Daily Mail*, Kano."
92. Schwartz, *Nigeria*, 162.
93. Ibelema, "The Nigerian Press and June 12," 173.
94. Ainslie, *The Press in Africa.*
95. Uche, *Mass Media, People and Politics in Nigeria*, 99.
96. Ibelema, "Nigeria Press and June 12," 173.
97. Ibelema, "Nigeria Press and June 12."
98. Elliot and Golding, "Mass Communication and Social Change," 247.
99. Uche, *Mass Media, People and Politics in Nigeria*, 99.
100. Ugboajah, "Nigerian Media Behavior on Development Issues of Conflict [sic]," 183. For a firsthand account how the *New Nigerian* opposed government policies in spite of being subsidized by the federal government, see Daura, "Editing a Government Newspaper in Nigeria," 43. In this article, Daura describes his experience of editing a newspaper "owned and subsidized by the Government

yet we criticize their action." He points out that it is an "anomaly neither properly understood by the people generally nor particularly liked by some government officials."

101. Eribo, "Internal and External Factors Affecting Press Freedom in Nigeria."
102. Agbese, *The Role of the Press*, 48.
103. Nwankwo and Kurian, "Nigeria."
104. Ogbondah, "The Pen is Mightier than the 'Koboko.'"
105. After twelve years of rule, the military decided voluntarily to hand over power to civilians. A radical military head of state had been assassinated in a coup in 1975 after only six months in office. His deputy, Olusegun Obasanjo, who became head of state, immediately started a transition program that culminated in the handover of power to civilians.
106. For a concise yet perceptive history of the penny press in the United States, see Thompson, *The Penny Press*. For a critical perspective on the popular notions of the penny press, see Nerone, "The Mythology of the Penny Press." See also Kperogi, "News with Views."
107. The military again overthrew the civilian government in 1983 and continued to rule until 1999.
108. Article 19, *Truth from Below: The Emergent Press in Africa*, 51.
109. Interestingly, the military used censorious, partisan news reports against the central government by the opposition press as a basis for taking over. The military called itself a "corrective regime."
110. Quoted in Agbese, *The Role of the Press*, 49.
111. Olorunyomi, "Defiant Publishing in Nigeria."
112. Flacks, *Youth and Social Change*. An instructive study also discovered that an increase in levels of higher education is more conducive to the sustenance of press freedom than economic prosperity. See Weaver, Buddenhaum, and Fair, "Press Freedom, Media, and Development, 1950–1979."
113. Ette, "Agents of Change or Stability."
114. Ogbondah, "The Pen is Mightier than the 'Koboko,'" 111.
115. Collins, *Words of Fire*, 48.
116. *Report by the Press Freedom Committee*, 8.
117. Agbese, *The Role of the Press*, 52.
118. Olukotun, "Authoritarian State, Crisis of Democratization," 317.
119. Ibelema, "The Nigerian Press and June 12," 195.
120. Hall, "Think Imperially," 257.
121. Ibelema, "The Nigerian Press and June 12," 174.
122. Ogbondah, "The Pen is Mightier Than the 'Koboko,'" 121.
123. Olukotun, "Authoritarian State, Crisis of Democratization," 322.
124. Ayo Akinkuotu, "*Tell and the Abacha Transition*," 133.
125. Ojo, "The Nigerian Media and the Process of Democratization," 548.
126. Collings, *Words of Fire*.

127. Ojo, "The Nigerian Media and the Process of Democratization," 548.
128. Olukotun, "Authoritarian State, Crisis of Democratization," 341.
129. According to Freedom House's mapping of historical trends in press freedom, in 1984, Nigeria's press was "partly free," in 1989 it was "free"—the only "free" press on the African continent—and it regressed to being "partly free" in 1994, 1999, 2004 and 2007. See Freedom House, "Freedom House's Annual Survey."
130. Ette, "Agent of Change or Stability?" 82.
131. After eight years of a southern Christian presidency, a northern Muslim was elected president in 2007. An informal power-sharing arrangement among the political elites has agreed to rotate the presidency between the North and the South every eight years.
132. For the most part, it was the independent media in the North that were critical of government. This might very well be because the president was a Christian southerner. When a Muslim northerner took over power in 2007 and in 2015, the independent press in the North went back to being lapdogs of government.

Chapter Three

1. Shain, *Kinship and Diasporas, 124.*
2. See, for instance, McCabe, "Harlaftis, and Minoglou, *Diaspora Entrepreneurial Networks*." In their introduction, they argued that diasporas have been traditionally "understood to be pariah communities."
3. See, for instance, Brinkerhoff, *Digital Diasporas*; Addis, "Imagining the Homeland from Afar"; and Dejung and Petersson, *The Foundations of Worldwide Economic Integration.*
4. Sayad, *The Suffering of the Immigrant*, 141.
5. Milne, *Letters, Postcards, Email.*
6. Licoppe, "'Connected' Presence."
7. See, for example, Byman, et al, *Trends in Outside Support for Insurgent Movements*; King and Melvin, "Diaspora Politics."
8. Collier and Hoeffler, "Greed and Grievances in Civil War."
9. Cohen, "Diasporas and the New Nation-State."
10. McLuhan and Powers, *The Global Village*, 148.
11. "Deliberative democracy" is the reconceptualization of democracy in more participatory and substantive terms. It expands the notion of democracy beyond such institutional rituals as periodic elections to more popular and practical civic and discursive engagement in the process of governance. For a useful introductory discussion on the origin and development of this concept, see Brandenburg, "Pathologies of the Virtual Public Sphere"; Elster, "Introduction," 1; and Dryzek, *Deliberative Democracy and Beyond*, 162.
12. See Chyko, *Portable Communities*, 5.

13. See Castells, *End of Millennium.*
14. The Frankfurt School, also known as the Institute of Social Research, was founded in Frankfurt, Germany in 1923 by the German Jewish Marxists Theodor Adorno, Herbert Marcuse, Max Horkheimer, and Erich Fromm. As a result of Nazi persecution, they fled Germany and went into exile first to Geneva and later to Moscow, California, and Columbia University in New York. For a discussion of the influence they brought to bear on the social sciences and philosophy, see McLaughlin, "Origin Myths in the Social Sciences."
15. Habermas, *The Structural Transformation of the Public Sphere.*
16. See Koselleck, *Critique and Crisis.*
17. Dewey, *The Public and its Problems*, 64.
18. Lippmann, *Public Opinion*. See also Lippmann, "The Appeal to the Public."
19. Bakhtin, *Rabelais and His World.*
20. Bruner, "Carnivalesque Protest and the Humorless State," 138.
21. For another influential conception of the public sphere, see Arendt, *The Human Condition*. For an excellent comparison of the different traditions of public-sphere theorizing, see Benhabib, "Models of Public Space." Benhabib delineates three models of the public sphere and associates them with the work of particular theorists. She calls the first model, represented by the work of Hannah Arendt, the agonistic model. She characterizes the second model, represented by the work of Bruce Ackerman, as the legalistic model; and labels the third model, represented by the work of Jürgen Habermas, as the discursive model. My work is influenced by the discursive model of the public sphere.
22. Fraser, "Rethinking the Public Sphere," 111.
23. Habermas, "The Public Sphere," 398. Habermas was an assistant to Theodor Adorno in 1959. Nevertheless, he is distinguished from the Adorno-Horkeimer-Marcuse tendency of critical theory by his more sympathetic approach to science and technology.
24. Habermas, *The Structural Transformation of the Public Sphere*, 33.
25. See, for instance, Habermas, *Between Facts and Norms.*
26. This summary of Habermas's requirements for a rational-critical debate in the quintessential public sphere was adapted from the model developed in Dahlberg, "Computer-Mediated Communication and the Public Sphere." It encapsulates the whole range of Habermas's theoretical postulations, published in different books, on the public sphere.
27. See Neblo, "Thinking through Democracy."
28. Nieminen, "On the Formation of the National Public Sphere," 5.
29. Cited in Peters, "Distrust of Representation," 564.
30. Habermas responded to the criticisms of his conception of the public sphere in *The Inclusion of the Other.*
31. Lyotard, *The Postmodern Condition.*

32. For a review of the criticism of Habermas's public sphere, see Calhoun, "Introduction."
33. Fraser, "Rethinking the Public Sphere."
34. McLaughlin, "Feminism, the Public Sphere, Media and Democracy," 599.
35. Fernald, "A Feminist Public Sphere?"
36. A host of other feminist critics are included in Meehan, *Feminists Read Habermas.*
37. Dean, "Why the Net Is Not a Public Sphere," 96.
38. Dean, "Not a Public Sphere," 109.
39. Negt and Kluge, *Public Sphere and Experience.*
40. See Fraser, "Rethinking the Public Sphere" and Warner, *Publics and Counterpublics.*
41. Cited in Peters, "Distrust of Representation," 564.
42. Brandenburg, "Pathologies of the Virtual Public Sphere," 4.
43. Rheingold's seminal text, *The Virtual Community,* provides, in the view of many scholars, the first systematic, scholarly reflection on online sociability and the democratizing promise of the Internet (279). This book is basically a recounting of Rheingold's experiential encounters with online environments, particularly with the WELL (Whole Earth 'Lectronic Link—one of the Internet's earliest bulletin-board systems).
44. Robins and Webster, "Athens without Slaves . . . or Slaves without Athens?"
45. Rheingold, *The Virtual Community*, 279.
46. Buchstein, "Bytes that Bite," 250.
47. Kellner, "Intellectuals, the New Public Spheres, and Techno-politics."
48. Hauben and Hauben, *Netizens*, 69.
49. Dahlberg, "Computer-Mediated Communication and the Public Sphere."
50. Brook and Boal, *Resisting the Virtual Life*, vii.
51. O'Donnell, "Analyzing the Internet and the Public Sphere."
52. See Arthur, *Invisible Sojourners*. Arthur points out that although African immigration is still numerically insignificant in comparison with migrations from Latin America and other parts of the world, the period beginning in the early 1990s has seen the most massive influx of sub-Saharan Africans into the United States since the transatlantic slave trade. Also see Zeleza, "Contemporary African Migration in a Global Context"; Okome, "The Antinomies of Globalization."
53. See Hatton and Williamson, "Out of Africa?" Also see Takougang, "Contemporary African Immigrants to the United States." Nigeria leads in African immigration to the United States precisely because it is the most populous country in Africa and has the advantage of being English speaking, having been colonized by Britain.
54. For a comprehensive review of the role of civil society groups and the Nigerian diasporic public sphere in the restoration of constitutional rule, see Obadare,

"Second Thoughts on Civil Society"; Bradley, "Civil Society and Democratic Progression in Postcolonial Nigeria"; Njoku, "Deconstructing Abacha."

55. See Igbanoi, "How Nigerians in the Diaspora Significantly Aid Our Development."
56. See, for instance, Reynolds, "An African Brain Drain"; Fadayomi, "Brain Drain and Brain Gain in Africa."
57. It's important to mention that Nigeria's first indigenous postindependence president, Nnamdi Azikiwe, studied at the historically black Lincoln University, Pennsylvania, in the 1920s, graduating with a bachelor's degree in 1930. See Lincoln University, "About Lincoln: A Legacy of Producing Leaders," http://www.lincoln.edu/about.html; accessed March 28, 2019. For a history of Nigerian immigration to the United States, see Offoha, *Educated Nigerian Settlers in the United States.*
58. Mahmud, *State, Class and Underdevelopment in Nigeria and Early Meiji Japan*, 3.
59. Becker, "Bonanza Development and the New Bourgeoisie," 88.
60. Joseph, *Democracy and Prebendal Politics in Nigeria*, 236. This period witnessed what in Nigeria has come to be known as the "Udoji era," in reference to Justice Jerome Udoji, who recommended that the government increase the Nigerian national minimum wage exponentially in light of the windfall from crude-oil sales. The implementation of this recommendation dramatically increased the size of the middle class and generally led to hitherto unthought-of improvement in the general standard of living in the country. The head of state of Nigeria at the time, General Yakubu Gowon, was often quoted as saying that Nigeria's problem was not money but how to spend it.
61. There is a vast array of literature on the devastating consequences on structural adjustment on Nigeria. Julius Kómoláfé, for instance, traces the nexus between the increased flow of Nigerian ethnoscapes to the West and the consequences of structural adjustment in his "Searching for Fortune." Also see Mosley, "Policy-Making without Facts" and Olukoshi, *The Politics of Structural Adjustment in Nigeria*. For a neoliberal apologia of the politics and implementation of the structural adjustment program in Nigeria, see Lewis, "From Prebendalism to Predation."
62. See Reynolds, "'We Are Not Surviving, We Are Managing,'" 6.
63. Connor, "At Least a Million Sub-Saharan Africans Moved to Europe Since 2010."
64. Solomon, "African Immigrant Population on Rise in US."
65. As part of the Immigration and Nationality Act of 1952, fifty thousand diversity work visas (green cards) have been available yearly to people from countries with low rates of immigration to the United States. The National Visa Center of the State Department holds a lottery every year and chooses winners randomly from all qualified entries. Nigeria and Bangladesh have consistently

been in the top ten countries for lottery winners. For details, see Brettell, "Political Belonging and Cultural Belonging." Nigeria has been ineligible to participate in the lottery since 2014, after reaching its cap. The program currently is in danger of being discontinued by the Trump administration.

66. See Youngstedt, "The New Nigerien Hausa Diaspora in the U.S." Also see Stoller, *Jaguar: A Story of Africans in America*; Reynolds, "An African Brain Drain."
67. Page, "Black Immigrants Collect Most Degrees."
68. Jaschik, "Black (Immigrant) Admissions Edge."
69. Cowen, "Africa is Sending Us Its Best and Brightest."
70. Fosco, "The Most Successful Ethnic Group in the U.S. May Surprise You."
71. Fosco. The American Community Survey also points out, "A growing number of Nigerian-Americans are becoming entrepreneurs and CEOs, building tech companies in the U.S. to help people back home."
72. Page, "Black Immigrants Collect Most Degrees."
73. See Stevenson, *The Contested Murder of Latasha Harlins*, 226.
74. Morgan, "Exploratory Study of Problems of Academic Adjustment," 211.
75. Reynolds and Younstedt, "Globalization and African Ethnoscapes," 7.
76. Inda and Rosaldo, "Introduction."
77. Reynolds, "We Are Not Surviving, We Are Managing."
78. For a seminal and critically acclaimed ethnographic study of how the Nigerian diaspora in the United States deployed the Internet to nourish nostalgia for the homeland and to foster nationalist sentiments, see Bastian, "Nationalism in a Virtual Space."
79. Appadurai, *Modernity at Large*, 28.
80. O'Connor and Mackeogh, "New Media Communities."
81. Anderson, *Imagined Communities.*
82. Anderson, 6.
83. Anderson.
84. Anderson, 7.
85. Bastian, "Nationalism in a Virtual Space."
86. Bastian.
87. Everett, "The Revolution Will Be Digitized," 139.
88. Ebeling, "The New Dawn," 104.
89. Bastian, "Nationalism in a Virtual Space."

Chapter Four

1. The Chicago journalist and humorist Finley Peter Dunne pointed out, at the turn of the twentieth century, that "the job of the newspaper is to comfort the afflicted and afflict the comfortable." Bill Kovach and Tom Rosentiel explain

that the essence of this quip, which has now metamorphosed into a journalistic maxim, is its dramatization of the role the press is expected to play in "watching over the powerful few in society on behalf of the many to guard against tyranny." See Kovach and Rosentiel, "Are Watchdogs an Endangered Species?" For other interpretations of this phrase, see Benjaminson and Anderson, *Investigative Reporting*. Also see Teel and Taylor, *Into the Newsroom*. For a somewhat similar death of watchdog journalism in a developing country, see Pinto, "Muzzling the Watchdog."

2. There have been noticeable improvements in the real-time updating of breaking news stories among top homeland legacy newspapers such as *Vanguard, Daily Trust, Punch, Nigerian Tribune*, and *ThisDay*, but they still lag behind online-only homeland and diasporic newspapers.
3. See Kperogi, "Cooperation with the Corporation?" Also see Singer, "Changes and Consistencies"; Singer, "Still Guarding the Gate?"
4. Deuze, "The Web and Its Journalisms," 206.
5. Deuze, "The Web and Its Journalisms," 205.
6. Pavlik, "The Future of Online Journalism."
7. Deuze, "Journalism and the Web." Also see Boczkowski, "The Development and Use of Online Newspapers." Boczkowski cites several studies that show that a vast majority of newspaper websites were no more than "shovelware."
8. Nerone and Barnhurst, "Beyond Modernism." For other lively debates about the future of the newspaper in the age of the Internet, see Franklin, "The Future of Newspapers"; Conboy and Steele, "The Future of Newspapers"; Picard, "Shifts in Newspaper Advertising Expenditures and their Implication for the Future of Newspapers"; and Schultz and Voakes, "Prophets of Gloom."
9. The online version of the paper was called *Post Express Wired*. Although it is often said in popular Nigerian media narratives that the paper first went online in late 1996, Oladimeji Aborishade and Robert Mundt said *Post Express Wired* was actually formally launched on February 18, 1997. See Aborisade and Mundt, *Politics in Nigeria*.
10. See Ette, "Agents of Change or Stability."
11. Nworah, "The Impact of the Internet on Journalism Practice in Nigeria."
12. Thurman, "Forums for Citizen Journalists?"
13. Because of their rudimentary technical capacities, many Nigerian newspapers get hacked through the feedback mechanisms they provide on their sites. That is why many of them have backed out of providing interactive features to their sites. The up-and-coming Abuja-based *Peoples Daily* newspaper, for instance, was shut down for more than a week in 2010 because it was hacked through the reader-comments section. After getting back up, it banned reader comments entirely for more than a year.
14. Cited in Matheson, "Weblogs and the Epistemology of the News," 444.
15. Matheson, 446.

16. Gillmor, *We the Media*, 112.
17. SaharaTV, "Borno Governor, Senator Ali Modu Sheriff Dancing and Spraying Dollars in Dubai."
18. The homepage of this online paper can be found at https://www.elendureportsonline.com/. It lost it original URL of www.elendureports.com after years of inactivity. It ceased publication at some point, returned with a new URL, and is no longer as active and as influential as it used to be, for reasons that will be made clear later in the chapter.
19. Check the site at http://www.saharareporters.com/.
20. The Times of Nigeria shut down after the death of its owner, Sunny Ofili, in a car crash in 2014.
21. See www.nigeriavillagesquare.com.
22. See www.huhuonline.com.
23. See www.PointBlankNews.com.
24. Empowered Newswire operated like a wire service agency. It shut down after its owner, Laolu Akande, accepted an appointment as the spokesperson for the vice president of Nigeria in 2015.
25. See http://www.usafricaonline.com/news.html. USAfrica prided itself on being the "first African-owned U.S.-based professional newspaper to be published on the Internet."
26. This muckraking outlet (whose URL was located at http://ireports-ng.com) was published from Noblesville, Indiana. It was founded in 2008 and went dead in 2017. It attracted national attention when it exposed massive corruption scandals in *Punch*, one of Nigeria's most notable daily newspapers. The scandal is one of the case studies explored in this book.
27. See http://thewillnigeria.com/news/.
28. Harcup, "'I'm Doing This to Change the World,'" 370.
29. Among the prominent citizen journalists that made Elendu Reports a hit with Nigerians at home and in the diaspora is Omoyele Sowore, a former student-union activist who studied geography at the University of Lagos. He later relocated to the United States and earned a master's degree in public policy from Columbia University. Sowore later fell out with Elendu and set up his own independent citizen-media site called Sahara Reporters, which is profiled in the next section of this chapter.
30. Harcup, "'I'm Doing This to Change the World,'" 370.
31. The website actually started on November 30, 1999 but closed shop the same day after publishing just five low-impact stories that seemed like regular homeland newspaper stories. It reemerged in 2005 and has remained consistent since then. Its popularity peaked in 2006 and has been on the decline ever since.
32. Omoh, Babasola, and Igbikiowubo, "Obasanjo's Library Fund is Executive Extortion."

33. Since Elendu Reports lost its original URL, the link to the story is gone, but see Kperogi, "Webs of Resistance," 131.
34. See Kperogi, "Guerrillas in Cyberia."
35. For other stories that graphically exposed the president's corruption, see Elendu and Sowore, "War on Corruption"; Elendu and Sowore, "War on Corruption: Obasanjo's Oily Hands."
36. See Gentry and Poole, "GoodWorks Draws Criticism."
37. See Elendu and Sowore, "Olu Obasanjo's House."
38. See Osoba, "Corruption in Nigeria."
39. See, for, instance, this series of exposés on the corrupt property purchases of Nigerian governors in the United States, particularly in Potomac, Maryland (a reason it's dubbed the "Potomac bug") and London: Elendu and Sowore, "Potomac Mansions"; Elendu and Sowore, "More Corrupt Deals of Bayelsa Governor Uncovered"; Elendu and Sowore, "Sokoto Governor Has His Share of London"; Sowore and Elendu, "'The House Is Mine'"; Elendu and Sowore, "Sokoto Governor Paid £500,00.00 More for House"; and Elendu and Sowore, "Bayelsa Governor's 'Modest' Mansion in Potomac." In all of these exposés, documents and pictures were used to prove allegations. Many of the indicted owned up to their corruption but explained it away.
40. See Kperogi, "Webs of Resistance."
41. Kperogi, "Webs of Resistance."
42. The governor invited Elendu to Sokoto; Elendu wrote an incredibly laudatory account of the governor's governance.
43. Jimoh, "Blogger/Blackmailer Unmasked."
44. Elendu, "Sowore Disengages from Elendureports.com." The story says Sowore announced his disengagement by email, "which he distributed to his friends," indicating that the disengagement was acrimonious.
45. Kperogi, "Webs of Resistance," 134.
46. Spiegel, "From Safety of New York, Reporting on Distant Home."
47. For a fascinating account of this brand of journalism by a former editor of one of Nigeria's "guerrilla" newsmagazines, see Olorunyomi, "Defiant Publishing in Nigeria."
48. Sahara Reporters, "About Sahara Reporters."
49. Starr, *Naming the Enemy*, ix.
50. Ocheja, "Nigeria at the Mercy of Sahara Reporters." The editors of Sahara Reporters have never denied the letter. In fact, they published this account on their site.
51. Ocheja, "Nigeria at the Mercy of Sahara Reporters."
52. Adeyemo, "Why I Write."
53. Adeyemo, "Why I Write."
54. Olumhense, "Our SaharaReporters."
55. Spiegel, "From Safety of New York, Reporting on Distant Home."

56. Most Nigerian newspaper editors and reporters are fans of Sahara Reporters on Facebook and follow it on Twitter. The site also has a "thin media" service in the form of a periodic newsletter of its current stories distributed to an email list to which many editors, reporters, and the public are subscribed.
57. See *Time*, "Who is Umar Faruk Abdulmutallab?"; Gambrelle, "Bomb Suspect Came from Elite Family, Best Schools."
58. See, for instance, Akintayo, "Sahara Reporters Comes of Age."
59. Ifedigbo, "It's Been Three Years."
60. Oyekunle, "I Have Moles in OBJ's Home, Says Omoyele Sowore."
61. Sowore/Sahara Reporters, "Gbenga Obasanjo on Atiku, El-Rufai, Corruption, Otta, EPZ and More." Also see, Sowore, "Gbenga Obasanjo Speaks: Atiku is Greedy."
62. See Abati, "The Gbenga Obasanjo 'Interview.'"
63. See Ojekunle, "Treasonable Sex!"
64. Kperogi, "Guerrillas in Cyberia."
65. See Sahara Reporters, "As London Case Winds Up, Details of Case Against Ibori Money-Laundering Associates Exposed."
66. See Curran and Seaton, *Power without Responsibility.*
67. Ogwuda, "Delta Monarch, Governor's Aide Perish in Auto Crash." Ofili left the United States to take a political appointment as a senior special advisor to the Delta State governor on information and communication technology.
68. Akaeze, "How They Survived Hard Times in US."
69. See Kperogi, "Webs of Resistance."
70. About US, "Title for The Times of Nigeria."
71. Elendu, "Yar'adua Dead."
72. NVS News, "Breaking News Update: 'I'm Alive & Well, Yar'adua Speaks to TON."
73. Kperogi, "Guerrillas in Cyberia."
74. Koinange, "Big Guns, Big Oil Collide in Nigeria."
75. CNN.com, "CNN Denies Nigerian Allegations of Staging Report."
76. This correspondence is no longer available on Times of Nigeria's website. But it has been reproduced and archived on my blog. I also wrote a three-part reflection on this in my weekly column in the *Weekly Trust newspaper.* See Kperogi, "CNN, Niger Delta and Western Media Portrayals of Africa (I)"; Kperogi, "CNN, Niger Delta and Western Media Portrayals of Africa (II)"; and Kperogi, "CNN, Niger Delta and Western Media Portrayals of Africa (III)." These articles are archived on my blog and can be found at http://farooqkperogi.blogspot.com/2009/03/cnn-niger-delta-and-western-media.html.
77. Nairaland Forum, "Jeff Koinange Sacked From CNN." Koinange apparently confessed to his mistress in an email communication that he indeed paid a group of people to stage the Niger Delta report. After he fell out with the

mistress, she blogged about this. See my reflection on this in my newspaper column, Kperogi, "Now That CNN has Finally Dismissed Jeff Koinange."

78. James Ibori, the former governor of Delta State, was tried for corruption by Nigeria's Economic and Financial Crimes Commission (EFCC) and had become the byword for corruption in the country. He was later found guilty of corruption and jailed by a British court. Yet the Times of Nigeria relentlessly defended him.
79. See The Nigerian Village Square, "About Us."
80. The Nigerian Village Square, "About Us." For another insightful fictional reconstruction of precolonial deliberative practices in what were called village squares in Nigeria and, by extension, Africa, read Achebe's *Things Fall Apart.*
81. The iWitness news site can be found here: http://www.nigeriavillagesquare.com/witness/.
82. Albert, "Whose Deliberative Democracy?"
83. Concerned Nigerians in Diaspora, "Letter to President Obasanjo on Third Term Agenda."
84. Kanu, "NVS Members Donate $1200 to the Aikpitanhi Family, NTA Goes Haywire." "Haywire" is used to mean "overly excited" in Nigerian English; it does not mean insane or stupid, as it does in American and British English.
85. Adekola, "FG Probes Killing of Nigerian Aboard Spanish Plane."
86. *El País*, "Aikpitanhi's Death Causes Major Policy Change in Spain."
87. Adigun, "Nigerian President Declares Assets."
88. Guardian Editorial, "DYA Campaign."
89. P.M. News, "VP Jonathan Declare Assets."
90. Empowered Newswire, "I Am Here to Understudy the Americans."
91. Adeniyi, "Why the Hell Am I Here?"
92. Schudson, "Why Conversation Is Not the Soul of Democracy."
93. Ackerman, "Why Dialogue?" 6.
94. Bohman, "Expanding Dialogue," 146.
95. Fraser, "Transnationalizing the Public Sphere," 7.
96. Dean, "Virtually Citizens."
97. Oladimeji Abitogun left the team to found his own online citizen media outlet, www.sharpedgenews.com. Although it is modeled after SaharaReporters.com and PointBlankNews, its impact, if any, has been modest.
98. PointBlankNews, "About Us."
99. PointBlankNews, "About Us."
100. Ogan, "Development Journalism/Communication."
101. Domatob and Hall, "Development Journalism in Black Africa." Also see Musa and Domatob, "Who Is a Development Journalist?"
102. PointBlankNews, "U.S. Hospital Accuses Kalu of Forgery."
103. The original Punch story is no longer on the web, but the story has been preserved on the NigeriaWorld website. See Temple Ubochi, "As It Is for Orji

Uzoh Kalu, It Is Hard for 'The Leopard to Change Its Skin." Also see Sahara Reporters, "US Hospital Denies Knowledge of Surgery Letter on Kalu's Wife."

104. See PointBlankNews, "Turaki Plans Escape, Declares False Affidavit."
105. To see a comprehensive list of the anticorruption stories the site has published since its inception, visit PointBlankNews, "Exclusive News Archive."
106. The story has been taken down from Pointblanknews.com, but it was simultaneously published on CNN's defunct iReport. See Dasmile, "Newspaper Publishers' Wife Murder 14 Years for Rituals."
107. Dasmile.
108. Dasmile.
109. The digitally manipulated photos, some of which were published on CNN iReport, no longer appear on the PointBlankNews site.
110. *Vanguard*, "The Lies of www.PointBlankNews."
111. PointBlankNews, "Between PointBlankNews and VANGUARD Newspaper."
112. PointBlankNews, "Between PointBlankNews and VANGUARD Newspaper."
113. *Vanguard*, "Drama as Alleged Ritual Murder Victim Surfaces in Court."
114. The *Vanguard* wrote an editorial on the issue after *PointBlankNews* apologized. It called *PointBlankNews* a "conceited medium of deceit, extortion and blackmail." See *Vanguard*, "Editorial: www.PointBlankNews: Dealing with Online 'Character Assassins.'"
115. Some Nigerian newspapers, of which *ThisDay* is foremost, owe reporters several months', sometimes years', worth of back wages. They tell reporters that their work ID cards are their "meal tickets." As Omenugha and Oji explain, "In other words, the journalists are encouraged to make money on their own in whatever manner they deem fit, thus encouraging the popular brown envelope syndrome within journalism parlance in Nigeria." "Brown envelope" is a euphemism for the bribes given to Nigerian journalists to induce favorable coverage. See Omenugha and Oji, "News Commercialization, Ethics and Objectivitya." Also see Tony, "Mass Media Ethics"; Olufemi, "Poverty Militates Against Code of Ethics."
116. Huhuonline.com, "About Us."
117. Huhuonline.com, "About Us."
118. Huhuonline.com, "About Us."
119. Huhuonline, "South Africans Vow to Sack Christ Embassy."
120. See, for example, Ujah and Egwuatu, "AP Shares—Otedola Seeks N117 Billion Compensation." For a recap of the controversy, see Serafin, "Then There was One."

Chapter Five

1. Chung et al., "Uses and Perceptions of Blogs," 306.

2. *ThisDay*, "Governors Sign MoU with Harvard on Capacity Building."
3. See, for instance, Sahara Reporters, "ARG to Governors' Forum: If You Must Go to Harvard, Resign!" ARG stands for Afenifere Renewal Group. It was the most politically powerful group in southwest Nigeria in 2010. Also see Akintunde, "Outrage over Governors' Harvard Programme."
4. To get a sense of the history and nature of corruption among Nigerian political elites, see Aluko, "The Institutionalization of Corruption."
5. Amadi, "Who Needs Harvard Education?"
6. *Guardian*, "The Proposed Harvard Training for Governors."
7. Bamidele, "How We Planned to Fund Harvard Programme—Govs' Forum"; Ikuomola, "'Why Governors Seek Harvard Training.'"
8. See, for instance, Ihemeremadu, "Much Ado About Harvard" and Adibe, "Nigerian Governors and the MOU with Harvard University."
9. They got the editor of the thoroughly corrupt and compromised but popular *ThisDay* newspaper to defend the training agreement with Harvard in his column. See Kolawole, "What's Wrong with Harvard?" "Some of our governors," he wrote, "don't just have any clue about development. They need help. If Harvard would help to polish their brains, please let them go!"
10. Adega, "Citizen Investigation: Harvard University Denies Agreement with Governors."
11. Adega, "Citizen Investigation."
12. Adega, "Citizen Investigation."
13. See Adega, "Harvard Denies Agreement with Nigerian Governors."
14. See, for instance, Oyebode, "Nigerian Governors' Forum Lied—Harvard University."
15. Edomaruse and Akanbi, "Document Affirms Govs' Forum, Harvard Varsity Deal."
16. Sahara Reporters, "Adams Oshiomole Says Governors' Forum 'MOU' with Harvard Is False."
17. Pan African News Agency, "Nigerian Governors Forum Cancels Harvard Training after Storm."
18. Keck and Sikkink, *Activists beyond Borders*, x.
19. Keck and Sikkink, 23.
20. Keck and Sikkink.
21. Keck and Sikkink, 36.
22. Kumar, "Transnational Networks and Campaigns for Democracy," 136.
23. Shaw, "Civil Society and Global Politics," 655.
24. Hargrove and Stempel, "Use of Blogs as a Source of News Presents Little Threat."
25. Olasanmi, "EFCC Declares el-Rufai Wanted."
26. Ige and Nnochiri, "FG after My Life over Ibori, Says Ribadu."
27. Akinbanjo, "Yar'Adua Denied Me Passport—El-Rufai."

28. SaharaReporters, "El Rufai, Ribadu: 'No New Passport! No Renewal of Passport! No Passport!' Yar'Adua Orders."
29. See, for instance, the story in *Punch*: Fabiyi, "FG Stops New Passports for Ribadu, el-Rufai."
30. Aluko, "Diaspora Petition to President Yar'adua over Non-renewal of Passport."
31. Sahara Reporters, "About Face: Yar'Adua Repudiates NIA Memo on El Rufai and Ribadu, Fires DG Imohe for Memo." Also see Iffer, "Ribadu/El-Rufai Saga: Yar'Adua Fires NIA Boss"; Ugwoke, "FG Fires Security Chief over el-Rufai, Ribadu"; Chiedozie, "Presidency Lifts Ban on Passports of el-Rufai, Ribadu." Interestingly, all these papers depended almost entirely on Sahara Reporters' reporting for their stories, even though they are geographically closer to the source of the story.
32. Idonor, "Yar'Adua Orders Probe of Sacked NIA Boss."
33. Sahara Reporters, "It is Official: El-Rufai and Ribadu Can Enjoy Passport Services, Yar'Adua Now Says."
34. Oloja, "El-Rufai-Ribadu Passport Saga."
35. Chonoko, "How Yar'adua Betrayed Us, by el-Rufai."
36. El-Rufai, "The Moral of the Story."
37. See Okonkwor, "Nigeria's Sedition Laws."
38. Cited in Campbella and McIlroy, "'The Trojan Horse,'" 2.
39. Shenon, "Sahara Reporters."
40. Sahara Reporters, "IBB's N10 Million Photo-Op with Media Executives."
41. Idowu, "IBB, Sahara Reporters, and the Press." Also see Pointblanknewews.com, "IBB's Minna Parley."
42. See, for instance, Anaba, "IBB, Visit to Minna and Journalism."
43. Sahara Reporters, "Punch Newspaper Prohibits News Critical of Jonathan."
44. Sahara Reporters, "How Farida Waziri and Top Nigerian Editors Got Abuja Land Allocations."
45. A commentator picked up an old article written by Reuben Abati, at the time the editorial board chairman of the *Guardian*, who was mentioned in the report. In the article titled, "How Much Land Does a Man Need?" Abati pontificated about the virtues of modesty and railed against corruption, avarice, and prodigality. The commentator, Osita Mba, titled his critique of Abati, "How Much Land Does Reuben Abati Need?" See, Mba, "How Much Land Does Reuben Abati Need?"
46. iReports-ng.com, "Dirty War Over Money Tears Punch Apart."
47. iReports-ng.com, "Dirty War Over Money."
48. iReports-ng.com, "Dirty War Over Money."
49. *Punch*, "A Statement from PUNCH."
50. iReports-ng.com, "Punch Chairman in Desperate Moves to Cover Up Corruption Scandals."
51. iReports-ng.com, "PUNCH/Azugate Scandal."

52. iReports-ng.com, "Another Staff Opens Can of Worms on Azu."
53. Ayorinde, "Corruption in the Nigerian Media—Case of Azubuike Ishiekwene."
54. Olumhense, "The Nigerian Media on Trial," 29.
55. Fakoya, "Nigeria Mass Media—The Fourth Estate of Graft."
56. See Cowan, "The Rise of the Coffeehouse Reconsidered."
57. See Curran, "Rethinking the Media as a Public Sphere."
58. Media Matters, "Five-Man Panel Probes Ayorinde's Petition Against Azu."
59. Ibekwe, "Ishiekwene Leaves CNN Judges Panel."
60. See Ishiekwene, "An Era Ends, a Story Begins . . ."
61. Ibekwe, "Allegations Against Punch Director Sad, Says Journalism Teacher."
62. Lasisi Olagunju (editor, *Saturday Tribune*), in discussion with the author. April 7, 2019.
63. Joel Nwokeoma (editorial page editor, *Punch*), in discussion with the author, April 7, 2019.
64. Nuruddeen M. Abdallah (assistant editor of investigations, *Daily Trust*), in discussion with the author, April 9, 2019.
65. Ajibola Amzat (editor, International Center for Investigative Reporting), in discussion with the author, April 7, 2019.
66. Martins Oloja (executive head, editorial board, the *Guardian*), in discussion with the author, April 20, 2019.
67. Malakata, "Nigeria Claims Top Internet Spot in Africa."
68. See Workman, "Nigeria leads Africa's 7 Highest Internet Using Countries."

Chapter Six

1. See Kperogi, "Guerrillas in Cyberia," 83.
2. Skjerdal, "Research on Brown Envelope Journalism in the African Media," 369.
3. Akabogu, "The Ethical Journalist and Brown Envelope Syndrome," 303.
4. Arogundade, "Calls for Ethical Revival as Corruption Infects Media."
5. Mojeed, "SaharaReporters' Sowore."
6. Isine, "Federal Government Seeks Power to Intercept Internet Communications."
7. Chesa, "Presidency Administers Secrecy Oath on Staff."
8. See Ochonu, "SaharaReporters' Strategic Success."
9. Ochonu, "SaharaReporters' Strategic Success."
10. Aluko, "Re: SaharaReporters' Strategic Success."
11. Aluko, "Re: SaharaReporters' Strategic Success."
12. Ochonu, "Saharereporters' Strategic Success."
13. Sahara Admin, "'Mercedes Jeep' Bribe."
14. Sahara Admin, "'Mercedes Jeep' Bribe."

in particular newspapers started with gusto, go off the streets after a few years of publication. Nonetheless, it is conceivable, given Nigeria's youthful population that the number of daily readers of news pages on the web is bigger than the number of those who buy ink stained papers." Olukotun, "Governance and the Media in an Emergent Democracy," 10. As of June 2019, I counted more than fifty online-only Nigerian news sites.

29. Ibraheem Musa in discussion with the author, January 2018.
30. Ekwealor, "Mobile Internet Subscriptions in Nigeria Hit a 100.9 Million High."
31. Hersman, "The Mobile Continent."
32. Smith, "Internet Use on Mobile Phones in Africa Predicted to Increase 20-Fold."
33. Pew Research Center, "Cell Phones in Africa: Communication Lifeline."
34. Castells, *End of Millennium*, 162.
35. Olukoya, "Facebook Growing Fast in Nigeria."
36. Oludimu, "Facebook Now Has 26 Million Active Users in Nigeria."
37. Owen, "Slate's Facebook Traffic has Dropped by 87 Percent Since 2017."
38. Ogala, Ekott, and Bamidele, "Police Boss Denies Banning Camera Phones at Polling Units."
39. Ogala et al.
40. Olopade, "Change They Can Almost Believe In."
41. Edozien, "Social Media Was the Other Big Winner at Nigeria's Historic Elections."
42. Akinwale, "INEC: A Wasted N27bn Investment in Technology?"
43. Campbell, "Mobile Communication and Network Privatism," 3.
44. Foucault, "The Eye of Power,"155.
45. Adebayo, "How We Use Social Media to Source Stories, by Nigerian Journalists."
46. Jin-ah, "Social Media and the Evolution of Journalism," 5.
47. Kperogi, "Journalism Is Dying a Slow Death in Nigeria."
48. Marama, "Women Demobilise Boko Haram Insurgents in Borno."
49. Idris, "Women Arrest Boko Haram Fighters in Borno."
50. Starkey, "Women Are Bent on Revenge against Tuareg Rebels in Mali."
51. Coleman and Blumler, *The Internet and Democratic Citizenship*, 4.
52. Fung and Wright, "Deepening Democracy," 5.
53. Reader, "Free Press vs. Free Speech?" 489.
54. Nielsen, "Coproduction or Cohabitation," 473.
55. Suler, "The Online Disinhibition Effect," 321.
56. Suler, 322.
57. Lewinski, "Collective Argumentative Criticism."
58. Bastian, "Nationalism in a Virtual Space."

59. Gaffey, "Nigerians Protest Draft Social Media Bill That Carries $25,000 Fine for False Accusations."
60. Aborisade, "Senate Bows to Pressures, Throws Out 'Anti-social Media Law.'"
61. Busari, "New Senate Bill Proposes Death Sentence for Hate Speech."
62. See, for instance, Namubiru, "How Uganda Is Implementing Its Controversial Social Media Tax"; Matinde, "Taxing Technology"; and Chutel, "Zambia is the Latest African State Trying to Muzzle Social Media."
63. Sindorf, "Symbolic Violence in the Online Field."
64. Kaigo and Watanabe, "Ethos in Chaos?"
65. Bakhtin, *Toward a Philosophy of the Act*, 28.
66. Hirschkop, "Justice and Drama," 61.
67. Gardiner, "Wild Publics and Grotesque Symposiums."
68. Miller and Yudice, *Cultural Policy, 11.*
69. Quoted in Smith, "Freedom of Expression and the Marketplace of Ideas Concept," 49.

Chapter Eight

1. Olukotun, "Media Accountability and Democracy in Nigeria, 1999–2003."
2. Usua, "Citizen Media and the Future of Government-Owned Broadcast Organizations," 1.
3. Network journalism is multimedia, hyperlinked journalism targeted at specific audiences. For an analysis of what "network journalism" entails in practice, see Bardoel and Deuze, "Network Journalism."
4. Pavlik, "The Future of Online Journalism."
5. Obijiofor, "Singaporean and Nigerian Journalists' Perceptions of New Technologies."
6. For a thoughtful analysis of the phenomenon of Internet access through cell phones in the developing world, see Chinn and Fairlie, "ICT Use in the Developing World." Also see Kim, "A Study of Internet Penetration Percents of Africa Using Digital Divide Models." The UK *Guardian* notes that "in mobile phone journalism, Africa is ahead of the west" (Bunz, "In Mobile Phone Journalism, Africa Is Ahead of the West"). For a fascinating scholarly reflection on how mobile phones are aiding web-based journalism in the developing world, see Andjelkovic, "The Future Is Mobile."
7. To be sure, this is also the case in most advanced democracies in the world. Journalists can be subpoenaed by the courts to reveal their sources before a grand jury. See, for instance, Fargo, "Evidence Mixed on Erosion of Journalists' Privilege." However, it is highly improbable that a subpoena from a Nigerian court against an online diasporic citizen journalist in, say, the United States, can be enforced.

8. Sahara Reporters, "Nigerian Treasury Looters Have Moved over to China, India, and Persian Gulf Countries."
9. Merritt, "What Citizen Journalism Can Learn from Public Journalism," 28.
10. Lasica, "Blogs and Journalism Need Each Other."
11. Olumhense, "Nigeria's Citizen Reporters."
12. I know this because, being a former newspaper journalist in Nigeria and a regular reader of Nigerian newspapers, I am familiar with the names of Nigerian journalists. Being a Facebook fan and Twitter follower allows users to keep up with the latest updates of news organizations or personalities. It does not necessarily indicate friendship or approval.
13. Proposition 8, formally called the California Marriage Protection Act, was a 2008 ballot proposition on the constitutional legality of same-sex marriage.
14. Sayre, "Agenda Setting in a Digital Age," 26.
15. The canonical article on agenda setting is McCombs' and Shaw's "The Agenda-Setting Function of the Mass Media." For a notable revision of the agenda-setting paradigm, see Erbring, Goldenberg, and Miller, "Front-Page News and Real-World Cues: A New Look at Agenda-Setting by the Media." The explosion of new media and the new media landscape this reality has inspired had led communication theorists to refine and extend "agenda setting" to "agenda melding." See Shaw, McCombs, and Weaver, "Individuals, Groups, and Agenda Melding." Also see Ragas and Roberts, "Agenda Setting and Agenda Melding."
16. See Andrews, "Is Blogging Journalism?"; Baoill, "Weblogs and the Public Sphere"; Carroll, "Culture Clash."
17. Halavais, "The Web as News: September 11 and New Sources of Web News."
18. Singer, "The Political J-Blogger," 23.
19. Redden, "Read the Whole Thing," 162.
20. The term "crowdsourcing" was neologized by Jeff Howe, who defined it as "the act of taking a job traditionally performed by a designated agent (usually an employee) and outsourcing it to an undefined, generally large group of people in the form of an open call" (see Howe, "The Rise of Crowdsourcing"). In a journalistic context, crowdsourcing news reporting entails the solicitation of textual news, eyewitness photos, and citizen video and audio clips from non-professional journalists for use in professionally run news operations.
21. In the United States, for instance, web advertising officially overtook print newspaper advertising in 2010. See Schweizer, "U.S. Web Advertising Exceeds Newspaper Print Ads in 2010, eMarketer Says."
22. Quoted in Harcup, *Journalism*, 98.
23. Haas, "Alternative Media, Public Journalism and the Pursuit of Democratization,"116.
24. Atton, *Alternative Media*, 154.
25. Melucci, *Challenging Codes*, 379.

26. Whitaker, *News Limited*, 105.
27. Visiting the White House shortly after a US presidential inauguration has become a rite of passage for Nigerian presidents since 1999.
28. Keck and Sikkink, *Activists Beyond Borders*, 23.
29. For representative examples of studies that fall in these categories see, Mainsah, "Cameroonians in Oslo, Diaspora, and Uses of the Media"; Ghorashi and Boersma, "The 'Iranian Diaspora' and the New Media"; Shi, "Identity Construction of the Chinese Diaspora"; Mai, "The Albanian Diaspora-in-the-Making."
30. Bastian, "Nationalism in a Virtual Space."
31. *ThisDay* and the *Daily Trust* experimented with selling print copies of their papers in London and New York in the late 1990s. They discontinued the experiment when AllAfrica.com emerged as a news aggregator that paid major African newspapers to make their content available on its site. Thus, newspapers from Africa, especially from Nigeria, that did not have functional websites were viewable online on AllAfrica.com. This obviated the need to sell physical copies of the papers in the West.
32. See, for instance, Dahlgren, "Introduction" and Eason, "On Journalistic Authority."
33. Zelizer, "Achieving Journalistic Authority through Narrative."
34. Zelizer, "Journalists as Interpretive Communities," 226.
35. A good example is the New York-based *African Sun Times*, which won the Historical Black Press Foundation's Black Newspaper of the Year award in 2009, the first time an Africa-focused newspaper won this award. The paper, which is now defunct in the aftermath of the death of its publisher, described itself as "America's #1 African Newsweekly," although the preponderance of its editorial coverage centered on Nigerian immigrants in America.
36. Ogundamisi, "Starving Nigerian Journalists and Blood-Stained Proprietors."
37. Several scholars have chronicled instances of contraflows from other parts of the world, chiefly through the export of cultural goods to the West and the emergence of influential news organizations that attract the attention of the West and the rest of the world such as Al-Jazeera. See, for instance, Biltereyst and Meers, "The International Telenovela Debate and the Contra-Flow Argument"; Wessler and Adolphsen, "Contra-Flow from the Arab World?"; Kunz, "Prime-Time Island"; Miller, "Ugly Betty Goes Global"; Tal, "Resisting Peripheral Exports." African countries do not have the financial muscle to export their cultural and media products to the West through the traditional media. Diasporic citizen media could very well be a useful model for reversing the media flow from the West to African and other developing-world societies.
38. Traditionally, alternative-media scholars have posited that "courting advertising revenue leads to depoliticization" and that media progressivism is measured by the extent of freedom from commercial pressures (see Kim and Hamilton,

"Capitulation to Capital?" 542). This argument is, of course, problematic, as I have shown in this book.

39. "Netizen" is the popular short form for "Internet citizen." It's a blend of "net" and "citizen."
40. Kovach and Rosenstiel, *The Elements of Journalism*, 18.
41. Johnson and Wiedenback, "Enhancing Perceived Credibility of Citizen Journalism Web Sites," 333.
42. Lasica, "Blogs and Journalism Need Each Other."
43. Rosen, "The People Formerly Known as the Audience."
44. Nip, "Exploring the Second Phase of Public Journalism."
45. Bruns, "The Active Audience."
46. Rosen, "Chris Nolan: The Stand Alone Journalist is Here. . . ."
47. Shenon, "Africa's WikiLeaks."
48. Nip, "Exploring the Second Phase of Public Journalism," 218.
49. Sahara Reporters, "Our Philosophy and Editorial Policy."
50. *Comedia*, "The Alternative Press."
51. Peck, *Uncovering the Sixties.*
52. Khiabany, "Red Pepper."
53. Pimlott, "Mainstreaming the Margins."
54. Hass, "Alternative Media, Public Journalism and the Pursuit of Democratization."
55. Downing, "Audiences and Readers of Alternative Media."
56. See, for instance, Sreberny-Mohammadi, "Small Media for a Big Revolution" and Sreberny-Mohammadi and Mohammadi, *Small Media, Big Revolution.*
57. Becoming a citizen of another country or getting another country's permanent residence permit is a good indication of the absence of a desire to return "home." It is evidence of rootedness. It needs to be stated, though, that many diasporic Nigerians, such as the Sahara Reporters publisher Omoyele Sowore, choose not to become American citizens so that they can run for high political positions in Nigeria. Although the Nigerian constitution recognizes dual citizenship, it bars dual citizens from running for president.
58. The only times when Nigerian governments openly disagreed with the US government and strained diplomatic relations were in 1975 and in the late 1990s. In 1975, Murtala Muhammed, a radical military dictator, took power by a coup d'état and decided to confront the West, including the US government. He was toppled and assassinated after only six months in power in what many believed was a CIA plot. In the 1990s, General Sani Abacha rebuffed the United States when he was severely excoriated for his gross human rights violations, including his hanging of the environmental rights activist Ken Saro-Wiwa. He too died in office.
59. Freedom House, "Freedom House's Annual Survey."

60. The two-step flow theory was first conceptualized by Paul Lazarsfeld and his colleagues. See Lazarsfeld, Berelson, and Gaudet, *The People's Choice*. It was later fleshed out by Elihu Katz in many experiments, as his famous article "The Two-Step Flow of Communication." Although this theory has been criticized for being simplistic, it nonetheless offers a useful framework for conceptualizing how informational flows occur, especially in societies not yet permeated by the mass media.
61. See Kperogi, "How Buhari Is Turning Nigeria into a Fascist State."
62. See Chinnasamy and Griffiths, "Looking Back at Malaysia's GE2008."

Bibliography

Abati, Reuben. "The Gbenga Obasanjo 'Interview.'" [Nigerian] *Guardian*, January 13, 2006; http://www.nigerianmuse.com/opessays/?u=Abati_on_Gbenga_Obasanjo_interview_by_Sowore.htm&PHPSESSID=69a95bb996be7efdb8b862b2ff7fbdf8.

Abdulaziz, Abdulaziz. "EXCLUSIVE: Pressure Mounts on NYSC to Cover up #AdeosunGate." Premium Times, July 10, 2018, https://www.premiumtimesng.com/news/headlines/275663-exclusive-pressure-mounts-on-nysc-to-cover-up-adeosungate.html.

Abercrombie, Nicholas, Stephen Hill, and Bryan S. Turner. *Dictionary of Sociology*. 3rd edition. Harmondsworth, UK: Penguin, 1994.

Aborisade, Oladimeji, and Robert J. Mundt. *Politics in Nigeria*. New York: Longman, 1999.

Aborisade, Sunday. "Senate Bows to Pressures, Throws Out 'Anti-Social Media Law.'" *Punch*, May 17, 2016, http://punchng.com/senate-bows-pressures-throws-anti-social-media-law/.

About US. "Title for The Times of Nigeria." http://www.aboutus.org/TheTimesOfNigeria.com, accessed April 24, 2010.

Achebe, Chinua. *Things Fall Apart*. London: Heinemann, 1986.

Ackerman, Bruce. "Why Dialogue?" *Journal of Philosophy* 86, no. 1 (1989): 5–22.

Adams, Paul. "Network Topologies and Virtual Place." *Annals of the Association of American Geographers* 88 (1998): 88–89.

Adamu, Abdallah U. "Istanci, Imamanci and Bollywoodanci: Media and Adaption in Hausa Popular Culture." In *Hausa Home Videos: Technology, Economy and Society*, edited by Abdallah Adamu, Yusuf M. Adamu, and Umar Faruk Jibril. Kano, Nigeria: Center for Hausa Cultural Studies, 2004.

Adebowale, Segun. "Simon Kolawole Begins Online Newspaper." The Eagle Online, April 27, 2014, https://theeagleonline.com.ng/simon-kolawole-begins-online-newspaper/.

Addis, Adeno. "Imagining the Homeland from Afar: Community and Peoplehood in the Age of the Diaspora." *Vanderbilt Journal of Transnational Law* 45, no. 963 (2012): 991–92.

Adebayo, Bukola. "Nigeria Overtakes India in Extreme Poverty Ranking." CNN, June 26, 2018, https://www.cnn.com/2018/06/26/africa/nigeria-overtakes-india-extreme-poverty-intl/index.html.

Adebayo, Ismail. "How We Use Social Media to Source Stories, by Nigerian Journalists." Daily Trust, September 9, 2012, https://www.dailytrust.com.ng/news/others/how-we-use-social-media-to-source-stories-by-nigerian-journalists/94021.html.

Adega, Majek. "Citizen Investigation: Harvard University Denies Agreement with Governors." Nigerian Village Square, June 11, 2009, http://www.nigeriavillagesquare.com/articles/patrick-nwadike/harvard-university-denies-agreement-with-governors.html.

Adega, Majekodumi. "Harvard Denies Agreement with Nigerian Governors." Sahara Reporters, June 12, 2009, http://saharareporters.com/report/harvard-university-denies-agreement-nigerian-governors.

Adekola, Shola. "FG Probes Killing of Nigerian Aboard Spanish Plane." *Nigerian Tribune*, June 29, 2007, http://www.nigeriavillagesquare.com/index.php?option=com_content&view=article&id=6476&catid=169&Itemid=46.

Adeniyi, Olusegun. "Why the Hell Am I Here?" Nigerian Village Square, September 7, 2007, http://www.nigeriavillagesquare.com/index.php?option=com_content&view=article&id=7117&catid=336&Itemid=46.

Adetayo, Olalekan. "Buhari Says Rule of Law Must be Subject to National Interest." Punch, August 27, 2018, https://punchng.com/buhari-says-rule-of-law-must-be-subject-to-national-interest/.

Adeyemo, Tudun. "Why I Write: Omoyele Sowore," *Tell*, September 7, 2009, http://saharareporters.com/2009/09/18/why-i-write-omoyele-sowore.

Adibe, Jideofor. "Nigerian Governors and the MOU with Harvard University: A Contrary View." Nigeria Village Square, June 26, 2009, http://www.villagesquare.ng/xenforo/index.php?threads/nigerian-governors-and-the-mou-with-harvard-university-a-contrary-view.33066/.

Adigun, Bashir. "Nigerian President Declares Assets." Associated Press, June 28, 2007, http://www.nigeriavillagesquare.com/index.php?option=com_content&view=article&id=6470&catid=169&Itemid=46.

Afigbo, Adiele E. "Background to Nigerian Federalism: Federal Features in the Colonial State." *Publius* 21, no. 4 (1991): 13–29.

AFP. "Nigeria Shuts Down Private TV, Radio Stations Tied to Opposition." Al Jazeera, June 7, 2019, https://www.aljazeera.com/news/2019/06/nigeria-shuts-private-tv-radio-stations-tied-opposition-190607062834145.html.

Againstbabangida.com. "FG Shuts Saharareporters.com." October 16, 2006, http://www.againstbabangida.com/index.php/resources/news-2/500-fg-shuts-saharareporterscom.html.

Agamben, Giorgio. *Homo Sacer: Sovereign Power and Bare Life*. Palo Alto: Stanford University Press, 1988.

Agbaje, Adigun A. *The Nigerian Press, Hegemony, and the Social Construction of Hegemony, 1960–1983*. Ontario, CA: Edwin Mellen Press, 1992.

Agbese, Aje-Ori. *The Roles of the Press and Communication Technology in Democratization: The Nigerian Story*. New York: Routledge, 2006.

Ahmad, Gausu. "Gaskiya Ta Fi Kwabo: From Colonial Service to Community Beacon." In *Indigenous Language Media in Africa*, edited by Abiodun Salawu, 95–113. Lagos: Centre for Black and African Arts and Civilization, 2006.

Ahmad, Muhammad. "Kano Assembly Suspends Emir Sanusi Probe after 'Osinbajo, IBB Intervention.'" Premium Times, May 22, 2017, https://www.premiumtimesng.com/news/headlines/231836-kano-assembly-suspends-emir-sanusi-probe-after-osinbajo-ibb-intervention.html.

Akabogu, Chinwe E. "The Ethical Journalist and Brown Envelope Syndrome: The Way Forward." *International Journal of Communication* 3 (2006): 201–6.

Akaeze, Anthony. "How They Survived Hard Times in US." *Newswatch*, October 13, 2009; http://stevennajieme.blogspot.com/2009/10/how-they-survived-hard-times-in-us.html.

Akinbanjo, Idris. "Yar'Adua Denied Me Passport—El-Rufai." *NEXT*, September 17, 2009.

Akinfeleye, Ralph. "Religious Publication: Pioneers of Nigerian Journalism." In *Mass Communication in Nigeria: A Book of Readings*, edited by Onuora E. Nwuneli, 26–34. Enugu, Nigeria: Fourth Dimension Publishers, 1985.

Akinkuotu, Ayo. "*Tell* and the Abacha Transition." In *The Media, Transition and Nigeria*. Edited by Tunji Oseni, 131–39. Lagos, Nigeria: Tosen Consult, 1999.

Akinkuotu, Eniola. "PUNCH Reporter Wins Rotary Humanitarian Award." Punch, July 13, 2016, https://punchng.com/punch-reporter-wins-rotary-humanitarian-award/.

Akintayo, Akin. "Nigeria: Sahara Reporters Comes of Age." *NEXT*, January 3, 2010, http://saharareporters.com/2009/12/30/nigeria-sahara-reporters-comes-age.

Akintunde, Kazeem. "Outrage over Governors' Harvard Programme." *Newswatch*, June 28, 2009.

Akinwale, Adedayo. "INEC: A Wasted N27bn Investment in Technology?" ThisDay, April 14, 2019, https://www.thisdaylive.com/index.php/2019/04/14/inec-a-wasted-n27bn-investment-in-technology/.

Albert, Isaac Olawale. "Whose Deliberative Democracy? A Critique of Online Public Discourses in Africa." Nigerian Village Square, April 19, 2010, http://www.nigeriavillagesquare.com/index.php?option=com_content&view=article&id=15291&catid=67&Itemid=46.

Aluede, R. O. A. "Regional Demands and Contemporary Educational Disparities in Nigeria." *Journal of Social Science* 13, no. 3 (2006): 183–89.

Aluko, M. A. O. "The Institutionalization of Corruption and Its Impact on Political Culture and Behavior in Nigeria." *Nordic Journal of African Studies* 11, no. 3 (2002): 393–402.

Aluko, Mobolaji. "Re: SaharaReporters' Strategic Success." USAAfrica Dialogue Series, December 18, 2008, http://groups.google.com/group/USAAfricaDialogue/browse_thread/thread/b0045233d98cd8db.

Aluko, Mobolaji. "Diaspora Petition to President Yar'adua over Non-renewal of Passport." Nigerian Village Square, http://www.nigeriavillagesquare.com/articles/mobolaji-aluko/diaspora-petition-to-president-yaradua-over-non-renewal-of-passport.html, accessed June 12, 2018.

Amadi, Sam. "Who Needs Harvard Education?" AllAfrica.com, http://allafrica.com/stories/200906250567.html, accessed June 12, 2018.

Anaba, Eze. "IBB, Visit to Minna and Journalism." Vanguard, August 20, 2010, http://www.vanguardngr.com/2010/08/ibb-visit-to-minna-and-journalism/.

Anderson, Benedict. *Imagined Communities: Reflections on the Origin and Spread of Nationalism*. New York: Verso, 1983; rev. ed. London: Verso, 1991.

Andjelkovic, Maja. "The Future Is Mobile: Why Developing Country Entrepreneurs Can Drive Internet Innovation." *SAIS Review* 30, no. 2 (2010): 121–33.

Andrews, Paul. "Is Blogging Journalism?" *Nieman Reports* 57 (2003): 63–64.

Appadurai, Arjun. *Modernity at Large: Cultural Dimensions of Globalization*. Minneapolis: University of Minnesota Press, 1996.

Arendt, Hanna. *The Human Condition*. Chicago: University of Chicago Press, 1958.

Arogundade, Lanre. "Nigeria: Calls for Ethical Revival as Corruption Infects Media." Ethical Journalism Network, https://ethicaljournalismnetwork.org/resources/publications/untold-stories/nigeria, accessed June 21, 2018.

Arthur, John A. *Invisible Sojourners: African Immigrant Diaspora in the United States*. Westport, CT: Praeger, 2000.

Article 19. *Truth from Below: The Emergent Press in Africa*. London: Article 19, 1991.

Atonko, Ben, and Ronald Mutum. "Exclusive: Army Shares Out Barracks Land to Generals, Others." Daily Trust, June 4, 2014, https://www.dailytrust.com.ng/daily/top-stories/25788-e-x-c-l-u-s-i-v-e-army-shares-out-barracks-land-to-generals-others.

Atton, Chris. *An Alternative Internet*. Edinburgh: Edinburgh University Press, 2004.

———. *Alternative Media*. London: Sage, 2001.

———. "Alternative Media in Scotland: Problems, Positions and 'Product.'" *Critical Quarterly* 42, no. 4 (2000): 40–47.

———. "Ethical Issues in Alternative Journalism." In *Communication Ethics Today*, edited by R. Keeble, 15–27. Leicester, UK: Troubadour, 2005.

———. "News Cultures and New Social Movements: Radical Journalism and Mainstream Media." *Journalism Studies* 3 (2002): 491–505.

———, ed. *The Routledge Companion to Alternative and Community Media*. London: Routledge, 2015.

———. "Towards a Cultural Study of Alternative Media on the Internet." *Southern Review* 35, no. 3 (2002): 52–62.

———. "What Is 'Alternative' Journalism?" *Journalism: Theory, Practice and Criticism* 4 (2003): 267–72.

Atton, Chris, and James F. Hamilton. *Alternative Journalism*. London: Sage, 2008.

Atton, Chris, and Emma Wickenden. "Sourcing Routines and Representation in Alternative Journalism: A Case Study Approach." *Journalism Studies* 6 (2005): 347–59.

Ayorinde, Steve. "Corruption in the Nigerian Media—Case of Azubuike Ishiekwene." Nigeria Village Square, March 1, 2010, http://www.nigeriavillagesquare.com/articles/corruption-in-the-nigerian-media-case-of-azubuike-ishiekwene.html.

Babalola, Hakeem. "Elendu Released: Nigerian Press Vs Citizen Online Press." Nigerian Village Square, October 29, 2008, http://www.nigeriavillagesquare.com/articles/elendu-released-nigerian-press-vs-citizen-online-press.html.

Bakhtin, Mikhail M. *Toward a Philosophy of the Act*. Translated by Vadim Liapunov, edited by Michael Holquist. Austin: University of Texas Press, 1993.

Bamidele, Razak. "How We Planned to Fund Harvard Programme—Govs' Forum." NigerianBestForum, June 15, 2009, http://www.nigerianbestforum.com/general-topics/how-we-planned-to-fund-harvard-programme/Bahktin, Mikhail. *Rabelais and His World*. Translated by Helene Iswolsky. Bloomington: Indiana University Press, 1984.

Bailey, Olga G. *Bart Cammaert, and Nico Carpentier: Understanding Alternative Media*. London: Open University Press, 2007.

Baoill, Andrew. "Weblogs and the Public Sphere." University of Minnesota. Retrieved from the University of Minnesota Digital Conservancy, http://hdl.handle.net/11299/172814.

Bardoel, Jo, and Mark Deuze. "Network Journalism: Converging Competences of Media Professionals and Professionalism." *Australian Journalism Review* 23, no. 2 (2001): 91–103.

Bastian, Misty. "Nationalism in a Virtual Space: Immigrant Nigerians on the Internet." *West Africa Review* 1, no. 1 (July 1999): 13, http://www.africaresource.com/war/vol1.1/bastian.html.

Bauder, David. "Web Has Unexpected Effect on Journalism." *USA Today*, March 17, 2008, http://www.usatoday.com/news/nation/2008-03-17-3511532335_x.htm.

Becker, Bruce, and Jason Wehner. "Electronic Networks and Civil Society: Reflections on Structural Changes in the Public Sphere." In *Culture, Technology, Communication: Towards an International Global Village*, edited by Charles Ess, 67–85. Albany: State University of New York Press, 2001.

Becker, David G. "Bonanza Development and the New Bourgeoisie." *Comparative Political Studies* 15 (1982): 88–243.

Ben, Sayre, Leticia Bode, Dhavan Shah, Dave Wilcox, and Chirag Shah. "Agenda Setting in a Digital Age: Tracking Attention to California Proposition 8 in Social Media, Online News, and Conventional News." *Policy & Internet* 2, no. 2 (2010): 7–32.

Benbasat, Izak, David K. Goldstein, and Melissa Mead. "The Case Research Strategy in Studies of Information Systems." *MIS Quarterly* 11 (1987): 369–87.

Benedikt, Michael, ed. *Cyberspace: First Steps*. Cambridge, MA: MIT Press, 1991.

Benhabib, Seyla. "Models of Public Space: Hannah Arendt, the Liberal Tradition, and Jürgen Habermas." In *Habermas and the Public Sphere*. Edited by Craig Calhoun. Cambridge, MA: MIT Press, 1992.

Benjaminson, Peter, and David Anderson. *Investigative Reporting*. 2nd ed. Ames: Iowa State University, 1990.

Benson, Rodney. "Commercialism and Critique; California's Alternative Weeklies." In *Contesting Media Power: Alternative Media in a Networked World*, edited by James Curran and Nick Couldry, 111–27. Lanham, MD: Rowman & Littlefield, 2003.

Bernal, Victoria. "Diaspora, Cyberspace and Political Imagination: The Eritrean Diaspora Online." *Global Networks* 6, no. 2 (2006): 161–79.

Biltereyst, Daniel, and Philippe Meers. "The International Telenovela Debate and the Contra-Flow Argument: A Reappraisal." *Media, Culture & Society* 22, no. 4 (2000): 393–414.

Bittner, John R. *Mass Communication: An Introduction*. 5th ed. Englewood Cliffs, NJ: Prentice Hall, 1989.

Boczkowski, Pablo J. "The Development and Use of Online Newspapers: What Research Tells Us and What We Might Want to Know." In *Handbook of New Media: Social Shaping and Consequences of ICTs, L.A.*, edited by Leah A. Lievrouw and Sonia M. Livingstone, 270–86. London: Sage, 2002.

Bohman, James. "Expanding Dialogue: The Internet, the Public Sphere and Prospects for Transnational Democracy." In *After Habermas: New Perspectives on the Public Sphere*, edited by Nick Crossley and John M. Roberts, 131–54. Oxford: Blackwell Publishing, 2004.

Bourdieu, Pierre. *Language and Symbolic Power*. Cambridge, MA: Harvard University Press, 1991.

Bowman, Shayne, and Chris Willis. "We Media: How Audiences Are Shaping the Future of News and Information." http://www.hypergene.net/wemedia/, accessed September 11, 2009.

Boyd-Barrett, Oliver. "Media Imperialism: Towards an International Framework for the Analysis of Media Systems." In *Mass Communication and Society*, edited by James Curran, Michael Gurevitch, and Janet Woollacott, 116–41. London: Edward Arnold, 1977.

Bradley, Matthew T. "Civil Society and Democratic Progression in Postcolonial Nigeria: The Role of Non-Governmental Organizations." *Journal of Civil Society* 1, no. 1 (2005): 61–74.

Brandenburg, Heinz. "Pathologies of the Virtual Public Sphere." In *Civil Society, Politics and the Internet: A Comparative Perspective*, edited by S. Oates, D. Owen, and R. Gibson. London: Routledge, 2005.

Brettell, Caroline B. "Political Belonging and Cultural Belonging Immigration Status, Citizenship, and Identity among Four Immigrant Populations in a Southwestern City." *American Behavioral Scientist* 50, no. 1 (2006): 70–99.

Brinkerhoff, Jennifer M. *Digital Diasporas: Identity and Transnational Engagement.* Cambridge: Cambridge University Press, 2009.

Brook, James, and Iain A. Boal, eds. *Resisting the Virtual Life: The Culture and Politics of Information.* San Francisco: City Lights, 1995.

Bruner, Michael L. "Carnivalesque Protest and the Humorless State." *Text and Performance Quarterly* 25, no. 2 (2005): 136–55.

Bruns, Axel. "The Active Audience: Transforming Journalism from Gatekeeping to Gatewatching." In *Making Online News: The Ethnography of New Media Production* edited by Chris Patterson and David Domingo. New York: Peter Lang, 2008.

Buchstein, Hubertus. "Bytes that Bite: The Internet and Deliberative Democracy." *Constellations* 4, no. 2 (1997): 248–23.

Bunz, Mercedes. "In Mobile Phone Journalism, Africa is Ahead of the West." *The Guardian*, December 18, 2009, http://www.guardian.co.uk/media/pda/2009/dec/17/digital-media-mobilephone-usage-africa-leapfroging-ushahidi-swift-river.

Busari, Kemi. "New Senate Bill Proposes Death Sentence for Hate Speech." Premium Times, March 2, 2018, https://www.premiumtimesng.com/news/top-news/260466-new-senate-bill-proposes-death-sentence-hate-speech.html.

Byman, Daniel, Peter Chalk, Bruce Hoffman, William Rosenau, and David Brannan. *Trends in Outside Support for Insurgent Movements.* Santa Monica, CA: Rand Corporation, 2001.

Calhoun, Craig, Introduction to *Habermas and the Public Sphere*, edited by Craig Calhoun. Cambridge, MA: MIT Press, 1992.

Campbell, Scott W. "Mobile Communication and Network Privatism: A Literature Review of the Implications for Diverse, Weak, and New Ties." *Review of Communication Research* 3, no. 1 (2015): 1–21. https://doi.org/10.12840/issn.2255-4165.2015.03.01.006.

Campbella, Allan, and John McIlroy. "'The Trojan Horse': Communist Entrism in the British Labour Party, 1933–43." *Labor History* 59, no. 5 (2018): 513–54, https://doi.org/10.1080/0023656X.2018.1436938.

Campbell, Donald T. "Degrees of Freedom and the Case Study." *Comparative Political Studies* 8, no. 1 (1975): 178–91.

Campbell, Vincent. *Information Age Journalism: Journalism in an International Context.* London: Arnold, 2004.

Cammaerts, Bart, and Leo Van Audenhove. "Online Political Debate, Unbounded Citizenship, and the Problematic Nature of a Transnational Public Sphere." *Political Communication* 22 (2005): 179–96.

Carroll, Brian. "Culture Clash: Journalism and the Communal Ethos of the Blogosphere." University of Minnesota. Retrieved from the University of Minnesota Digital Conservancy, http://hdl.handle.net/11299/172831.

Castells, Manuel. *End of Millennium*. Malden, MA: Blackwell, 1998.

———. *The Internet Galaxy: Reflections on the Internet, Business, and Society*. Oxford: Oxford University Press, 2002.

Cecil, Matthew, ed. "Alternative Media." *Journal of Communication Inquiry* 24, no. 4 (2000): 355–56.

Chesa, Chesa. "Presidency Administers Secrecy Oath on Staff." *Daily Independent*, September 24, 2008.

———. "President's Health: Yar'Adua Sues Leadership Newspaper." *Sunday Independent*, November 9, 2008.

Chick, John D. "The Nigerian Press and National Integration." *Commonwealth & Comparative Politics* 9, no. 2 (1971): 115–33.

Chiedozie, Ihuoma. "Presidency Lifts Ban on Passports of el-Rufai, Ribadu." *Punch*, October 15, 2009.

Chinnasamy, Sara, and Mary Griffiths. "Looking Back at Malaysia's GE2008: An Internet Election and its Democratic Aftermath." *IAFOR Journal of Media, Communication and Film* 1, no. 1 (2013): 59–74.

Chinn, Menzie D., and Robert W. Fairlie. "ICT Use in the Developing World: An Analysis of Differences in Computer and Internet Penetration." *Review of International Economics* 18, no. 1 (2010): 153–67.

Cho, Hiromi, Hugh Martin, and Stephen Lacy. "An Industry in Transition: Entry and Exit in Daily Newspaper Markets, 1987–2003." *Journalism & Mass Communication Quarterly* 83, no. 2 (2006): 381–96.

Chonoko, Ibrahim. "How Yar'adua Betrayed Us, By el-Rufai." *Daily Trust*, October 22, 2009.

Chung, Deborah S., Eunseong Kim, Kaye D. Trammell, and Lance V. Porter. "Uses and Perceptions of Blogs: A Report on Professional Journalists and Journalism Educators." *Journalism & Mass Communication Educator* 62, no. 3 (2007): 305–32.

Chutel, Lynsey. "Zambia Is the Latest African State Trying to Muzzle Social Media with Arbitrary Laws." Quartz Africa, July 6, 2018, https://qz.com/1322814/zambia-considers-social-media-clampdown-through-new-laws-or-tighter-regulation/.

Chyko, Mary. *Portable Communities: The Social Dynamics of Online and Mobile Connectedness*. Albany: State University of New York Press, 2008.

CNN. "CNN Denies Nigerian Allegations of Staging Report." February 13, 2007, http://www.cnn.com/2007/WORLD/africa/02/12/nigeria.reaction/index.html.

Cohen, Robin. "Diasporas and the New Nation-State: From Victims to Challengers." *International Affairs* 72, no. 3 (1996): 507–20.

Coleman, James S. *Nigeria: A Background to Nationalism*. Berkeley: University of California Press, 1960.

Coleman, Stephen, and Jay G. Blumler. *The Internet and Democratic Citizenship: Theory, Practice and Policy*. Cambridge: Cambridge University Press, 2009.

Collier, Paul, and Anke Hoeffler. "Greed and Grievances in Civil War." Policy Research Working Paper No. 2355. Washington, DC: World Bank, 2001.

Collins, Anthony. *Words of Fire: Independent Journalists Who Challenge Dictators, Drug Lords, and Other Enemies of a Free Press.* New York: New York University Press, 2001.

Collins, Chuks. "Daniel, Timothy Elombah Plead Not Guilty to 'Biafra Terrorism,' Cyber Bullying Ibrahim Idris." News48Hours Nigeria, March 4, 2018, https://www.news48hrs.com/2018/03/daniel-timothy-elombah-plead-not-guilty.html.

Comedia. "The Alternative Press: The Development of Underdevelopment." *Media, Culture & Society* 6 (1984): 95–102.

Committee to Protect Journalists. "Nigerian Journalist Jones Abiri Arrested Again in Bayelsa State." CPJ.com, March 30, 2019, https://cpj.org/2019/03/nigerian-journalist-jones-abiri-arrested-again-in-.php.

———. "Second U.S.-based Nigerian Blogger Held." CPJ.com October 31, 2008, https://cpj.org/2008/10/second-us-based-nigerian-blogger-held.php.

———. "Three Journalists Killed in Nigeria." CPJ.com, April 26, 2010, https://cpj.org/2010/04/three-journalists-killed-in-nigeria.php.

Conboy, Martin, and John Steele. "The Future of Newspapers." *Journalism Studies* 9, no. 5 (2008): 650–61.

Concerned Nigerians in Diaspora. "Letter to President Obasanjo on Third Term Agenda—On His Visit to the White House." Nigerian Village Square, March 29, 2006, http://www.nigeriavillagesquare.com/index.php?option=com_content&view=article&id=2718&catid=111&Itemid=46.

Connor, Phillip. "At Least a Million Sub-Saharan Africans Moved to Europe Since 2010: Sub-Saharan Migration to the United States also Growing." Pew Research Center, March 22, 2018, http://www.pewglobal.org/2018/03/22/at-least-a-million-sub-saharan-africans-moved-to-europe-since-2010/#nigeria-and-ghana-have-been-major-sources-of-sub-saharan-migrants-to-both-europe-and-the-united-states.

Conway, Janet, and Jakeet Singh. "Is the World Social Forum a Transnational Public Sphere? Nancy Fraser, Critical Theory and the Containment of Radical Possibility." *Theory, Culture & Society* 26, no. 5 (2009): 61–84.

Cottle, Simon. "Rethinking News Access." *Journalism Studies* 1, no. 3 (2000): 427–48.

Couldry, Nick. "Mediation and Alternative Media, or Relocating the Centre of Media and Communication Studies." *Media International Australia Incorporating Culture and Policy* 103 (2002): 24–31.

———. *The Place of Media Power: Pilgrims and Witnesses in the Media Age*. London: Routledge, 2000.

Cowan, Brian. "The Rise of the Coffeehouse Reconsidered." *Historical Journal* 47, no. 1 (2004): 21–46.

Cowen, Tyler. "Africa is Sending Us Its Best and Brightest." *Chicago Tribune*, January 16, 2018; http://www.chicagotribune.com/news/opinion/commentary/ct-perspec-africa-immigration-trump-norway-slur-0116-20180112-story.html.

Curran, James. "Globalization Theory: The Absent Debate." In *Media and Power*, 166–84. London: Routledge, 2002.

———. "Rethinking the Media as a Public Sphere." In *Communication and Citizenship: Journalism and the Public Sphere*, edited by Peter Dahlgren and Colin Sparks, 1–57. London: Routledge, 1991.

Curran, James, and Jean Seaton. *Power Without Responsibility: The Press, Broadcasting, and New Media in Britain*. London: Routledge, 2003.

Dahlberg, Lincoln. "Computer-Mediated Communication and the Public Sphere: A Critical Analysis." *Journal of Computer-Mediated Communication* 7, no. 1 (2001): n.p., http://jcmc.indiana.edu/vol7/issue1/dahlberg.html.

Dahlgren, Peter. Introduction to *Journalism and Popular Culture*, edited by Peter Dahlgren and Collin Sparks, 1–23. London: Sage, 1992.

Dare, Sunday. *Guerrilla Journalism: Dispatches from the Underground*. Ibadan, Nigeria: Kraft Books Limited, 2007.

Darke, Peter, Graeme Shanks, and Marianne Broadbent. "Successfully Completing Case Study Research: Combining Rigour, Relevance and Pragmatism." *Information Systems Journal* 8 (1998): 273–89.

Dasmile. "Newspaper Publishers' Wife Murder 14 Years for Rituals." CNN iReport, February 25, 2009, http://ireport.cnn.com/docs/DOC-220064.

Daura, Mamman. "Editing a Government Newspaper in Nigeria." In *Reporting Africa*, edited by Olav Stokke, 39–46. New York: Africana Publishing Corporation, 1971.

Davis, Steve. "Public Journalism: The Case Against." *Journalism Studies* 1, no. 4 (2000): 686–89.

De St. Jorre, John. *The Nigerian Civil War*. London: Hodder and Stoughton, 1972.

Dean, Jodi. "Virtually Citizens." *Constellations* 4, no. 2 (1997): 264–82.

———. "Why the Net Is Not a Public Sphere." *Constellations* 10, no. 2 (2003): 95–112.

Dejung, Christof, and Niels P. Petersson, eds. *The Foundations of Worldwide Economic Integration: Power, Institutions, and Global Markets, 1850–1930*. Cambridge: Cambridge University Press, 2013.

Deuze, Mark. "Journalism and the Web: An Analysis of Skills and Standards in an Online Environment." *Gazette* 61, no. 5 (1999): 373–90.

———. "The Web and its Journalisms: Considering the Consequences of Different Types of Newsmedia Online." *New Media & Society* 5, no. 2 (2003): 203–30.

Dewey, John. *The Public and its Problems*. Athens: University of Ohio Press, 1927.

Dick, Murray. "Search Engine Optimisation in UK News Production." *Journalism Practice* 5, no. 4 (2011): 462–77.

Dike, Akobundu U. "Strategies for Preservation and Increased Access to Newspapers in Nigerian University Libraries." In *Library Philosophy and Practice 2009*, edited by University of Idaho, http://www.webpages.uidaho.edu/~mbolin/ugah7.htm, accessed September 30, 2009.

Dimitrova, Daniela V., and Matt Neznanski. "Online Journalism and the War in Cyberspace: A Comparison between U.S. and International Newspapers." *Journal of Computer-Mediated Communication* 12 (2006): 248–63.

Dirlik, Arif. "Intimate Others: [Private] Nations and Diasporas in an Age of Globalization." *Inter-Asia Cultural Studies* 5, no. 3 (2004): 491–502.

Dodge, Martin, and Robert Kitchin. *Mapping Cyberspace*. London: Routledge, 2001.

Downing, John D. H. "Audiences and Readers of Alternative Media: The Absent Lure of the Virtually Unknown." *Media, Culture & Society* 25 (2003): 625–65.

———. *Radical Media: The Political Experience of Alternative Communication*. Boston: South End Press, 1984.

———. *Radical Media: Rebellious Communication and Social Movements*. Thousand Oaks, CA: Sage, 2001.

Dryzek, John. *Deliberative Democracy and Beyond: Liberals, Critics, Contestations*. Oxford: Oxford University Press, 2000.

Duyile, Dayo. *Makers of Nigerian Press: An Historical Analysis of Newspaper Development, the Pioneer Heroes, the Modern Press Barons and the New Publishers from 1859–1987*. Ibadans: Gong Communications Ltd, 1987.

Dyson, Esther, George Gilder, George Keyworth, and Alvin Toffler. "Cyberspace and the American Dream: A Magna Carta for the Knowledge Age." Progress and Freedom Foundation, August 1994, http://www.pff.org/issues-pubs/futureinsights/fi1.2magnacarta.html.

Eason, David L. "On Journalistic Authority: The Janet Cooke Scandal." In *Media, Myths and Narratives: Television and the Press*, edited by James Carey, 246–61. Newbury Park, CA: Sage, 1988.

Ebeling, Mary F. "The New Dawn: Black Agency in Cyberspace." *Radical History Review* 87 (2003): 96–108.

Edomaruse, Collins, and Festus Akanbi. "Document Affirms Govs' Forum, Harvard Varsity Deal." ThisDay, June 14, 2009.

Edozien, Frankie. "Social Media Was the Other Big Winner at Nigeria's Historic Elections." Quartz, April 7, 2015, https://qz.com/377777/social-media-was-the-other-big-winner-at-nigerias-historic-elections/.

Ehrlich, Matthew C. *The Journalism of Outrageousness: Tabloid Television News vs. Investigative News*. Columbia, SC: Association for Education in Journalism and Mass Communication, 1996.

Eisenhardt, Kathleen M. "Building Theories from Case Study Research." *Academy of Management Review* 14, no. 4 (1989): 532–50.

Ekine, Sokari. "Nigeria Joins List of Countries Harassing Bloggers." *BPS Media Shift*, November 10, 2008; http://mediashift.org/2008/11/nigeria-joins-list-of-countries-harassing-bloggers315/.

Ekwealor, Victor. "Mobile Internet Subscriptions in Nigeria Hit a 100.9 Million High." *Techpoint*, April 18, 2018, https://techpoint.ng/2018/04/18/nigeria-mobile-Internet-subscription-february-2018/.

Elendu, Jonathan. "Sowore Disengages from Elendureports.com." Elendu Reports, January 4, 2006; http://nigeriavillagesquare.com/forum/threads/what-motivates-elendu-and-sowore.2607/.

———. "Yar'adua Dead." Elendu Reports, March 7, 2007, http://oyibo-in-nigeria.blogspot.com/2007/03/.

Elendu, Jonathan, and Omoyele Sowore. "Bayelsa Governor's 'Modest' Mansion in Potomac." Elendu Reports, October 13, 2005, http://nigeriavillagesquare.com/forum/threads/bayelsa-governors-modest-mansion-in-potomac.1772/.

———. "More Corrupt Deals of Bayelsa Governor Uncovered." Elendu Reports, September 30, 2005, http://nigeriavillagesquare.com/forum/threads/more-corrupt-deals-of-bayelsa-governor-uncovered.1703/.

———. "Olu Obasanjo's House: Lies, Half-Truths, and Threats." Elendu Reports, September 12, 2005, http://www.nigerialinks.com/Articles/Sowore/2005/09/olu-obasanjos-house-lies-half-truths.html.

———. "Potomac Mansions: Kalu and Atiku Are Neighbours." Elendu Reports, August 30, 2005, http://nigeriavillagesquare.com/forum/threads/buy-america-olu-obasanjo-felicia-wabara-and-orji-kalu-and-the-anti-corruption.1730/.

———. "Sokoto Governor Has His Share of London." OnlineNigeria, October 10, 2005, http://nm.onlinenigeria.com/templates/?a=5518.

———. "Sokoto Governor Paid £500,00.00 More for House." Elendu Reports, October 9, 2005, http://www.nigerianmuse.com/nigeriawatch/officialfraud/?u=Bafarawa_London_property.htm.

———. "War on Corruption: Obasanjo is Complicit." Nigeria Village Square, September 6, 2005, http://nigeriavillagesquare.com/forum/threads/corruption-incorporated.8525/.

———. "War on Corruption: Obasanjo's Oily Hands." ElenduReports, September 10, 2005, http://www.nigeriavillagesquare.com/articles/war-on-corruption-obasanjos-oily-hands.html.

Elliot, Philip, and Peter Golding. "Mass Communication and Social Change: The Imagery of Development and the Development of Imagery." In *Sociology and Development*, edited by Emanuel Jehuda De Kadt and Gavin Williams, 229–54. London: Tavistock, 1974.

Elombah, Daniel. "Umaru Yar'adua Joins the 'Battle on Cyberspace.'" June 17, 2009, http://saharareporters.com/2009/06/18/yar%E2%80%99adua-joins-%E2%80%98battle-cyber-space%E2%80%99.

Elombah.com. "Nigerians Kick Against Harvard Training for Governors." June 14, 2009.

ElombahNews. "I Was Abducted By SARS—Daniel Elombah." Elombah.com, January 4, 2018, https://elombah.com/index.php/special-reports/i-was-abducted-by-sars-daniel-elombah/.

Elster, Jon. Introduction to *Deliberative Democracy: Essays on Reason and Politics*, edited by James Bohman and William Rehg. Cambridge, MA: MIT Press, 1997.

Emmanuel, Ogala. "Sahara Reporters Publisher, Sowore, Accuses Saraki of Identity Theft." Premium Times, April 14, 2016, https://www.premiumtimesng.com/news/top-news/201802-sahara-reporters-publisher-sowore-accuses-saraki-identity-theft.html.

Empowered Newswire. "I Am Here to Understudy the Americans—Adeniyi, Yar'Adua's Spokesman, on US Visit." Nigerian Village Square, September 4, 2007, http://www.nigeriavillagesquare.com/index.php?option=com_content&view=article&id=7094&catid=22&Itemid=46.

Erbring, Lutz, Edie N. Goldenberg, and Arthur H. Miller. "Front-Page News and Real-World Cues: A New Look at Agenda-Setting by the Media." *American Journal of Political Science* 24, no. 1 (1980): 16–34.

Escobar, Arturo. "Welcome to Cyberia: Notes on the Anthropology of Cyberculture." *Current Anthropology* 35, no. 3 (1994): 56–76.

Ette, Mercy. "Agents of Change or Stability: The Nigerian Press Undermines Democracy." *Harvard International Journal of Press and Politics* 5, no. 3 (2000): 67–86.

Evans, Michael R. "Hegemony and Discourse: Negotiating Cultural Relationships through Media Production." *Journalism: Theory, Practice & Criticism* 3, no. 3 (2002): 309–29.

Everett, Anna. "The Revolution Will Be Digitized: Afrocentricity and the Digital Public Sphere." *Social Text* 71/20, no. 2 (2002): 125–46.

Ezimakor, Tony. "DSS Arrested Abiri For Pipeline Vandalism, Militant Activities—FG." Daily Independent, June 24, 2018, https://independent.ng/dss-arrested-abiri-for-pipeline-vandalism-militant-activities-fg/.

Fabiyi, Olusola. "FG Stops New Passports for Ribadu, el-Rufai." *Punch*, October 10, 2009.

Fadayomi, Theophilus O. "Brain Drain and Brain Gain in Africa: Causes, Dimensions, and Consequences." In *International Migration in and from Africa: Dimensions, Challenges, and Prospects*, edited by Adeanti Adepoju and Tomas Hammer. Stockholm: Population, Human Resources and Development in Africa, Centrum for Invandringsforskning, 1996.

Fagbenle, Kunle. "Cease and Desist Letter: Re: Invasion of the Privacy of Chief (Mrs.) Lamide Adegbenro by www.saharareporters.com, et al." Nigerian Village Square, December 13, 2006, http://www.nigeriavillagesquare.com/news/update-re-cease-and-desist-letter-to-saharareporters-letter-of-response-to-kunle-fagbenle.html.

———. "Re: Malicious Defamation of President Olusegun Obasanjo." Nigerian Village Square, November 7, 2006, http://www.nigeriavillagesquare.com/articles/nvs/malicious-defamation.html.

Fakoya, Olusegun. "Nigeria Mass Media—The Fourth Estate of Graft." Point-BlankNews, March 26, 2010, http://www.PointBlankNews/artopn2542.html.

Falola, Toyin. *The History of Nigeria*. Westport, CT: Greenwood Press, 1999.

Fargo, Anthony. "Evidence Mixed on Erosion of Journalists' Privilege." *Newspaper Research Journal* 22, no. 2 (2003): 50–63.

Fernald, Anne E. "A Feminist Public Sphere? Virginia Woolf's Revisions of the Eighteenth Century." *Feminist Studies* 31, no. 1 (2005): 125–58.

Fiske, John. "British Cultural Studies and Television." In *Channels of Discourse, Reassembled*. 2nd ed., edited by Robert C. Allen, 284–326. London: Routledge, 1992.

Flacks, Richard. *Youth and Social Change*. Chicago: Markham, 1971.

Flew, Terry. *New Media: An Introduction*. 3rd edition. Melbourne: Oxford University Press, 2005.

Flyvbjerg, Bent. "Five Misunderstandings about Case-Study Research." *Qualitative Inquiry* 12, no. 2 (2006): 219–45.

Forde, Susan. *Challenging the News: The Journalism of Alternative and Community Media*. New York: Palgrave, 2011.

Fosco, Molly. "The Most Successful Ethnic Group in the U.S. May Surprise You." Ozy, June 6, 2018, https://www.ozy.com/fast-forward/the-most-successful-ethnic-group-in-the-us-may-surprise-you/86885?li_source=LI&li_medium=default-widget.

Foucault, Michel. "The Eye of Power." In *Power/Knowledge: Selected Interviews and Other Writings 1972–1977*, edited by Colin Gordon, 146–65. Sussex: Harvester Press, 1980.

Frank, Thomas. *New Consensus for Old: Cultural Studies from Left to Right*. Chicago: Prickly Paradigm Press, 2002.

Franklin, Bob. "The Future of Newspapers." *Journalism Practice* 2, no. 3 (2008): 306–17.

Fraser, Nancy. "Rethinking the Public Sphere." *Social Text* 25/26 (1990): 56–80.

———. "Transnationalizing the Public Sphere: On the Legitimacy and Efficacy of Public Opinion in a Post-Westphalian World." *Theory, Culture & Society* 24, no. 4 (2007): 7–30.

Freedom House. "Freedom House's Annual Survey of Global Media Independence: An Historical Review, 1984–2007," http://freedomhouse.org/template.cfm?page=359; accessed February 28, 2010.

———. "Freedom on the Net 2018—Nigeria." Refworld, November 1, 2018, https://www.refworld.org/docid/5be16b02a.html.

Friedland, Lewis A. *Public Journalism: Past and Future*. Dayton, OH: Kettering Foundation Press, 2003.

Fung, Archon, and Erik Olin Wright. "Deepening Democracy: Innovations in Empowered Participatory Governance." *Politics and Society* 29, no. 1 (2001): 5–51.

Furuholt, Bjørn, and Stein Kristiansen. "Internet Cafés in Asia and Africa: Venues for Education and Learning?" *Journal of Community Informatics* 3, no. 2 (2007): 1–12.

Gaffey, Conor. "Nigerians Protest Draft Social Media Bill that Carries $25,000 Fine for False Accusations." *Newsweek*, December 4, 2015, https://www.newsweek.com/nigerians-protest-draft-social-media-bill-which-carries-25000-fine-false-401084.

Gambrelle, Jon. "Bomb Suspect Came from Elite Family, Best Schools." Associated Press, December 28, 2009, http://www.richmond.com/news/bomb-suspect-came-from-elite-family-best-schools/article_d07fd39f-dc40-5fdc-ac78-a6be63d99dd2.html.

Gardiner, Michael E. "Wild Publics and Grotesque Symposiums: Habermas and Bakhtin on Dialogue, Everyday Life and the Public Sphere." *Sociological Review* 52, no. 1 (2004): 28–48.

Gentry, Mae, and Shelia M. Poole. "GoodWorks Draws Criticism: Andrew Young's Lobbying Firm under Fire for Ties with Nigerian President Obasanjo." *Atlanta Journal Constitution*, March 18, 2007.

George, Alexander L., and Andrew Bennett. *Case Studies and Theory Development in the Social Sciences*. Cambridge. MA: MIT Press, 2005.

Ghorashi, Halleh, and Kees Boersma. "The 'Iranian Diaspora' and the New Media: From Political Action to Humanitarian Help." *Development & Change* 40, no. 4 (2009): 667–91.

Gibbs, Patricia, and James Hamilton, eds. "Special Issue of Media History: Alternative Media." *Media History* 7, no. 2 (2001): 117–18.

Gibson, William. *Neuromancer*. New York, Fantasia Press, 1984.

Giddens, Anthony. Runaway World. BBC Reith Lectures, 1999, http://news.bbc.co.uk/hi/english/static/events/reith_99; accessed August 29, 2009.

Gillmor, Dan. "A New Brand of Journalism Is Taking Root in South Korea." *San Jose Mercury News*, May 18, 2003.

———. *We the Media: Grassroots Journalism by the People, for the People*. Sebastopol, CA: O'Reilly Media, 2004.

Giomelakis, Dimitrios, and Andreas Veglis. "Employing Search Engine Optimization Techniques in Online News Articles." *Studies in Media and Communication* 3, no. 1 (2015): 22–33.

Glasser, Theodore L., ed. *The Idea of Public Journalism*. New York: Guilford Press, 1999.

———. "The Politics of Public Journalism." *Journalism Studies* 1, no. 4 (2000): 683–86.

Goldfarb, Jeffery C. *Civility and Subversion: The Intellectual in Democratic Society.* New York: Cambridge University Press, 1998.

Golding, Peter. "Media Professionalism in the Third World: The Transfer of an Ideology." In *Mass Communication and Society,* edited by James Curran, Michael Gurevitch, and Janet Woollacott, 291–308. London: Edward Arnold/Open University Press, 1977.

Goujard, Clothilde. "Why News Websites are Closing Their Comments Sections." Medium.com, last modified September 8, 2016, https://medium.com/global-editors-network/why-news-websites-are-closing-their-comments-sections-ea31139c469d.

Guardian Editorial. "DYA Campaign: The Vice President's Assets." [Nigerian] Guardian, August 8, 2007, http://www.nigeriavillagesquare.com/index.php?option=com_content&view=article&id=6801&catid=111&Itemid=46.

———. "The Proposed Harvard Training for Governors." *The [Nigerian] Guardian,* June 11, 2009.

Guidry, John A., Michael D. Kennedy, and Mayer N. Zald. *Globalizations and Social Movements: Culture, Power, and the Transnational Public Sphere.* Ann Arbor: University of Michigan Press, 2000.

Haas, Tanni. "Alternative Media, Public Journalism and the Pursuit of Democratization." *Journalism Studies* 5 (2004): 115–21.

———. "From 'Public Journalism" to the 'Public's Journalism'? Rhetoric and Reality in the Discourse on Weblogs." *Journalism Studies* 6, no. 3 (2005): 387–96.

Habermas, Jürgen. *Between Facts and Norms: Contributions to a Discourse Theory of Law and Democracy.* Translated by William Rehg. Cambridge: Polity Press, 1996.

———. *The Inclusion of the Other: Studies in Political Theory.* Edited by Ciaran Cronin and Pablo De Greiff. Cambridge, MA: MIT Press, 1998.

———. "The Public Sphere." In *Rethinking Popular Culture,* edited by Chandra Mukerji and Michael Schudson, 338–40. Berkeley: University of California Press, 1991.

———. *The Structural Transformation of the Public Sphere: An Inquiry into a Category of Bourgeois Society.* Translated by Thomas Burger. London: Polity Press, 1989.

Halavais, Alexander. "The Web as News: September 11 and New Sources of Web News." Paper presented at the Annual Convention of the Association of Internet Researchers, Maastricht, The Netherlands, October, 2002.

Hall, Philippa. "'Think Imperially': The Private Press Mediation of State Policy and the Global Economy within Colonial and Postcolonial Nigeria." *Journal of African Media Studies* 1, no. 2 (2009): 247–62.

Hall, Stuart. "Encoding/Decoding." In *Culture, Media, Language,* edited by the Centre for Contemporary Cultural Studies, 128–38. London: Hutchinson, 1980.

Halleck, DeeDee. *Hand Held Visions: The Impossible Possibilities of Community Media.* Bronx, New York: Fordham University Press, 2002.

Haller, André, Kristoffer Holt, and Renaud de La Brosse, eds. "The 'Other' Alternatives: Political Right-Wing Alternative Media." Special issue, *Journal of Alternative and Community Media* 4, no. 1 (2019): 1–91.

Hamilton, James. "Alternative Media: Conceptual Difficulties, Critical Possibilities." *Journal of Communication Inquiry* 24, no. 4 (2000): 357–78.

Hannerz, Ulf. *Transnational Connections: Cultures, People, Places*. London: Routledge, 1996.

Hansen, Thomas B., and Finn Stepputat. *Sovereign Bodies: Citizens, Migrants and States in the Postcolonial World*. Princeton, NJ: Princeton University Press, 2005.

Harcup, Tony. *Alternative Journalism, Alternative Voices*. London: Routledge, 2013.

———. "'I'm Doing This to Change the World': Journalism in Alternative and Mainstream Media." *Journalism Studies* 6, no. 3 (2005): 361–74.

———. *Journalism: Principles & Practice*. London: Sage, 2009.

———. "The Unspoken Said: The Journalism of Alternative Media." *Journalism* 4, no. 3 (2003): 256–376.

Hargrove, Thomas, and Guido Stempel III. "Use of Blogs as a Source of News Presents Little Threat to Mainline News Media." *Newspaper Research Journal* 28, no. 1 (2007): 99–102.

Haruna, Mohammed. "The Life and Times of Abubakar Imam: Lessons for Today." *Weekly Trust*, April 30–May 6, 2005.

Hassane, Muolaye. "Ajami in Africa: The Use of Arabic Script in the Transcription of African Languages." In *The Meanings of Timbuktu*, edited by Souleymane Shamil Jeppie and Bachir Diagne, 109–21. Cape Town: Human Sciences Research Council, 2008.

Hatchten, William. *Muffled Drums: The News Media in Africa*. Ames: Iowa State University Press, 1971.

Hatton, Timothy J., and Jeffery G. Williamson. "Out of Africa? Using the Past to Project African Emigration Pressure in the Future." *Review of International Economics* 10, no. 3 (2002): 556–73.

Hauben, Michael, and Rhonda Hauben, eds, *Netizens: On the History and Impact of Usenet and the Internet*. Los Alamitos, CA: IEEE Computer Society Press, 1997.

Hersman, Erik. "The Mobile Continent." *Stanford Social Innovation Review*, https://ssir.org/articles/entry/the_mobile_continent, accessed July 19, 2018.

Hirschkop, Ken. "Justice and Drama: On Bakhtin as a Complement to Habermas." *Sociological Review* 52, no. 1 (2004): 49–66.

Hochheimer, John. "Organizing Democratic Radio: Issues in Practice." *Media, Culture & Society* 15, no. 4 (1993): 473–86.

Holeton, Richard. *Composing Cyberspace: Identity, Community, and Knowledge in the Electronic Age*. New York: McGraw-Hill, 1998.

Howe, Jeff. "The Rise of Crowdsourcing." *Wired*, June 1, 2006, http://www.wired.com/wired/archive/14.06/crowds.html.

Hughes, Kevin. *From Webspace to Cyberspace.* Menlo Park, CA: Enterprise Integration Technologies, 1995.

Huhuonline. "About Us." http://huhuonline.com/hunew/index.php/login-contact-chat/about-us, accessed April 16, 2018.

———. "South Africans Vow to Sack Christ Embassy . . . As Authorities Humiliate Chris Oyakhilome at Airport." http://www.nairaland.com/257670/south-africans-vow-sack-christ, accessed April 16, 2018.

Huhuonline. "How Aliko Dangote Blackmailed, Bribed His Way to NSE Presidency." https://www.modernghana.com/news/233026/1/how-aliko-dangote-blackmailed-bribed-his-way-to-ns.html, accessed April 6, 2018.

Hujanen, Jaana, and Sari Peitikainen. "Interactive Uses of Journalism: Crossing Between Technological Potential and Young People's News-Using Practices." *New Media & Society* 6, no. 3 (2004): 383–401.

Ibekwe, Nicholas. "Allegations Against Punch Director Sad, Says Journalism Teacher." *NEXT*, March 11, 2010.

———. "Ishiekwene Leaves CNN Judges Panel." *NEXT*, April 7, 2010.

Ibelema, Minabere. "The Nigerian Press and June 12: Pressure and Performance during a Political Crisis." *Journalism Communication Monographs* 4, no. 4 (2003): 163–209.

Ibrahim, Jibrin. "Towards a Political Economy of Mass Communication in Nigeria." Paper presented at the Graduate Political Economy Seminar, Ahmadu Bello University, Zaria, Nigeria, November 5, 1979.

Idonor, Daniel. "Yar'Adua Orders Probe of Sacked NIA Boss." *Vanguard*, October 15, 2009.

Idowu, Lanre. "IBB, Sahara Reporters, and the Press." *NEXT*, September 1, 2010.

Idris, Hamza. "Women Arrest Boko Haram Fighters in Borno." Daily Trust, May 27, 2014, https://www.dailytrust.com.ng/news/others/women-arrest-boko-haram-fighters-in-borno/47261.html.

Ifedigbo, Sylva Nze. "It's Been Three Years: An Anniversary Message to SaharaReporters." January 24, 2009, http://www.nigeriavillagesquare.com/articles/sylva-nze-ifedigbo/it-s-been-three-years-an-anniversary-message-to-sahararepor.html.

Iffer, Emmanuel. "Ribadu/El-Rufai Saga: Yar'Adua Fires NIA Boss." *Leadership*, October 14, 2009.

Ige, Ise-Oluwa, and Ikechukwu Nnochiri. "FG after My Life over Ibori, Says Ribadu." Vanguard, September 24, 2009, http://www.vanguardngr.com/2009/09/fg-after-my-life-over-ibori-says-ribadu/.

Ihemeremadu, Johnson. "Much Ado about Harvard." *Nation*, June 7, 2009.

Ikuomola, Vincent. "'Why Governors Seek Harvard Training.'" *Nation*, June 23, 2009.

Inda, Jonathan Xavier, and Renato Rosaldo. "Introduction: A World in Motion." In *The Anthropology of Globalization: A Reader*, edited by J. X. Inda and R. Rosaldo. Malden, MA: Blackwell Publishing, 2002.

iReports-ng.com. "Another Staff Opens Can of Worms on Azu, Punch's Deep-Rooted Corruption." iReports-ng, March 12, 2010.

———. "Dirty War over Money Tears Punch Apart, as Editor Opens Can of Worms on Multi-Million Naira Corruption Scandal." March 14, 2010, http://saharareporters.com/2010/03/04/dirty-war-over-money-tears-punch-apart-editor-opens-can-worms-multi-million-naira.

———. "Punch Chairman in Desperate Moves to Cover Up Corruption Scandals." iReports-ng, March 30, 2010.

———. "PUNCH/Azugate Scandal: Media Group Calls for Probe as EFCC Steps in." iReports-ng, March 8, 2010.

Iser, Wolfang. *The Act of Reading: A Theory of Aesthetic Response*. Baltimore: Johns Hopkins University Press, 1978.

Ishiewene, Azubuike. "An Era Ends, a Story Begins. . . ." SaharaReporters, April 17, 2010, http://www.saharareporters.com/article/era-ends-story-begins%E2%80%A6.

Isine, Ibanga. "Federal Government Seeks Power to Intercept Internet Communications." *Punch*, February 7, 2007.

Inyang, Ifreke. "Why We Are Investigating Emir Sanusi—Kano Assembly." Daily Post, May 11, 2017, http://dailypost.ng/2017/05/11/investigating-emir-sanusi-kano-assembly/.

Jaafar, Jaafar. "Another Word for Emir Sanusi." *Daily Nigerian*, April 15, 2017, https://dailynigerian.com/another-word-for-emir-sanusi-by-jaafar-jaafar/.

———. "EXCLUSIVE VIDEO: Kano Governor, Abdullahi Ganduje, Caught Receiving Bribe." Daily Nigerian, October 14, 2018, https://dailynigerian.com/exclusive-video-kano-governor-abdullahi-ganduje-caught-receiving-bribe/.

Jacubowicz, Karol. "Musical Chairs? The Three Public Spheres of Poland." *Media Culture & Society* 12 (1990): 195–212.

Jaschik, Scott. "Black (Immigrant) Admissions Edge." *Inside Higher Ed*, March 17, 2009, http://www.insidehighered.com/news/2009/03/17/immigrant.

Jimoh, Mike. "Blogger/Blackmailer Unmasked." Nigerian Village Square, March 3, 2007, http://www.nigeriavillagesquare.com/j2/articles/nvs/bloggerblackmailer-unmasked.html.

Jin-ah, Seol. "Social Media and the Evolution of Journalism." *Korea Journalism Review* 5, no. 1 (2011): 1–124.

Johnson, Kristen A., and Susan Wiedenback. "Enhancing Perceived Credibility of Citizen Journalism Web Sites." *Journalism & Mass Communication Quarterly* 86, no. 2 (2009): 332–48.

Jordan, Tim. *Cyberpower: The Culture and Politics of Cyberspace and the Internet*. London: Routledge, 1999.

Joseph, Richard. *Democracy and Prebendal Politics in Nigeria*. Cambridge: Cambridge University Press, 1987.

Jude, Igbanoi. "How Nigerians in the Diaspora Significantly Aid Our Development." *This Day*, February 19, 2007.

Kahn, Richard, and Douglas Kellner, "Techopolitics, Blogs, and Emergent Media Ecologies: A Critical Reconstructive Approach." In *Small Tech: The Culture of Digital Tools*, edited by Byron Hawk, David M. Rieder, and Ollie Oviedo, 27–37. Minneapolis: University of Minnesota Press, 2008.

Kaigo, Muneo, and Isao Watanabe. "Ethos in Chaos? Reaction to Video Files Depicting Socially Harmful Images in the Channel 2 Japanese Internet Forum." *Journal of Computer-Mediated Communication* 12, no. 4 (2007): 1248–68.

Kanu, Ahaoma. "NVS Members Donate $1200 to the Aikpitanhi Family, NTA Goes Haywire." Nigerian Village Square, August 13, 2007; http://www.nigeriavillagesquare.com/articles/nvs-projects/nvs-members-donate-1200-to-the-aikpitanhi-family-nta-goes-haywire.html.

Karim, Karim H. "From Ethnic Media to Global Media: Transnational Communication Networks Among Diasporic Communities." Economic and Social Research Council, Oxford University, 1998, Available from http://www.transcomm.ox.ac.uk/working%20papers/karim.pdf.

———, ed. *The Media of Diaspora: Mapping the Globe*. London: Routledge, 2003.

———. "Mapping Diasporic Mediascapes." In *The Media of Diaspora: Mapping the Globe*, 1–18. London: Routledge Press, 2003.

Katz, Elihu. "The Two-Step Flow of Communication: An Up-to-Date Report on a Hypothesis." *Public Opinion Quarterly* 21, no. 1 (1957): 61–78.

Keck, Margaret E., and Kathryn Sikkink. *Activists Beyond Borders: Advocacy Networks in International Politics*. Ithaca, NY: Cornell University Press, 1998.

Kellner, Douglas. "Intellectuals, the New Public Spheres, and Techno-politics." In *The Politics of Cyberspace: A New Political Science Reader*, edited by Chris Toulouse and Timothy W. Luke, 167–86. New York: Routledge, 1998.

———. *Media Culture: Cultural Studies, Identity and Politics between the Modern and the Postmodern*. London, Routledge, 1995.

Khiabany, Gholan. "Red Pepper: A New Model for the Alternative Press." *Media, Culture & Society* 22 (2000): 447–63.

Kidd, Dorothy, and Bernadette Barker-Plummer, eds. "Social Justice Movements and the Internet." *Peace Review* 13, no. 3 (2001): 331–37.

Killson, Martin. *Political Change in a West African State: A Study of the Modernization Process in Sierra Leone*. Cambridge, MA: Harvard University Press, 1966.

Kim, Chaiho. "A Study of Internet Penetration Percents of Africa Using Digital Divide Models." Technology Management for Global Economic Growth (PICMET), 2010 Proceedings of PICMET, October 14, 2010.

Kim, Eun-Gyoo, and James W. Hamilton. "Capitulation to Capital? OhmyNews as Alternative Media." *Media, Culture & Society* 28, no. 4 (2006): 541–60.

King, Charles, and Neil J. Melvin. "Diaspora Politics: Ethnic Linkages, Foreign Policy, and Security in Eurasia." *International Security* 47, no. 3 (Winter 1999/2000): 108–38.

King, Russell, and Nancy Wood, eds. *Media and Migration: Constructions of Mobility and Difference*. London: Routledge, 2001.

Koinange, Jeff. "Big Guns, Big Oil Collide in Nigeria." CNN, February 12, 2007; http://www.cnn.com/2007/WORLD/africa/02/06/btsc.koinange.nigeria/index.html.

Kolawole, Simon. "What's Wrong with Harvard?" *ThisDay*, June 14, 2009.

Kómoláfé, Julius. "Searching for Fortune: The Geographical Process of Nigerian Migration to Dublin, Ireland." Ìrìnkèrindò: A Journal of African Migration 2 (2003), http://www.africamigration.com/archive_01/j_komolafe_searching.htm.

Koselleck, Reinhart. *Critique and Crisis: Enlightenment and the Pathogenesis of Modern Society*. Cambridge, MA: MIT Press, 1988.

Kovach, Bill, and Tom Rosentiel. "Are Watchdogs an Endangered Species?" *Columbia Journalism Review* 40, no. 1 (May 2001): 50.

———. *The Elements of Journalism: What Newspeople Should Know and the Public Should Expect*. New York: Crown Publishers, 2001.

Kperogi, Farooq A. "Clash of Civilization or Clash of Newspaper Ideologies? An Analysis of the Ideological Split in British Newspaper Commentaries on the 2002 Miss World Riots." *Asia Pacific Media Educator* 23, no. 1 (2013): 121–43.

———. "CNN, Niger Delta and Western Media Portrayals of Africa (I)." Weekly Trust, February 24, 2007, http://farooqkperogi.blogspot.com/2009/03/cnn-niger-delta-and-western-media.html.

———, Farooq A. "CNN, Niger Delta and Western Media Portrayals of Africa (II)." Weekly Trust, March 3, 2007. http://farooqkperogi.blogspot.com/2009/03/cnn-niger-delta-and-western-media.html.

———, Farooq A. "CNN, Niger Delta and Western Media Portrayals of Africa (III)." Weekly Trust, March 10, 2007. http://farooqkperogi.blogspot.com/2009/03/cnn-niger-delta-and-western-media.html.

———. "Cooperation with the Corporation? CNN and the Hegemonic Cooptation of Citizen Journalism Through iReport.com." *New Media & Society* 13, no. 2 (2011): 314–29.

———. "Guerrillas in Cyberia: The Transnational Alternative Online Journalism of the Nigerian Diasporic Public Sphere." *Journal of Global Mass Communication* 1, no. 1 (2008): 72–87.

———. "How Buhari is Turning Nigeria into a Fascist State." *Nigerian Tribune*, March 23, 2019, https://www.tribuneonlineng.com/197620/.

———. "Journalism Is Dying a Slow Death in Nigeria." Daily Trust, May 31, 2014.

———. "News with Views: Postobjectivism and Emergent Alternative Journalistic Practices in America's Corporate News Media." *Review of Communication* 13, no 1 (2013): 48–65.

———. "Now That CNN has Finally Dismissed Jeff Koinange." Weekly Trust, June 12, 2007; https://www.farooqkperogi.com/2009/03/now-that-cnn-has-finally-dismissed-jeff.html.

———. "Webs of Resistance: The Citizen Online Journalism of the Nigerian Digital Diaspora." PhD diss., Georgia State University, 2011.

Kumar, Chetan. "Transnational Networks and Campaigns for Democracy." In *The Third Force: The Rise of Transnational Civil Society*, edited by Ann M. Florini, 5–142. Washington, DC: Carnegie Endowment for International Peace, 2000.

Kumolu, Charles. "Court Awards N5m against Police for Arresting Elombah Brothers." Vanguard, April 23, 2018, https://www.vanguardngr.com/2018/04/court-awards-n5m-police-arresting-elombah-brothers/.

———. "Journalist Arrested over Publication." Vanguard, January 2, 2018, https://www.vanguardngr.com/2018/01/journalist-arrested-publication/.

Kunz, William M. "Prime-Time Island: Television Program and Format Importation into the United States." *Television & New Media* 11, no. 4 (2010): 308–24.

Kyem, Peter A. Kwakwu, and Peter Kewku LeMaire. "Transforming Recent Gains in the Digital Divide into Digital Opportunities: Africa and the Boom in Mobile Phone Subscription." *Electronic Journal on Information Systems in Developing Countries* 28, no. 5 (2006): 1–16.

Laguerre, Michel S. "Homeland Political Crisis, the Virtual Diasporic Public Sphere, and Diasporic Politics." *Journal of Latin American Anthropology* 10, no. 1 (2008): 206–25.

Lasica, J. D. "Blogs and Journalism Need Each Other." Nieman Reports, Fall 2003, http://www.nieman.harvard.edu/reports/03-3NRfall/V57N3.pdf, accessed May 5, 2009.

Lazarsfeld, Paul F., Bernard Berelson, and Hazel Gaudet. *The People's Choice: How the Voter Makes Up His Mind in a Presidential Campaign*. New York: Columbia University Press, 1944.

Leadership. "Aiding Boko Haram—Army Court-Martials 10 Generals, Five Others." Leadership, June 3, 2014, https://allafrica.com/stories/201406030392.html.

Legun, Colin. "The Mass Media: The Institution of the African Political Systems." In *Reporting Africa*, edited by Olav Stokke, 27–38. Uppsala: Scandinavian Institute of African Studies, 1971.

Lewinski, Marcin. "Collective Argumentative Criticism in Informal Online Discussion Forums." *Argumentation and Advocacy* 47, no. 2 (2010): 86–105.

Lewis, Peter. "From Prebendalism to Predation: The Political Economy of Decline in Nigeria." *Journal of Modern African Studies* 34, no. 1 (1996): 79–103.

Licoppe, Christian. "'Connected' Presence: The Emergence of a New Repertoire for Managing Social Relationships in a Changing Communication Technoscape." *Environment and Planning D: Society and Space* 22 (2004): 135–56.

Lippmann, Walter. "The Appeal to the Public." In *Public Opinion*, 398–410. New York: Macmillan, 1922.

Lippmann, Walter. *Public Opinion*. New York: Free Press, 1922.

Loba, André da. "Have Comment Sections on News Media Websites Failed?" *New York Times*, last modified April 18, 2016, https://www.nytimes.com/roomfordebate/2016/04/18/have-comment-sections-on-news-media-websites-failed.

Luke, Timothy W. "Cybercritique: A Social Theory of Online Agency and Virtual Structures." In *Critical Theory: Diverse Objects, Diverse Subjects*, edited by J. Lehmann, 133–59. Current Perspectives in Social Theory 22. Bingley, UK: Emerald Group Publishing Ltd., 2002.

Lyotard, Jean-François. *The Postmodern Condition: A Report on Knowledge*. Translated by Geoff Bennington and Brian Massumi. Minneapolis: University of Minnesota Press, 1984.

MacArthur Foundation. "Sahara Reporters Was Awarded $600,000 in 2016, Including 1 grant in On Nigeria," https://www.macfound.org/grantees/9430/.

Macha, Ndesanjo. "Nigerian Blogger Arrested for Sponsoring a 'Guerrilla News Agency.'" Global Voices, Oct. 24, 2008, http://globalvoicesonline.org/2008/10/24/nigerian-blogger-arrested-for-sponsoring-a-guerrilla-news-agency/.

Mahmud, Sakah Saidu. *State, Class and Underdevelopment in Nigeria and Early Meiji Japan*. London: Macmillan, 1996.

Mai, Nicola. "The Albanian Diaspora-in-the-Making: Media, Migration and Social Exclusion." *Journal of Ethnic & Migration Studies* 31, no. 3 (2005): 543–61.

Mainsah, Henry. "Cameroonians in Oslo, Diaspora, and Uses of the Media." *NORDICOM Review* 30, no. 1 (2009): 83–94.

Malakata, Michael. "Nigeria Claims Top Internet Spot in Africa." *ComputerWorld*, August 10, 2010, http://news.idg.no/cw/art.cfm?id=5DBFEB28-1A64-67EA-E470DF5BE0AA9E10.

Manson, Katrina, and David Pilling. "Africa Looks for Something New Out of Donald Trump." *Financial Times*, August 27, 2018, https://www.ft.com/content/2795662c-a8aa-11e8-94bd-cba20d67390c.

Marama, Nadhi. "Women Demobilise Boko Haram Insurgents in Borno." Vanguard, May 27, 2017, https://www.vanguardngr.com/2014/05/women-demobilise-boko-haram-insurgents-borno/.

Massey, Brian, and Mark Levy. "Interactivity, Online Journalism, and English-Language Web Newspapers in Asia." *Journalism and Mass Communication Quarterly* 76, no. 1 (1999): 138–52.

Matheson, Donald. "Weblogs and the Epistemology of the News: Some Trends in Online Journalism." *New Media & Society* 6, no. 4 (2004): 443–68.

Matinde, Vincent. "Taxing Technology: Why This African Trend Can Pull Back Connectivity Gains." *IDG Connect*, July 10, 2018, https://www.idgconnect.com/abstract/30963/taxing-technology-why-african-trend-pull-connectivity-gains.

Mba, Osita. "How Much Land Does Reuben Abati Need?" Nigerian Village Square, January 18, 2009, http://www.nigeriavillagesquare.com/articles/osita-mba/how-much-land-does-reuben-abati-need.html.

Mbembe, Achille. "Necropolitics." *Public Culture* 15 (2003): 11–40.

McCabe, Ina B., Gelina Harlaftis, and Ioanna Pepelasis Minoglou (eds). *Diaspora Entrepreneurial Networks: Four Centuries of History*. Oxford: Berg, 2005.

McChesney, Robert. *Rich Media, Poor Democracy: Communication Politics in Dubious Times*. New York: New Press, 2000.

McCombs, Maxwell, and Donald Shaw. "The Agenda-Setting Function of the Mass Media." *Public Opinion Quarterly* 6, no. 2 (1972): 176–87.

McLaughlin, Neil. "Feminism, the Public Sphere, Media and Democracy." *Media, Culture & Society* 15, no. 4 (1993): 599.

———. "Origin Myths in the Social Sciences: Fromm, the Frankfurt School and the Emergences of Critical Theory." *Canadian Journal of Sociology* 24, no. 1 (1999): 109–39.

McLuhan, Marshal, and Bruce Powers. *The Global Village: Transformations in World Life and Media in the 21st Century*. New York: Oxford University Press, 1989.

Media Legal Defence Initiative. "Nigeria Case Is Real-Life Thriller: Africa Graft Story Ends Up in New York, via Texas." Sahara Reporters, March 2, 2010. http://saharareporters.com/2010/03/02/nigeria-case-real-life-thriller-africa-graft-story-ends-new-york-texas.

Media Matters. "Five-Man Panel Probes Ayorinde's Petition Against Azu." October 10, 2010.

Meehan, Johanna, ed. *Feminists Read Habermas: Gendering the Subject of Discourse*. New York: Routledge, 1995.

Mehlman, Jeffrey. "The 'Floating Signifier' from Lévi-Strauss to Lacan." *Yale French Studies* 48 (1972): 10–37.

Melucci, Alberto. *Challenging Codes: Collective Action in the Information Age*. Cambridge: Cambridge University Press, 1996.

Merritt, Davis. "What Citizen Journalism Can Learn from Public Journalism." In *Public Journalism 2.0: The Promise and Reality of a Citizen-Engaged Press*, edited by Jack Rosenberry and Burton St. John III, 21–31. New York: Routledge, 2010.

Miles, Matthew, and A. Michael Huberman. *Qualitative Data Analysis: An Expanded Sourcebook*. Thousand Oaks, CA: Sage, 1994.

Miller, Jade L. "Ugly Betty Goes Global: Global Networks of Localized Content in the Telenovela Industry." *Global Media & Communication* 6, no. 2 (2010): 198–217.

Miller, Toby, and George Yudice. *Cultural Policy*. London: Sage, 2002.

Milne, Esther. *Letters, Postcards, Email: Technologies of Presence*. New York: Routledge, 2012.

Mojeed, Musikilu. "SaharaReporters' Sowore: A Thorn in the Flesh of Corrupt Nigerian Officials." Premium Times, January 22, 2012, https://www.premiumtimesng.com/features-and-interviews/3551-saharareporters-sowore-a-thorn-in-the-flesh-of-corrupt-nigerian-officials.html.

Mora, Abdulrahman, ed. *The Abubakar Imam Memoirs*. Zaria, Nigeria: Northern Nigeria Publishing Company, 1989.

Morgan, Gordon D. "Exploratory Study of Problems of Academic Adjustment of Nigerian Students in America." *Journal of Negro Education* 32, no. 3 (1963): 208–17.

Morris, Meaghan. "Banality in Cultural Studies." In *What is Cultural Studies? A Reader*, edited by John Storey, 147–67. London: Arnold, 1996.

Mosley, Paul. "Policy-Making without Facts: A Note on the Assessment of Structural Adjustment Policies in Nigeria, 1985–1990." *African Affairs* 91(1992): 227–40.

Mott, Frank Luther. *The News in America*. Cambridge, MA: Harvard University Press, 1952.

Mowlana, Hamid. *Global Information and World Communication* 2nd ed. Thousand Oaks, CA: Sage, 1997.

Musa, Mohammed, and Jibril Mohammed. "The Political Economy of Media Ownership in Nigeria." In *Who Owns the Media? Global Trends and Local Resistances*, edited by Pradip Thomas and Zaharom Nain, 227–47. London: Zed Books, 2004.

Nah, Seungahn, and Deborah S. Chung. "When Citizens Meet Both Professional and Citizen Journalists: Social Trust, Media Credibility, and Perceived Journalistic Roles among Online Community News Readers." *Journalism* 13, no. 6 (2011): 714–30.

Nairaland Forum. "Jeff Koinange Sacked from CNN over His Story on the Niger-Delta Based Mend Group." http://www.nairaland.com/nigeria/topic-57196.128.html, accessed April 7, 2018.

Nairaland.com. "Elendu Reports—Cutting Edge Investigative Journalism." http://www.nairaland.com/nigeria/topic-2845.0.html#msg263767, accessed April 7, 2018.

Namubiru, Lydia. "How Uganda Is Implementing Its Controversial Social Media Tax." Quartz, July 3, 2018, https://qz.com/1319826/how-ugandas-social-media-tax-works-with-whatsapp-facebook-twitter-blocked/amp/?

Neblo, Michael. "Thinking through Democracy: Between the Theory and Practice of Deliberative Politics." *Acta Politica* 40, no. 2 (2005): 169–81.

Negt, Oskar, and Alexander Kluge. *Public Sphere and Experience: Toward an Analysis of the Bourgeois and Proletarian Public Sphere*. Translated by Peter Labanyi et al. Minneapolis: University of Minnesota Press, 1993.

Nerone, John C. "The Mythology of the Penny Press." *Critical Studies in Mass Communication*, 4, no. 4 (1987): 376–404.

Nerone, John, and Kevin G. Barnhurst. "Beyond Modernism: Digital Design, Americanization and the Future of Newspaper Form." *New Media & Society* 3, no. 4 (2001): 467–83.

"News Blogger Detained in Nigeria." *BBC News*, October 23, 2008; http://news.bbc.co.uk/2/hi/africa/7686119.stm.

Ngom, Fallou. *Muslims Beyond the Arab World: The Odyssey of 'Ajami and the Murīdiyya*. New York: Oxford University Press, 2016.

Nielsen, Carolyn E. "Coproduction or Cohabitation: Are Anonymous Online Comments on Newspaper Websites Shaping News Content?" *New Media & Society* 16, no. 3 (2014): 470–87.

Nieminen, Hannu. "On the Formation of the National Public Sphere." Paper presented at the International Association for Media and Communication Research Conference, Porto Alegre, Brazil, August 25–30, 2004.

Nigerian Village Square. "About Us." http://www.nigeriavillagesquare.com/about-us.html.

Nip, Joyce. "Exploring the Second Phase of Public Journalism." *Journalism Studies* 7, no. 2 (2006): 212–36.

Njoku, Raphael C. "Deconstructing Abacha: Demilitarization and Democratic Consolidation in Nigeria after the Abacha Era." *Government and Opposition* 36, no. 1 (2001): 71–96.

NVS News. "Breaking News Update: 'I'm Alive & Well, Yar'adua Speaks to TON." Nigerian Village Square, March 6, 2007, http://www.nigeriavillagesquare.com/index.php?option=com_content&view=article&id=5213&catid=168&Itemid=46.

———. "US Court Dismisses Paul Orhili's Lawsuit Against Saharareporters." Nigerian Village Square, April 2, 2009, http://www.nigeriavillagesquare.com/articles/newsflash/us-court-dismisses-paul-orhilis-lawsuit-against-saharareporters.html.

Nwabughuogu, Anthony. "The Role of Propaganda in the Development of Indirect Rule in Nigeria." *International Journal of African Historical Studies* 14, no. 1 (1981): 65–92.

Nwankwo, Joe. "Writers Decry Continued Detention of Online Journalist." *Daily Independent*, October 27, 2008.

Nwankwo, Robert L., and George T. Kurian. "Nigeria." *World Press Encyclopedia*, edited by George T. Kurian, 687–97. New York: Fact on File, 1982.

Nworah, Uche. "The Impact of the Internet on Journalism Practice in Nigeria." Chicken Bones: A Journal for Literary & Artistic African-American Themes. http://www.nathanielturner.com/journalisminnigeria.htm, accessed April 7, 2018.

Obadare, Ebenezer. "Second Thoughts on Civil Society: The State, Civic Associations and the Antinomies of the Public Sphere in Africa." *Journal of Civil Society* 1, no. 3 (2005): 267–81.

Obijiofor, Levi. "Singaporean and Nigerian Journalists' Perceptions of New Technologies." *Australian Journalism Review* 23, no. 1 (2001): 131–51.

Ocheja, Joshua. "Nigeria at the Mercy of Sahara Reporters." Gamji.com. http://www.gamji.com/article8000/NEWS8584.htm, accessed April 6, 2018.

Ochonu, Moses. *Colonial Meltdown: Northern Nigeria in the Great Depression*. Athens: Ohio University Press, 2009.

Ochonu, Moses E. "Saharareporters' Strategic Success." Nigerian Village Square, December 18, 2008, http://www.nigeriavillagesquare.com/articles/moses-ebe-ochonu/saharareporters-strategic-success-12.html.

O'Connor, Barbara, and Carol Mackeogh. "New Media Communities: Performing Identity in an Online Women's Magazine." *Irish Journal of Sociology* 16, no. 2 (2007): 97–116.

O'Donnell, Susan. "Analyzing the Internet and the Public Sphere: The Case of Womenslink." *Javnost—The Public* 8, no. 1 (2001): 39–58.

Odunsi, Wale. "IG of Police Breaks Silence on Arrest of Elombah Brothers." Daily Post, January 5, 2018, http://dailypost.ng/2018/01/05/ig-police-breaks-silence-arrest-elombah-brothers/.

Offoha, Marcellina U. "Educated Nigerian Settlers in the United States: The Phenomenon of Brain Drain." PhD diss., Temple University, 1989.

Ogala, Emmanuel, Ini Ekott, and Soji Bamidele. "Police Boss Denies Banning Camera Phones at Polling Units." *NEXT*, March 9, 2011.

Ogan, Christine L. "Development Journalism/Communication: The Status of the Concept." *International Communication Gazette* 29, no. 1–2 (1982): 3–13.

Ogbondah, Chris W. "Nigerian Journalism: A Bibliographical Essay." *International Communication Gazette* 36, no. 3 (1985): 175–91.

———. "Nigerian Press under Imperialists and Dictators, 1903–85." *ERIC*, July 1, 1988.

———. "The Pen Is Mightier than the 'Koboko': A Critical Analysis of the Amakiri Case in Nigeria." *Political Communication and Persuasion* 8 (1991): 109–24.

Ogbondah, Chris, and Emmanuel U. Onyedike. "Origins and Interpretations of Nigerian Press Laws." *African Media Review* 5, no. 2 (1991): 59–70.

Ogundamisi, Kayode. "Starving Nigerian Journalists and Blood-Stained Proprietors." P.M. News, May 21, 2010, http://pmnewsnigeria.com/2010/05/21/starving-nigerian-journalists-and-blood-stained-proprietors/.

Ogundipe, Samuel. "Nigerian Woman Loses Job after Criticising Vice President Osinbajo Online." Premium Times, June 2, 2018, https://www.premiumtimesng.com/news/headlines/270744-nigerian-woman-loses-job-after-criticising-vice-president-osinbajo-online.html.

———. "Police Raid PREMIUM TIMES Head Office; Arrest Publisher, Journalist." Premium Times, January 19, 2017, https://www.premiumtimesng.com/news/more-news/221012-breaking-police-raid-premium-times-head-office-arrest-publisher-journalist.html.

———. "REPORTER'S DIARY: Detained PREMIUM TIMES Journalist, Samuel Ogundipe, Narrates Ordeal in Police Custody." Premium Times, August 30, 2018, https://www.premiumtimesng.com/features-and-interviews/281931-reporters-diary-detained-premium-times-journalist-samuel-ogundipe-narrates-ordeal-in-police-custody.html.

———. "SSS Arrests Social Media Users for Posting 'Inciting Materials.'" Premium Times, June 12, 2019, https://www.premiumtimesng.com/news/top-news/334711-just-in-sss-arrests-social-media-users-for-posting-inciting-materials.html.

———. "SPECIAL REPORT: How a Nigerian Law Is Suppressing Citize ns' Freedom on the Internet." Premium Times, October 17, 2017, https://www.premiumtimesng.com/news/headlines/246348-special-report-nigerian-law-suppressing-citizens-freedom-Internet.html.

Ogwuda, Austin. "Delta Monarch, Governor's Aide Perish in Auto Crash." Vanguard, August 9, 2014, https://www.vanguardngr.com/2014/08/delta-monarch-governors-aide-perish-auto-crash/.

Ohuegbe, Chuks. "FG Withdraws Channels TV Licence." *Leadership*, September 18, 2008.

Ojekunle, Jobola. "Treasonable Sex! 'You Slept with My Wife,' Gbenga Accuses Dad, Ex-President Obasanjo and Father-in-law, Doubts Paternity of Kids, Seeks DNA Tests." *The Sun*, January 13, 2008, http://www.nigerianmuse.com/20080112230541zg/spotlight/Son_Gbenga_Accuses_Obasanjo_and_father_in_law_of_sleeping_with_his_wife_asks_for_paternity_test_and_divorce.

Ojo, Tokunbo. "The Nigerian Media and the Process of Democratization." *Journalism* 8, no. 5 (2007): 545–50.

Okakwu, Evelyn. "Alleged Libel: Sahara Reporters Floors Saraki at Appeal Court." Premium Times, December 5, 2018, https://www.premiumtimesng.com/news/top-news/299223-alleged-libel-sahara-reporters-floors-saraki-at-appeal-court.html.

Okome, Mojúbàolú O. "The Antinomies of Globalization: Some Consequences of Contemporary African Immigration to the United States of America." Ìrìnkèrindò: A Journal of African Migration 1, no. 1 (2002), africamigration.com.

Okonkwor, Chude R. "Nigeria's Sedition Laws—Their Effects on Free Speech." *Journalism Quarterly* 60, no. 1 (1983): 54–60.

Olasanmi, Kunle. "EFCC Declares el-Rufai Wanted." *Nigerian Compass*, December 22, 2008.

Olatunji, Haleem. "Judges Now Afraid to Perform Their Duties, Says NBA President." TheCable, June 21, 2019, https://www.thecable.ng/judges-now-afraid-to-perform-their-duties-says-nba-president.

Olawoyin, Oladeinde. "Celebrations at PREMIUM TIMES as Panama Papers Wins Pulitzer Prize." Premium Times, April 11, 2017, https://www.premiumtimesng.com/news/headlines/228572-celebrations-at-premium-times-as-panama-papers-wins-pulitzer-prize.html.

Oloja, Martins. "El-Rufai—Ribadu Passport Saga: How Nigeria Escaped International Embarrassment." *Guardian*, October 18, 2009.

Olopade, Dayo. "Change They Can Almost Believe In: How Nigerian Voters, Especially the Young, Are Using Technology to Prove a Point." Slate, April 14, 2011, http://www.slate.com/articles/news_and_politics/foreigners/2011/04/change_they_can_almost_believe_in.single.html.

Olorunyomi, Dapo. "Defiant Publishing in Nigeria." In *Journalism in Peril*, edited by Nancy J. Woodhull and Robert W. Snyder, 53–63. New Brunswick, NJ: Transaction Publishers, 1998.

Oludimu, Tititola. "Facebook Now Has 26 Million Active Users in Nigeria." Techpoint, https://techpoint.ng/2018/05/23/26-million-nigerians-use-facebook/, accessed July 19, 2018.

Olufemi, Adelusi. "Poverty Militates Against Code of Ethics." In *Ethics and Regulation: Formulating a Working Agenda for Journalists and the Media*, edited by International Press Centre, 39–43. Lagos, Nigeria: IPC, 2000.

Olukoshi, Adebayo O., ed. *The Politics of Structural Adjustment in Nigeria*. London: James Carey, 1993.

Olukotun, Ayo. "Authoritarian State, Crisis of Democratization and the Underground Media in Nigeria." *African Affairs* 101 (2002): 317–42.

———. "Governance and the Media in an Emergent Democracy: A Study of the Role, Record and Changing Profile of the Nigerian Media 1999–2017." Inaugural lecture delivered at Adeola Odutola Hall, Ijebu Ode, Department of Political Science, Olabisi Onabanjo University, Ago Iwoye, Nigeria, May 10, 2017, https://obaadetonachair.oouagoiwoye.edu.ng/wp-content/uploads/2019/04/Governance-and-the-Media-in-an-Emergent-Democracy.pdf.

———. "Media Accountability and Democracy in Nigeria, 1999–2003." *African Studies Review* 47, no. 3 (2004): 69–90.

Olukoya, Sam. "Facebook Growing Fast in Nigeria." Deutsche Welle, https://www.dw.com/en/facebook-growing-fast-in-nigeria/a-17408466, accessed July 19, 2018.

Olumhense, Sonala. "Keep SaharaReporters Alive." [Nigerian] *Guardian*, December 20, 2008, http://www.nigeriavillagesquare.com/articles/sonala-olumhense/keep-saharareporters-alive-13.html.

———. "Our SaharaReporters." Nigerian Village Square, August 10, 2008, http://www.nigeriavillagesquare.com/articles/sonala-olumhense/our-saharareporters.html.

———. "The Nigerian Media on Trial." [Nigerian] *Guardian*, March 21, 2010, p. 29.

———. "Nigeria's Citizen Reporters." *Nigerian Tribune*, January 9, 2011.

———. "Popular Investigative Nigeria Website Sued For $25 Billion." Black Star News, December 26, 2008, http://www.blackstarnews.com/others/extras/popular-investigative-nigeria-website-sued-for-25-billion.html.

Olurounbi, Ruth, and Emele Onu. "EU Observers Say Nigeria 2019 Elections Weren't Transparent." Bloomberg, June 15, 2019, https://www.bloomberg.com/news/articles/2019-06-15/eu-observers-say-nigeria-s-2019-elections-weren-t-transparent.

Omenugha, Kate Azuka, and Majority Oji. "News Commercialization, Ethics and Objectivity in Journalism Practice in Nigeria: Strange Bedfellows?" *Estudos em Comunicação* 3 (2008): 13–28.

Omoh, Gabriel, Sina Babasola, and Hector Igbikiowubo. "Obasanjo's Library Fund Is Executive Extortion—Soyinka." Vanguard, May 17, 2005, http://allafrica.com/stories/200505171507.html.

Omu, Fred I. *Press and Politics in Nigeria 1800–1937*. London: Longman, 1978.

Our Reporter. "Kalu's Wife Not Our Patient Now—US Hospital." *Punch*, August 14, 2007.

Owen, Laura Hazard. "Slate's Facebook Traffic Has Dropped by 87 Percent Since 2017." NiemanLab, June 27, 2018, http://www.niemanlab.org/2018/06/slates-facebook-traffic-has-dropped-by-87-percent-since-2017/.

Owolabi, Femi. "Zamfara Awards Contracts for Rehabilitation of Primary Schools." TheCable, July 31, 2017, https://www.thecable.ng/zamfara-awards-contracts-for-rehabilitation-of-primary-schools.

Oyebode, Olayinka. "Nigerian Governors' Forum Lied—Harvard University." *Punch*, June 13, 2009.

Oyedoyin, Tunde. "Omoyele Sowore: The 10-Year-Old Boy Who Became an Activist." https://nigeriaworld.com/feature/publication/oyedoyin/2003/021703p.html.

Oyekunle, Jibola. "I Have Moles in OBJ's Home, Says Omoyele Sowore." *The Sun*, Sunday, December 2, 2007, http://www.nigerianmuse.com/nigeriawatch/20071201202522zg/I_have_moles_in_OBJ_s_home_says_Omoyele_Sowore.

Oyewobi, Akin, and Kemi Busari. "Premium Times Journalists Win Global Shining Light Award." Premium Times, November 18, 2017, https://www.premiumtimesng.com/news/headlines/249933-premium-times-journalists-win-global-shining-light-award.html.

Page, Clarence. "Black Immigrants Collect Most Degrees but Affirmative Action is Losing Direction." *Chicago Tribune*, March 18, 2007, http://articles.chicagotribune.com/2007-03-18/news/0703180344_1_black-immigrants-high-achieving-immigrants-biracial-couples.

El País. "Aikpitanhi's Death Causes Major Policy Change in Spain." Nigeria Village Square, November 11, 2007, http://nigeriavillagesquare.com/index.php?option=com_content&view=article&id=7781&Itemid=46.

Palmer, H. R. *Sudanese Memoirs, Being Mainly Translations of a Number of Arabic Manuscripts Relating to the Central and Western Sudan*. London: Frank Cass, 1967.

Pan African News Agency. "Nigerian Governors Forum Cancels Harvard Training after Storm." *Pan African News Agency*, June 15, 2009.

Panagakos, Anastasia N., and Heather A. Horst. "Return to Cyberia: Technology and the Social Worlds of Transnational Migrants." *Global Networks* 6, no. 2 (2006): 109–24.

Pavlik, John V. "The Future of Online Journalism." *Columbia Journalism Review* 36, no. 2 (1997): 30–38.

Peck, Abe. *Uncovering the Sixties: The Life and Times of the Underground Press*. New York: Citadel Press, 1991.

Peters, John D. "Distrust of Representation: Habermas on the Public Sphere." *Media, Culture and Society* 15, no. 4 (1993): 541–71.

Pew Research Center. "Cell Phones in Africa: Communication Lifeline." Pew Research Center, April 15, 2015, http://www.pewglobal.org/2015/04/15/cell-phones-in-africa-communication-lifeline/.

Philips, Anza. "Keep Your Mouth Shut." *Newswatch*, October 4, 2008.

Picard, Robert G. "Shifts in Newspaper Advertising Expenditures and Their Implication for the Future of Newspapers." *Journalism Studies* 9, no. 5 (2008): 704–16.

Pimlott, Herbert F. "Mainstreaming the Margins: The Transformation of Marxism Today." In *Media Organizations in Society*, edited by James Curran. London: Arnold, 2000.

Platon, Sara, and Mark Deuze. "Indymedia Journalism: A Radical Way of Making, Selecting and Sharing News?" *Journalism: Theory, Practice & Criticism* 4 (2003): 336–55.

P.M. News. "Online Publishers Association Rejects Terrorism Allegation." P.M. News, February 28, 2018, https://www.pmnewsnigeria.com/2018/02/28/online-publishers-association-rejects-terrorism-allegation/.

———. "VP Jonathan Declare Assets." P.M. News, August 8, 2007, http://www.nigeriavillagesquare.com/index.php?option=com_content&view=article&id=6804&catid=111&Itemid=46.

PointBlankNews. "About Us." http://pointblanknews.com/pbn/about-us/, accessed April 16, 2018.

———. "Between PointBlankNews and VANGUARD Newspaper: An Anatomy of a Smear." http://www.pointblanknews.com/os1506.html, accessed April 16, 2018.

———. "Exclusive News Archive." http://www.pointblanknews.com/exclusivenewshome.html; accessed April 16, 2018.

———. "IBB's Minna Parley: How Punch's Editorial Board Chairman Was Fired." September 1, 2010, http://www.ointblanknews.com/News/os3828.

———. "Turaki Plans Escape, Declares False Affidavit . . . As Singaporean Hospital Denies Him." http://www.pointblanknews.com/os614.html; accessed April 16, 2018.

———. "U.S. Hospital Accuses Kalu of Forgery." http://www.pointblanknews.com/os486.html, accessed April 6, 2018.

Post, Kenneth, and George D. Jenkins. *The Price of Liberty: Personality and Politics in Colonial Nigeria*. Cambridge: Cambridge University Press, 1973.

Premium Times. "PREMIUM TIMES Shines in London; Wins One World Media Award." Premium Times, May 8, 2014, https://www.premiumtimesng.com/news/160416-premium-times-shines-in-london-wins-one-world-media-award.html.

———. "SPECIAL REPORT: How Buhari's Govt Detained Nigerian Journalist for Two Years Without Trial." Premium Times, July 1, 2018, https://www.premiumtimesng.com/news/headlines/274467-special-report-how-buharis-govt-detained-nigerian-journalist-for-two-years-without-trial.html.

———. "US Court Dismisses Defamation Lawsuit Against Sahara Reporters." Premium Times, November 27, 2012; https://www.premiumtimesng.com/news/108817-us-court-dismisses-defamation-lawsuit-against-sahara-reporters.html.

Press Reference. "Nigeria Press, Media, TV, Radio, Newspapers." http://www.press-reference.com/Ma-No/Nigeria.html, accessed September 30, 2009.

Punathambekar, Aswin. "Bollywood in the Indian-American Diaspora: Mediating a Transitive Logic of Cultural Citizenship." *International Journal of Cultural Studies* 8, no. 2 (2005): 151–73.

Punch. "A Statement from PUNCH." *Punch*, March 20, 2010, http://www.punchng.com/Articl.aspx?theartic=Art20100320462910.

Punke, Harold Herman. *Education, Lawlessness, and Political Corruption in America*. North Quincy, MA: Christopher Publishing House, 1978.

Ragas, Matthew W., and Marylyn S. Roberts. "Agenda Setting and Agenda Melding in an Age of Horizontal and Vertical Media: A New Theoretical Lens for Virtual Brand Communities." *Journalism & Mass Communication Quarterly* 86, no. 1 (2009): 46–64.

Ragin, Charles C. "'Casing' and the Process of Social Inquiry." In *What Is a Case? Exploring the Foundations of Social Inquiry*, edited by Charles C. Ragin and Howard S. Becker, 217–26. Cambridge: Cambridge University Press, 1992.

Rauch, Jennifer. "Activists as Interpretive Communities: Rituals of Consumption and Interaction in an Alternative Media Environment." *Media, Culture & Society* 29, no. 6 (2007): 994–1013.

Reader, Bill. "Free Press vs. Free Speech? The Rhetoric of 'Civility' in Regard to Anonymous Online Comments." *Journalism and Mass Communication Quarterly* 89, no. 3 (2012): 495–513.

Redden, Guy. "Read the Whole Thing: Journalism, Weblogs and the Remediation of the War in Iraq." *Media International Australia Incorporating Culture & Policy* 109 (2003): 153–66.

Reese, Stephen D., Lou Rutigliano, Kideuk Hyun, and Jaekwan Jeong, "Mapping the Blogosphere: Professional and Citizen-Based Media in the Global News Arena." *Journalism* 8, no. 3 (2007): 235–61.

A Report by the Press Freedom Committee of the Nigerian Union of Journalists. Lagos: NUJ, 1993.

Reporters without Borders. "Army Seizes Newspaper Issues Day after Day on 'Security' Grounds." June 11, 2014, updated January 20, 2016, https://rsf.org/en/news/army-seizes-newspaper-issues-day-after-day-security-grounds.

Reuters. "2 Journalists Freed by Nigerian Authorities." *New York Times*, May 8, 1997, https://www.nytimes.com/1997/05/08/world/2-journalists-freed-by-nigerian-authorities.html.

Reynolds, Rachel R. "An African Brain Drain: Nigerian (Igbo) Decisions to Immigrate to the U.S." *Review of African Political Economy* 29, no. 92 (2002): 273–84.

———. "'We Are Not Surviving, We Are Managing': The Constitution of a Nigerian Diaspora along the Contours of the Global Economy." *City & Society* 16, no. 1 (2004): 15–37.

Reynolds, Rachel R., and Scott M. Younstedt. "Globalization and African Ethnoscapes: Contrasting Nigerien Hausa and Nigerian Igbo Migratory Orders in the U.S." *City & Society* 16, no. 1 (2004): 5–13.

Rheingold, Howard. *The Virtual Community: Homesteading on the Electronic Frontier*. New York: Basic Books, 1993.

Robins, Kevin, and Frank Webster. "Athens without Slaves . . . or Slaves without Athens? The Neurosis of Technology." *Science as Culture* 1, no. 3 (1988): 7–53.

Rodriguez, Clemencia. *Fissures in the Mediascape: An International Study of Citizens' Media*. Cresskill, NJ: Hampton Press, 2001.

Rosen, Jay. "Chris Nolan: The Stand Alone Journalist is Here. . . ." PressThink: Ghost of Democracy in the Media Machine, April 21, 2005, http://archive.pressthink.org/2005/04/21/nol_stnd.html.

———. "The People Formerly Known as the Audience." PressThink: Ghost of Democracy in the Media Machine, June 27, 2006, http://archive.pressthink.org/2006/06/27/ppl_frmr.html.

———, Jay. *What Are Journalists For?* New Haven: Yale University Press, 1999.

Rufai, Nasir el-. "The Moral of the Story." Nigerian Village Square, October 21, 2009, http://www.nigeriavillagesquare.com/articles/nasir-el-rufai/the-moral-of-the-story.html.

Sahara Admin. "'Mercedes Jeep' Bribe: EFCC Chair Plans Arrest of Supplier, as EFCC's International Image Plummets." January 7, 2009, http://www.sahara-reporters.com/real-news/hot-topic/436-qmercedes-jeepq-bribe-efcc-chair-plans-arrest-of-supplier-as-efccs-international-image-plummets.html?showall=1.

Sahara Reporters. "About Face: Yar'Adua Repudiates NIA Memo on El Rufai and Ribadu, Fires DG Imohe for Memo." Sahara Reporters, October 13, 2009, http://saharareporters.com/news-page/about-face-yaradua-repudiates-nia-memo-el-rufai-and-ribadu-fires-dg-imohe-memo.

———. "About Sahara Reporters." Sahara Reporters, http://www.saharareporters.com/index.php?option=com_content&view=article&id=584, accessed April 12, 2018.

———. "Adams Oshiomole Says Governors' Forum 'MOU' with Harvard Is False." Sahara Reporters, June 22, 2009, http://www.saharareporters.com/press-release/adams-oshiomole-says-governors-forum-mou-harvard-false.

———. "ARG to Governors' Forum: If You Must Go to Harvard, Resign!" Sahara Reporters, June 8, 2009, http://www.saharareporters.com/press-release/arg-governors-forum-if-you-must-go-harvard-resign.

———. "As London Case Winds Up, Details of Case Against Ibori Money-Laundering Associates Exposed; Governor Uduaghan, David Edevbie Also Cited." Sahara Reporters, May 9, 2010, http://www.saharareporters.com/real-news/sr-headlines/6037-as-london-case-winds-up-details-of-case-against-ibori-money-laundering-associates-exposed-governor-uduaghan-david-edevbie-also-cited.html.

———. "The Drama Behind Closure of Channels Television." Sahara Reporters, September 17, 2008, http://saharareporters.com/2008/09/17/drama-behind-closure-channels-television.

———. "El Rufai, Ribadu: 'No New Passport! No Renewal of Passport! No Passport!' Yar'Adua Orders." Sahara Reporters, October 10, 2009, http://saharareporters.com/news-page/el-rufai-ribadu-%E2%80%9Cno-new-passport-no-renewal-passport-no-passport%E2%80%9D-yar%E2%80%99adua-orders.

———. "Federal Court Declares the Arrest and Detention of US-based Blogger Emmanuel Asiwe Illegal." Sahara Reporters, Feb. 3, 2009, http://saharareporters.com/2009/02/02/federal-court-declares-arrest-and-detention-us-based-blogger-emmanuel-asiwe-illegal.

———. "FG Grants Ugwuonye, Embattled Washington DC Lawyer Who Withheld Embassy Funds, Authority to Sue Ambassador, Howard University Professor, and Saharareporters." Sahara Reporters, March 18, 2009, http://saharareporters.com/2009/03/18/fg-grants-ugwuonye-embattled-washington-dc-lawyer-who-witheld-embassy-funds-authority-sue.

———. "How Farida Waziri and Top Nigerian Editors Got Abuja Land Allocations." Sahara Reporters, January 4, 2009, http://www.saharareporters.com/news-page/how-farida-waziri-and-top-nigerian-editors-got-abuja-land-allocations.

———. "It Is Official: El-Rufai and Ribadu Can Enjoy Passport Services, Yar'Adua Now Says." Sahara Reporters, October 14, 2009, http://www.saharareporters.com/news-page/it-official-el-rufai-and-ribadu-can-enjoy-passport-services-yaradua-now-says.

———. "IBB's N10 Million Photo-Op with Media Executives." Sahara Reporters, August 19, 2010, http://www.saharareporters.com/photo/ibbs-n10-million-photo-op-media-executives?page=1.

———. "Nigerian Ambassador to the UN, Joy Ogwu, to Commence Multi-Million Dollar Lawsuit against Sahara Reporters." Sahara Reporters, April 21, 2010, http://saharareporters.com/2010/04/21/nigerian-ambassador-un-joy-ogwu-commence-multi-million-dollar-lawsuit-against.

———. "Nigerian Treasury Looters Have Moved Over to China, India, and Persian Gulf Countries." Sahara Reporters, December 7, 2010, http://www.saharareporters.com/news-page/nigerian-treasury-looters-have-moved-over-china-india-and-persian-gulf-countries.

———. "Our Philosophy and Editorial Policy." Sahara Reporters, October 25, 2010, http://www.saharareporters.com/press-release/saharareporters-our-philosophy-and-editorial-policy.

———. "Punch Newspaper Prohibits News Critical of Jonathan." Sahara Reporters, September 19, 2010, http://www.saharareporters.com/news-page/punch-newspaper-prohibits-news-critical-jonathan?page=2.

———. "SSS Plans to Re-Arrest Jonathan Elendu from the EFCC as He Embarks on Hunger Strike." Sahara Reporters, October 25, 2008, http://saharareporters.com/2008/10/25/sss-plans-re-arrest-jonathan-elendu-efcc-he-embarks-hunger-strike.

———. "Umaru Yar'adua Regime Launches $5 Million Online War." Sahara Reporters, June 16, 2009, http://saharareporters.com/2009/06/15/umaru-yar%E2%80%99adua-regime-launches-5-million-online-war.

———. "US Hospital Denies Knowledge of Surgery Letter on Kalu's Wife." Sahara Reporters, August 08, 2010, http://67.192.103.155/reports/exclusive/1871-us-hospital-deny-knowledge-of-surgery-letter-on-kalus-wife-.html.

SaharaTV. "Borno Governor, Senator Ali Modu Sheriff Dancing and Spraying Dollars in Dubai." SaharaTV, November 05, 2008, http://www.youtube.com/watch?v=RRCuvQZPlgw.

Salawu, Abiodun. "Not Iwe Irohin but Umshumayeli: A Revisit of the Historiography of the Early African Language Press." *African Identities* 13, no. 2 (2015): 157–70.

———. "Paradox of a Milieu: Communication in African Indigenous Languages in the Age of Globalization." In *Indigenous Language Media in Africa*, edited by Abiodun Salawu, 1–20. Lagos, Nigeria: Center for Black and African Arts and Civilization, 2006.

Saleh, Jimeh. "Ramen Noodles and the Prospects of Web-Only Journalism in Nigeria: An In-Depth Study of Premium Times." MA thesis, London Metropolitan University, 2015.

Samoriski, Jan. *Issues in Cyberspace: Communication, Technology, Law, and Society on the Internet Frontier*. Boston: Allyn & Bacon, 2002.

Sayad, Adbelmalek. *The Suffering of the Immigrant*. Cambridge: Polity, 2004.

Sayre, Ben. "Agenda Setting in a Digital Age: Tracking Attention to California Proposition 8 in Social Media, Online News, and Conventional News." *Policy & Internet* 2, no. 2 (2010): 7–32.

Schiffrin, Anya, Beatrice Santa-Wood, Susanna De Martino, Nicole Pope, and Ellen Hume. *Bridging the Gap: Rebuilding Citizen Trust in Media*. New York: Open Society Foundations, 2017.

Schiller, Herbert I. *Communication and Cultural Domination*. White Plains, NY: International Arts and Sciences Press, 1976.

———. *Culture Inc.: The Corporate Takeover of Public Expression*. New York: Oxford University Press, 1989.

———. *Mass Communications and American Empire*. Boston: Beacon Press, 1969.

Schneider, Volker. "Evolution in Cyberspace: The Adaption of National Videotext Systems to the Internet." *Information Society* 16, no. 4 (2000): 319–28.

Schramm, Wilbur. *Mass Media and National Development*. Stanford: Stanford University Press, 1964.

Schudson, Michael. "Why Conversation Is Not the Soul of Democracy." *Critical Studies in Mass Communication* 14, no. 4 (1997): 297–309.

Schultz, Tanjev, and Paul S. Voakes. "Prophets of Gloom: Why Do Newspaper Journalists Have So Little Faith in the Future of Newspapers?" *Newspaper Research Journal* 20, no. 2 (1999): 23–41.

Schwartz, Frederick. *Nigeria*. Cambridge, MA: MIT Press, 1965.

Schweizer, Kristen. "U.S. Web Advertising Exceeds Newspaper Print Ads in 2010, eMarketer Says." Bloomberg Businessweek, December 20, 2010, http://www.bloomberg.com/news/2010-12-20/u-s-web-ads-exceed-newspaper-print-ads-in-2010-emarketer-says.html.

Scott, James C. *Weapons of the Weak: Everyday Forms of Peasant Resistance*. New Haven: Yale University Press, 1985.

Scott, Martin, Kate Wright, and Mel Bunce. "'Doing Good' and 'Looking Good' in Global Humanitarian Reporting: Is Philanthro-journalism Good News?" In *Communication in International Development*, edited by Florencia Enghel and Jessica Noske-Turner. London: Routledge, 2018.

Searcey, Dionne, and Emmanuel Akinwotu. "Nigeria Military Raids Newspaper, Seizes Computers and Arrests Journalists." *New York Times*, January 7, 2019, https://www.nytimes.com/2019/01/07/world/africa/nigeria-military-daily-trust-boko-haram.html.

Serafin, Tatiana. "Then There Was One: Nigeria Loses One of Its Billionaires as Its Two Wealthiest Citizens Battle It Out." Forbes.com, March 27, 2009, http://www.forbes.com/2009/03/27/nigeria-dangote-otedola-business-billionaires-feud.html.

Sharp, Charles. "Gaskiya Corporation and the Establishment of the Ahmadu Bello University Press, Creation of a Daily Newspaper to Serve Northern Nigeria and the Possible Amalgamation of *Daily Mail*, Kano." Memorandum Submitted on Instruction of the Minister of International Affairs, Norfolk, UK, 1963.

Shaw, Martin. "Civil Society and Global Politics: Beyond a Social Movements Approach." *Millennium: Journal of International Studies* 23, no. 3 (1994): 647–67.

Shaw, Donald L., Maxwell McCombs, David H. Weaver, and Bradley J. Hamm. "Individuals, Groups, and Agenda Melding: A Theory of Social Dissonance." *International Journal of Public Opinion Research* 11, no. 1 (1999): 2–24.

Shain, Yossi. *Kinship and Diasporas in International Affairs*. Ann Arbor: University of Michigan Press, 2007.

Shehu, Garba D. "The Role of Mass Media in National Development: A Case Study of Gaskiya Ta Fi Kwabo," MA thesis, Department of Mass Communication, University of Nigeria, Nsukka, 1991.

Shenon, Philip. "Sahara Reporters: Uncovering Nigeria's Corruption." Daily Beast, https://www.thedailybeast.com/sahara-reporters-uncovering-nigerias-corruption, accessed June 12, 2018.

Shi, Yu. "Identity Construction of the Chinese Diaspora, Ethnic Media Use, Community Formation, and the Possibility of Social Activism." *Continuum: Journal of Media & Cultural Studies* 19, no. 1 (2005): 55–72.

Sholle, David. "Access through Activism: Extending the Ideas of Negt and Kluge to American Alternative Media Practice." *Javost—The Public* 2, no. 4 (1995): 21–35.

Silverstone, Roger. *Why Study the Media*? London: Sage, 1999.

Sindorf, Shannon. "Symbolic Violence in the Online Field: Calls for 'Civility' in Online Discussion." *Fibreculture Journal* 162, no. 22 (2013): 194–215.

Singer, Jane B. "Changes and Consistencies: Newspaper Journalists Contemplate Online Future." *Newspaper Research Journal* 18, no. 1 (1997): 2–18.

———. "The Political J-Blogger." Paper Presented at the Annual Convention of the Association for Education in Journalism and Mass Communication, Toronto, Canada, August 2004.

———. "Still Guarding the Gate? The Newspaper Journalist's Role in an On-line World." *Convergence* 3, no. 1 (1997): 72–89.

Skjerdal, Terje S. "Research on Brown Envelope Journalism in the African Media." *African Communication Research* 3, no. 3 (2010): 367–67.

Smith, David. "Internet Use on Mobile Phones in Africa Predicted to Increase 20-Fold." *Guardian*, June 5, 2014, https://www.theguardian.com/world/2014/jun/05/Internet-use-mobile-phones-africa-predicted-increase-20-fold.

Smith, Jeffery. "Freedom of Expression and the Marketplace of Ideas Concept from Milton to Jefferson." *Journal of Communication Inquiry* 7, no. 1 (1981): 47–63.

Sobowale, Idowu I. "The Historical Development of the Nigerian Press." In *Mass Communication Culture and Society in West Africa*, edited by Frank Ugboajah. Oxford: Hans Zell, 1985.

Solomon, Salem. "African Immigrant Population on Rise in US." Voice of America, February 17, 2017; https://www.voanews.com/amp/african-immigrant-population-on-the-rise-in-us/3728715.html.

Sowore, Omoyele. "Exclusive and Explosive: Gbenga Obasanjo on Atiku, El-Rufai, Corruption, Otta, EPZ and More." Nigerian Village Square, January 6, 2006, http://www.nigeriavillagesquare.com/index.php?option=com_content&task=view&id=2241.

Sowore, Omoyele. "Gbenja Obasanjo Speaks: Atiku Is Greedy." Sahara Reporters, January 15, 2006, http://www.saharareporters.com/interviews/interview-political/452-gbenga-obasanjo-speaks-atiku-is-greedy-html.

Sowore, Omoyele, and Jonathan Elendu. "'The House is Mine': Sokoto Governor." Elendu Reports, October 6, 2005, http://nm.onlinenigeria.com/templates/?a=5519&z=17.

Spiegel, Brenda. "From Safety of New York, Reporting on Distant Home." *New York Times*, November 19, 2011, https://www.nytimes.com/2011/11/20/nyregion/from-safety-of-new-york-reporting-on-a-distant-homeland.html.

Spitulnik, Debra. "Alternative Small Media and Communicative Spaces." In *Media and Democracy in Africa*, edited by Goran Hyden, Michael Leslie, and Folu F. Ogundimu, 177–205. New Brunswick, NJ: Transaction Publishers, 2002.

Sreberny-Mohammadi, Annabelle. "Globalization, Communication and Transnational Civil Society: Introduction." In *Globalization, Communication and Transnational Civil Society*, edited by Sandra Braman and Annabelle Sreberny-Mohammadi, 1–19. Cresskil, NJ: Hampton Press, 1996.

———. "Small Media for a Big Revolution: Iran." *International Journal of Politics, Culture and Society* 3, no. 3 (1990): 341–71.

Sreberny-Mohammadi, Annabelle, and Ali Mohammadi. *Small Media, Big Revolution: Communication, Culture and the Iranian Revolution*. Minneapolis: University of Minnesota Press, 1994.

Stake, Robert E. *The Art of Case Study Research*. Thousand Oaks, CA: Sage, 1995.

Starkey, Jerome. "Women Are Bent on Revenge against Tuareg Rebels in Mali." *Times*, November 23, 2012, https://www.thetimes.co.uk/article/women-are-bent-on-revenge-against-tuareg-rebels-in-mali-xrq7r6br088.

Starr, Amory. *Naming the Enemy: Anti-Corporate Movements Confront Globalization*. London: Zed Books, 2002.

Stevenson, Brenda. *The Contested Murder of Latasha Harlins: Justice, Gender, and the Origins of the LA Riots*. Oxford: Oxford University Press, 2013.

Stoller, Paul. *Jaguar: A Story of Africans in America*. Chicago: University of Chicago Press, 1999.

Straubhaar, Joseph D. "Beyond Media Imperialism: Asymmetrical Interdependence and Cultural Proximity." *Critical Studies in Mass Communication* 8 (1991): 39–59.

Streitmatter, Rodger. *Voices of Revolution: The Dissident Press in America*. New York: Columbia University Press, 2001.

Suler, John. "The Online Disinhibition Effect." *CyberPsychology & Behavior* 7, no. 3 (2004): 321–26.

Sun News. "Stanley Macebuh (1942–2010)." Sun News, http://www.sunnewsonline.com/Webpages/opinion/editorial/2010/mar/17/editorial-1703-2010-001.htm, accessed April 10, 2010.

Takougang, Joseph. "Contemporary African Immigrants to the United States." *Ìrìnkèrindò: A Journal of African Migration* 2 (2003), http://africamigration.com/issue/dec2003/j_takougang.pdf.

Tal, Azran. "Resisting Peripheral Exports: Al Jazeera's War Images on US Television." *Media International Australia Incorporating Culture & Policy*, 113 (2004): 75–86.

Teel, Leonard R., and Ron Taylor. *Into the Newsroom: An Introduction to Journalism*. 2nd ed. Chester, CT.: Globe Pequot Press, 1988.

ThisDay. "Governors Sign MoU with Harvard on Capacity Building." ThisDay, May 24, 2009.

Thompson, Susan. *The Penny Press: The Origins of the Modern News Media, 1883–1861*. Northport, AL: Vision Press, 2004.

Thurman, Neil. "Forums for Citizen Journalists? Adoption of User-Generated Content Initiatives by Online News Media." *New Media & Society* 10, no. 1 (2008): 139–57.

Thurman, Neil, and Susan Jones. "From Nexus to Newslog: Online Journalism from the Grassroots." In *Print Journalism: A Critical Introduction*, edited by R. Keeble, 252–63. London: Taylor & Francis, 2005.

Thussu, Daya Kishan. Introduction to *Media on the Move: Global Flow and Contra-Flow*. London: Routledge, 2007.

TIME. "Who is Umar Faruk Abdulmutallab?" *TIME*, http://www.time.com/time/photogallery/0,29307,1950292_2017642,00.html#ixzz0b8mAvQ6n, accessed April 6, 2018.

Times of Nigeria. "Delta Shares in Oceanic Not Used in Paying Ascot Loan." Times of Nigeria, April 18, 2010, http://www.thetimesofnigeria.com/Article.aspx?id=2555.

———. "EFCC Continued Investigation in Delta Shows They Have No Evidence Against Me—Ibori." Times of Nigeria, April 22, 2010, http://www.thetimesofnigeria.com/TON/Article.aspx?id=2565.

Tomaselli, Kenya, and Eric Louw. "Alternative Media and Political Practice: The South African Struggle." In *Communication for and against Democracy*, edited by Marc Raboy and Peter Bruck, 203–20. Montreal: Black Rose, 1990.

Tony, Onyisi. "Mass Media Ethics: Analyzing the 'Brown Envelope' or 'AWUFU' Syndrome." In *Mass Media and Marketing Communications*, edited by Ikechukwu Nwosu and Uchenna Ekwo, 79–91. Enugu, Nigeria: Thoughts Communications Publishers, 1996.

Tukur, Sani. "Presidency Defends Military Attack on Nigerian Newspapers, Exonerates Jonathan." Premium Times, June 7, 2014, https://www.premiumtimesng.com/news/162296-presidency-defends-military-attack-nigerian-newspapers-exonerates-jonathan.html.

Turkle, Sherry. *Life on the Screen: Identity in the Age of the Internet*. London: Phoenix, 1997.

Turner, Graeme. Editorial. *Media International Australia, Incorporating Culture & Policy* 103 (2002), http://www.uq.edu.au/emsah/mia/issues/miacp103.html.

Turner, Terisa. "Commercial Capitalism and the 1975 Coup." In *Soldiers and Oil: The Political Transformation of Nigeria*, edited by Keith Panter-Brick, 166–97. London: Frank Cass, 1978.

Ubochi, Temple C. "As It Is for Orji Uzoh Kalu, It Is Hard for 'the Leopard to Change Its Skin.'" NigeriaWorld, August 14, 2007, http://nigeriaworld.com/feature/publication/ubochi/081407.html.

Uche, Luke U. *Mass Media, People and Politics in Nigeria*. New Delhi: Concept Publishing, 1989.

Ugboajah, Frank Okwu. "Four Options for Press Regulation." In *Communication Training and Practice in Nigeria: Issues and Perspectives*, edited by Frank O. Ogboajah, Ikechukwu E. Nwosu, and Tom Adaba, 129–40. Nairobi, ACCE, 1987.

———. "Nigerian Media Behaviour on Development Issues of Conflict." *Instant Research on Peace and Violence* 6, no. 4 (1976): 183–94.

Ugwoke, Francis. "FG Fires Security Chief over el-Rufai, Ribadu." ThisDay, October 15, 2009.

Ujah, Emma, and Peter Egwuatu. "AP Shares—Otedola Seeks N117 Billion Compensation." Vanguard, April 24, 2009, http://allafrica.com/stories/200904240020.html.

Usua, N. "Citizen Media and the Future of Government-Owned Broadcast Organizations: A Study of Radio Nigeria." *Lwati: A Journal of Contemporary Research* 7, no. 2 (2010): 1–19.

Vanguard. "Drama as Alleged Ritual Murder Victim Surfaces in Court." Vanguard, June 25, 2009, http://www.vanguardngr.com/2009/06/25/drama-as-alleged-ritual-murder-victim-surfaces-in-court/.

———. "Editorial: www.PointBlankNews: Dealing with Online 'Character Assassins.'" Vanguard, June 8, 2009; http://www.vanguardngr.com/2009/06/08/editorial-wwwPointBlankNewscom-dealing-with-online-%E2%80%9Ccharacter-assassins%E2%80%9D/.

———. "The Lies of www.PointBlankNews: Police Report on Blackmailer Steve Chinuwa Ogwu and Others." *Vanguard,* August 08, 2009, http://www.vanguardngr.com/2009/06/08/the-lies-of-wwwPointBlankNewscom-police-report-on-blackmailer-steve-chinuwa-ogwu-and-others/.

———. "Reactions as SARS Reportedly Arrests Journalist Daniel Elombah over Alleged Criticism of Buhari's Govt." Vanguard, January 1, 2018, https://www.vanguardngr.com/2018/01/reactions-as-sars-reportedly-arrests-journalist-daniel-elombah-over-alleged-criticism-of-buhari/.

Vertovec, Steve. "Conceiving and Researching Transnationalism." *Ethnic and Racial Studies* 22 (1999): 447–62.

Villareal, Tamara F., and Genève Gil. "Radical Internet Use." In *Radical Media: Rebellious Communication and Social Movements,* edited by John D. Downing, 201–34. Thousand Oaks, CA: Sage, 2001.

Viner, Katherine. "The Guardian's Reader Funding Model Is Working. It's Inspiring." *Guardian,* November 18, 2018, https://www.theguardian.com/membership/2018/nov/12/katharine-viner-guardian-million-reader-funding.

Violanti, Anthony. "Alternative News Made Its Mark." *Buffalo News,* November 4, 2004, p. C1.

Warner, Michael. *Publics and Counterpublics.* New York: Zone Books, 2005.

Waterson, Jim. "Guardian Media Group Digital Revenues Outstrip Print for First Time." *Guardian,* July 24, 2018, https://www.theguardian.com/media/2018/jul/24/guardian-media-group-digital-revenues-outstrip-print-for-first-time.

Weaver, David H., Judith M. Buddenhaum, and Jo Ellen Fair. "Press Freedom, Media, and Development, 1950–1979: A Study of 134 Nations." *Journal of Communication* 35 (1985): 104–17.

Wessler, Hartmut, and Manuel Adolphsen. "Contra-Flow from the Arab World? How Arab Television Coverage of the 2003 Iraq War Was Used and Framed on Western International News Channels." *Media, Culture & Society* 30, no. 4 (2008): 439–61.

Whitaker, Brian. *News Limited: Why You Can't Read All about It.* London: Minority Press Group, 1981.

White, Bob W. "Talk about School: Education and the Colonial Project in French and British Africa (1860–1960)." *Comparative Education* 32, no. 1 (1996): 9–25.

Whitehead, Clive. "The Historiography of British Imperial Education Policy, Part II: Africa and the Rest of the Colonial Empire." *History of Education* 34, no. 4 (2005): 441–54.

Wiener-Bronner, Danielle. "Nigerian Military Officers Court-Martialed for Giving Boko Haram Weapons." *Atlantic,* June 3, 2004, https://www.theatlantic.com/international/archive/2014/06/nigerian-generals-arrested-for-giving-boko-haram-weapons/372052/.

Woodstock, Louise. "Public Journalism's Talking Cure: An Analysis of the Movement's 'Problem' and 'Solution' Narratives." *Journalism: Theory Practice and Criticism* 3, no. 1 (2002): 37–55.

Woollacott, Janet. "Messages and Meanings." In *Culture, Society and the Media,* edited by Michael Gurevitch, Tony Bennett, James Curran, and Janet Woollacott, 91–111. London: Methuen, 1982.

Workman, Dean. "Nigeria leads Africa's 7 Highest Internet Using Countries." IT News Africa, http://www.itnewsafrica.com/2017/03/nigeria-leads-africas-7-highest-Internet-using-countries, accessed June 7, 2018.

Yahya, I. Y. *Hausa a Rubuce: Tarihin Rubuce-Rubuce Cikin Hausa.* Zaria, Nigeria: Northern Nigerian Publishing Company, 1988.

Yin, Robert K. *Case Study Research: Design and Methods.* 4th ed. Thousand Oaks, CA: Sage, 2008.

Youngstedt, Scott M. "The New Nigerian Hausa Diaspora in the U.S.: Surviving and Building Community on the Margins of the Global Economy." *City & Society* 16, no. 1 (2004): 39–67.

Yu, Yeon-Jung. "OhmyNews Makes Every Citizen a Reporter." *Japan Media Review,* September 17, 2003.

Zeleza, Paul T. "Contemporary African Migration in a Global Context." *African Issues* 30, no. 1 (2002): 12–25.

Zelizer, Barbie. "Achieving Journalistic Authority through Narrative." *Critical Studies in Media Communication* 7, no. 4 (1990): 366–76.

———. "Journalists as Interpretive Communities." *Critical Studies in Mass Communication* 10, no. 3 (1993), 219–37.

Index